AMERICA
A PROPHECY

INTRODUCTION

■ *"The business of art . . . is to live in the actual present, that is the complete actual present, and to completely express that complete actual present."*

—GERTRUDE STEIN

■ *"It is dawn at Jerusalem while midnight hovers above the Pillars of Hercules. All ages are contemporaneous in the mind."*

—EZRA POUND

■ *"You always insist on knowing things from the beginning,"* he said. *"But there's no beginning; the beginning is only in your thought."*

—DON JUAN, to CARLOS CASTANEDA

AMERICA A PROPHECY

A New Reading of American Poetry
from Pre-Columbian Times to the Present

Edited by **GEORGE QUASHA**
and **JEROME ROTHENBERG**

Random House New York

Copyright © 1973 by George Quasha and Jerome Rothenberg

All rights reserved under International
and Pan-American Copyright Conventions.
Published in the United States
by Random House, Inc., New York,
and simultaneously in Canada
by Random House of Canada Limited, Toronto.

Library of Congress Cataloging in Publication Data
Quasha, George, comp.
America, a prophecy.
1. American poetry (Selections: Extracts, etc.)
2. Indian poetry—Translations into English.
3. American poetry—Translations from Indian languages.
I. Rothenberg, Jerome, 1931–   joint comp.
II. Title.
PS586.Q37   811'.008   73–4811
ISBN 0–394–48083–X

Manufactured in the United States of America

9   8   7   6   5   4   3   2

vii

Theodore Enslin: "Forms XIII" Copyright © 1970 by Theodore Enslin.

Frontier Press: "The Lawg of the Winterbook" by Edward Dorn.

Fulcrum Press: "Wintergreen Ridge" by Lorine Niedecker, from *North Central.* Copyright © 1968 by Lorine Niedecker.

Allen Ginsberg: "Psalm IV" by the author.

John Giorno: "A Coven" by John Giorno, from *Balling Buddha.*

Grossman Publishers: "Old Man Sam Ward's History of the Gee-Haw Whimmy Diddle" by Jonathan Williams. From *Blues and Roots/Rue and Bluets,* by Jonathan Williams and Nicholas Dean. Copyright © 1971 by Jonathan Williams.

Grove Press, Inc.: Excerpt from *Human Universe and Other Essays* by Charles Olson. Copyright 1951, © 1959, 1965, 1967 by Charles Olson.

Harcourt Brace Jovanovich, Inc.: "The Face in the Barroom Mirror" and "The People v. The People" from *Stranger at Coney Island* by Kenneth Fearing. Copyright 1948 by Kenneth Fearing. "The Lawyers Know Too Much" from *Smoke and Steel* by Carl Sandburg. Copyright 1920 by Harcourt Brace Jovanovich, Inc., and renewed 1948 by Carl Sandburg. "my mind is," "5," and "at the ferocious phenomenon" from *Poems 1923–1954* by E.E. Cummings. Copyright 1925 and renewed 1953 by E. E. Cummings. "brIght" from *Poems 1923–1954* by E. E. Cummings. Copyright 1935 by E. E. Cummings and renewed 1954 by Marion Morehouse Cummings. Twenty-one lines from "Little Gidding" in *Four Quartets* by T. S. Eliot, copyright 1943 by T. S. Eliot; renewed 1971 by Esme Valerie Eliot. Reprinted by permission of Harcourt Brace Jovanovich, Inc., and Faber and Faber Ltd. "Magical Incantation" from *On Bear's Head* by Philip Whalen. Copyright © 1969 by Philip Whalen.

Harper & Row Publishers, Inc.: "Looking into a Face" from *The Light Around the Body* by Robert Bly. Copyright © 1965 by Robert Bly. "Sermon: Behold the Rib" from *Mules and Men* by Zora Neal Hurston. Copyright 1935 by Zora Neal Hurston.

Jim Harrison: "Suite to Fathers" from *Locations* by Jim Harrison (W. W. Norton, 1968). Copyright © 1968 by Jim Harrison. Reprinted by permission of the author.

Harvard University Press: "In Winter in my Room," "The first day's night," "One need not be a chamber," "I years had been from home," "I think I was enchanted," "I cannot live with you" and "Banish air from air" from *The Poems of Emily Dickinson,* edited by Thomas H. Johnson. Reprinted by permission of the publishers and the Trustees of Amherst College from Thomas H. Johnson, Editor: The Belknap Press of Harvard University Press, Copyright 1951, © 1955 by The President and Fellows of Harvard College. Extract from Letter No. 233 from

Gerrit Lansing: "Exercises for Ear # CLV" by Stephen Jonas. "The Compost" by Gerrit Lansing.

Liveright Publishing Corporation: "Cutty Sark" from *The Complete Poems and Selected Letters and Prose of Hart Crane* by Hart Crane. Copyright 1933, © 1958, 1966 by Liveright Publishing Corporation. "Identity a Poem" from *What Are Masterpieces* by Gertrude Stein.

Sterling Lord Agency, Inc.: "Black Dada Nihilismus" from *The Dead Lecturer* by LeRoi Jones, published by Grove Press. Copyright © 1964 by LeRoi Jones. 211th Chorus from *Mexico City Blues* by Jack Kerouac, published by Grove Press. Copyright © 1959 by Jack Kerouac. "Ghost Tantra, no. 8," from *Ghost Tantras* by Michael McClure, published by Four Seasons Foundation. Copyright © 1964 by Michael McClure.

Walter Lowenfels: "For Ludwig Wittgenstein" from *Some Deaths* by the author. Copyright © 1964 by Walter Lowenfels.

David McAllester: Permission to reprint 14 one-line verses and 160 words of prose from *Peyote Music* by the author.

The M.I.T. Press: Pages 52–55, 9 pairs of Hopi words and definitions, from *Language, Thought and Reality* by Benjamin Lee Whorf. Copyright © 1956, 1964 by Benjamin Lee Whorf.

Jackson Mac Low: "Paracelsus" from *Stanzas for Iris Lezak* by the author. Copyright © 1972 by Jackson Mac Low (Something Else Press). "The Presidents of the United States of America" from *Some/Thing No. 1.* Copyright © 1965 by David Antin and Jerome Rothenberg, copyright © 1973 by Jackson Mac Low. "5th Gatha" copyright © 1973 by Jackson Mac Low. "2nd Light Poem: For Diane Wakoski-10 June 1962," copyright © 1968 by Jackson Mac Low (Black Sparrow Press).

The Macmillan Company: "Spenser's Ireland" from *Collected Poems* by Marianne Moore. Copyright 1941 and renewed 1969 by Marianne Moore.

Ellen Masters: "Euripides Alexopoulos" from *The New Spoon River* by Edgar Lee Masters, published by Macmillan Company. Copyright 1924 by Edgar Lee Masters. Reprinted by permission of Mrs. Ellen Masters.

Bernadette Mayer: "Fiction," from *Story* published by OTO9, 1968.

David Meltzer: "Yetsiradicals," section 1, by David Meltzer, first appeared in *Tree: 2.*

Monica McCall (I.F.A.): "Dam" from *U.S. 1* by Muriel Rukeyser. Copyright 1938 by Muriel Rukeyser.

W.S. Merwin: "Fear" from *The Carrier of Ladders* by W.S. Merwin. Reprinted by permission of the author.

New Directions Publishing Corporation: "Food" from *The Happy Birthday of Death* by Gregory Corso. Copyright © 1960 by New Directions Publishing Corporation. "The Last Poem to

liam Carlos Williams. "To Elsie," "Flowers by the Sea" and "The Attic Which is Desire" from *Collected Earlier Poems* by William Carlos Williams. Copyright 1938 by New Directions Publishing Corporation. Extract of approximately 400 words from *In the American Grain* by William Carlos Williams. Copyright 1925 by James Laughlin, copyright 1933 by William Carlos Williams.

W. W. Norton and Company, Inc.: #5 from "Song of Degrees" and "A Sea" from *All: The Collected Short Poems 1956–1964* by Louis Zukofsky. Copyright © 1966 by Louis Zukofsky.

Harold Ober Associates, Inc.: "American Spring Song" from *Mid-American Chants* by Sherwood Anderson, published by Frontier Press. Copyright 1918 and renewed in 1945 by Eleanor Copenhaver Anderson. "The Man in the Brown Coat" from *The Triumph of the Egg* by Sherwood Anderson, published by B.W. Huebsch Company. Copyright 1921 by B.W. Huebsch Company and renewed 1948 by Eleanor C. Anderson. "Hope," and "Gauge," "Request," and "Fact" from *Montage of a Dream Deferred* by Langston Hughes, published by Henry Holt. Copyright 1951 by Langston Hughes.

Simon Ortiz: "Telling About Coyote" by the author.

Norman Holmes Pearson: "The Walls do not Fall, section 36," "Tribute to the Angels, sections 29–32, 35–43," and "Heat" from *Selected Poems* by H.D.

Hilda N. Petri: Extracts from pages 186 and 191, also complete pages 187–190 from *Black Elk Speaks* by John G. Neihardt. Copyright 1932, © 1959, 1961 by John G. Neihardt.

Allan Planz: Twenty-two lines of "High Summer" by the author. Copyright © 1969 by Swallow Press, Inc.

Arthur Okamura: For permission to reproduce 6 illustrations to accompany the text of "People" by Robert Creeley.

Oklahoma Historical Society: "History of Nez Percé Indians from 1805 up to the Present Time 1880" by James Reuben, *The Chronicles of Oklahoma,* Volume 12, September 1934.

Joel Oppenheimer: "cartography" from *Love Bit and Other Poems* by the author (Corinth Books).

Rochelle Owens: "O mi darling" from *Elga's Incantation* by the author.

Princeton University Press: Quotes from the Foreword and from the 64th Hexagram, from *The I Ching, or Book of Changes,* translated by Richard Wilhelm, rendered into English by Cary F. Baynes, Bollingen Series XIX, copyright 1950, © 1967 by the Bollingen Foundation.

Random House, Inc., and Alfred A. Knopf, Inc.: Pages 160–161, from *Love's Body* by Norman O. Brown. Copyright © 1966 by Norman O. Brown. Reprinted by permission of Random House, Inc. "Anecdote of Men by the Thousand," "Metaphor as Degen-

University of California Press: "A Novel: Who Was He" pages 27–30 from *Mark Twain's Satires & Burlesques,* edited with an Introduction by Franklin R. Rogers.

University of Oklahoma Press: "A Chapter of Questions and Answers," from *The Book of Chilam Balam of Chumayel* by Ralph L. Roys. New edition copyright © 1967 by the University of Oklahoma Press.

University of Utah Press: "Definition of *Eye,*" "Definition of *Owl,*" "Definition of tzontecomannacatl," "Definition of nanacatl" from *Florentine Codex, Book XI,* translated by Arthur J. O. Anderson and Charles E. Dibble, published by School of American Research and the University of Utah. Copyright © 1963 by the University of Utah.

The Viking Press, Inc.: "Migration Symbols," page 125, and Song and Symbol, page 46, from *Book of the Hopi* by Frank Waters. Copyright © 1963 by Frank Waters.

Diane Wakoski: "The Ice Eagle," "George Washington and the Loss of His Teeth" by the author.

John Weatherhill, Inc.: Calligraphy by Shunryu Suzuki from *Zen Mind, Beginner's Mind.*

Tom Weatherly: "Honeymoon Weather" by the author. Copyright © 1970 by Tom Weatherly (Corinth Books, Inc.)

Wesleyan University Press: "Milkweed" from *Collected Poems* by James Wright. Copyright © 1962 by James Wright. "Ritual One" from *Rescue the Dead* by David Ignatow. Copyright © 1967 by David Ignatow. "The Inner Part" from *At the End of the Open Road* by Louis Simpson. Copyright © 1963 by Louis Simpson. "Hands   birds" from *Centering* by Mary Caroline Richards. Copyright © 1962, 1964 by Mary Caroline Richards. Extracts from *Silence* by John Cage. Copyright 1949 by John Cage.

William Alanson White Psychiatric Foundation: "New Words and Neologisms, with a Thesaurus of Coinages by a Schizophrenic Savant" by David V. Forrest, eight definitions on pages 47–48, from *Psychiatry* (1969).

Emmett Williams: "do you remember," copyright © 1966 by Emmett Williams. "like attracts like," copyright © 1958 by Emmett Williams.

Keith Wilson: "Coyote" from *Homestead* by the author. Copyright © 1969 by Keith Wilson.

Yale University Press: Extracts from *Stanzas in Meditation* by Gertrude Stein. Copyright © 1956 by Alice B. Toklas. Extracts from *Bee Time Vine* by Gertrude Stein. Copyright 1953 by Alice B. Toklas. Extracts from *Painted Lace* by Gertrude Stein. Copyright © 1955 by Alice B. Toklas. "Meditations (Second Series)," #31, #163, from *The Poems of Edward Taylor,* edited by Donald E. Stanford. Copyright © 1960 by Yale University Press.

Contents

Introduction   xxvii

RE BEGINNINGS

[IROQUOIS]: The Tree of the Great Peace   3

WALT WHITMAN: *From* Song of Myself   4

EZRA POUND: Religio or, The Child's Guide to Knowledge   5

GERTRUDE STEIN: *From* Winning His Way   7

H. D.: *From* The Walls Do Not Fall   8

WALLACE STEVENS: Not Ideas about the Thing
    but the Thing Itself   9

MAP ONE: ORIGINS

[MAYA]: *From* The Popol Vuh: Beginnings   13

[DELAWARE]: *From* The Walam Olum, or Red Score   16

ROBINSON JEFFERS: The Great Explosion   19

CHARLES OLSON: Maximus, from Dogtown—I   20

ROBERT DUNCAN: Tribal Memories (Passages 1)   27

[SERMON]: Behold the Rib!   29

ALLEN GINSBERG: The End   32

[SIOUX]: Three for Bear   33

EZRA POUND: Canto XLVII   34

SANTO BLANCO: A Series of Seri Songs / Whales   37

HERMAN MELVILLE: The Head of the Whale   39

CHARLES SIMIC: The Animals   41

EMILY DICKINSON: "In Winter in My Room"   41

EDGAR ALLAN POE: The Lynx   43

ROBERT KELLY: The Masks   43

WALT WHITMAN: This Compost   48

RED CORN [OSAGE]: Map of Earth & Sky: Migrations   51

BOOK OF THE HOPI [I]: Migration Symbols   52

BOOK OF THE HOPI [II]: Song of the Humpbacked Flute Player
    53

"MOUNDBUILDERS": The Great Serpent Mound of Adams County, Ohio   54

WILLIAM CULLEN BRYANT: The Prairies   55

RALPH WALDO EMERSON: Hamatreya   59

KENNETH IRBY: Relation   61

KENNETH REXROTH: A Lesson in Geography   64

WALLACE STEVENS: Anecdote of Men by the Thousand   67

MARSDEN HARTLEY: Lewiston Is a Pleasant Place   68

HART CRANE: Cutty Sark   71

GERTRUDE STEIN: A Landscape from Four Saints in Three Acts   74

GARY SNYDER: The Hump-Backed Flute Player   75

A BOOK OF RITES & NAMINGS

Definitions & Namings   81

WALT WHITMAN: Words   81

[PAPAGO]: From "Naming Events"   83

GREGORY CORSO: Food   83

[FLORENTINE CODEX]: Aztec Definitions   85

COTTON MATHER: Stones   86

GERTRUDE STEIN: Chicken   87

DANIEL SPOERRI/EMMETT WILLIAMS: Nail   88

[ANONYMOUS]: Schizophrenic Definitions   90

HARRY CROSBY: Short Introduction to the Word   91

MARCEL DUCHAMP: From Notes and Projects for the Large Glass   93

BENJAMIN LEE WHORF: Movements from the Punctual and Segmentative Aspects of Some Hopi Verbs   95

GEORGE BRECHT: Excerpts from Gloss for an Unknown Language   96

JACK SPICER: Five Words for Joe Dunn on His 22nd Birthday   97

Rites & Events   99

ENOCH HOAG [CADDO]: A Moon Peyote Altar   99

[THE SHAKERS]: Shaker Events   100

SADAKICHI HARTMANN: Sadakichi's 1895 Psychedelic Light Show   101

AMOS BRONSON ALCOTT: Conversation VIII. Nativity of Spirit. Family Relation.   104

DICK HIGGINS: *From* twenty-seven episodes for the aquarian
theater   105

JOHN CAGE: 2 Pages, 122 Words on Music and Dance   106

Sound-Poems & Incantations   108

CHÖGYAM TRUNGPA: Past and Present   108

RICHARD JOHNNY JOHN, JEROME ROTHENBERG, IAN TYSON: *Song
from* Shaking the Pumpkin [SENECA]   109

[THE SHAKERS]: Sound-Poem   110

LAFCADIO HEARN: Charcoal Man   111

ELSE VON FREYTAG-LORINGHOVEN: Kling—Hratzvenga
(DEATHWAIL)   112

MICHAEL McCLURE: Ghost Tantra No. 8   113

JACKSON MAC LOW: "5th Gatha"   114

ANSELM HOLLO: 2 Useful Poems that Traveled Across the
Atlantic   115

PHILIP WHALEN: Magical Incantation   116

JAIME de ANGULO: Coyote Shaman Songs   117

E. E. CUMMINGS: bright   119

MAP TWO: LOSSES

[MAYA]: *From* The Popol Vuh: Blood-Girl and the Chiefs of
Hell   124

SMOHALLA [NEZ PERCÉ]: The Mother   126

ARCHIBALD MacLEISH: Empire Builders   126

RALPH WALDO EMERSON: Ode Inscribed to W. H. Channing
130

WILLIAM CARLOS WILLIAMS: *From* Paterson, Book Three   133

CHARLES REZNIKOFF: Testimony   137

NATHANIEL TARN: *From* The Beautiful Contradictions   139

ALLEN GINSBERG: Mescaline   140

WALT WHITMAN: Respondez!   143

DIANE WAKOSKI: The Ice Eagle   147

JOHN LEE HOOKER: Black Snake   150

SHERWOOD ANDERSON: American Spring Song   151

[ANONYMOUS]: The Boasting Drunk in Dodge   153

EUGENE JOLAS: Wyof   154

LOUIS SIMPSON: The Inner Part   156

[NEZ PERCÉ]: Three Songs of Mad Coyote   156

DENISE LEVERTOV: The Goddess   158

ROBERT BLY: *From* The Teeth-Mother Naked at Last   159

IMAMU AMIRI BARAKA [LEROI JONES]: Black Dada Nihilismus   162

EZRA POUND: Canto 116   165

[AZTEC]: *From* The Birth of the War God   167

A BOOK OF HISTORIES

[MANDAN]: A Tree of History   175

[DAKOTA]: *From* Battiste Good's Winter Count   176

[ANONYMOUS REVOLUTIONARY PAMPHLET]: *From* The First Book of the American Chronicles of the Times   179

JOSEPH SMITH: *From* The Book of Mormon: Christ's Crucifixion Witnessed in America   181

JACOB CARPENTER: *From* Deaths on Three-Mile Creek: 1841–1915   182

JOHN GREENLEAF WHITTIER: Letter   183

WALT WHITMAN: To the States   185

MARK TWAIN: A Novel: Who Was He?   186

JAMES REUBEN [NEZ PERCÉ]: History of Nez Percé Indians from 1805 up to the Present Time 1880   189

WILLIAM VAUGHN MOODY: I Am the Woman   192

CARL SANDBURG: The Lawyers Know Too Much   195

EDGAR LEE MASTERS: Euripides Alexopoulos   196

SHERWOOD ANDERSON: The Man in the Brown Coat   197

ERNEST HEMINGWAY: They All Made Peace—What Is Peace?   199

JOHN DOS PASSOS: Newsreel LXVI   201

LIGHTNING HOPKINS: Mister Charlie   202

MELVIN B. TOLSON: Rho   205

MURIEL RUKEYSER: The Dam   207

ROBERT DUNCAN: Passages 24 Orders   211

EDWARD DORN: Thesis   215

LAWRENCE FERLINGHETTI: "In Goya's greatest scenes"   217

HAROLD DICKER: For the Day of Atonement/1963   218

JIMMY BELL: The Signifying Monkey and the Lion   219

JONATHAN WILLIAMS: Old Man Sam Ward's History

of the Gee-Haw Whimmy-Diddle   222

CHARLES BUKOWSKI: Drawing of a Band Concert on a Matchbox
223

JOEL OPPENHEIMER: Cartography   225

DAVID ANTIN: history   226

JACKSON MAC LOW: *From* The Presidents of the United States
of America   229

DIANE WAKOSKI: George Washington and the Loss of His Teeth
232

GERRIT LANSING: The Compost   234

SIMON ORTIZ: Telling About Coyote   235

[ANONYMOUS]: Horoscope of a Tentative North American
Republic   239

MAP THREE: VISIONS

Magic & Vision   243

HERMAN MELVILLE: Lines—After Shakespeare   243

HERMAN MELVILLE: Pip's Soliloquy   243

EMILY DICKINSON: Three Poems   244

ELSE von FREYTAG-LORINGHOVEN: *From* Mineself—Minesoul—
and—Mine—Cast-Iron Lover   247

HARRY CROSBY: Vision   249

HARRY CROSBY: Five Prose Poems   253

NORMAN O. BROWN: *From* Love's Body   254

[SIOUX]: Vision Event   256

[WINTU]: Spirit Song   256

HEHAKA SAPA [BLACK ELK]: The Dog Vision   256

WALT WHITMAN: *Fragment from* "The Sleepers"   259

EDGAR ALLAN POE: *From* The Narrative of A. Gordon Pym
260

FITZHUGH LUDLOW: *From* The Hasheesh Eater   261

EMILY DICKINSON: "I Think I Was Enchanted"   262

STEPHEN CRANE: Poem   264

GERTRUDE STEIN: Birds   265

BOB BROWN: Houdini   265

EUGENE JOLAS: We Meet the Old Griper [A Mythdream]   267

[Hoodoo]: *From* Hoodoo—Conjuration—Witchcraft—Rootwork
269

WILLIAM FAULKNER: Coffin   271

KENNETH FEARING: The Face in the Bar Room Mirror   272

KENNETH FEARING: The People v. The People   273

ANAÏS NIN: *From* The House of Incest   274

KENNETH PATCHEN: The Outlaw of the Lowest Planet   276

THEODORE ROETHKE: Unfold! Unfold!   279

DAVID IGNATOW: Ritual One   281

KEITH WILSON: Coyote   283

ALLEN GINSBERG: Psalm IV   284

PAUL BLACKBURN: At the Well   284

RUSSELL EDSON: The Angel   287

PHILIP LAMANTIA: The Diabolic Condition   287

GALWAY KINNELL: The Hen Flower   289

JOHN GIORNO: "A Coven"   293

ISHMAEL REED: I Am a Cowboy in the Boat of Ra   293

HARVEY BIALY: A Waratah Blossom   295

ANDREW PEYNETSA [ZUNI] thru DENNIS TEDLOCK: The Shumeekuli   296

Sacred Plants   301

[AZTEC]: Two Mushrooms   301

JOANNA KITCHEL [SHAKER]: Song of the East   302

EDWARD TAYLOR: Meditation 31. Joh. 15.13.
    Greater Love hath no man etc.   303

COMANCHE: Peyote Songs   304

RALPH WALDO EMERSON: Blight   305

GARY SNYDER: For Plants   307

CHARLES SIMIC: Forest   309

J. D. [JELLY JAW] SHORT: Snake Doctor Blues   310

GEORGE OPPEN: But So As by Fire   311

HENRY DAVID THOREAU: Th' Ambrosia of the Gods 's a Weed on
    Earth   312

HENRY DAVID THOREAU: And Once Again   313

WILLIAM CARLOS WILLIAMS: The Yellow Flower   313

CARL RAKOSI: The Code   315

VACHEL LINDSAY: Celestial Trees of Glacier Park   317

EZRA POUND: Canto XVII   319

A BOOK OF MUSIC

WILLIAM BILLINGS: The Pleasures of Variety   325

[THE SHAKERS]: Heavenly Display   326

JONES VERY: The Garden   327

EDGAR ALLAN POE: *From* X-ing a Paragrab   327

WALT WHITMAN: Sea-Shore Fancies   328

EMILY DICKINSON: "I Cannot Live with You"   329

SIDNEY LANIER: The Marshes of Glynn   331

FRANCES DENSMORE: American Indian Songs   335

EZRA POUND: The Return   338

ELSE VON FREYTAG-LORINGHOVEN: Love—Chemical Relationship   339

GERTRUDE STEIN: Sonnets that Please   341

MARIANNE MOORE: Spenser's Ireland   342

JAMES LAUGHLIN: The Last Poem To Be Written   344

CHARLIE PATTON: *From* Hang It on the Wall   345

LOUIS ZUKOFSKY: *A*: 4   347

LANGSTON HUGHES: Four Poems   350

JOSE GARCIA VILLA: Poem   351

WILLIAM CARLOS WILLIAMS: *From* Spring and All   352

ROBERT DUNCAN: The Structure of Rime I   355

CHARLES OLSON: *From* "Projective Verse"   357

PAUL BLACKBURN: The Watchers   359

JACK SPICER: Phonemics   365

JOHN CAGE: *From* Lecture on Nothing   369

JACKSON MAC LOW: *From* Stanzas for Iris Lezak   372

LARRY EIGNER: The Music, The Rooms   374

THEODORE ENSLIN: Forms XIII   377

ALLEN GINSBERG: Sunflower Sutra   383

JACK KEROUAC: "211th Chorus" *from* Mexico City Blues   385

STEPHEN JONAS: Exercises for Ear   385

SONIA SANCHEZ: on seeing paroah sanders blowing   386

ROCHELLE OWENS: *From* Elga's Incantation   388

EMMETT WILLIAMS: do you remember   390

ALLAN PLANZ: *From* High Summer   390

TED BERRIGAN: *From* Sonnets   391

CHARLES STEIN: The day of the bell   393

GEORGE OPPEN: The Translucent Mechanics   394

TOM WEATHERLY: Maumau American Canto 31   395

ARMAND SCHWERNER: Tablet XII   396

MAP FOUR: RENEWALS

Image-Making   403

MAYAN GLYPHS: A Frame from the Dresden Codex   404

[TOLTEC]: *From* The Blue House of Tlaloc   405

[THE SHAKERS]: Emblem Poems   406

EDGAR ALLAN POE: Prose Poem   407

WILLIAM CULLEN BRYANT: *From* October   409

JAMES RUSSELL LOWELL: *From* The Biglow Papers   409

WALT WHITMAN: The Runner   409

WALT WHITMAN: Visor'd   410

HENRY DAVID THOREAU: Two Poems   410

LOUIS AGASSIZ: Cyanea Arctica   411

EMILY DICKINSON: "Banish Air from Air"   412

WILLIAM HAMILTON GIBSON: *Three Definitions from* Sharp Eyes
    412

STEPHEN CRANE: Two Untitled Poems   413

TRUMBULL STICKNEY: Dramatic Fragment   414

FRANCES DENSMORE: *From* Chippewa Music   414

ERNEST FENOLLOSA: *From* The Chinese Written Character
    as a Medium for Poetry   415

H. D.: Oread   417

EZRA POUND: Canto XLIX   418

GERTRUDE STEIN: A White Hunter   421

GERTRUDE STEIN: *From* A Geographical History of America
    421

GERTRUDE STEIN: *From* Before the Flowers of Friendship Faded
    Friendship Faded   421

GERTRUDE STEIN: *From* Lifting Belly   421

WALTER CONRAD ARENSBERG: Arithmetical Progression
    of the Verb "To Be"   423

KENNETH REXROTH: *From* A Prolegomenon to a Theodicy   424

ELSE VON FREYTAG-LORINGHOVEN: Affectionate   426

MAX ERNST: Natural History   426

EUGENE JOLAS: *Hypnologues:* Panopticon   427

HARRY CROSBY: Photoheliograph   428

WALLACE STEVENS: Metaphor as Degeneration   429

WILLIAM FAULKNER: *A Chapter from* As I Lay Dying   430

WILLIAM CARLOS WILLIAMS: Flowers by the Sea   430

WILLIAM CARLOS WILLIAMS: The Attic Which Is Desire   431

LOUIS ZUKOFSKY: A Sea   432

LOUIS ZUKOFSKY: Julia's Wild   432

GEORGE OPPEN: *From* Discrete Series   433

GEORGE HERRIMAN: "Krazy Kat"   434

CHARLES HENRI FORD: Reptilia   435

PHILIP LAMANTIA: Animal Snared in His Revery   435

JOHN CAGE: Translating Basho's Haiku   437

M. C. RICHARDS: Poem   438

JACKSON MAC LOW: 2nd Light Poem: for Diane Wakoski—10
    June 1962   439

FRANK KUENSTLER: Three Poems   442

EMMETT WILLIAMS: "Like Attracts Like"   443

CHARLES OLSON: *From* The Mayan Letters   444

ROBERT DUNCAN: Passages 23   445

DENISE LEVERTOV: Turning   446

ED SANDERS: Soft-Man 6   446

JEROME ROTHENBERG: Sightings II   449

JAMES WRIGHT: Milkweed   450

ROBERT BLY: Looking into a Face   451

BERNADETTE MAYER: "Fiction" *from* Story   451

Symposium of the Whole   453

TORLINO [NAVAJO]: Therefore I Must Tell the Truth   453

WALT WHITMAN: *From Preface to* Leaves of Grass   454

GERTRUDE STEIN: Identity a Poem   455

E. E. CUMMINGS: *From* Portraits   461

FRANK O'HARA: In Memory of My Feelings   464

MINA LOY: Parturition   470

ARMAND SCHWERNER: Tablet XV   474

ARTURO GIOVANNITTI: *From* The Nuptials of Death   476

JEROME ROTHENBERG: Cokboy, Part One   477

ELI SIEGEL: Hot Afternoons Have Been in Montana   481

WALTER LOWENFELS: For Ludwig Wittgenstein   486

WALT WHITMAN: I Sing the Body Electric   488

HERMAN MELVILLE: [Sperm]   496

JAMES KOLLER: Poem   498

GEORGE ECONOMOU: *From* Poems for Self-Therapy   499

HANIEL LONG: Heavenly Bodies   501

CLAYTON ESHLEMAN: Ode to Reich   502

DAVID MELTZER: *From* Yetsiradicals   507

THOMAS MCGRATH: *From* Letter to an Imaginary Friend   507

CHARLES OLSON: Enyalion   509

A BOOK OF CHANGES

CHILAM BALAM [MAYA]: "A Chapter of Questions and Answers"
516

TAHIRUSSAWICHI: *From* The Hako: A Pawnee Ceremony   520

JOHN FISKE: Upon the much-to-be lamented desease
of the Reverend Mr John Cotton   525

EDWARD TAYLOR: Meditation 163. Cant. 2.3.
His fruit was Sweet to my Tast.   528

JONES VERY: The Hand and Foot   531

NATHANIEL HAWTHORNE: *From* The American Notebooks   532

HERMAN MELVILLE: *From* Journal up the Straits   534

EMILY DICKINSON: "To Recipient Unknown"   536

GERTRUDE STEIN: *From* Stanzas in Meditation   537

WALLACE STEVENS: The Rock   540

H. D.: *From* Tribute to the Angels   544

LOUIS ZUKOFSKY: *From* Song of Degrees   553

JAMES AGEE: *From* Let Us Now Praise Famous Men   555

LORINE NIEDECKER: Wintergreen Ridge   557

THOMAS MERTON: *From* The Geography of Lograire   563

W. S. MERWIN: Fear   566

ROBERT CREELEY: People   570

ARTHUR OKAMURA: 1.2.3.4.5.6.7.8.9.0   570

JOHN ASHBERY: Clepsydra   575

SPENCER HOLST: Three   582

EDWARD DORN: The Lawg of the Winterbook   583

DAVID ANTIN: 7th separation meditation   585

ROBERT KELLY: The Tower   587

JIM HARRISON: Suite to Fathers   590

DAVID HENDERSON: Egyptian Book of the Dead   593

GEORGE QUASHA: Somapoetics 45   594

T. S. ELIOT: *From* Little Gidding   597

From the I Ching: 64. Wei Chi / Before Completion   597

I: PRELIMINARIES

Poetry over the past hundred years has not only changed radically, it has transformed our idea of what poetry is or ever has been. In this century, especially since World War II, conscious experimentation has shown us the great range of language possibilities at our disposal. And we have learned to look for that "language charged with meaning to the utmost degree" that reveals new powers of communication at the center of our lives. The reader who opens the pages of this book and no more than scans them will come (even before getting to the deeper issues) on a picture of poetry that would have been impossible a hundred or even fifty years ago and hardly probable as recently as twenty years ago. This is not only because this collection includes so much contemporary poetry, but because as editors and poets we have deliberately applied the expanded sense of poetry in our own time to the history of poetry on the North American continent. Only in this way can we start to see how rich that history is: how much more there is than most of us had previously imagined.

Every important change in poetry opens the way for new work in the future and for a redefinition of the past. The 1855 *Leaves of Grass*, for example, is a Declaration of Independence from the "bondage" of British and European conventions that both heralds the 1950s— Charles Olson's "projective verse" or Allen Ginsberg's *Howl*—and frees us to see and express the structural particularities of archaic and tribal poetries at a similar remove from those conventions. All these developments share the sense of poetry as an act of vision, charged with the immediate energies of authentic speech and shaped by its moment in history. Any truly new work, such as that of Ezra Pound, Gertrude Stein, William Carlos Williams, Louis Zukofsky, or John Cage, is an invitation to read, think, and speak differently; it permits a reader (or hearer) to experience, as nothing else quite does, new "levels" of consciousness and verbal meaning. After the Surrealist experiments with "dream" states and "automatic writing," we are more attentive to what used to be called the "irrational." Similarly, the efforts of Dada poets of the 1920s to make use of "pure sound" link up in our minds with the wordless poetries of pre-literate societies (once thought "meaningless"), the meditative chants of the East and certain ritual, magical, and mystical texts of the West. So, too, the partly or wholly

xxix

visual devices of concrete poetry have reminded us that the separation of the verbal and the pictorial is comparatively recent; it did not exist for the Egyptians, Mayans, and Medieval Europeans, or for William Blake. In many such ways—some subtle, some extreme—the domain of poetry has been extended to include virtually any use of language.

Yet anthologies and literary histories have mostly failed to take notice of these extensions and have thus ignored the power of a live tradition to "make new" whatever in the past can grow in the present. When we understand that tradition as an active force, we are able to make genuine use of the discoveries of archaeologists, linguists, anthropologists, historians, and translators who have brought to light whole bodies of poetry and whole cultures long lost to us. (American Indian poetry, going back to pre-Columbian times, is a case in point.) The spread of information about the past and the culturally remote has made the present generation, in Gary Snyder's words, "the first human beings in history to have all of man's culture available to our study" and to be "free enough of the weight of traditional cultures to seek out a larger identity." But for these acquired meanings to be more than a burden of information, we must put them to active use—must employ them, that is, to bring about an actual change in our modes of perception. In this process, present and past will continue to shape each other through a contemporary poetry that creates new means of reawakening and refining our attentions.

This collection attempts to "map" some of the lines of recovery and discovery, of the old and the new, as they relate specifically to the place we inhabit. A map is a guide to unknown terrain, and American poetry remains largely just that—a vast region of which we're not yet fully conscious. The title, *America a Prophecy*, comes from the poem "Printed by William Blake in the year 1793": first, because today Blake seems more than ever to have "prophetically" initiated so much of what this poetry is about; and, second, because his poem projects the image of an American revolution whose demand for freedom would evolve long obscured poetic, sexual, and visionary powers.* If we can begin to map our native poetry in the light of that prophecy, we may also contribute to the high end of which Pound wrote: "Yeats . . . long

---

* Blake's sense of prophecy should not be confused with the easy optimism or pessimism that avoids sharp poetic, historical, and political distinctions. His symbol of Revolutionary Man is Orc (see pages 161 and 508, below), who himself must fail (rigidify) many times before the deepest humanity, Albion, is resurrected in Jerusalem.

ago prayed for a new sacred book. Every age has tried to compound such a volume. Every culture has had such a major anthology."

II: PERSPECTIVES

In mapping the ground for that future anthology, we have tried to avoid locking the reader or ourselves into a new set of rules and theories about poetry. The process, as we see it, calls for many such mappings, and we would hope to encourage directions different from our own. Even so, we have continually had to clarify our two perspectives, and in doing so, four working assumptions have served as guides to the selection.

First, we read American poetry as containing a "prophecy," an "inner truth" linked to the process of change. From the visionary predictions and meditative practice of Chilam Balam, the Mayan jaguar-priest and poet, to the mystical mental travels in Whitman's *Song of Myself*, there has been a tradition (several traditions, in fact) of explicitly prophetic poetry on this continent. But in a broader sense of the visionary as the accurate voice of meaning at work in history, the American Prophecy is present in all that speaks to our sense of "identity" and our need for renewal.

Second, we observe that at a certain point in the history of consciousness, around the time of Blake and Goethe, the process of change began to accelerate. Recently it has been recognized (as it wasn't earlier in this century) that Romanticism was a permanent step forward in the evolution of consciousness. In the work of Blake, Goethe, Coleridge, Keats, and Shelley, to name the most obvious, American poets from Emerson to Robert Duncan have found keys to a tradition of individual vision. Thoreau, for example, seems to bridge Wordsworth and William Carlos Williams in his *Journal*, writing on November 30, 1841: "Good poetry seems so simple and natural a thing that when we meet it we wonder that all men are not always poets. Poetry is nothing but healthy speech. . . ." And Whitman assumes an attitude shared with both Blake and our twentieth-century contemporaries when he speaks of *Leaves of Grass* as a "language experiment" or writes, in 1888: "No one will get at my verses who insists upon viewing them as a literary performance, or as aiming mainly toward art or aestheticism." The aim is rather toward a revelation through authentic speech, and in the last two centuries this has meant an active search for new language structures.

Third, we see this prophetic sense as affirming the oldest function of poetry, which is to interrupt the habits of ordinary consciousness by means of more precise and highly charged uses of language and to provide new tools for discovering the underlying relatedness of all life. Revitalized communication is the means of affirming a true social bond. And, historically, poetry has revealed the hidden commune of human meanings. It reminds us, as Pound wrote in 1918: "Our only measure of truth is . . . our own perception of truth. The undeniable tradition of metamorphoses teaches us that things do not remain always the same. They become other things by swift and unanalysable process. It was only when men began to mistrust the myths and tell nasty lies about the Gods for a moral purpose that these matters became hopelessly confused."

Fourth, we believe that poetry "evolves," not in quality or aesthetic merit, but in awareness of its role and the resources at its disposal. This means that the invention of language possibilities is a cumulative process which has created what might be called a "tradition of changes" or "metapoetry." And this evolution invites us to view the past through the eyes—that is, the *work*—of what Gertrude Stein called "the continuous present."

III: THE SOURCES

Anyone who goes at American poetry with his bare hands, free of existing opinions about its virtues, flaws, and limits, will be astonished at its numerous "unrepresented selves." As this was our experience, we have emphasized many of the more hidden aspects, in the belief that they are necessary to reconstitute an actual "center" of American poetry, truer to our total human experience on this continent than anything we had previously imagined. We have avoided the "old favorites" as much as possible. And where we have decided to keep familiar works for one reason or another, we have placed them in unfamiliar contexts in order to see them anew.

We have drawn materials from many sources—ancient and modern, ruggedly American or related to international movements in poetry and art. Some of these sources are common to all collections of American poetry, while others are rare or new within this book. Among the latter are four general traditions broadly defined, the first two primarily oral or nonliterate or produced by very particularized ethnic/religious communities and the last two coming mainly from the written culture:

[1] The aboriginal poetry of the American continent, which includes pre-Columbian works (written classics like the Mayan *Popol Vuh,* as well as the monumental "concrete poetry" of the Mound-

Quartets, Williams' *Paterson*, Zukofsky's *A*, Stevens' *Notes toward a Supreme Fiction*, H. D.'s *Tribute to the Angels*, Olson's *Maximus Poems*, Duncan's *Passages*, Snyder's *Mountains and Rivers*, Ginsberg's *Kaddish*, Ashbery's *Three Poems*, Mac Low's *Stanzas for Iris Lezak*, Enslin's *Forms*, Emmett Williams' *Sweathearts*, Schwerner's *Tablets*, Kelly's *The Common Shore*, and Antin's *Meditations* begin a long list of what has been possible in American poetry. The present book can, however, do no more than suggest the meaning and range of such work.

A NOTE ON KINDRED PUBLICATIONS: Early anthologies defining what we are here calling the "poetry of changes" or "metapoetry" (but limiting their selections to the twentieth century and to literary poetry in English) include Pound's *Active Anthology* (1933) and Zukofsky's *An "Objectivists" Anthology* (1932). Among recent anthologies defining new areas of this poetry in the post-World-War-II period are *The New American Poetry: 1945–1960*, ed. Donald Allen (Grove Press, 1960); *An Anthology*, ed. La Monte Young and Jackson Mac Low (Heiner Friedrich, 1963); *A Controversy of Poets*, ed. Robert Kelly and Paris Leary (Anchor Books, 1965); *An Anthology of Concrete Poetry*, ed. Emmett Williams (Something Else Press, 1967); *A Caterpillar Anthology*, ed. Clayton Eshleman (Anchor Books, 1971); and *Open Poetry*, containing "Four Anthologies of Expanded Poems" ed. George Quasha, Emmett Williams, Robert Colombo, and Walter Lowenfels (Simon & Schuster, 1973). Since the 1920s the important poetry of this order has been published mainly by small, often noncommercial presses and magazines, most of them run by poets. Here we would mention, among others of comparable value: *The Little Review* (ed. Margaret Anderson and Jane Heap, guest ed. Ezra Pound), Contact Editions (ed. Robert McAlmon), *Transition* (ed. Eugene Jolas), Black Sun Press (ed. Harry Crosby), Objectivist Press (ed. George Oppen), New Directions (ed. James Laughlin), View Editions (ed. Charles Henri Ford), *Experimental Review* (ed. Robert Duncan and Sanders Russell), *Black Mountain Review* (ed. Robert Creeley), *Origin* (ed. Cid Corman), Fluxus (ed. George Maciunas), Jargon Books (ed. Jonathan Williams), City Lights Books (ed. Lawrence Ferlinghetti), *The Fifties* and *The Sixties* (ed. Robert Bly), Totem Press (ed. LeRoi Jones), Trobar Books (ed. George Economou and Robert Kelly), Hawk's Well Press (ed. Jerome Rothenberg), Corinth Books (ed. Ted Wilentz), "C" (ed. Ted Berrigan), *Fuck You* (ed. Ed Sanders), Something Else Press (ed. Dick Higgins and Emmett Williams), *Umbra* (ed. David Henderson), Fulcrum Press (ed. Stuart and Deirdre Montgomery), *Measure* (ed. John Wieners), *Set* (ed. Gerrit Lansing), *Matter* (ed. Robert Kelly), *Caterpillar* (ed.

Clayton Eshleman), Black Sparrow Press (ed. John Martin), Kulchur Press (ed. Lita Hornick), Broadside (ed. Dudley Randall), Angelhair (ed. Anne Waldmann and Lewis Warsh), Frontier Press (ed. Harvey Brown), Sumac Press (ed. Dan Gerber and Jim Harrison), Unicorn Press (ed. Alan Brilliant), *Stony Brook* (ed. George Quasha), Tree Books (ed. David Meltzer), Goliard Editions (ed. Barry Hall), White Rabbit Press, Oyez, Four Seasons Foundation. To all of these we are deeply indebted, and to all of them in some sense our own book is dedicated.

GEORGE QUASHA	JEROME ROTHENBERG
New York City	Salamanca, New York

" Properly, we shd. read for power. Man reading shd. be man intensely alive. The book shd. be a ball of light in one's hands. "

—EZRA POUND, *Guide to Kulchur* [1938]

RE BEGINNINGS

[IROQUOIS]

The Tree of the Great Peace   [c. 1450]

I am Dekanawideh and with the chiefs of the Five Nations
I plant the Tree of the Great Peace. . . .

Roots have spread out from the Tree of the Great Peace. . . .
the Great White Roots of Peace. . . .

Any man of any nation
may trace the roots to their source and be welcome
to shelter
beneath the Great Peace. . . .

I
Dekanawideh
and the chiefs of our Five Nations of the Great Peace
we now uproot the tallest pine

> into the cavity thereby made
> we cast all weapons of war

> Into the depths of the earth
> into the deep underneath. . . .

> we cast all weapons of war

We bury them from sight forever. . . .
and we plant again the tree. . . .

Thus shall the Great Peace be established. . . .

—Adapted by WILLIAM BRANDON, after Arthur C. Parker

WALT WHITMAN

From Song of Myself   [1855]

Dazzling and tremendous how quick the sunrise would kill
      me,
If I could not now and always send sunrise out of me.

We also ascend dazzling and tremendous as the sun,
We found our own my soul in the calm and cool of the
      daybreak.

My voice goes after what my eyes cannot reach,
With the twirl of my tongue I encompass worlds and volumes
      of worlds.

Speech is the twin of my vision . . . . it is unequal to measure
      itself.

It provokes me forever,
It says sarcastically, Walt, you understand enough . . . . why
      don't you let it out then?

Come now I will not be tantalized . . . . you conceive too much
      of articulation.

Do you not know how the buds beneath are folded?
Waiting in gloom protected by frost,
The dirt receding before my prophetical screams,
I underlying causes to balance them at last,
My knowledge my live parts . . . . it keeping tally with the
      meaning of things,
Happiness . . . . which whoever hears me let him or her set
      out in search of this day.

My final merit I refuse you . . . . I refuse putting from me the
      best I am.

Encompass worlds but never try to encompass me,
I crowd your noisiest talk by looking toward you.

Writing and talk do not prove me,
I carry the plenum of proof and every thing else in my face,
With the hush of my lips I confound the topmost skeptic.

EZRA POUND

Religio
or, The Child's Guide to Knowledge   [1918]

What is a god?
A god is an eternal state of mind.
What is a faun?
A faun is an elemental creature.
What is a nymph?
A nymph is an elemental creature.
When is a god manifest?
When the states of mind take form.
When does a man become a god?
When he enters one of these states of mind.
What is the nature of the forms whereby a god is manifest?
They are variable but retain certain distinguishing characteristics.
Are all eternal states of mind gods?
We consider them to be so.
Are all durable states of mind gods?
They are not.
By what characteristic may we know the divine forms?
By beauty.
And if the presented forms are unbeautiful?
They are demons.
If they are grotesque?
They may be well-minded genii.
What are the kinds of knowledge?
There are immediate knowledge and hearsay.
Is hearsay of any value?
Of some.
What is the greatest hearsay?

The greatest hearsay is the tradition of the gods.
Of what use is this tradition?
It tells us to be ready to look.
In what manner do gods appear?
Formed and formlessly.
To what do they appear when formed?
To the sense of vision.
And when formless?
To the sense of knowledge.
May they when formed appear to anything save the
sense of vision?
We may gain a sense of their presence as if they were
standing behind us.
And in this case they may possess form?
We may feel that they do possess form.
Are there names for the gods?
The gods have many names. It is by names that they are
handled in the tradition.
Is there harm in using these names?
There is no harm in thinking of the gods by their
names.
How should one perceive a god, by his name?
It is better to perceive a god by form, or by the sense of
knowledge, and, after perceiving him thus, to consider his
name or to "think what god it may be."
Do we know the number of the gods?
It would be rash to say that we do. A man should be
content with a reasonable number.
What are the gods of this rite?
Apollo, and in some sense Helios, Diana in some of her
phases, also the Cytherean goddess.
To what other gods is it fitting, in harmony or in
adjunction with these rites, to give incense?

To Koré and to Demeter, also to lares and to oreiads and to certain elemental creatures?

How is it fitting to please these lares and other creatures?

It is fitting to please and to nourish them with flowers.

Do they have need of such nutriment?

It would be foolish to believe that they have, nevertheless it bodes well for us that they should be pleased to appear.

Are these things so in the East?

This rite is made for the West.

GERTRUDE STEIN

From Winning His Way   [1931]

What is poetry. This. Is poetry.
Delicately formed. And pleasing. To the eye.
What is fame. Fame is. The care of. Their. Share.
And so. It. Rhymes better.
A pleasure in wealth. Makes. Sunshine.
And a. Pleasure. In sunshine. Makes wealth.
They will manage very well. As they. Please. Them.
What is fame. They are careful. Of awakening. The. Name.
And so. They. Wait. With oxen. More. Than one.
They speak. Of matching. Country oxen. And.
They speak. Of waiting. As if. They. Had won.
By their. Having. Made. A pleasure. With. Their.
May they. Make it. Rhyme. All. The time.
This is. A pleasure. In poetry. As often. As. Ever.
They will. Supply it. As. A measure.
Be why. They will. Often. Soften.
As they may. As. A. Treasure.

H. D.

From The Walls Do Not Fall   [1944]
Section 36

In no wise is the pillar-of-fire
that went before

different from the pillar-of-fire
that comes after;

chasm, schism in consciousness
must be bridged over;

we are each, householder,
each with a treasure;

now is the time to re-value
our secret hoard

in the light of both past and future,
for whether

coins, gems, gold
beakers, platters,

or merely
talismans, records or parchments,

explicitly, we are told,
it contains

for every scribe
which is instructed,

things new
and old.

WALLACE STEVENS

Not Ideas about the Thing
but the Thing Itself   [1954]

At the earliest ending of winter,
In March, a scrawny cry from outside
Seemed like a sound in his mind.

He knew that he heard it,
A bird's cry, at daylight or before,
In the early March wind.

The sun was rising at six,
No longer a battered panache above snow . . .
It would have been outside.

It was not from the vast ventriloquism
Of sleep's faded papier-mâché . . .
The sun was coming from outside.

That scrawny cry—it was
A chorister whose c preceded the choir.
It was part of the colossal sun,

Surrounded by its choral rings,
Still far away. It was like
A new knowledge of reality.

MAP ONE: ORIGINS

In this **Map,** the poet appears as the singer-of-first-things
—creation and emergence, the gods and sacred animals,
the primal unity of all living things, migrations
of the tribes, the land as seen by the men
who travel it, mappings, geographies, and landscapes.
This is a map of things in place, with only
the first signs of those losses and
disruptions that occur in history.

POEMS-OF-ORIGIN were part of the sacred oral tradition of all those tribes inhabiting the North American continent before the European conquests. All spoke of the creation or emergence of animals and gods, and of the evolving geography that men learned in their movements through the land. Of these monumental poems, the Quiché Mayan *Popol Vuh,* literally "book of the community," is the oldest written survival. "Not the story of a hero," writes translator Munro Edmonson, "[but] of a people. . . . The rise and fall of Quiché glory is placed in the cosmic cycling of all creation, and when it is ended, like the cycles of Mayan time, it stops. . . . The next cycle will be something else, perhaps the epoch suggested by the closing line of the work, something called 'Holy Cross.' "

The opening of the selection herein is from the translation by Delia Goetz and Sylvanus G. Morley (1950), while the versified section is from Munro Edmonson's (1971) version that reconstructs an original "entirely composed in parallelistic (i.e. semantic) couplets."

[MAYA]

From The Popol Vuh: Beginnings

This is the account of how all was in suspense, all calm, in silence; all motionless, still, and the expanse of the sky was empty.

This is the first account, the first narrative. There was neither man, nor animal, birds, fishes, crabs, trees, stones, caves, ravines, grasses, nor forests; there was only the sky.

The surface of the earth had not appeared. There was only the calm sea and the great expanse of the sky.

There was nothing brought together, nothing which could make a noise, nor anything which might move, or tremble, or could make noise in the sky.

There was nothing standing; only the calm water, the placid sea, alone and tranquil. Nothing existed.

There was only immobility and silence in the darkness, in the night. Only the Creator, the Maker, Tepeu, Gucumatz, the Forefathers, were in the water surrounded with

13

light. They were hidden under green and blue feathers,
and were therefore called Quetzal Serpent. By nature they
were great sages and great thinkers. In this manner the
sky existed and also the Heart of Heaven, which is the
name of God and thus He is called.

•　　•　　•

So then came his word here.
　　It reached
To Majesty
　　And Quetzal Serpent
There in the obscurity,
　　In the nighttime.
It spoke to Majesty
　　And Quetzal Serpent, and they spoke.
Then they thought;
　　Then they pondered.
Then they found themselves;
　　They assembled
Their words,
　　Their thoughts.
Then they gave birth—
　　Then they heartened themselves.
Then they caused to be created
　　And they bore men.
Then they thought about the birth,
　　The creation
Of trees
　　And shrubs,
And the birth of life
　　And humanity
In the obscurity,
　　In the nighttime
Through him who is the Heart of Heaven,
　　1 Leg by name.
1 Leg Lightning is the first,
　　And the second is Dwarf Lightning.
Third then is Green Lightning,

So that the three of them are the Heart of Heaven.
Then they came to Majesty
And Quetzal Serpent, and then was the invention
Of light
And life.
"What if it were planted?
Then something would brighten—
A supporter,
A nourisher.
So be it.
You must decide on it.
There is the water to get rid of,
To be emptied out,
To create this,
The earth
And have it surfaced
And levelled
When it is planted,
When it is brightened—
Heaven
And earth."

The Walam Olum (below) was the tribal chronicle of the Lenni Lenape or Delaware Indians and is the oldest epic surviving in written form north of Mexico. Its name means "red score" or "painted records," from the symbols painted onto sticks and kept together in bundles. Each symbol, according to C. F. Voeglin, "represented a verse of the chronicle. None of these sticks survive today," only copies of the pictographs and the Lenape verses in the 1833 manuscript of Constantine S. Rafinesque, a nineteenth-century botanist and a natural historian.

The Walam Olum, again according to Voeglin, was "divided into five books or songs, each made up of a varying number of verses. In total length it runs to 183 verses. The songs relate the tribal story from the Creation to the coming of the White man to North America. The main themes are the migration from Asia to Alaska and south and east across the North American continent, and the chronological representation of the chief by which time was measured in the epic." The sixteen verses presented here comprise the second song, in which

Turtle Island may be taken as the world (seen as fastened to a turtle's back) or, geographically, the northeast coast of Asia. It has elsewhere been taken as North America, but that is probably represented in another part of the poem by Snake Island.

long ago a strong snake lived
when men—the big men
stayed there

the strong snake who was hated
& those young men
stayed there—
who was hated who invaded
sacred places

were destroying things—
were badly living—
were both living without peace

both quarrelsome
still living there
were lazy—
both were fighting

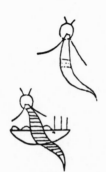

the strong snake quickly
making up his mind
would wipe those people out

& brought it on—
brought floods—
brought rapids

running running—
hollow on hollow—
was lightning (entered like
lightning)—to
ruins ruins

on Turtle Island where
Nanaboush great rabbit god was—
grandfather's grandfather

windy-but-crawling-
along
& unties the young turtle

people & men all
crawling—river of rapids
downstream—to
Turtle Island

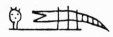

where water monster ate
some—of many
many people

manito's daughter
helped out with a boat
some came from
elsewhere—someone else helped

Nanaboush Nanaboush
everyone's grandfather—grand-
father to people to men
grandfather to turtle

the Delaware were where
the turtle was—turtle
tied down with a belt

& knew fear of the turtle—
& prayer to the turtle—
to end it—make good
what he'd done

in water—running to
dryness
in long hollow places—
in caves—
then the snake god got out
(got going)

SOURCE: Pictographs reproduced from DANIEL G. BRINTON, *The Lenape and their Legends,* 1885; text adapted from "The Walam Olum, or Red Score," *Indiana Historical Society* (1954).

■ *"I have heard what the talkers were talking . . . . the talk of the beginning and the end,*
But I do not talk of the beginning or the end.

There was never any more inception than there is now,
Nor any more youth or age than there is now;
And will never be any more perfection than there is now,
Nor any more heaven or hell than there is now.

Urge and urge and urge,
Always the procreant urge of the world.

Out of the dimness opposite equals advance . . . . Always substance and increase,
Always a knit of identity . . . . always distinction . . . . always a breed of life. "

—WALT WHITMAN, Song of Myself [1855]

A concern with first things continues into twentieth-century poetry, incorporating new visions from physical science and anthropology, as well as older myths long known to European man. The gods are introduced as primal values, "eternal states of mind."

ROBINSON JEFFERS

The Great Explosion

The universe expands and contracts like a great heart.
It is expanding, the farthest nebulae
Rush with the speed of light into empty space.
It will contract, the immense navies of stars and galaxies,
      dust-clouds and nebulae
Are recalled home, they crush against each other in one
      harbor, they stick in one lump
And then explode it, nothing can hold them down; there is no
      way to express that explosion; all that exists
Roars into flame, the tortured fragments rush away from each
      other into all the sky, new universes
Jewel the black breast of night; and far off the outer nebulae
      like charging spearmen again
Invade emptiness.
              No wonder we are so fascinated with
      fire-works
And our huge bombs: it is a kind of homesickness perhaps for
      the howling fire-blast that we were born from.

But the whole sum of the energies
That made and contained the giant atom survives. It will
      gather again and pile up, the power and the glory—
And no doubt it will burst again; diastole and systole: the
      whole universe beats like a heart.
Peace in our time was never one of God's promises; but back
      and forth, die and live, burn and be damned,

The great heart beating, pumping into our arteries His
      terrible life.
                  He is beautiful beyond belief.
And we, God's apes—or tragic children—share in the beauty.
      We see it above our torment, that's what life's for.
He is no God of love, no justice of a little city like Dante's
      Florence, no anthropoid God
Making commandments: this is the God who does not care
      and will never cease. Look at the seas there
Flashing against this rock in the darkness—look at the
      tide-stream stars—and the fall of nations—and dawn
Wandering with wet white feet down the Carmel Valley to
      meet the sea. These are real and we see their beauty.
The great explosion is probably only a metaphor—I know not
      —of faceless violence, the root of all things.

Charles Olson's *Maximus Poems,* like the *Cantos* of Ezra Pound, Wil-
liam Carlos Williams' *Paterson,* and Robert Duncan's *Passages,* is a
long, continuous work, throughout which Maximus, the archetypal
man, speaks. Like James Joyce's Dublin in *Ulysses,* Olson's setting is
an actual town, Gloucester, Mass. (where he lived), whereas Duncan's
City in "Tribal Memories," below, shares with these principally the
mythic plane of meaning.

CHARLES OLSON

Maximus, from Dogtown—I
proem

The sea was born of the earth without sweet union of love Hesiod
    says

But that then she lay for heaven and she bare the thing which
    encloses
every thing, Okeanos the one which all things are and by which
    nothing
is anything but itself, measured so

screwing earth, in whom love lies which unnerves the limbs and
    by its
heat floods the mind and all gods and men into further nature

                  Vast earth rejoices,

deep-swirling Okeanos steers all things through all things,
everything issues from the one, the soul is led from drunkenness
to dryness, the sleeper lights up from the dead,
the man awake lights up from the sleeping

        WATERED ROCK
of pasture meadow orchard road where Merry
died in pieces tossed by the bull he raised himself to fight
in front of people, to show off his
              Handsome Sailor ism

died as torso head & limbs
in a Saturday night's darkness
drunk trying
to get the young bull down
to see if Sunday morning again he might
before the people show off
once more
his prowess—braggart man to die
among Dogtown meadow rocks

           "under" the dish
           of the earth
           Okeanos <u>under</u>
           Dogtown
           through which (inside of which) the sun passes
           at night—
                she passes the sun back to
           the east through her body
           the Geb (of heaven) at night

Nut is water
above & below, vault
above and below
watered rock on which
by which Merry
was so many pieces
Sunday morning

<u>subterranean</u> and celestial
primordial water holds
Dogtown high
            And down
the ice holds
Dogtown, scattered
boulders little bull
who killed
Merry
        who sought to manifest
his soul, the stars
manifest their souls

                my soft sow the roads
of Dogtown trickling like from underground rock
springs under an early cold March moon

                        or hot summer and my son
                        we come around a corner
                        where a rill
                        makes Gee Avenue in a thin
                        ford

                        after we see a black duck
                        walking across a populated
                        corner

                            life spills out

Soft soft rock
Merry died by
in the black night

fishermen lived
in Dogtown and came
when it was old to whore
on Saturday nights
at three girls' houses

Pisces eternally swimming
inside her overhead
their boots or the horse
clashing the sedimentary
rock tortoise shell
she sits on the maternal beast
of the moon and the earth

Not one mystery
nor man
possibly not even a bird
heard Merry
fight that bull by
(was Jeremiah Millett's house

Drunk
to cover his shame,
blushing Merry
in the bar
walking up

to Dogtown to try
his strength,
the baby bull
now full grown

waiting,
not even knowing
death
was in his power over
this man who lay
in the Sunday morning sun
like smoked fish

in the same field
fly-blown and a colony
of self-hugging grubs—handsome
in the sun, the mass
of the dead and the odor
eaten out of the air
by the grubs sticking
moving by each other
as close as sloths

she is the goddess
of the earth, and night
of the earth and fish
of the little bull
and of Merry

Merry
had a wife

She is the heavenly mother
the stars are the fish swimming
in the heavenly ocean she has
four hundred breasts

Merry could have used
as many could have drunk
the strength he claimed
he had, the bravo

Pulque in Spain
where he saw the fight
octli in Mexico
where he wanted to
show off
dead in Gloucester
where he did

The four hundred gods
of drink alone

sat with him
as he died
in pieces

In 400 pieces
his brain shot
the last time the bull
hit him pegged him
to the rock

      before he tore him
to pieces

      the night sky
looked down

Dogtown is soft
in every season
high up on her granite
horst, light growth
of all trees and bushes
strong like a puddle's ice
the bios
of nature in this
park of eternal
events is a sidewalk
to slide on, this
terminal moraine:

the rocks the glacier tossed
toys
Merry played by
with his bull

      400 sons of her only
      would sit
      by the game

      All else was in the sky
      or in town
      or shrinking solid rock

We drink
or break open
our veins solely
to know. A drunkard
showing himself in public
is punished
by death

The deadly power of her
was there that night
Merry was born
under the pulque-sign

The plants of heaven
the animals of the soul
were denied

Joking men
had laughed
at Merry

Drink
had made him
brave

Only the sun
in the morning
covered him
with flies

Then only
after the grubs
had done him
did the earth
let her robe
uncover and her part
take him in

ROBERT DUNCAN

from the Emperor Julian *Hymn to the Mother of the Gods:*
And Attis encircles the heavens like a tiara, and thence sets out as though to descend to earth.

For the even is bounded, but the uneven is without bounds and there is no way through or out of it.

Tribal Memories   Passages 1

And to Her-Without-Bounds I send,
wherever She wanders,   by what
        campfire at evening,

among tribes setting each the City where
                we Her people are
at the end of a day's reaches   here
        the Eternal
lamps lit, here   the wavering human
    sparks of heat and light
glimmer, go out, and reappear.

For this is the company of the living
and the poet's voice speaks from no
        crevice in the ground between
            mid-earth and underworld
breathing fumes of what is deadly to know,
            news larvae in tombs
            and twists of time do feed upon,

but from the hearth stone, the lamp light,
            the heart of the matter where the

            house is held

yet here, the warning light at the edge of town!
The City will go out in time, will go out
    into time, hiding even its embers.

And we were scattered thruout the countries and times of man

for we took alarm in ourselves,
                    rumors of the enemy
spread among the feathers of the wing that coverd us.

Mnemosyne, they named her, the
                    Mother with the whispering
              featherd wings.   Memory,
the great speckled bird who broods over the
              nest of souls, and her egg,
         the dream in which all things are living,
I return to, leaving my self.

I am beside myself with this
              thought of the One in the World-Egg,
enclosed,   in a shell of murmurings,

                    rimed round,
                    sound-chamberd child.

It's that first!   The forth-going to be
                    bursts into green as the spring
              winds blow watery from the south
and the sun returns north.   He hides

         fire among words in his mouth

and comes racing out of the zone of dark and storm

                    towards us.

I sleep in the afternoon, retreating from work,
reading and dropping away from the reading,
as if I were only a seed of myself,
         unawakend,   unwilling
                    to sleep or wake.

BLACK TRADITION: A vast area of American poetry is to be found in the Black oral tradition. The sermons of Black preacher-poets, for example (commonly set up in verse lines in the printed versions), are instances both of speech in complex motion and of a process of ongoing *mythos,* i.e. of ancient story made or remade in the telling. The contemporary poet Tom Weatherly writes: "Our tradition is composed of those work songs, field hollers, gospels, and blues. . . . That's our poetry, our tradition, my main main, and if you put it down, you put down most of what is good in American song lyric and poetry, and you put down most of the base I build on." The sermon-poem below originally appeared in Zora Neale Hurston's *Mules and Men* (1935).

[SERMON]
Behold the Rib!

I take my text from Genesis two and twenty-one (Gen. 2:21)

Behold de Rib!
Now, my beloved,
Behold means to look and see.
Look at dis woman God done made,
But first thing, ah hah!
Ah wants you to gaze upon God's previous works.
Almighty and arisen God, hah!
Peace-giving and prayer-hearing God,
High-riding and strong armded God
Walking acrost his globe creation, hah!
Wid de blue elements for a helmet
And a wall of fire round his feet
He wakes de sun every morning from his fiery bed
Wid de breath of his smile
And commands de moon wid his eyes.
And Oh—
Wid de eye of Faith
I can see him

Even de lion had a mate
So God shook his head
And a thousand million diamonds
Flew out from his glittering crown
And studded de evening sky and made de stars.
So God put Adam into a deep sleep
And took out a bone, ah hah!
And it is said that it was a rib.
Behold de rib!
A bone out of a man's side.
He put de man to sleep and made wo-man,
And men and women been sleeping together ever since.
Behold de rib!
Brothers, if God
Had taken dat bone out of man's head
He would have meant for woman to rule, hah
If he had taken a bone out of his foot,
He would have meant for us to dominize and rule.
He could have made her out of back-bone
And then she would have been behind us.
But, no, God Almighty, he took de bone out of his side
So dat places de woman beside us;
Hah! God knowed his own mind.
Behold de rib!
And now I leave dis thought wid you,
Standing out on de eaves of ether
Breathing clouds from out his nostrils,
Blowing storms from 'tween his lips
I can see!!
Him seize de mighty axe of his proving power
And smite the stubborn-standing space,
And laid it wide open in a mighty gash—
Making a place to hold de world
I can see him—
Molding de world out of thought and power
And whirling it out on its eternal track,
Ah hah, my strong armded God!
He set de blood red eye of de sun in de sky
And told it,

Wait, wait! Wait there till Shiloh come
I can see!
Him mold de mighty mountains
And melting de skies into seas.
Oh, Behold, and look and see! hah
We see in de beginning
He made de bestes every one after its kind,
De birds that fly trackless air,
De fishes dat swim de mighty deep—
Male and fee-male, hah!
Then he took of de dust of de earth
And made man in his own image.
And man was alone,
Let us all go marchin' up to de gates of Glory.
Tramp! tramp! tramp!
In step wid de host dat John saw.
Male and female like God made us
Side by side.
Oh, behold de rib!
And less all set down in Glory together
Right round his glorified throne
And praise his name forever.

                          AMEN.

ALLEN GINSBERG
The End

I am I, old Father Fisheye that begat the ocean, the worm at
  my own ear, the serpent turning around a tree,
I sit in the mind of the oak and hide in the rose, I know if any
  wake up, none but my death,
come to me bodies, come to me prophecies, come all
  foreboding, come spirits and visions,
I receive all, I'll die of cancer, I enter the coffin forever, I
  close my eye, I disappear,
I fall on myself in winter snow, I roll in a great wheel
  through rain, I watch fuckers in convulsion,
car screech, furies groaning their basso music, memory
  fading in the brain, men imitating dogs,
I delight in a woman's belly, youth stretching his breasts and
  thighs to sex, the cock sprung inward
gassing its seed on the lips of Yin, the beasts dance in Siam,
  they sing opera in Moscow,
my boys yearn at dusk on stoops, I enter New York, I play my
  jazz on a Chicago Harpsichord,
Love that bore me I bear back to my Origin with no loss, I
  float over the vomiter
thrilled with my deathlessness, thrilled with this endlessness I
  dice and bury,
come Poet shut up eat my word, and taste my mouth in your
  ear.

TOTEMIC ANIMALS: Speaking of the (totemic) connection between
tribal men of different clans and their animal allies, Gary Snyder writes:
"People of primitive cultures appreciate animals as other people off on
various trips. Snakes move without limbs, and are like free penises.
Birds fly, sing, and dance; they gather food for their babies; they disap-

pear for months and then come back. Fish can breathe water and are brilliant colors. Mammals are like us, they fuck and give birth to babies while panting and purring; their young suck their mothers' breasts; they know terror and delight, they play." *(Earth House Hold,* 1969*)*

[SIOUX]

Three for Bear

    1.

He comes from the north
he comes to fight
he comes from the north
see him there

I throw dust on me
it changes me
I am a bear
when I go to meet him

2.

Send word, bear father
send word, bear father
I'm having a hard time
send word, bear father
I'm having a bad time

3.

My paw is holy
herbs are everywhere
my paw
herbs are everywhere

My paw is holy
everything is holy
my paw
everything is holy

    —Working by JAMES KOLLER, from Frances Densmore

EZRA POUND
Canto XLVII

Who even dead, yet hath his mind entire!
>This sound came in the dark
>First must thou go the road
>>to hell
And to the bower of Ceres' daughter Proserpine,
Through overhanging dark, to see Tiresias,
Eyeless that was, a shade, that is in hell
So full of knowing that the beefy men know less than he,
Ere thou come to thy road's end.
>>Knowledge the shade of a shade,
Yet must thou sail after knowledge
Knowing less than drugged beasts. *phtheggometha
thasson*
φθεγγώμεθα θᾶσσον
>The small lamps drift in the bay
And the sea's claw gathers them.
Neptunus drinks after neap-tide.
Tamuz! Tamuz!!
The red flame going seaward.
>By this gate art thou measured.
From the long boats they have set lights in the water,
The sea's claw gathers them outward.
Scilla's dogs snarl at the cliff's base,
The white teeth gnaw in under the crag,
But in the pale night the small lamps float seaward
>>Τυ Δώνα
>>TU DIONA

Καὶ Μοῖραιτ' "Αδονιν
Kai MOIRAI' ADONIN
The sea is streaked red with Adonis,
The lights flicker red in small jars.
Wheat shoots rise new by the altar,
>flower from the swift seed.
Two span, two span to a woman,
Beyond that she believes not. Nothing is of any importance.
To that is she bent, her intention

To that art thou called ever turning intention,
Whether by night the owl-call, whether by sap in shoot,
Never idle, by no means by no wiles intermittent
Moth is called over mountain
The bull runs blind on sword, *naturans*
To the cave art thou called, Odysseus,
By Molü hast thou respite for a little,
By Molü art thou freed from the one bed
   that thou may'st return to another
The stars are not in her counting,
   To her they are but wandering holes.
Begin thy plowing
When the Pleiades go down to their rest,
Begin thy plowing
40 days are they under seabord,
Thus do in fields by seabord
And in valleys winding down toward the sea.
When the cranes fly high
   think of plowing.
By this gate art thou measured
Thy day is between a door and a door
Two oxen are yoked for plowing
Or six in the hill field
White bulk under olives, a score for drawing down stone,
Here the mules are gabled with slate on the hill road.
Thus was it in time.
And the small stars now fall from the olive branch,
Forked shadow falls dark on the terrace
More black than the floating martin
   that has no care for your presence,
His wing-print is black on the roof tiles
And the print is gone with his cry.
So light is thy weight on Tellus
Thy notch no deeper indented
Thy weight less than the shadow
Yet hast thou gnawed through the mountain,
   Scylla's white teeth less sharp.
Hast thou found a nest softer than cunnus
Or hast thou found better rest

Hast'ou a deeper planting, doth thy death year
Bring swifter shoot?
Hast thou entered more deeply the mountain?

The light has entered the cave. Io! Io!
The light has gone down into the cave,
Splendour on splendour!
By prong have I entered these hills:
That the grass grow from my body,
That I hear the roots speaking together,
The air is new on my leaf,
The forked boughs shake with the wind.
Is Zephyrus more light on the bough, Apeliota
more light on the almond branch?
By this door have I entered the hill.
Falleth,
Adonis falleth.
Fruit cometh after. The small lights drift out with the tide,
sea's claw has gathered them outward,
Four banners to every flower
The sea's claw draws the lamps outward.
Think thus of thy plowing
When the seven stars go down to their rest
Forty days for their rest, by seabord
And in valleys that wind down toward the sea
Καὶ Μοῖραι᾽ Ἄδονιν
KAI MOIRAI' ADONIN
When the almond bough puts forth its flame,
When the new shoots are brought to the altar,
Τυ Διώνα, Καὶ Μοῖραι
TU DIONA, KAI MOIRAI
Καὶ Μοῖραι᾽ Ἄδονιν
KAI MOIRAI' ADONIN
     that hath the gift of healing,
That hath the power over wild beasts.

GLOSS TO FOREIGN WORDS: (Canto XLVII). *phtheggometha / thasson:*
"Let us raise our voices without delay" *(Odyssey,* Book X). *Tu
Diona, kai Moirai:* "You, Dione, and the Fates" (from Bion's *Lament for Adonis*).

SANTO BLANCO, a Seri Indian from the island of Tiburon off the coast of Baja California, communed with the singing god of the cave and received the power to carry on an ancient tradition of song. (Transposed by George Quasha, from Dane and Mary Roberts Coolidge, *The Last of the Seris, 1939.*)

SANTO BLANCO
A Series of Seri Songs / Whales

I

The sea
is calm, no
wind. Warm sun
plays me
on the surface, haie!
my many, many
companions, torque
of many clouds,
all know the joy.

II

Mother
whale knows it,
slices the surface
with speed—no
sharks here, but speed
over surface.
        She sinks
to the bottom: four
whales
born.

III

One
surfaces,
leaps around Mother
over surfaces.
Now three

leaping over surfaces.
Now gone
below surfaces, with Mother,
eight days
out of our sight.

IV

Comes then the old,
old whale, bearing no
young, swims the near
and never far from
the shore of her sadness,
she of pity, old, that cannot
feed as whales.
Mouth on the surface,
sheer breath—
        hrrrrr
small fish, lame birds
are such a meal.

V

She is sick, sharks
gnaw her bowels, meat
of opposites, clinging
at any shore.
Slow travel, no bowels,
death, and no travel.

VI

Fifty sharks, looped
in hunger, a belly
moves inward
of fifty jaws, flesh,
bowels, old
red cunnus, death, and
she without teeth
to fight sharks.

HERMAN MELVILLE
The Head of the Whale
(from Moby Dick)

In thought, a fine human brow is like the East when troubled with the morning. In the repose of the pasture, the curled brow of the bull has a touch of the grand in it. Pushing heavy cannon up mountain defiles, the elephant's brow is majestic. Human or animal, the mystical brow is as that great golden seal affixed by the German emperors to their decrees. It signifies—"God: done this day by my hand." But in most creatures, nay in man himself, very often the brow is but a mere strip of alpine land lying along the snow line. Few are the foreheads which like Shakspeare's or Melancthon's rise so high, and descend so low, that the eyes themselves seem clear, eternal, tideless mountain lakes; and all above them in the forehead's wrinkles, you seem to track the antlered thoughts descending there to drink, as the Highland hunters track the snow prints of the deer. But in the great Sperm Whale, this high and mighty god-like dignity inherent in the brow is so immensely amplified, that gazing on it, in that full front view, you feel the Deity and the dread powers more forcibly than in beholding any other object in living nature. For you see no one point precisely; not one distinct feature is revealed; no nose, eyes, ears, or mouth; no face; he has none, proper; nothing but that one broad firmament of a forehead, pleated with riddles; dumbly lowering with the doom of boats, and ships, and men. Nor, in profile, does this wondrous brow diminish; though that way viewed, its grandeur does not domineer upon you so. In profile, you plainly perceive that horizontal, semi-crescentic depression in the forehead's middle, which, in man, is Lavater's mark of genius.

But how? Genius in the Sperm Whale? Has the Sperm Whale ever written a book, spoken a speech? No, his great genius is declared in his doing nothing particular to prove it. It is moreover declared in his pyramidical silence. And this reminds me that had the great Sperm Whale been known to the young Orient World, he would have been deified by their child-magian thoughts. They deified the crocodile of the Nile, because the crocodile is tongueless; and the Sperm Whale has no tongue, or at least it is so exceedingly small, as to be incapable of protrusion. If hereafter any highly cultured, poetical nation shall lure back to their birthright, the merry May-day gods of old; and livingly enthrone them again in the now egotistical sky; on the now unhaunted hill; then be sure, exalted to Jove's high seat, the great Sperm Whale shall lord it.

Champollion deciphered the wrinkled granite hiero-glyphics. But there is no Champollion to decipher the Egypt of every man's and every being's face. Physiognomy, like every other human science, is but a passing fable. If then, Sir William Jones, who read in thirty languages, could not read the simplest peasant's face in its profounder and more subtle meanings, how may unlettered Ishmael hope to read the awful Chaldee of the Sperm Whale's brow? I but put that brow before you. Read it if you can.

THE POETRY OF WHALE SONGS: Melville's Ishmael places the whale among the "merry May-day gods," and to hear the singing of the Humpback whales is to know a reason why. The ethereal sea-sounds reported by sailors for centuries may have been these songs, transmitted by "impedance matching" or the "coupling of sound from water to air [which] occurs at all times through the hull of a wooden boat at sea." Dr. Roger Payne's recordings (*The Whale,* the New York Zoological Society's long-playing record) and studies of whale sounds suggest that they "can properly be called songs because they occur in complete sequences that are repeated." They differ from bird songs in that they are longer (six to thirty minutes) and more complexly structured (e.g., beginning and ending anywhere in a given sequence). *Hypothesis:* the apparent resemblance between whales' songs and certain man-made structures (oral-tribal poetry; serial, electronic, and jazz music; etc.) may be a key to an interspecies poetics and psychic process.

CHARLES SIMIC

The Animals

I have no news of the animals.
Do they still exist? Those toads
I used to know so well. And the foxes,
Are they still out there in the dark?

Impossible. Where a horse used to graze
In my dream—an emptiness, edge of a cliff
On which I balance myself
With no skill and plenty of luck.

I can see now that I'll have to construct
My bestiary in some other manner:
Without a bone or an eye,
Without even a track of blood in the snow,
And the barking
Reaching over my shoulders.

Alone, without a model—
It will be up to me
To imagine, out of the stones and debris
That are left, a new species—

A tooth,
An udder
Full of milk.

EMILY DICKINSON

"In Winter in My Room"

In Winter in my Room
I came upon a Worm—
Pink, lank and warm—
But as he was a worm

And worms presume
Not quite with him at home—
Secured him by a string
To something neighboring
And went along.

A Trifle afterward
A thing occurred
I'd not believe it if I heard
But state with creeping blood—
A snake with mottles rare
Surveyed my chamber floor
In feature as the worm before
But ringed with power—
The very string with which
I tied him—too
When he was mean and new
That string was there—

I shrank—"How fair you are"!
Propitiation's claw—
"Afraid," he hissed
"Of me"?
"No cordiality"—
He fathomed me—
Then to a Rhythm *Slim*
Secreted in his Form
As Patterns swim
Projected him.

That time I flew
Both eyes his way
Lest he pursue
Nor ever ceased to run
Till in a distant Town
Towns on from mine
I set me down
This was a dream.

EDGAR ALLAN POE

The Lynx

(from *Silence—A Fable*)

Now there are fine tales in the volumes of the Magi— in the iron-bound, melancholy volumes of the Magi. Therein, I say, are glorious histories of the Heaven, and of the Earth, and of the mighty sea—and of the Genii that overruled the sea, and the earth, and the lofty heaven. There was much lore too in the sayings which were said by the Sibyls; and holy, holy things were heard of old by the dim leaves that trembled around Dodona—but, as Allah liveth, that fable which the demon told me as he sat by my side in the shadow of the tomb, I hold to be the most wonderful of all! And as the Demon made an end of his story, he fell back within the cavity of the tomb and laughed. And I could not laugh with the Demon, and he cursed me because I could not laugh. And the lynx which dwelleth forever in the tomb, came out therefrom, and lay down at the feet of the Demon, and looked at him steadily in the face.

ROBERT KELLY

The princes in their masks come carrying wheat
step by step through the wet maple leaves)
                                        thunder's bird

                    I caught you
                in my first sleep
but suffered the deceitful tongue of dream
to go on singing
                & in the last
true dream of the almost waking
you were far above me filling the air with my name

I heard my name among the trees
where it was so dark not even
my wife's face could tell me where the sun was

1 THE MASKS

were everyone. Moon Wind Thunder Famine Death
wolves & mosquitoes, a whale dying on the beach.

(The sun was pressed tight to my face
my long blond hair streamed out around the basswood

when I wear this mask the children scream)

                                        Hens Cocks

When did we become such things as mushrooms & eagles
fish scales shredded on bark, scales stuck to my true love's
        fingers,
she knows how long to cook fish

        2

My dream when I was five was broken stone old man
who had ground wheat in his stomach's mill,
he was stone ate stone

                        was a face that did not move.
                                        Our fishermen
learned to eat salmon from bears

We catch them with our masks
the face changes only in water
the fish is good
                truly we can eat anything we like

Fish dry in the sun All winter keep
the wolves away
                Come in the wolf mask

(stone lion I was four years old)
stone chair I sat on)

                        Put a fish or parts of a fish
in each hillock of corn

The mask said:
an animal turns grasses into flesh
you people turn flesh to spirit
                              we come
every winter to eat your spirit
make us strong

                    Take this mask
                    Eat these animals

                                        Fishermen
wear this mask   This mask eats fish

    3

Flame
        The housedoor faces west
all winter
we'll catch sunlight

                        The tenderness of my people, the names
they bear & their problems

                        If you put on this mask
the wet log will break into flame
                                    heat stones. The stones
boil water & cook meat
                        breaking down the protein chains.

This is important to know

                        Wear my mask, the one
of an animal that lives in fire

    4

Moon mask
Wear a mask & bite the moon,
                        who said anything different?

        I wanted to apologize to him
because I have no sons
     Look I will probably never want children
are we both clear about that? I keep telling her
I want her dance around the World as center
not the child not the child
         Is the child the world
         Is the child the world

then sometimes my body hurts
& I think of my friends with children

          Sun mask & wear
this mask The power
   is IN the world
is in your body & my body
       I say it like that
to keep it always happening.
      The window The masked
house we live in
    Now

   5

And Mercury's signature (Cornelius Agrippa says)
is the Shee-Beare
     patient by the rapids catching salmon

These masks also we put on,
       young men of the tribe
come back open-mouthed from our empty hunting

          Yesterday
I saw two deer too far away too young way up the ridge

The mask pursues me, has rotten teeth
tells me what I want to eat, hints
      at where the daisies go
after October

The mask is brown, wants women
comes when I call & remembers every address
Dont you know I can write down all your names
& find your house wherever you live?

Mask-confidence,

mask-fear.

I am the wolf   I am the sudden wind
scattering cloud   I am the dreamer doubting his dream
the dream-carver hollowing a mask
that will fit anybody's face
The power

is in that hollow
The mask makes noise
when the wind blows through

6

Eagle   Loon   Whale   Teeth
of a large animal, for tearing meat

Blue round, white eyes
the shells catch the light, store
some glint of time's power in themselves
When everything is dark

burn this candle
Work through   Woman
came to our house to use the phone
she'd walked for a mile & could find no other
who did she call   what did she say

The bugs make mask-eyes
in the leaves, big linden leaves, big
enough for a child's face

Each turns
turns into other.
I have no brother
from my mother's womb.

There are powers in whom we can live:
masked with their energies
our eyes seek a familiar world

hold it, hold the wolves away from the settlement
hold the street in place
                              because in dream a mask
calls out a man's name
& I hear it waking, summoned by my name
& our tender hands rise to take the mask away

we see a face nakeder than wood
come home to the world

WALT WHITMAN

This Compost

1.

Something startles me where I thought I was safest,
I withdraw from the still woods I loved,
I will not go now on the pastures to walk,
I will not strip the clothes from my body to meet my lover the
    sea,
I will not touch my flesh to the earth as to other flesh to
    renew me.

O how can it be that the ground itself does not sicken?
How can you be alive you growths of spring?
How can you furnish health you blood of herbs, roots,
    orchards, grain?
Are they not continually putting distemper'd corpses within
    you?
Is not every continent work'd over and over with sour dead?

Where have you disposed of their carcasses?

Those drunkards and gluttons of so many generations?
Where have you drawn off all the foul liquid and meat?
I do not see any of it upon you to-day, or perhaps I am
      deceiv'd,
I will run a furrow with my plough, I will press my spade
      through the sod and turn it up underneath,
I am sure I shall expose some of the foul meat.

        2.

Behold this compost! behold it well!
Perhaps every mite has once form'd part of a sick person—yet
      behold!
The grass of spring covers the prairies,
The bean bursts noiselessly through the mould in the garden,
The delicate spear of the onion pierces upward,
The apple-buds cluster together on the apple-branches,
The resurrection of the wheat appears with pale visage out of
      its graves,
The tinge awakes over the willow-tree and the mulberry-tree,
The he-birds carol mornings and evenings while the she-birds
      sit on their nests,
The young of poultry break through the hatch'd eggs,
The new-born of animals appear, the calf is dropt from the
      cow, the colt from the mare,
Out of its little hill faithfully rise the potato's dark green
      leaves,
Out of its hill rises the yellow maize-stalk, the lilacs bloom in
      the dooryards,
The summer growth is innocent and disdainful above all
      those strata of sour dead.

What chemistry!
That the winds are really not infectious,
That this is no cheat, this transparent green-wash of the sea
      which is so amorous after me,
That it is safe to allow it to lick my naked body all over with
      its tongues,

That it will not endanger me with the fevers that have deposited
    themselves in it,
That all is clean forever and forever,
That the cool drink from the well tastes so good,
That blackberries are so flavorous and juicy,
That the fruits of the apple-orchard and the orange-orchard, that
    melons, grapes, peaches, plums, will none of them poison
    me,
That when I recline on the grass I do not catch any disease,
Though probably every spear of grass rises out of what was once
    a catching disease.

Now I am terrified at the Earth, it is that calm and patient,
It grows such sweet things out of such corruptions,
It turns harmless and stainless on its axis, with such endless
    successions of diseas'd corpses,
It distills such exquisite winds out of such infused fetor,
It renews with such unwitting looks its prodigal, annual, sump-
    tuous crops,
It gives such divine materials to men, and accepts such leavings
    from them at last.

. . . the myth of origins as an account of historical migrations . . .

RED CORN [Osage]
Map of Earth & Sky: Migrations

THE CHART accompanies a history chanted by the members of a secret society of the Osage nation. It images the world and early man's emergence: tree-of-life and river at the top; sun, moon, and stars beneath; four heavens or upper worlds at center, through which the ancestors passed before coming to this earth, etc. The pictographs are (mnemonic) clues to songs, but the whole map is more than that: part of a dream-time poem of earth and sky. (SOURCE: GARRICK MALLERY, *Picture-Writing of the American Indians,* 1888–1889.)

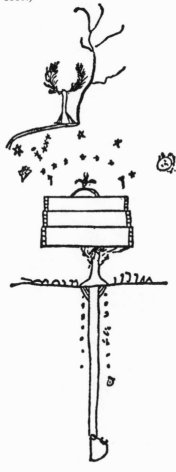

■ "*Ethnoastronomy is the map of archaeological sites geometrized by the heavens* (geo-metron); *in the stars lies the key to Stonehenge and the Mayan temples, the shape of the earth bent, by time, continental drift, migration, and galactic speed. So the Shoshoneans wandered across stars into the Aztec oikumene; the Osage and Salish followed a galactic trail, language families bending the sky out of into shape. The star temples of the Caribbean move thru stars into the Mississippi Valley. Genghis Khan sweeps across the skies of Europe; and the magi use conjunction to find the birth-time-place of Christ. Ethnoastronomy is the route taken to the New World, taken originally by the Indians, lost in snow-blind ice, is the route taken again by the Norsemen, the Sufis, moving thru the clear geometric temple of the sky, delivered suddenly into other promised lands, Newfoundland, Vinland, and Boston harbor; is the map of East by West taken by Columbus, the French and Cartier, is the map, sprung into three dimensions, by which the starships locate the earth. For the earth-lands move on the X-Y axis, and the earth itself moves thru X-Y-Z coordinates; the Niña, Pinta, and Santa Maria sighting stars for position on the surface, the great unknown starships moving thru stars as they sight them.*"

—RICHARD GROSSINGER, *Book of the Earth and Sky*
(Book I) [1971]

BOOK OF THE HOPI [I]
Migration Symbols

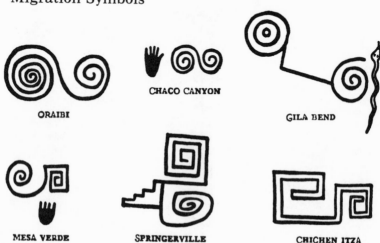

ORAIBI

CHACO CANYON

GILA BEND

MESA VERDE

SPRINGERVILLE

CHICHEN ITZA

PICTURE-WRITING: Cut into rocks of the Southwest, in fact all along the spine of America from Chile to Canada, pictographs mark the emergence and migration patterns of an ancient people, called "ancestors" by such as the Hopi. "The circles," writes Frank Waters in *The Book of the Hopi* (1963), "record the number of rounds or pasos covered, north, east, south and west." At Oraibi, the oldest continuous settlement in the United States, resting on a six-hundred foot high mesa in the Arizona desert, the double coil of interlacing movements "shows the completed four circles, with three points covered on the return." Could these graphs have been a sort of mapping of the internal sense of space-time in the minds of voyaging people? Such "torsion maps" would record the dynamisms of history in a way related both visually and functionally to Wilhelm Reich's sexual energy graphs (see below, page 406). Tentative "translation": *The journey over Earth is a union with Her body.* The torsion patterns, like the suggested myth behind them, are a global presence, some other examples appearing on the walls of a burial chamber at New Grange, Ireland, or the Temple of Hal Tarxien, Malta (circa 4000 B.C.).

BOOK OF THE HOPI [II]
Song of the Humpbacked Flute Player

Kitana-po, ki-tana-po, ki-tana-po,
　　ki-tana-PO!
Ai-na, ki-na-weh, ki-na-weh
Chi-li li-cha, chi-li li-cha
Don-ka-va-ki, mas-i-ki-va-ki
Ki-ve, ki-ve-na-meh
HOPET!

SEEDING POWER: Frank Waters writes that the "locust *máhu* [insect which has the heat power] is known as the Humpbacked Flute Player, the *kachina* [spirit of the invisible forces of life] named Kókopilau, because he looked like the wood [*koko*—wood; *pilau*—hump]. In the hump on his back he carried seeds of plants and flowers"—the *kachina* doll often depicted with long penis to signify the sexual root of the power—"and with the music of his flute he created warmth." During the migrations Kókopilau "would stop and scatter seeds from the hump on his back. Then he would march on, playing his flute and singing a song. His song is still remembered, but the words are so ancient that nobody knows what they mean." The resulting text bears inevitable resemblance to many varieties of wordless poetry, such as Indian songs, magical spells and mantras, medieval tropes, and the conscious "sound poetry" of more recent years (see below, **Sound-Poems & Incantations,** pages 108–119).

"MOUNDBUILDERS" [Adena]

The Great Serpent Mound of Adams County, Ohio [circa 1000 B.C.]

Photograph courtesy of Museum of the American Indian, Heye Foundation

MOUNDS / EARTHWORKS / MONUMENTAL POEMS: In *Mound Builders of Ancient America: The Archeology of a Myth* (Greenwich, Conn., 1968), Robert Silverberg has recounted the story of the mounds of the Mississippi Valley and Southeastern United States and their colorful play upon the mind of America during the last two centuries. Mounds, often containing artifacts of great beauty, flank the rivers of the Midwest, some ten thousand in the Ohio Valley alone. Though almost certainly Indian in origin, they led to myths of a vanished race, a lost pre-Indian civilization; treatises appeared, postulating immigrations from Mexico, refugees from Atlantis, traveling Danes, Malays, and remnants of the Ten Lost Tribes of Israel—works like *The Book of Mormon* and William Pidgeon's *Traditions of De-coo-dah* (1858). The latter speaks of the mound as "the hieroglyphical sign through which the traditions were taught, and the knowledge of past events preserved." Frank Waters records the Hopi belief that the great Serpent Mound in Adams County, Ohio, may have been built by their migrating ancestors in the absence of cliffs on which to mark their pictographs. Whoever the author, it is the largest known serpent effigy in the world: length, 1,254 feet; average width, 20 feet; height, 4 or 5 feet. Physical structures with the power to convey tradition and call men to exegesis continue to figure among the possibilities of poetry—as witness the Mexican concrete poet Mathias Goeritz's "architectural poems": e.g., a gate, built of the word "ororororororo . . ." etc. (in Spanish, alternately "gold" and "horror").

Among those who celebrate the mounds as emblems of a sacred past, William Cullen Bryant produced memorable works like "Thanatopsis," written in his eighteenth year and published in 1817 *(North American Review)* in an atmosphere of great public interest in the mounds, and "The Prairies," written in 1832 after riding horseback over the ancient sites, a poem invoking a sense of space peculiar to American poetry.

WILLIAM CULLEN BRYANT

The Prairies

These are the gardens of the Desert, these
The unshorn fields, boundless and beautiful,
For which the speech of England has no name—
The Prairies. I behold them for the first,
And my heart swells, while the dilated sight
Takes in the encircling vastness. Lo! they stretch,
In airy undulations, far away,
As if the ocean, in his gentlest swell,
Stood still, with all his rounded billows fixed,
And motionless forever.—Motionless?—

No—they are all unchained again. The clouds
Sweep over with their shadows, and, beneath,
The surface rolls and fluctuates to the eye;
Dark hollows seem to glide along and chase
The sunny ridges. Breezes of the South!
Who toss the golden and the flame-like flowers,
And pass the prairie-hawk that, poised on high,
Flaps his broad wings, yet moves not—ye have played
Among the palms of Mexico and vines
Of Texas, and have crisped the limpid brooks
That from the fountains of Sonora glide
Into the calm Pacific—have ye fanned
A nobler or a lovelier scene than this?
Man hath no power in all this glorious work:
The hand that built the firmament hath heaved
And smoothed these verdant swells, and sown their slopes
With herbage, planted them with island groves,
And hedged them round with forests. Fitting floor
For this magnificent temple of the sky—
With flowers whose glory and whose multitude
Rival the constellations! The great heavens
Seem to stoop down upon the scene in love,—
A nearer vault, and of a tenderer blue,
Than that which bends above our eastern hills.

As o'er the verdant waste I guide my steed,
Among the high rank grass that sweeps his sides
The hollow beating of his footstep seems
A sacrilegious sound. I think of those
Upon whose rest he tramples. Are they here—
The dead of other days?—and did the dust
Of these fair solitudes once stir with life
And burn with passion? Let the mighty mounds
That overlook the rivers, or that rise
In the dim forest crowded with old oaks,
Answer. A race, that long has passed away,
Built them;—a disciplined and populous race
Heaped, with long toil, the earth, while yet the Greek

Was hewing the Pentelicus to forms
Of symmetry, and rearing on its rock
The glittering Parthenon. These ample fields
Nourished their harvests, here their herds were fed,
When haply by their stalls the bison lowed,
And bowed his manèd shoulder to the yoke.
All day this desert murmured with their toils,
Till twilight blushed, and lovers walked, and wooed
In a forgotten language, and old tunes,
From instruments of unremembered form,
Gave the soft winds a voice. The red man came—
The roaming hunter tribes, warlike and fierce,
And the mound-builders vanished from the earth.
The solitude of centuries untold
Has settled where they dwelt. The prairie-wolf
Hunts in their meadows, and his fresh-dug den
Yawns by my path. The gopher mines the ground
Where stood their swarming cities. All is gone;
All—save the piles of earth that hold their bones,
The platforms where they worshipped unknown gods,
The barriers which they builded from the soil
To keep the foe at bay—till o'er the walls
The wild beleaguerers broke, and, one by one,
The strongholds of the plain were forced, and heaped
With corpses. The brown vultures of the wood
Flocked to those vast uncovered sepulchers,
And sat unscared and silent at their feast.
Haply some solitary fugitive,
Lurking in marsh and forest, till the sense
Of desolation and of fear became
Bitterer than death, yielded himself to die.
Man's better nature triumphed then. Kind words
Welcomed and soothed him; the rude conquerors
Seated the captive with their chiefs; he chose
A bride among their maidens, and at length
Seemed to forget—yet ne'er forgot—the wife
Of his first love, and her sweet little ones,
Butchered, amid their shrieks, with all his race.

Thus change the forms of being. Thus arise
Races of living things, glorious in strength,
And perish, as the quickening breath of God
Fills them, or is withdrawn. The red man, too,
Has left the blooming wilds he ranged so long,
And, nearer to the Rocky Mountains, sought
A wilder hunting-ground. The beaver builds
No longer by these streams, but far away,
On waters whose blue surface ne'er gave back
The white man's face—among Missouri's springs,
And pools whose issues swell the Oregon—
He rears his little Venice. In these plains
The bison feeds no more. Twice twenty leagues
Beyond remotest smoke of hunter's camp,
Roams the majestic brute, in herds that shake
The earth with thundering steps—yet here I meet
His ancient footprints stamped beside the pool.

Still this great solitude is quick with life.
Myriads of insects, gaudy as the flowers
They flutter over, gentle quadrupeds,
And birds, that scarce have learned the fear of man,
Are here, and sliding reptiles of the ground,
Startlingly beautiful. The graceful deer
Bounds to the wood at my approach. The bee,
A more adventurous colonist than man,
With whom he came across the eastern deep,
Fills the savannas with his murmurings,
And hides his sweets, as in the golden age,
Within the hollow oak. I listen long
To his domestic hum, and think I hear
The sound of that advancing multitude
Which soon shall fill these deserts. From the ground
Comes up the laugh of children, the soft voice
Of maidens, and the sweet and solemn hymn
Of Sabbath worshippers. The low of herds
Blends with the rustling of the heavy grain
Over the dark brown furrows. All at once
A fresher wind sweeps by; and breaks my dream,
And I am in the wilderness alone.

GEOGRAPHY AND TRADITION: The "poetry of names," a cornerstone of Emerson's doctrine of Nature, makes any journey across the land a poetic process, an intersection of the ancient Adamic act of naming and the present history of our driving through actual places. "All times are contemporaneous in the mind" (Pound, 1910) when we read the signposts on U.S. 40 from the Atlantic to the Pacific: FIRSTVIEW, VERMILLION RIVER, CONOCOCHEAGUE, KINGDOM CITY, EMBARRASS, AUXVASSE CREEK, PHONETON . . . "Conococheague (Maryland) is an example of an Indian name, meaning something in the nature of 'far away,' and probably applied because the stream lay at some distance from a particular Indian village." (George R. Stewart) Poems like *The Odyssey* of Homer or the *Cantos* of Pound differ from travelogues in the complexity of their rendering of permanent states of mind, that is, the energy of their language; but at base the metaphor is the journey, and the places traveled through are real:

> periplum, not as land looks on a map
> but as sea bord seen by men sailing.   [CANTO LIX]

Homer is found to be accurate. Carl Ortwin Sauer, an American geographer, has (in books like *The Early Spanish Main; Land and Life; Northern Mists;* and *Sixteenth Century North America: The Land and the People as Seen by the Europeans)* been rewriting history according to a principle of direct observation and the accounts of those who directly observed. The fact that Whitman's *Song of Myself* is a song of the land, that Thoreau's *A Week on the Concord and Merrimac Rivers* views the journey of his mind toward inner "concord" against the grid of a real seven days of travel, or that Joyce rediscovers Ulysses in the story of eighteen hours in Dublin, is enough to make interesting this notion: Tradition lies buried in the land, and geography, like poetry, is an essential mode of attention. Whitman: "Once I pass'd through a populous city imprinting my brain for future use with its shows, architecture, customs, traditions. . . ."

RALPH WALDO EMERSON

Hamatreya

Bulkeley, Hunt, Willard, Hosmer, Meriam, Flint,
Possessed the land which rendered to their toil
Hay, corn, roots, hemp, flax, apples, wool and wood.
Each of these landlords walked amidst his farm,
Saying, "'Tis mine, my children's and my name's.
How sweet the west wind sounds in my own trees!

How graceful climb those shadows on my hill!
I fancy these pure waters and the flags
Know me, as does my dog: we sympathize;
And, I affirm, my actions smack of the soil."

Where are these men? Asleep beneath their grounds:
And strangers, fond as they, their furrows plough.
Earth laughs in flowers, to see her boastful boys
Earth-proud, proud of the earth which is not theirs;
Who steer the plough, but cannot steer their feet
Clear of the grave.
They added ridge to valley, brook to pond,
And sighed for all that bounded their domain;
"This suits me for a pasture; that's my park;
We must have clay, lime, gravel, granite-ledge,
And misty lowland, where to go for peat.
The land is well—lies fairly to the south.
'Tis good, when you have crossed the sea and back,
To find the sitfast acres where you left them."
Ah! the hot owner sees not Death, who adds
Him to his land, a lump of mold the more.
Hear what the Earth says:

EARTH-SONG

"Mine and yours;
Mine, not yours.
Earth endures;
Stars abide—
Shine down in the old sea;
Old are the shores;
But where are old men?
I who have seen much,
Such have I never seen.

"The lawyer's deed
Ran sure,
In tail,

To them, and to their heirs
Who shall succeed,
Without fail,
Forevermore.

"Here is the land,
Shaggy with wood,
With its old valley,
Mound and flood.
But the heritors?
Fled like the flood's foam.
The lawyer, and the laws,
And the kingdom,
Clean swept herefrom.

"They called me theirs,
Who so controlled me;
Yet every one
Wished to stay, and is gone,
How am I theirs,
If they cannot hold me,
But I hold them?"

When I heard the Earth-song,
I was no longer brave;
My avarice cooled
Like lust in the chill of the grave.

KENNETH IRBY

Relation

Mesas, erosion—
who was it, Dutton, Hayden, Gilbert, or Powell, said, it was
the *least* eroded country in America? The rest
all more worn down, long ago, to a nubbin—

Bryce's "hell of a place to lose a cow in" canyon
rims its ampitheater open toward the south
the river there, way south, roads its way
toward lower California, sawn—

    the year the fathers rallied
    round the bell in Philadelphia

    the fathers west crossed
    the crossing of the fathers
    now silt and muddy water
    backed up over the whole long canyon

    toward the home
    stretch, through
    Moquis and Navajos
    toward Albuquerque

    having circled north from Taos
    into the Colorado gorges, west
    through the Uintas, south along the Wasatch
    and across
        looking for California
        and the way thither

* The sun is out here in Palo Alto, and the flame red
        pyracantha
clacks its berries against the clapboards, windblown
as the clouds blown simultaneously show and recover
the direct sun
        such elements as only lately
        eroded those flats and ranges
        —the "Plateau Province" Powell called it
It takes such soft wool
as Escalante and his fathers wore, such
pain and ease among, such
care to even see
        to live in that land

—on any land, the care, that the wear
is of our feet across
not inundations planned

Cabeza de Vaca and Escalante
went through the trek, into the land traversed, the heavy
foot lift, over old and used again tracks—
    Sauer and Hallenbeck traced the trails Nuñez used, still
    visible and followable today, from the Texas shore
    to the Guadalupe and Sacramento mountains,
    south along the road to Cíbola—

through the land
is its own experience, care for
what care the land demands

And the interior distance,
the brain pan, the heaviness there

        —for Escalante only came back
        where he had begun, a great
        circle without touching
                  California
        or that western sea—

the plains in the mind
eroded to the Ground
the self lost on off
in those steep and wandering canyons

while the soft wool robes, the soft
touch of the
hand of the
naked bearded
wanderer
        created them anew
        who touched

KENNETH REXROTH

A Lesson in Geography

*"of Paradys ne can not I speken
propurly ffor I was not there"*—MANDEVILLE

The stars of the Great Bear drift apart
The Horse and the Rider together northeastward
Alpha and Omega asunder
The others diversely
There are rocks
On the earth more durable
Than the configurations of heaven
Species now motile and sanguine
Shall see the stars in new clusters
The beaches changed
The mountains shifted
Gigantic
Immobile
Floodlit
The faces appear and disappear
Chewing the right gum
Smoking the right cigarette
Buying the best refrigerator
The polished carnivorous teeth
Exhibited in approval
The lights
Of the houses
Draw together
In the evening dewfall on the banks
Of the Wabash
Sparkle discreetly
High on the road to Provo
Above the Salt Lake Valley
And
The mountain shaped like a sphinx
And
The mountain shaped like a finger
Pointing

On the first of April at eight o'clock
Precisely at Algol
There are rocks on the earth
And one who sleepless
Throbbed with the ten
Nightingales in the plum trees
Sleepless as Boötes stood over him
Gnawing the pillow
Sitting on the bed's edge smoking
Sitting by the window looking
One who rose in the false
Dawn and stoned
The nightingales in the garden
The heart pawned for wisdom
The heart
Bartered for knowledge and folly
The will troubled
The mind secretly aghast
The eyes and lips full of sorrow
The apices of vision wavering
As the flower spray at the tip of the windstalk
The becalmed sail
The heavy wordless weight
And now
The anguishing and pitiless file
Cutting away life
Capsule by capsule biting
Into the heart
The coal of fire
Sealing the lips
There are rocks on earth

And

In the Japanese quarter
A phonograph playing
"Moonlight on ruined castles"
Kojo n'suki
And

The movement of the wind fish
Keeping time to the music
Sirius setting behind it
(The Dog has scented the sun)
Gold immense fish
Squirm in the trade wind
"Young Middle Western woman
In rut
Desires correspondent"
The first bright flower
Cynoglossum
The blue hound's tongue
Breaks on the hill
"The tide has gone down
Over the reef
I walk about the world
There is great
Wind and then rain"
"My life is bought and paid for
So much pleasure
For so much pain"
The folded fossiliferous
Sedimentary rocks end here
The granite batholith
Obtrudes abruptly
West of the fault line
Betelgeuse reddens
Drawing its substance about it
It is possible that a process is beginning
Similar to that which lifted
The great Sierra fault block
Through an older metamorphic range

(The Dog barks on the sun's spoor)

Now
The thought of death
Binds fast the flood of light
Ten years ago the snow falling

All a long winter night
I had lain waking in my bed alone
Turning my heavy thoughts
And no way might
Sleep
Remembering divers things long gone
Now
In the long day in the hour of small shadow
I walk on the continent's last western hill
And lie prone among the iris in the grass
My eyes fixed on the durable stone
That speaks and hears as though it were myself

WALLACE STEVENS
Anecdote of Men by the Thousand

The soul, he said, is composed
Of the external world.

There are men of the East, he said,
Who are the East.
There are men of a province
Who are that province.
There are men of a valley
Who are that valley.

There are men whose words
Are as natural sounds
Of their places
As the cackle of toucans
In the place of toucans.

The mandoline is the instrument
Of a place.

Are there mandolines of western mountains?
Are there mandolines of northern moonlight?

The dress of a woman of Lhassa,
In its place,
Is an invisible element of that place
Made visible.

MARSDEN HARTLEY

Lewiston Is a Pleasant Place

I admire my native city because
it is part of the secret sacred rite
of love of place.
My childhood which was hard, it is always
hard to be alone at the wrong time,
brought seizures of intensity to the years;
the harsh grinding of the mills rang in
my ears for years—and a sordid sort of music
came out of it.
I return to instances that are the basic images
of my life as it now is.

I go back to the Franklin pasture which for
us children was the Asia and Africa of
our first impressions.

Spring—
and myself walking with my father along the
edges of a cool clear stream, gathering water cresses,
trilliums, dogtooth violets, and in
the fall—at times—mushrooms;
white violets and blue, growing on little hillocks
with trailing evergreens and boxberry leaves
with pink edges of baby-tender leaves,
and here and there, pushing up out of the snow,
the arbutus or, as we called them, Mayflowers.

Drama number one,
the image of all that was to come after:

the death of the white kitten—
wrapping it carefully in something soft—
laying it gently in a wooden saltbox—
fastening the lid down—
burying it deep in a hollow, with tears,
and my sister, Lillie May, joining in the rites.

There were toboggans in winter, made of end to end
joined barrel staves, seat in middle, gliding
dangerously into the Asiatic valleys below.
Scene-shifting a little later, the pasture a
deep, religious memory;
the Androscoggin
forever flowing solemnly through my brain,
coursing in and out of my flesh and bone,
as it still does, sacredly.

There was Dr. Alonzo Garcelon, always known to us
as Dr. "Gasselon," flying through Haymarket Square
behind his racing steed, spitting tobacco juice
as he went; and the amazing vision of his beautiful
daughter Edith, at church of a Sunday morning.
Mamie Straw and Lizzie Janes, sharp images of a day
so somehow past—
Miss Janes at the organ, pumped by a boy at the
back, out of sight—with the Ascension of Christ
over us all in not too good stained glass, as we
sang magnificats and epiphanies—and
"Lead kindly light amid. . . ." "Lord, now lettest thy
servant depart in peace, according to thy word."

Skinny Jinny was a tall, dark-clothed woman with
her thin arms akimbo under her black shawl,
wan-white, frightened of the solitudes that
enveloped her being, we children running madly for
home when we saw her—because "she has a butcher knife
under her shawl"—as if she hated little children, and
maybe she did—so many do.

The Canadians came to the city—giving it new
life, new fervors, new charms, new vivacities, lighter
touches, pleasant shades of cultivation, bringing no
harm to the city, bringing what it now has—a freshening
of city style, richer sense of plain living.
Recently I walked the streets of my native city
and there was gaiety in the air.
My thoughts returned to a white house in Howe Street,
a home with green blinds, the front ones always shut,
where a poet of distinction lived, wrote fine poetry,
cooked Savarinesque foods, writing poetry that few knew
the worth of—and almost none know the value, now.
Wallace Gould, if he is still fact, is a man of great
male beauty and gigantic proportion; he is almost a complete
legend to us now, none of us know where he is,
or if he even lives at all.
Gould was, in the careful use of the word, a genius;
he had high vision and plain habits; he was
a great cook, a superior pianist, with a frantic
worship of Byron.
He has image after image in photo of his idol,
and an impressive replica in plaster.

Gould devoted himself to Greek outline, Horatian
simplicity, with pagan notions of the
livingness of the moment.
He cared nothing for traditions, customs, mechanical
habits—lived the quiet life of a thinking being,
worshiping also his foster mother, genial in his
behaviors,
out of which evolved
The Children of the Sun.

The mills and factories that were once gigantic
in the vision of a child, monstrous, terrifying,
prison-like, are now mere objects on the horizon,
just as the garages and the filling stations have become.
The Androscoggin flows by them all, giving them
power through the solemn canals, minding none of

them, going onward because it has business with the sea.
Lumber was once a great industry; we all saw the
log-drives and jams above the falls, tumbling down
over the waters at West Pitch, settling into
jackstraw patterns as they may now be seen in places
like Trois-Rivières in Quebec—these logs later turning
into paper, turning into stockings, extraneous lingerie;
I myself having seen the moment when wood becomes syrup,
then silk.

On the breast of David's Mountain
many an adolescent dream was slain,
later to be snatched from early death
when manhood gave them back their breath
again.

> MARSDEN HARDLEY was one of the fathers of abstract painting,
> briefly joined the New York Dada movement around 1919, radical-
> ized his poetry, and wrote the essay, *"Importance of Being Dada."*
> Later he devoted both his poetry and painting to *"the secret sacred
> rite / of love of place,"* primarily the landscape of his native Maine.

HART CRANE

Cutty Sark

> *O, the navies old and oaken,*
> *O, the Temeraire no more!* —MELVILLE

I met a man in South Street, tall—
a nervous shark tooth swung on his chain.
His eyes pressed through green grass
—green glasses, or bar lights made them
so—
    shine—
           GREEN—
                   eyes—
stepped out—forgot to look at you
or left you several blocks away—

in the nickel-in-the-slot piano jogged
"Stamboul Nights"—weaving somebody's nickel—sang—

O Stamboul Rose—dreams weave the rose!

Murmurs of Leviathan he spoke,
and rum was Plato in our heads . . .

"It's S.S. Ala—Antwerp—now remember kid
to put me out at three she sails on time.
I'm not much good at time any more keep
weakeyed watches sometimes snooze—" his bony hands
got to beating time . . . "A whaler once—
I ought to keep time and get over it—I'm a
Democrat—I know what time it is—No
I don't want to know what time it is—that
damned white Arctic killed my time . . ."

O Stamboul Rose—drums weave—

"I ran a donkey engine down there on
in Panama—got tired of that—
then Yucatan selling kitchenware—beads—
have you seen Popocatepetl—birdless mouth
with ashes sifting down—?
　　　　　　　　　and then the coast again . . ."

Rose of Stamboul O coral Queen—
teased remnants of the skeletons of cities—
and galleries, galleries of watergutted lava
snarling stone—green—drums—drown—

Sing!
"—that spiracle!" he shot a finger out the door . . .
"O life's a geyser—beautiful—my lungs—
No—I can't live on land—!"

I saw the frontiers gleaming of his mind;
or are there frontiers—running sands sometimes

running sands—somewhere—sands running . . .
Or they may start some white machine that sings.
Then you may laugh and dance the axletree—
steel—silver—kick the traces—and know—

 ATLANTIS ROSE drums wreathe the rose,
 the star floats burning in a gulf of tears
 and sleep another thousand—

     interminably
long since somebody's nickel—stopped—
playing—

A wind worried those wicker-neat lapels, the
swinging summer entrances to cooler hells . . .
Outside a wharf truck nearly ran him down
—he lunged up Bowery way while the dawn
was putting the Statue of Liberty out—that
torch of hers you know—

I started walking home across the Bridge . . .

    ●   ●   ●

Blithe Yankee vanities, turreted sprites, winged
    British repartees, skilful savage sea-girls
that bloomed in the spring—Heave, weave
ʿthose bright designs the trade winds drive . . .

 Sweet opium and tea, Yo-ho!
 Pennies for porpoises that bank the keel!
 Fins whip the breeze around Japan!

Bright skysails ticketing the Line, wink round the Horn
to Frisco, Melbourne . . .
    Pennants, parabolas—
clipper dreams indelible and ranging,
baronial white on lucky blue!

 Perennial-*Cutty*-trophied-*Sark!*

Thermopylae, Black Prince, Flying Cloud through Sunda
—scarfed of foam, their bellies veered green esplanades,
locked in wind-humors, ran their eastings down;

> *at Java Head freshened the nip*
> *(sweet opium and tea!)*
> *and turned and left us on the lee . . .*

Buntlines tusseling (91 days, 20 hours and anchored!)
> > > > > > *Rainbow, Leander*
(last trip a tragedy)—where can you be
Nimbus? and you rivals two—

> a long tack keeping—
> > > > *Taeping?*
> > > > *Ariel?*

> From *The Bridge,* Crane's attempt in the 1920s at a poem of epic
> length and scope, lyric intensity, etc., focused on such archetypal
> U.S. images as Brooklyn Bridge.

GERTRUDE STEIN

A Landscape from *Four Saints in Three Acts*

Pigeons on the grass alas.
Pigeons on the grass alas.
Short longer grass short longer longer shorter yellow
grass. Pigeons large pigeons on the shorter longer yellow
grass alas pigeons on the grass.
If they were not pigeons what were they.
If they were not pigeons on the grass alas what were
they. He had heard of a third and he asked about it it was
a magpie in the sky. If a magpie in the sky on the sky can
not cry if the pigeon on the grass alas can alas and to pass
the pigeon on the grass alas and the magpie in the sky on
the sky and to try and to try alas on the grass alas the
pigeon on the grass the pigeon on the grass and alas. They

might be very well very well very well they might be they
might be very well they might be very well very well they
might be.
  Let Lucy Lily Lily Lucy Lucy let Lucy Lucy Lily Lily
Lily Lily Lily let Lily Lucy Lucy let Lily. Let Lucy Lily.

Of the visionary landscapes in *Four Saints* (1929), Gertrude Stein
wrote elsewhere: "I made the saints the landscape. . . . Magpies are
in the landscape that is they are in the sky of a landscape . . . and look
flat gainst the sky. . . . They look exactly like the birds in the Annuncia-
tion pictures the bird which is the Holy Ghost and rests flat against the
side sky very high."

GARY SNYDER

The Hump-Backed Flute Player

The hump-backed flute player
      walks all over.
      sits on the boulders around the Great Basin
      his hump   is a pack.

Hsuan Tsang (original name Ch'en I
      went to India 629 AD
      returned to China 645
      with 657 sutras, images, pictures,
      and 50 relics)
      a curved frame pack with a parasol,
      embroidery   carving
      incense censer swinging as he walked
      the Pamir   the Tarim   Turfan
      the Punjab   the doab
      of Ganga and Yamuna,

Sweetwater, Quileute, Hoh
Amur, Tanana, Mackenzie, Old Man,
Bighorn, Platte, the San Juan

```
he carried
        "emptiness"
he carried
        "mind only"
        vijnaptimatra
```

The hump-backed flute player
Kokopilau
his hump is a pack.
                •
In Canyon de Chelly on the North Wall up by a cave
is the hump backed flute player laying on his back,
playing his flute. Across the flat sandy canyon wash,
wading a stream and breaking through the ice, on the
south wall, the pecked-out pictures of some Mountain Sheep
with curling horns. They stood in the icy shadow of the
south wall two hundred feet away; I sat with my
shirt off in the sun facing south, with the hump
backed flute player just above my head.
They whispered; I whispered; back and forth
across the canyon, clearly heard.
                •
In the plains of Bihar, near Rajgir, are the
ruins of Nalanda. The name Bihar comes from "vihara"
—Buddhist temple—the Diamond Seat is in Bihar, and
Vulture Peak—Tibetan pilgrims come down to these
plains. The six-foot-thick walls of Nalanda, the
monks all scattered—books burned—banners tattered—
statues shattered—by the Turks.
Hsuan Tsang describes the high blue tiles, the delicate
debates; Logicians of Emptiness, worshippers of Tara,
Joy of Starlight, naked breasted, "She who saves."
                •
Ghost Bison, Ghost Bears, Ghost Bighorns, Ghost Lynx,
Ghost Pronghorns, Ghost Panthers, Ghost Marmots, Ghost
Owls:
Swirling and gathering, sweeping down, in the power
of a dance and a song. Then the White Man will be gone.
Then the butterflies will sing
on slopes of grass and aspen;

thunderheads the deep blue of Krishna
rise on rainbows; and falling shining rain—
each drop—
tiny people gliding slanting down: a little Buddha
seated in each pearl—
and join the million waving Grass-Seed Buddhas
on the ground.
          •
Ah, what am I carrying? What's this load?
     Who's that out there in the dust
sleeping on the ground?
with a black hat, and a feather stuck in his sleeve.

—It's old Jack Wilson,
Wovoka, the prophet,

          Black Coyote saw the whole world
          in Wovoka's empty hat

     the bottomless sky

     the night of starlight, lying on our sides

     the ocean, slanting higher

     all manner of beings
     may swim in my sea
     echoing up conch spiral corridors

     the mirror: countless ages back
     dressing   or laughing
     what world today?

     pearl crystal jewel
     taming and teaching
     the dragon in the spine—

     spiral, wheel,
     or breath of mind

desert sheep with curly horns.
the ringing in your ears

is the cricket in the stars.

up in the mountains that edge the Great Basin
it was whispered to me
by the oldest of trees.
by the oldest of beings,

the Oldest of Trees.

and all night long, sung on
by a vast throng
of Pinyon
Pine

For more on the hump-backed flute player in Amerindian religion and poetry, see above, page 53.

A BOOK OF RITES & NAMINGS

At root poetry is a ritual bringing about an awakening of consciousness and a renewal of the social bond between men. In its primary processes—naming and defining—language is itself a poetic act, which becomes remarkable when it revives its latent power to bring about change. **A Book of Rites & Namings** attempts to reveal the variety of poetic uses in the bare operation of language—its vocabulary and grammar— as well as the deliberate extension of those uses in the work of individual poets. In addition **A Book of Rites & Namings** focuses on the relation of poetry to actual rituals and events: formal or ceremonial occasions, performances, and acts of celebration, including the conception of the poem as pure sound and incantation.

■ *"If Adam in the Garden is a model of the prophet-poet in his role as Namer, Adam out of the Garden, or in History, is a model of the public poet in his role as Definer. Definition reheals the split in the Mother Tongue by giving Her form, i.e., presence, usefulness, accessibility. The poet's profession, as Rilke says, is the domain of the sayable, and his tools are all modes of definition imaginable. "*

—N.P. KREPID, *Theopoetics and the Idea of History* [1943]

Definitions & Namings

EXPANSION OF THE LINGUISTIC FIELD OF POETRY: What follows is a gathering of poems based on the linguistic assumption of a "creative aspect of language use" (Chomsky) and the metapoetic assumption of poetry as an activity of mind beyond the limitations of conventional literary modes. From the time of Whitman, American poets have been freeing themselves from the restrictions of a narrowly defined poetic language, until the domain of poetry has become more or less that of language itself—as a rite and an event.

In *An American Primer* (circa 1860), Whitman announced a range of words for poetry that would move its vocabulary out of previously restrictive bounds.

And if we now read his list as a poem . . . ?

WALT WHITMAN

Words

Words of the Laws of the Earth,
Words of the Stars, and about them,
Words of the Sun and Moon,
Words of Geology, History, Geography,
Words of Ancient Races,
Words of the Medieval Races,
Words of the progress of Religion, Law, Art, Government,
Words of the surface of the Earth, grass, rocks, trees, flowers,
        grains and the like,
Words of like climates,
Words of the Air and Heavens,
Words of the Birds of the air, and of insects,
Words of Animals,

Words of Men and Women—the hundreds of different nations,
 tribes, colors, and other distinctions,
Words of the Sea,
Words of Modern Leading Ideas,
Words of Modern Inventions, Discoveries, engrossing Themes,
 Pursuits,
Words of These States—the Year I, Washington, the Primal
 Compact, the Second Compact (namely the Constitution)
 —trades, farms, wild lands, iron, steam, slavery,
 elections, California, and so forth,
Words of the Body, Senses, Limbs, Surface, Interior,
Words of dishes to eat, or of naturally produced things to
 eat,
Words of clothes,
Words of implements,
Words of furniture,
Words of all kinds of Building and Constructing,
Words of Human Physiology,
Words of Human Phrenology,
Words of Music,
Words of Feebleness, Nausea, Sickness, Ennui, Repugnance,
 and the like.

■ *"Poetry did then in beginning include everything and it was natural
that it should because then everything including what was happening
could be made real to anyone by just naming what was happening in
other words by doing what poetry always must do by living in nouns.*

*"Nouns are the name of anything. Think of all that early poetry,
think of Homer, think of Chaucer, think of the Bible and you will see
what I mean you will really realize that they were drunk with nouns, to
name to know how to name earth sea and sky and all that was in them
was enough to make them live and love in names, and that is what poetry
is it is a state of knowing and feeling a name. "*

—GERTRUDE STEIN, *Poetry & Grammar* [1935]

[PAPAGO]

From "Naming Events"

1. A shaman has a dream & names a child for what he dreams in it. Among such names are Circling Light, Rushing Light Beams, Daylight Comes, Wind Rainbow, Wind Leaves, Rainbow Shaman, Feather Leaves, A-Rainbow-as-a-Bow, Shining Beetle, Singing Dawn, Hawk-Flying-over-Water-Holes, Flowers Trembling, Chief-of-Jackrabbits, Water-Drops-on-Leaves, Short Wings, Leaf Blossoms, Foamy Water.

2. A person receives a name describing something odd & sexual about the namer. Here the namer is a woman or a transvestite, who makes the name public by shouting it after the man named when others are present. The man invariably accepts it & is regularly called by it, even by his wife & family. Such names include: Down-Dangling-Pussy-Hairs, Big Cunt, Long Asshole.

3. A person buys a name or trades names with another person. For example, Devil-Old-Man exchanges names with Contrary, or Looking-for-Girls-at-a-Dance changes with Big Crazy, but has to give him four pints of whiskey in addition because of the desirability of the name.

SOURCE: RUTH UNDERHILL, *Social Organization of the Papago Indians,* 1939. (Adaptation from JEROME ROTHENBERG, *Shaking the Pumpkin,* 1972.)

GREGORY CORSO

Food

Surely there'll be another table.
Whortdye spread on nepenthean beans;
Southernhorns alight on Hesiod carrots;
Hare visionary astrologer stew:
Talc and dolphinheart mixed kangaroonian weep;

Spanish knights brandishing piteous forks;
Dutch kitchens, rosy-cheeked cooks,
Still-life ducks and rabbits,
Piles of silver fish, vast orange pies;
Global Rex kettles volcanoing away—

The farmer will never love me,
He feeds me purposelessly.
I do not wish to eat
With the knowledge of his wheat;
Mine with the knowledge of love
Has put down his murdered meat—

Hunger! petty agent of Death,
If anything to mature me, *you!*
Five-day sister making paper of me.
Sadder than the Last Supper
I eat nothing
—Melancholy learns to starve.
And even if I did eat
—The hand from soup absurdity
Reaches the mouth's enameling;
There's not much loveliness in that.

Wisconsin provisions
Insufficient when I have absolute dairy visions:
Corduroy eggs, owl cheese, pipe butter,
Firing squad milk;
The farmer will never love me
Nor I, he.
I'd rather go hungry
Than assist his chicken slaughter,
Attend his State Fair,
Or screw his famous daughter.

Because restaurant eating is noticeable
And I am no longer that boy to lean against the window
And pick my nose mischievously;
Because now my eyes are sad on the plate

And envy the eaters their fabulous shriek of
SOMEPLACE ELSE LET'S EAT!
Yes, eat! Eat!
Hammer your pork chops with blows of love!
I mean, hammer your fantastic jowl!
Each swallow to roar the grace of your sweet fist!
The table must go!
Terrorize the smooth plates! The thick spoons!
O mummy roots! Stomachic dire of Thoth!

Augh! eat a steak of pine! A cut of spruce! Boil rock!
What else so dreadful a nourishment to wage a soul
Who dreams to beat an overseer to death
In a field of magnificent peas.

I am no sad hunter of what I eat.
It is for God to deny the foody ka of Egypt
The calf that never looks West.
And well I know some food is demonstrate of denial.
Osiris, I join thee! unnoticed in the calf's eye.

[FLORENTINE CODEX]

Aztec Definitions

(1)

The Precipice

It is deep—a difficult, a dangerous place, a deathly place.
It is dark, it is light. It is an abyss.

(2)

Owl

It is round, like a ball. The back is rounded. The eyes are
like spindle whorls; shiny. It has horns of feathers. The
head is ball-like, round; the feathers thick, heavy. It is
blinded during the day. It is born in crags, in trees. It feeds
by night, because it sees especially well in the dark. It has
a deep voice when it hoots; it says, *tecolo, tecolo, o, o.*

(3)

Eye

The eye, the bird's eye, the eye of a bird; the turkey's eye, the eye of a turkey. With it, it looks, it looks in different directions, it becomes blind.

I blind one; I smash it in the eye; I smash it in the eyeball. I put fear in its eye. It opens its eye. I remove its eyeball.

Translated by ARTHUR J. O. ANDERSON and CHARLES E. DIBBLE from texts compiled a quarter-century after the Spanish conquest by Bernardino de Sahagún, a Spanish monk. The Aztec elders—who had been through the highly developed pre-Conquest schools— provided him with a compendium of their culture (songs, myths, histories, rituals, etc.) at a time of crisis. The "definitions" (a kind of glossary of "earthly things") comprise the eleventh book of his Florentine Codex.

COTTON MATHER

Stones

There are many sorts of *Stones* found in *lesser Masses*.

Of these there are many who do *not* exceed the hardness of *Marble*.

Seven or eight of these are of an *indeterminate Figure*.

Twice as many have a *determinate Figure*.

Among these the Wonders of the *Osteo-colla*, to join and heal our *broken Bones*.

But then there are others which *do* exceed *Marble* in hardness.

To this Article belong those that are usually called *Gems* or *precious Stones*.

[Pebbles and Flints are of the *Agate-kind.]*

Some of these are *opake*.

Three of the opake have a Body of *one Colour*.

Here the Wonders of the *Nephritick Stone!*

Three of the *opake* have *different Colours* mixed in the same Body.

Here the Wonders of the *Blood-stone!*

Some are *pellucid*.

Two with *Colours changeable*, according to their different position in the Light.

Nine or ten with *Colours permanent.*
Some are *diaphanous.*
Two *yellow* (or partaking of it.)
Three *red.*
Three *blue.*
Two *green.*
Four *without any Colours.*
'But an excellent Writer observing, *Deus est Figurus*
'Lapidum, carries on his Observation, That the God who
'makes *precious* as well as *common Stones,* has made *Men*
'with as much of a *Difference,* and not altogether without
'such a *Proportion.'*
'Good God, Thy heavenly Graces in the Soul are
'brighter Jewels than any that are dug out of the Earth!
'A *poor* Man may be adorn'd with these; those who are so,
'they shall be mine, saith the Lord, in the Day when I
make 'up my Jewels.'
'How often have I seen a Jewel in the *Snout of a Swine!'*
'And how many *Counterfeits* in the World!'

COTTON MATHER, the well-known seventeenth-century divine, also
wrote natural history as a mode of revelation. See Pound's remarks
on "the medieval philosopher," page 164. *Deus est Figurus Lapi-
dum:* God is the potter who makes the stones.

GERTRUDE STEIN

Chicken
(from *Tender Buttons)*

CHICKEN

Pheasant and chicken, chicken is a peculiar bird.

CHICKEN

Alas a dirty word, alas a dirty third alas a dirty third, alas a
dirty bird.

CHICKEN

Alas a doubt in case of more go to say what it is cress. What
is it. Mean. Potato. Loaves.

CHICKEN

Stick stick call then, stick stick sticking, sticking with a chicken. Sticking in a extra succession, sticking in.

> The complete *Tender Buttons* (written in 1911, published in 1914) was like a glossary in form: a book of definitions divided into three sections: objects, foods, rooms. Here Gertrude Stein's attempt was to "make poetry but and it seriously troubled me, dimly I knew that nouns made poetry but in prose I no longer needed the help of nouns and in poetry did I need the help of nouns. Was there not a way of naming things that would not invent names, but mean names without naming them." *(Poetry and Grammar,* 1935) In the process she came to the conception of a "continuous present," which, she said, it was "the business of art . . . to live in . . . that is the complete actual present and to completely express that complete actual present."

> (FURTHER COMMENTARY): "A continuous present is a continuous present."— Gertrude Stein.

DANIEL SPOERRI/EMMETT WILLIAMS
Nail [with commentaries]

3.5 cm long, brought from Sweden, square. In France, as far as I have been able to find out, nails are round and make wood fart. *Tr. Note 1.* Square nails are the only ones that don't have this defect, as ULTVEDT pointed out to me.

> TRANSLATOR'S NOTE *Pêter* means "to fart" in French, and that is what the author says ULTVEDT told him square nails prevent wood from doing. But it seemed a harsh word for such an activity, and I queried another sculptor, LAURENCE WHITFIELD, in London, who obliged with the following data:

>> Nope, I ain't never heard of any wood that farts. I've known wood that splits, warps, dries in, swells out, twists, cracks, shakes and runs, but no sir I ain't never heard of any wood that farts. I thought I knew every kind of wood in GOD's creation but this is a new one on me. . . . Happy to say that I do know something about your other query, though. I think the term "square nail" is a misnomer though there is

an actual square nail made, which is used largely in packing-case manufacture, but I don't think that it has any advantages over the ordinary round nail, though perhaps it can be clenched over easier when it comes through the other side of the wood as it does in packing cases. But I think the ones you mean are called "cut nails" or "brads." Nails were at one time made individually by blacksmiths, each one beaten out on an anvil, and so they had square corners. The first machine-made nails were stamped out from sheets of steel and so these too had square corners, and because of their rough edges gripped the fibres of the timber well. They don't have a sharp point like wire nails have, but have a flat tip. A thickish nail with a sharp point, when driven through a piece of timber, parts the fibres to allow the shaft of the nail through, but is really acting like a wedge and has a tendency to split the wood. With the cut nail, however, the square flat tip severs the fibres as it is driven in, in effect making a hole for itself, and so this lessens the chances of splitting, anyoldhow, that's enough about nails. Tap-Tap-Tap. . . . Q: What is a grub screw? A: A poke in the lunch hour. [E.W.]

From *An Anecdoted Topography of Chance* [1966]

The Rumanian-French artist Daniel Spoerri did the original work in French with the help of poet Robert Filliou, and it was later translated into English and "further anecdoted at random" by Emmett Williams, the American concrete poet. The book consists of a series of item-by-item descriptions of the objects that happened to be on Spoerri's blue table at 3:47 p.m. in the afternoon of October 17, 1961. With Williams' notes and comments, the book is an example of an international effort toward communal composition that has informed modern poetry from the Dadaists and Surrealists on. [G.Q./J.R.]

LOGOGENESIS: Presented below are eight of ninety new words coined and defined by a "chronic schizophrenic." Psychiatrist David V. Forrest labels the process-of-mind "poesis," and defines it by such characteristics as a tendency to concrete thinking; a use of self-created symbols "which have no consensual validation"; a logic of punning, metaphor, and "transient resemblances" to establish relations between things in the real world. Unlike related processes among primitives, surrealists, etc., the poesis is without a cultural context, dooming the patient (it would seem) to greater isolation and lack of communal outlet. The patient himself, "when asked at what age he began to coin words . . . replied, 'Age 20, when I developed a sense of humor.'"

[ANONYMOUS]

Schizophrenic Definitions

Py'ro•im'pe•tra'tion: Firestarting. From *pyro* meaning fire, *im* meaning in, and *petration,* a form of rock, *peter* meaning rock. Fire and rocks. Grass burns in connection with rocks. Rocks can burn.

Pho'to•chro•nog'ra•phy: Study of time by light with a timepiece.

Hor'o•le•ga'tion: Horology and separation; to keep apart in time. On April 28, 1964, I was alone with my clocks and jewelry—clocks, watches and diamond rings, sometimes pearls—watching TV, having a good time, talking with my parents, keeping away from bad company, with my clocks standing far apart, separating those that work and didn't. All people are like clocks with a heart ticking inside.

Pho'to•sec'tion•al'i•ty: Sectioning by light, of oranges and other fruits into quarters, eights, and sixteens.

Cir'clin•gol'o•gy: Study of a rolling circle. A fruit can in the form of a cylinder rolling. Rollers of presses.

Ster'e•o•trans•la'tion: Solid change of language, solid changing of interpretation, word of overidolization. The most cherished word of English. Respected, cherished, lovable words, solid, hard. Solid understanding. Cherishing, begetting. One word begets another, with a similar meaning and opposite.

Os'te•o•pho'to•car'di•ol'o•gy: Bones, lights and hearts. Bones to begin with. Light in the form of scintillation, illuminating, lighting up. One of the most brilliant words, because of "photo." Like superillumination.

Sem'i•cen'ti•os'te•o•pho'to•seis'mo•phys'i•o•ple'o•pol'y•
com'pu•ta'tion: The longest word, having 50 letters. The
act of boning up to count up to 50, a counting done by light,
on earth, by nature (from natural resources), more than 25,
many.

HARRY CROSBY

Short Introduction to the Word [1929]

1

Take the word Sun which burns permanently in my brain.
It has accuracy and alacrity. It is monomaniac in its inten-
sity. It is a continual flash of insight. It is the marriage of
Invulnerability with Yes, of the Red Wolf with the Gold
Bumblebee, of Madness with Rā

2

Birdileaves, Goldabbits, Fingertoes, Auroramor, Bar-
barifire, Parabolaw, Peaglecock, Lovegown, Nombrilo-
mane

3

I understand certain words to be single and by themselves
and deriving from no other words as for instance the
word I

4

I believe that certain physical changes in the brain result
in a given word—this word having the distinguished char-
acteristic of unreality being born neither as a result of
conotation nor of conscious endeavor: Starlash

5

There is the automatic word as for instance with me the word Sorceress; when the word goes on even while my attention is focused on entirely different subjects just as in swimming my arms and legs go on automatically even when my attention is focused on subjects entirely different from swimming such as witchcraft for instance or the Sorceress

6

A nursery game called Hunt-the-Slipper. A flower called Lady-Slipper. Running in the Gold Cup a horse called Slipper. Drinking champagne out of Her Red Slipper. From these magic sources the development of the word Slipper in my mind so that it becomes the word internal and therefore as much a part of me as my eyes or feet.

7

Honorificabilitudinity, Incircunscriptibleness, Antidisestablishment-Arians.

8

The evolution of a word in the mind requires despotic power and unlimited elimination. How could Yes for instance flourish among words such as dog or corset or safety-pin or hot-water-bag or eunuch.

For more on Crosby, see page 249, below.

Marcel Duchamp came from Paris to the United States in 1915, where he had an immediate influence during the time of "New York Dada" and an even more significant one on the art and poetry of the fifties and sixties. The "large glass" (or "Bride Stripped Bare by Her Bachelors, Even"), for which these are some of the verbal notes, was his big work, begun in 1913 and continued to the point of his withdrawal from art ten years later. George Hugnet wrote of him: "Duchamp opened the era of poetic experience in which chance and the concrete thing constitute a poetry that you can pick up in your hand or repluse with a kick."

MARCEL DUCHAMP
From Notes and Projects for the Large Glass

[22]

Conditions of a language
   the search for "prime
words"
("divisible" only
by themselves and
by unity).

[23]

Buy a dictionary
and cross out the words
  to be crossed out

     Sign, revised and corrected

[24]

Look through a dictionary
  and scratch out all the "undesirable" words.

Perhaps add a few—

sometimes replace the scratched out words
with another.

Use this dictionary for the
written part of the glass.

[26]

Dictionary

   of a language in which each word
would be translated into French (or other)
by several words, when necessary by a
   whole sentence
   —of a language which one could
   translate in its elements into
   known languages but which
   would not, reciprocally,
express the translation of
French words, or of
   or other

French or other sentences.
————Make this dictionary by means of cards
—find how to classify these cards
   (alphabetical order, but which alphabet)
   Alphabet—or rather a few
   elementary signs, like a dot
   a line, a circle, etc. (to be seen).
   which will vary according to the position etc—
—Sound of this language, is it
               speakable ?
      No.

[27]

   Dictionary=
   with films, taken close up, of parts
of very large objects, obtain
photographic records which no longer
look like photographs of
something—With these
semimicroscopies,
constitute a dictionary of which each
film would be the representation of a
group of words in a sentence or separated
so that this film would assume a

new significance or rather that
the concentration on this film of the
sentences or words chosen would give
a form of meaning to this film
and that once learned, this
relation between film and meaning
translated into words would be "striking."
and would serve as a basis for a kind
of writing which no longer has an
   alphabet or words but
      signs (films) already freed
      from the "baby talk" of all
   ordinary languages.
   —Find a means of
   filing all these films in such order
   that one could refer ^{to} them
   as in a dictionary

THE POETRY OF A GRAMMAR: The particular process in the Hopi language that linguist Benjamin Lee Whorf classified in 1936 as "the punctual and segmentative aspects of its verbs" is a highly abbreviated image of the relation between phenomena at rest and phenomena in motion, between a single instance and a repeated series. Thus Whorf's hypothesis also belongs to the history of poetry: that the grammar of a language (as a system of condensations) embodies a *Weltanschauung* and conditions the speaker's view of reality.

BENJAMIN LEE WHORF

Movements from the Punctual and Segmentative Aspects of Some Hopi Verb

ha'rï	it is bent in a rounded angle	harï'rïta	it lies in a meandering line
ho"ci	it forms a sharp acute angle	hoci'cita	it is zigzag
pa"ci	it is notched	paci'cita	it is serrated
wa'ya	it makes a waving shake, like a small tree shaken	waya'yata	it is shaking

na'ya	it makes a sway from one side to the other	naya'yata	it is swaying
ro'ya	it makes a turn or twist	roya'yata	it is rotating
rï"pi	it gives a flash	rïpï'pïta	it is sparkling
ʔï'wi	it flames up	ʔïwi'wïta	it is flaming
ʔï'mi	it explodes, goes off like a gun	ʔïmi'mïta	it is thundering

GEORGE BRECHT

Excerpts from Gloss for an Unknown Language

Tablet 3

Line	Character	
17	9	Image formed by a moving object for the duration of one breath.
31	7	An object formed by the intersection of an imaginary sphere with objects of the reference language. (Here used to describe a plano-convex section of flesh/earth).
31	8	Used by an observer standing at the edge of a body of water to denote an area of water surface in front of the observer and an area of earth of equal size and shape behind the observer, considered as one surface.

Tablet 10

Line	Character	
6	4	Everything within the bounds of an imaginary cube having its center congruent with that of the observer, and an edge of length equal to the observer's height.
23	9	A verb apparently denoting the motion of a static object. (The meaning is not clear.)

Tablet 15

Line	Character	
19	3	A unit of time derived from the duration of dream-events.
45	2	The independent action of two or more persons, considered as a single action.

JACK SPICER

Five Words for Joe Dunn on His 22nd Birthday

I shall give you five words for your birthday.

The first is *anthropos*
Who celebrates birthdays.
He is withered and tough and blind, babbler
Of old wars and dead beauty.
He is there for the calmness of your heart as the days race
And the wars are lost and the roses wither.
No enemy can strike you that he has not defeated.
No beauty can die in your heart that he will not remember.

The second word is *andros*
Who is proud of his gender,
Wears it like a gamecock, erects it
Through the midnight of time
Like a birthday candle.
He will give you wisdom like a Fool
Hidden in the loins
Crying out against the inelegance
Of all that is not sacred.

The third word is *eros*
Who will cling to you every birthnight
Bringing your heart substance.
Whomever you touch will love you,
Will feel the cling of His touch upon you
Like sunlight scattered over an ancient mirror.

The fourth word is *thanatos,* the black belly
That eats birthdays.
I do not give you *thanatos.* I bring you a word to call Him
Thanatos, devourer of young men, heart-biter, bone-licker.
Look, He slinks away when you name Him.
Name him! *Thanatos.*

The last word is *agape,*
The dancer that puts birthdays in motion.
She is there to lead words.
Counter to everything, She makes words
Circle around Her. Words dance.
See them. *Anthropos* ageless,
Andros made virgin, *Eros* unmirrored
Thanatos devoured.
Agape, Agape, ring-mistress,
Love
That comes from beyond birthdays,
That makes poetry
And moves stars.

Rites & Events

■ *". . . There is a curious parallel between [the] generalized collapse of life at the root of our present demoralization and our concern for a culture which has never been coincident with life, which in fact has been devised to tyrannize over life."*

—ANTONIN ARTAUD, *The Theater and Its Double*

■ *"Art's obscured the difference between art and life. Now let life obscure the difference between life and art."*

—JOHN CAGE

ENOCH HOAG [CADDO]

A Moon Peyote Altar

(SOURCE: WESTON LA BARRE, *The Peyote Cult*, 1959.) From the time of John Wilson (also called Nishkuntu or Moon-Head), an early revealer of peyote in the 1890s, the poetic and religious imagination of many leading peyotists has gone into the devising of highly symbolic altars or "moons," which can themselves be read as (concrete) poems. As with poems, the readings of the altars vary from maker to maker, while elements like the crescent-shaped upper portion remain basically fixed. In the present Enoch Hoag moon (in use among the Caddo), the elements make up a face: "a star and a heart at the hair-parting or forehead, . . . ash mounds simulating eyes, an inverted heart at the crossing of the altar-lines as a nose, four concentric lozenges for an oracular mouth, and another heart east of this resembling a cleft chin; the moon itself is the figure's hair." Among the Osage, they "call the three hearts of the altar the

99

'Heart of Goodness,' the 'Heart of the World,' and the 'Heart of Jesus'; others interpret the 'world' as the 'sun.' The ashes are the graves of Christ and Wilson for some, the dividing of the Red Sea for others. Some say the whole firepit is the grave of Christ, and the ash mounds his lungs, as the figure under the fire is his heart." The altar may also be marked with the leader's initials or "footprints" —as W's or M's for Wilson or Moon-Head. With a cross at center, the whole altar may be said, in the words of Wilson's vision, to map "the 'Road' which led from the grave of Christ to the Moon in the sky, which Christ had taken in his ascent."

THE SHAKERS: The United Society of Believers in Christ's Second Appearing—called "Shakers"—originated in England in the mid-eighteenth century and soon centered around the person of Ann Lee (Mother Ann, or Mother Wisdom), who became "the reincarnation of the Christ Spirit . . . Ann the Word . . . Bride of the Lamb." The group practiced communal living and equality of the sexes, along with a reputedly complete abstention from sexual intercourse. After persecutions and jailings in England, Ann brought them to America in 1774, where for many years they thrived on conversions, reaching a maximum size of 6,000 before their demise in the twentieth century.

[THE SHAKERS]
Shaker Events

1. *Sweeping Events.* Participants march through houses and out-buildings, pretending to be sweeping and cleaning wherever they go, while singing a song of vengeance, often "in the voice of God." They roar and howl at the appropriate time, stamp their feet, and shake wherever they come on any unclean spot. Returning to the place of worship, all fall on their knees "to scour and scrub from this floor the stains of sin."

2. *Bathing Event.* Two large white tubs—one for the Brethren and one for the Sisters—are placed on either side of a fountain. In the pantomime that follows, dippers and sponges are filled from the fountain, and the men and women, from their positions on separate sides of the enclosure, go through the motions of scrubbing each other clean.

3. *Fool Events.* After drinking spiritual wine, the partici-
pants get "merry" and an instument shouts: "I feel just
about ready to sing the fool song." Then all join in singing:
    Come, come
    Who will be a fool
    I will be a fool—
at the same time "throwing fool" to each other, catching
it, and acting as foolishly as possible.

4. *Spirit Food Event.* Participants eat a meal of spiritual
foods—such as apples, pears, peaches, pineapples, plums,
cherries, apricots, grapes, berries, pomegranates, oranges,
pies, sweet-cakes, bread and butter, locusts and wild
honey, milk and honey, white wine and manna—which
have been gathered from imaginary trees and gardens.

SADAKICHI HARTMANN
Sadakichi's 1895 Psychedelic Light Show

To Students of Color Psychology

DARKNESS IN SPACE

Poetical license imagines that at Buddha's entering Nir-
vana, a color revery takes place in the universe.

This scene, a concert of self-radiant colors, is to be
represented by pyrotechny brought by chemistry, elec-
tricity, and future light-producing sciences to such perfec-
tion and beauty that it becomes the new Optic Art, in
which Color will rival Sound as a vehicle of pure emotion.

SCENE: Bluish-black darkness in space: a minute section
of the universe, represented by a stage of at least 800 yards
length and 500 yards height and depth.

I. Out of darkness the earth, in the ban of the sun and
followed by her pallid paramour the moon, ever revolving
rolls majestically forward, displaying the phenomena of a
lunar and solar eclipse, and growing larger and larger
until she has become so large that one can discern: the
ultramarine of the oceans, the glaucous of the steppes, the
pallid gold of the deserts, the crystal fretwork of the poles

and glaciers, and here and there the dark flyspecks of the largest cities, which become scintillant as the other colors fade in earthly night. It impresses the beholder like the colossal ideal of human vanity and then rolls backward into darkness.

II. Confused tumbling of meteors through space—a symbol of man's life, propelled from some unknown bourn and rushing to some unknown goal, proving its momentary existence merely by a luminous line, lit and extinguished without change of course. The meteors, varying continually in the rhythm of entrance and exit, mobility, richness, and intensity of fire, shoot forth in every direction, also in every possible angle, towards the audience.

III. Incessant rain of luminous stellar dust, in the midst of which a battle of stars, comets, planets with rings and satellites, takes place. They rush towards each other, and recede, encircle each other and create endless variations of figures. Now and then stars crush into each other with a great explosion of fire, united into larger stars and, continuing their course, emit a light produced by a combination of their colors when separate. Suddenly the stars grow larger and larger, the smaller ones disappearing behind the larger, until a few dozens have reached the diameter of 50 yards, who in turn repeat a crescendo of concussions. An orange and a blue star collide and form a still larger one radiating a greenish light of painful hope. A roseate and blue star also collide to a violet glow of melancholy bliss. Thereupon these two collide, and before they grow into one, all the other stars crush into them, causing an incandescent firebrand that radiates the entire space with its irisating light. This fire wall is suddenly cleft in two, and in innumerable hues and palpitations melts away in "diminuendo."

IV. The lower (¼) part of the stage represents the sea of chaos over which by some caprice the light effects of an earthly day, from a blood-red dawn to a moonlit night, are performed in color gradations of subtlest purity, accompanied by descriptive music.

Intermezzo, entitled "Alhambra Arabesques." In succession the famous patterns in luminous gold, blue, and faded red interlace, overlap, and link before the eyes of the audience, and finally change into an improvisation of new designs of the same character. (For other intermezzos the author suggests "The Shattered Jewel Casket," "Flowers Growing in Cloudland," etc.)

v. A kaleidoscopical symphony of color effects continually changing in elation and depression, velocity, intensity, variety, and sentiment, continually developing and composing new forms and designs, not merely of mathematical symmetry, but also as suggested from the endless constructions, textures, phenomena revealed in astronomy, microscopy, mineralogy, geology, paleontology, etc., beginning with a *Lhargetto* in light bluish-grey, muddy yellowish-green, greenish-blue, and dark greyish-blue; followed by an *Andante* in color containing blue from green to purple; by an *Allegretto* of complimentary colors with a tendency towards yellow and red; and by a *Finale vivace* in all colors, ending at last with a flower star, emitting rocket-like fire lines, trills, radiations of various propelling power, at first paraphrasing in the colors of the solar spectrum, and at last improvising an outburst of new colors, like ultra red and violet, for which optical instruments have first to be invented before the human eye can perceive and enjoy them.

From *Buddha* [1897]

In the Foreword to Sadakichi Hartmann's *White Chrysanthemums* (ed. George Knox and Harry Lawton: Herder and Herder, 1971), Kenneth Rexroth writes: "Sadakichi . . . was one of the main links joining American intellectual life to the international revolutionary culture of the fifty years before the First War." Whitman praised him, and Pound wrote: "If one had not been oneself, it wd. have been worthwhile being Sadakichi."

EDUCATION AS DEFINITION: Amos Bronson Alcott was a Transcendentalist and a radical educator, whose innovations included the abolition of physical punishment, organized play, a pleasant school environment, and the honor system. His *Record of Conversations on the Gospel Held in Mr. Alcott's School, Unfolding the Doctrine and Discipline of Human Culture* (1836/1837) was based on Piaget-like experimental sessions with children, in which he read them excerpts from the New Testament in order "to *investigate* the *Consciousness of Childhood* . . . [to see if] these *testimonies* of *children* confirm the views of adults—that *Christianity is grounded in the essential Nature of Man.* . . ." Writes Perry Miller: "Alcott employed the children as divining rods for a proper reading of the text," in line with "the Transcendentalist supposition that the natural intuition is freshest and least unspoiled in children."

AMOS BRONSON ALCOTT

Conversation VIII.
Nativity of Spirit. Family Relation.

Idea of Birthplace and Birth

MR. ALCOTT . . . Now what came into your minds while I was reading?

JOSIAH. The deserts seemed to me a great space covered with sand, like that in the hour-glass. The sun was shining on it, and making it sparkle. There were no trees. John was there alone.

EDWARD J. I thought the deserts meant woods, with paths here and there.

LUCY. I thought of a space covered with grass and some wild flowers, and John walking about.

CHARLES. I thought of a prairie.

ALEXANDER. I thought of a rocky country.

AUGUSTINE. I thought of a few trees scattered over the country, with bees in the trunks.

GEORGE K. I thought of a place without houses, excepting John's; and flowers, trees, and bee-hives.

DICK HIGGINS

From twenty-seven episodes
for the aquarian theater
to the recognition of Antonin Artaud

i—the moon rises

the back of the theater is opened up
the rising moon is seen
the moon rises up and out of sight
the back of the theater is closed

there is ceremony

ii—the burning bush

the curtains open
there is quiet
there is darkness on the face of the earth

flames appear
a burning scarecrow
or a burning cross
or a small and twisted tree

the flames have their dinner
then they leave

when the glows and glowing are gone
there is silence and darkness

and the curtains close

JOHN CAGE

2 Pages, 122 Words on Music and Dance

This piece appeared in Dance Magazine, November 1957. *The two pages were given me in dummy form by the editors. The number of words was given by chance operations. Imperfections in the sheets of paper upon which I worked gave the position in space of the fragments of text. That position is different in this printing, for it is the result of working on two other sheets of paper, of another size and having their own differently placed imperfections.*

To obtain the value
of a sound, a movement,
measure from zero. (Pay
attention to what it is,
just as it is.)

A bird flies.

Slavery is abolished.

the woods

A sound has no legs to stand on.

The world is teeming: anything can
happen.

sound   movement

Points in   Activities which are different
time, in   love   happen in a time which is a space:
space   mirth   are each central, original.
                  the heroic
                  wonder
The emotions   tranquillity   are in the audience.
                  fear
                  anger   The telephone rings.
                  sorrow   Each person is in the best seat.
                  disgust

   Is there a glass of water?   War begins at any moment.

                              Each now is the time, the space.

      lights

          inaction?
                                   Are eyes open?

      Where the bird flies, fly.   ears?

Sound-Poems

& Incantations

CHÖGYAM TRUNGPA

Past and Present

CHÖGYAM TRUNGPA RINPOCHE, whose sacred lineage as "reincarnated Lama" is recounted in his autobiography, *Born in Tibet,* is presently teaching the practice of Tantric Buddhism to Americans. He has published a volume of poetry, *Mudra* (Shambala Press, Berkeley, 1972), a meditation manual called *Meditation in Action,* and is editor of the magazine *Garuda.* With Ginsberg, Snyder, and others, he shares a concern for creating an American practice of oriental philosophy. His own poetry includes both traditional Tibetan forms in translation, visual poems (as here), and modern experimentation (in one case a collaboration with Allen Ginsberg).

RICHARD JOHNNY JOHN
JEROME ROTHENBERG
IAN TYSON

Song from Shaking the Pumpkin [Seneca]

```
YOHOHEYHEYYEYHEYHAHYEYHEYHAHYEYEYHAHYEYEYHAHHEH
I WAS GOING THRU THE BIG SMOKE HEYHEYHEYHEYHAHYEYEYHAHYEYEYHAHHEH
YOHOHEYHEYHEYHEYHAHYEYHEYHAHYEYEYHAHYEYEYHAHHEH
YOHOHEYHEYHEYHEYHAHYEYHEYHAHYOHOHEYHEYHEYHEYHAHYEYEYHAHYEYEYHAHHEH
YOHOHEYHEYHEYHEYHAHYEYHEYHAHYOHOHEYHEYHEYHEYHAHYEYEYHAHYEYEYHAHHEH
YOHOHEYHEYHEYHEYHAHYEYHEYHAHYOHOHEYHEYHEY I WENT THRU THIS BIG SMOKE EH
YOHOHEYHEYHEYHEYHAHYEYHEYHAHYOHOHEYHEYHEYHEYHAHYEYEYHAHYEYEYHAHHEH
YOHOHEYHEYHEYHEYHAHYEYHEYHAHHEH I WAS GOING THRU THE BIG SMOKE HEYHEYHEYHEYHAHYEYEYHAHYEYEYHAHHEHE
YOHOHEYHEYHEYHEYHEY I WENT THRU THIS BIG SMOKE YHEYHEYHAHYEYHEYHAHYEYEYHAHYEYEYHAHHEH
YOHOHEYHEYHEYHEYHEY I WENT THRU THIS BIG SMOKE YHEYHEYHAHHEHYOHOHEYHEYHEYHEYHAHYEYEYHAHHEH
YOHOHEYHEYHEYHEYHEYHEYHEYHAHYEYHEYHAH I WAS GOING THRU THE BIG SMOKE
YOHOHEYHEYHEYHEYHEYHEYHEYHAHYEYHEYHAHHEHYOHOHEYHEYHEYHEYHAHYEYEYHAHHEH
YOHOHEYHEYHEY I WENT THRU THIS BIG SMOKE YHEYHEYHAHHEHYOHOHEYHEYHEYHEYHAHYEYEYHAHHEH
YOHOHEYHEYHEYHEY I WAS GOING THRU THE BIG SMOKE
YOHOHEYHEYHEYHEYHEYHAHYEYHAHYEYHAHHEHYOHOHEYHEYHEYHEYHAHYEYEYHAHHEH
YOHOHEYHEYHEYHEYHEYHAHYEYHAHYEYHAHHEHYOHOHEYHEYHEYHEYHAHYEYEYHAHHEH
YOHOHEYHEYHEYHEYHEYHAHYEYHAHYEYHAHHEHYOHOHEYHEYHEYHEYHAHYEYEYHAHHEH
YOHOHEYHEYHEYHEYHEYHAHYEYHAHYEYHAHHEHYOHOHEYHEYHEYHEYHAHYEYEYHAHHEH
KE OHEYHEYHEYHEYHEYHAHYEYHAHYEYHAHHEHYOHOHEYHEYHEYHEYHAHYEYEYHAHHEH
YOHOHEYHEYHEYHEYHEYHEYHAHYEYHEYHAHYEYEYHAHHEH
```

Derived from a sacred curing song of The Society of the Mystic Animals (also called: Society of Shamans), this version uses all elements of the original (including the nonverbal), representing the sounds (mantra) by yantra-like visual patterns. The present version by British artist IAN TYSON comes from the Seneca of RICHARD JOHNNY JOHN and an earlier translation by JEROME ROTHENBERG in *Shaking the Pumpkin: Traditional Poetry of the Indian North Americas* (1972).

■ *"A* mantra *is primarily a mental sound and regarded as fundamental in both the creation and dissolution of all form. The function does not end in expressing an ordinary meaning; the very sound aspect of a word or a combination of words has the capacity to activate the divine forms invoked. A* mantra *exerts its power, not so much through expressing the meaning as we understand it, but more deeply through its sound-vibrations. . . . Seers of ancient times who knew the secrets of the power of sounds composed the* mantras *by joining symbolic syllables in accordance with certain laws laid down in Tantric texts. . . .* Mantra *gives formula and equation;* yantra, *diagram and pattern; and what correlates both systems of relations is* Tantra.*"*

—AJIT MOOKERJEE, *Tantra Art, Its Philosophy and Physics* [1971]

[THE SHAKERS]
Sound-Poem

Ah pe-an t-as ke t-an te loo
O ne vas ke than sa-na was-ke
   lon ah ve shan too
Te wan-se ar ke ta-ne voo te
   lan se o-ne voo
Te on-e-wan tase va ne woo te wan-se o-ne van
Me-le wan se oo ar ke-le van te
   shom-ber on vas sa la too lar var sa
   re voo an don der on v-tar loo-cum an la voo
O be me-sum ton ton ton tol a wac—er tol-a wac-er
   ton ton te s-er pane love ten poo

     By "Jack." Holy Ground. Oct. 6th 1847

     "The first Shaker songs were wordless tunes," writes EDWARD DEM-ING ANDREWS, from whose *The Gift to be Simple* the various entries in the present mapping have been taken. Given "in tongues" by spiritual messengers that included not only Mother Ann and other dead Shaker elders, but also Indians, Blacks, Persians, Jews, Chinese, and William Penn, George Washington, Napoleon, Mahomet, Leo X, St. Patrick, and Alexander Pope, they were in fact "sound-poems" preceding the experiments of Dadaists, etc., by over a century. See also page 100, above.

LAFCADIO HEARN
Charcoal Man

Char–coal, Lady! Char-coal! Chah-ah-coal, Lady!
Black—coalee—coalee!
Coaly—coaly; coaly—coaly—coal—coal—coal.
Coaly—coaly!
Coal—eee! Nice!
Chah—coal!
Twenty-five! Whew!
O Charco-oh-oh-oh-h-oh-lee!
Oh—lee—eee!
(You get some coal in your mout', young fellow, if you don't
    keep it shut!)
Pretty coalee—oh—lee!
Charcoal!
Cha—ah—ahr—coal!
Charbon! Du charbon, Madame! Bon charbon? Point! Ai-ai!
Tonnèrre de dieu!
Cha-r-r-r-r-r-r-rbon!
A-a-a-a-a-a-aw!
Vingt-cinq! Nice coalee! Coalee!
Coaly-coal-coal!
Pretty coaly!
Charbon de Paris!
De Paris, Madame; de Paris!

New Orleans street-cries gathered by Hearn at the turn of the
century and collaged by him into a sound-poem that creates an
immediate aural image. About these there's nothing magical or
mantric on the face of it, except the Black charcoal seller's attempt
to call-into-presence and to persuade by celebration. And that
would also seem to be what Hearn was doing in his transmission.

Else von Freytag-Loringhoven's sound-poem (below) is from 1920, part of a conscious Dadaist experiment that was also a replaying of a much older kind of wordless poetry. Michael McClure's *Ghost Tantras* (1964) extend the experiment and posit its connection to forms of communication throughout the animal world: the creation of what he calls a "beast language."

ELSE von FREYTAG-LORINGHOVEN

Klink—Hratzvenga

(Deathwail)

Narin—Tzarissamanili

(He is dead!)

Ildrich mitzdonja—astatootch
Ninj—iffe kniek—
Ninj—iffe kniek!
Arr—karr—
Arrkarr—barr
Karrarr—barr—
Arr—
Arrkarr—
Mardar
Mar—dóórde—dar—

Mardoodaar! ! !

Mardoodd—va—hist—kniek— —
Hist—kniek?
Goorde mee—niss— — —
Goorde mee! ! !
Narin—tzarissamanilj—
Narin—tzarissamanilj! ! !
Hee—hassee?
O—voorrr!

Kardirdesporvorde—hadoorde—klossnux
Kalsinjevasnije—alquille—masré
Alquille masréje paquille—paquille
Ojombe—ojoombe—ojé— — — —

Narin—tzarissamanilj—
Narin—tzarissamanilj ! ! !
Vé—O—voorrr—!
Vévoorrr—
Vrmbbbjjj—sh—
Sh—sh— —
Ooh ! ! !
Vrmbbbjjj—sh—sh—
Sh—sh—
Vrmm.

MICHAEL McCLURE

Ghost Tantra No. 8

Awaken grahhh nameless brahh beauty brahhh sense:
SENZOR BRAHH-GRAHH GROOOOOWEE!
Hrrruh! Rahhr. Gragma huhrr vreeeemagtarb.
OH!
Ohhhh ooooie more superb than Anita Ekberg.
YOU!
Proud cones of Grecian breasts
and thighs and belly. Smile in the darkness.
Groooooooooooooooooh! Goooooooor
mowkarg-lang voooooo mahh tah.
Rose and lily lovely cheek mate;
GROOOOOOOOOOOOO
OOOOOOOOOOOIE
Gooooooooor. HRAHH!

JACKSON MAC LOW
"5th Gatha"

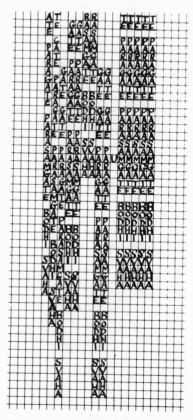

The "5th Gatha" is part of an extensible series of grid poems, in which the letters of any mantra (here the Sanskrit Great Praj-naparamita Mantram, *Gate Gate Paragate Parasamgate Bodhi Svaha,* "gone, gone, far gone, gone over to the other shore—awak-ening svaha!") are arranged by chance operation off a central axis containing the Hindu seed-syllable AUM. The gathas are generally performed as "simultaneities" by a group of readers using the same or different realizations of a single prayer. In working from the notation, the reader begins at any square (empty spaces are silences). He moves to any adjacent square horizontally, vertically, or diagonally, and continues this process until the end of the piece. Letters are read as any sound they can stand for alone or grouped —syllables, words, word groups, complete sentences, or the sound or name of the letter itself, in any language.

ANSELM HOLLO'S versions (below) are from Finnish originals collected by Marjorie Edgar from "settlers from Finland and their descendants in the iron mining towns of Minnesota and the lake country surrounding them." Charms were originally used by professional *loihtija* or wise women. Hollo, born and raised in Finland, writes in a distinctively American idiom, as well as translating in and out of several languages (e.g., Williams' *Paterson* into German, Voznesensky into English, etc.).

ANSELM HOLLO

2 Useful Poems
that Traveled Across the Atlantic

TO PREVENT FROSTBITE

Frost, Son of Blizzard, i tell you:
STOP freezing my fingernails
& STOP freezing my fingers, too:
go freeze the willows by the river,
go freeze the dumb birchtrees, wherever!

—Kangasniemi/Finland—Winton/Minnesota
Iowa City/Iowa/2:iv:72

TO MAKE THE COWS COME HOME

here, let me tie this bell round your neck
                    this bell round your neck, my dearest cow
clang, bell
                    bell, clang
clang from the farthest range
bell them right back to the Big House

you are the biggest & strongest
you'll bring home all the others

clang clang back to the Big House
                    back to evening smokes rising
while the Sun still shines, & mid-evening
is mellow, clang, bell, clang, yellow

all in a row, all in a row

bring the holy cows home, bring them home

The Cows of Our Bounteous Mother

> —Oulu/Finland—Crooked Lake/Minnesota
> Iowa City/Iowa/2:iv:72

PHILIP WHALEN
Magical Incantation

Pig fuck pig baby pig shit. ham, bacon, pig
        sausage, Charles Lamb

        A beautiful sunset
        A gorgeous broad

        *

Fallen stars, fallen arches at Nimes,
        broken dick, fallen womb, Chagrin Falls
           Ohio for the view,
        no fun for anybody.
Farewell Wilhelm Reich.

GARY SNYDER SAYS: "Jaime de Angulo you must realize was a great culture hero on the West Coast. He was a Spaniard with a Paris M.D., came to the South West, quit to live with Indians, moved to California. Self-taught linguist, a good one. He never had a regular appointment, he was just too wild. Burned a house down one night when drunk, rode about naked on a horse at Big Sur, member of the Native American Church, great friend of Jeffers—the only man Jeffers ever allowed to visit him day or night. . . . So: at the end of World War II, Jaime de Angulo was one of the few people alive to jazz up California."

JAIME de ANGULO

Coyote Shaman Songs

"Grandfather," Fox Boy said, "Will you teach me the songs of the Shaman, good medicine songs full of power? I want to have power!"

"How can I? I'm just an old man Coyote. I don't know any."

"Oh, YES you do, Grandfather! You could teach me if you wanted to. You know everything!!"

"All right," grumbled the old Coyote, "but you're just a LITTLE BOY. You won't understand."

Fox sat on a stump and listened with all his might.

These are the songs of the Shaman that Grandfather Coyote sang.

Wildcat who stalks the trail alone,
I never yet told of you
And of your bitterness in the brush.
The sun is setting, Wildcat, in the western sea.

Serpent on the rock, stretched in the sun,
Crawl into your hole

And tell the rain to come:
My heart is drying in my belly.

Raven perching on the dead tree,
Fly to the mother of the sun,
Old-Spider-in-the-sky,
And tell her that my heart
Is slowly freezing under my ribs.

Busy bee flying back to crowded hive,
You are no totem for shaman seeking power!
I am looking for a locust in the grass,
A locust whirring in the sunlight.

Fox lurking in the night,
I see your eyes.
Go tell the waxing moon
That my mind is dark.

I am Pis'wis'na, the hawk.
I am myself.
I thought I was myself
But I am only a head.
I am a head crying in the desert.

E. E. CUMMINGS
brIght

bRight s??? big
(soft)

soft near calm
(Bright)
calm st?? holy

(soft briGht deep)
yeS near sta? calm star big yEs
alone
(wHo

Yes
near deep whO big alone soft near
deep calm deep
? ? ? ? Ht ? ? ? ? ? T)
Who(holy alone)holy(alone holy)alone

MAP TWO: LOSSES

Primal unity is shattered. Recurrently in our history
man loses his sense of a radiant world of meanings
and turns to a pattern of violence toward himself and
toward others from whom he is divided. In **Map Two**
the Great Mother—the Native Land—has become
a stony virgin, symbol of the closed self, and the
Father, a tyrant and agent of sexual and political
repression and of a long process of despair,
impotence, and psychic decay. The Son of this unholy
union is a rapist and insurrectionary, who gives rise to
terrifying change and the wobble of modern history.

■ *"The* Shekinah—*literally in-dwelling, namely of God in the world—is taken to mean simply God himself in His omnipresence and activity in the world. . . . In the usage of the Kabbalah . . . the* Shekinah *becomes an aspect of God, a quasi-independent feminine element within Him. . . . As complement to the universally human and masculine principle, [She is] seen at once as mother, as wife, and as daughter. . . . [The conception of] the exile of the* Shekinah *goes back to the Talmud. 'In every exile into which the children of Israel went, the* Shekinah *was with them.' In the Talmud this means only that God's presence was always with Israel in its exiles. In the Kabbalah, however, it is taken to mean that* a part of God Himself is exiled from God. . . . The exile of Shekinah . . . in other words . . . [is] the separation of the masculine and feminine principles in God.*

"The exile of the Shekinah *is sometimes represented as the banishment of the queen or of the king's daughter by her husband or father. Sometimes the* Shekinah *is represented as overpowered by the demonic powers of the 'other side,' which break into her realm, subjugate her, and make her subservient to their activities of stern judgment."*

—GERSHOM G. SCHOLEM, *Kabbalah & Its Symbolism* [1960]

AMERICA AS WOMAN: In *In the American Grain,* William Carlos Williams writes: "One is forced on the conception of the New World as a woman." In that form he has her speaking to De Soto, he who would soon be buried in her waters, "this solitary sperm . . . into the liquid, the formless, the insatiable belly of sleep; down among the fishes." She had told him while alive to

> . . . ride upon the belly of the waters, building your boats to carry all across. Calculate for the current; the boats move with a force not their own, up and down, sliding upon that female who communicates to them, across all else, herself. And still there is that which you have not sounded, under the boats, under the adventure—giving to all things the current, the wave, the onwash of my passion. So cross and have done with it you are safe—and I am desolate. . . . Follow me—if you can. Follow me, Señor, this is your country. I give it to you. Take it.

We have encountered that woman-thing before—a nearly universal myth of "Mother Earth," or of the land, that which we wrench from Earth, with pleasure at first, then in a dream of losses endlessly repeated. She is Blake's Jerusalem (*and* Oothoon-Enitharmon): the one the Jews called the Shekinah; the Gnostics called Sophia; the Tantrists called Goddess-of-Wisdom-Whose-Substance-Is-Desire and in her terrifying aspect, Kali. The Indian nations knew her too, as the mother sometimes or grandmother, sometimes as the woman on a journey, like the one for whom the mound in Upper Michigan was called Where-she-with-the-full-belly-turned-over.

In the story of American poetry she turns up often. She is earth or god, wisdom or muse—or that woman always one town ahead of our pursuit, say, or like the poor-old-soul of Bukka White's blues, singing

> I ain't got nobody
> To take me to this train
> Mmmmmmmmmmmmmmmmmmmmmmmm
> Mmmmmm mmmm mm mm mm

as real in her desolation as America in hers. Wrote Edgar Allan Poe, "The death, then, of a beautiful woman is, unquestionably, the most poetical topic in the world."

[MAYA]

From The Popol Vuh: Blood-Girl
and the Chiefs of Hell

[After the Twin Gods, 1 and 7 Hunter, had been murdered
by the Chiefs of Hell, their skulls were hung like fruit from
a tree at Dusty Court. Blood-Girl found them there, and
while they spoke to her, spittle from the skulls dripped in
her womb and filled her. Six months pregnant when her
father, Blood Chief, discovered it and cursed her for her
fornication; sent four owls to kill her and bring her heart
back in a jar. To whom she pleaded, and they, having
decided they would spare her, asked what they could bring
back as her heart.]

"Take the fruit of this tree,"
    Said the maiden then.
For red was the sap of the tree
    That she went and gathered in the jar,
And then it swelled up
    And became round
And so then it became an imitation heart,
    The sap of the red tree.
Just like blood the sap of the tree became
    An imitation of blood.
Then she gathered up there in it
    What was red tree sap
And the bark became just like blood,
    Completely red when placed inside the jar.
When the tree was cut by the maiden
    Cochineal Red Tree it was called,
And so she called it blood
    Because it was said to be the blood of the croton.
"So there you will be loved then;
    On earth there will come to be something of yours,"
She said then
    To the Owls.
"Very well,

Oh maiden,
We must go back
And appear directly;
We shall go right back.
We feel it must be delivered,
This seeming imitation of your heart,
Before the lords,"
Then said
The messengers.
So then they came before the lords,
Who were all waiting expectantly.
"Didn't it get done?"
Then asked 1 Death.
"It is already done,
Oh Lords,
And here in fact is her heart.
It is down in the jar."
"All right,
Then I'll look,"
Said 1 Death then.
And when he poured it right out,
The bark was soggy with fluid,
The bark was bright crimson with sap.
"Stir the surface on the fire well
And put it over the fire," said 1 Death then.
So then they dried it over the fire
And those of Hell then smelled the fragrance.
They all wound up standing there,
Bending over it.
It really smelled delicious to them,
The aroma of the sap.
Thus it was that they were still crouching there
When the Owls came who were guiding the maiden,
Letting her climb up through a hole to the earth.
Then the guides turned around and went back down.
And thus were the lords of Hell defeated.
It was by a maiden that they were all blinded.

SMOHALLA [NEZ PERCÉ]
The Mother

My young men shall never work. Men who work cannot dream, & wisdom comes in dreams.

You ask me to plow the ground. Shall I take a knife & tear my mother's breast? Then when I die she will not take me to her bosom to rest.

You ask me to dig for stone. Shall I dig under her skin for bones? Then when I die I cannot enter her body to be born again.

You ask me to cut grass & make hay & sell it, & be rich like white men. But how dare I cut off my mother's hair?

It is a bad law, & my people cannot obey it. I want my people to stay with me here. All the dead men will come to life again. We must wait here in the house of our fathers & be ready to meet them in the body of our mother.

SMOHALLA was the founder of the nineteenth-century Dreamer Religion, which abandoned Christianity in favor of the native concepts of a benevolent Earth Mother and of the dream-vision as the major vehicle for communication with her powers. Contrast the screwing-of-the-earth in MACLEISH'S vision of the Empire Builders.

ARCHIBALD MacLEISH
Empire Builders

THE MUSEUM ATTENDANT:

This is *The Making of America in Five Panels:*

This is Mister Harriman making America:
Mister-Harriman-is-buying-the-Union-Pacific-at-Seventy:
The Santa Fe is shining on his hair.

This is Commodore Vanderbilt making America:
Mister-Vanderbilt-is-eliminating-the-short-interest-in-
      Hudson:

Observe the carving on the rocking chair.

This is J. P. Morgan making America:
(The Tennessee Coal is behind to the left of the Steel
        Company.)
Those in mauve are braces he is wearing.

This is Mister Mellon making America:
Mister-Mellon-is-represented-as-a-symbolical-figure-in-
        aluminum-
Strewing-bank-stocks-on-a-burnished-stair.

This is the Bruce is the Barton making America:
Mister-Barton-is-selling-us-Doctor's-Deliciousest-Dentifrice.
This is he in beige with the canary.

You have just beheld the Makers making America:
This is The Making of America in Five Panels:
America lies to the west-southwest of the switch-tower:
There is nothing to see of America but land.

THE ORIGINAL DOCUMENT
UNDER THE PANEL PAINT:

        "To Thos. Jefferson Esq. his obd't serv't
        M. Lewis: captain: detached:
                        Sir:

Having in mind your repeated commands in this matter,
And the worst half of it done and the streams mapped,

And we here on the back of this beach beholding the
Other ocean—two years gone and the cold

Breaking with rain for the third spring since St. Louis,
The crows at the fishbones on the frozen dunes,

The first cranes going over from south north,
And the river down by a mark of the pole since the
      morning,

And time near to return, and a ship (Spanish)
Lying in for the salmon: and fearing chance or the

Drought or the Sioux should deprive you of these
      discoveries—
Therefore we send by sea in this writing.

                        Above the
Platte there were long plains and a clay country:
Rim of the sky far off, grass under it,

Dung for the cook fires by the sulphur licks.
After that there were low hills and the sycamores,

And we poled up by the Great Bend in the skiffs:
The honey bees left us after the Osage River:

The wind was west in the evenings, and no dew and the
Morning Star larger and whiter than usual—

The winter rattling in the brittle haws.
The second year there was sage and the quail calling.

All that valley is good land by the river:
Three thousand miles and the clay cliffs and

Rue and beargrass by the water banks
And many birds and the brant going over and tracks of

Bear, elk, wolves, marten: the buffalo
Numberless so that the cloud of their dust covers them:

The antelope fording the fall creeks, and the mountains
      and
Grazing lands and the meadow lands and the ground

Sweet and open and well-drained.
                              We advise you to
Settle troops at the forks and to issue licenses:

Many men will have living on these lands.
There is wealth in the earth for them all and the wood
        standing

And wild birds on the water where they sleep.
There is stone in the hills for the towns of a great
        people . . ."

You have just beheld the Makers Making America:

They screwed her scrawny and gaunt with their seven-year
        panics:
They bought her back on their mortgages old-whore-cheap:
They fattened their bonds at her breasts till the thin blood
        ran from them.
Men have forgotten how full clear and deep
The Yellowstone moved on the gravel and the grass grew
When the land lay waiting for her westward people!

SAND CREEK MASSACRE: On November 29, 1864, Colonel J. M. Chivington and his Colorado Volunteers attacked the Cheyenne encampment at Sand Creek, Colorado. The Cheyenne leader, Black Kettle, had promoted the pacification of his people in the face of a continuing gold and land rush, and as a sign of his allegiance, was flying an American flag over his tipi. In the action that followed, wrote Robert Bent, a local rancher:

There seemed to be indiscriminate slaughter of men, women, and children. There were some thirty or forty squaws collected in a hole for protection; they sent out a little girl about six years old with a white flag on a stick; she had not proceeded but a few steps when she was shot and killed. All the squaws in that hole were afterwards killed, and four or five bucks outside. The squaws offered no resistance. Every one I saw dead was scalped. I saw one squaw cut open with an unborn child, as I thought, lying by her side. Captain Soule afterwards told me that such was the fact. I saw the body of White Antelope with the privates cut off, and I heard a soldier say he was going to make a tobacco pouch out of them. I saw one squaw whose privates had been cut out.

Added Lieutenant James Connor: "I also heard of numerous instances in which men had cut out the private parts of females and stretched them over the saddle-bows and wore them over their hats while riding in the ranks." Some time before the massacre Chivington had summarized his own position thus: "I have come to kill Indians, and believe it is right and honorable to use any means under God's heaven to kill Indians." He added: "Nits make lice."

BROMION–URIZEN: In *Visions of the Daughters of Albion* (1793), Blake presents the slavemaster Bromion as rapist of the innocent Oothoon (America as a young girl); having "rent" her, he withdraws into repressive morality, crying: "Behold this harlot here on Bromion's bed / . . . Thy soft American plains are mine, and mine thy north & south: / Stampt with my signet are the swarthy children of the sun: / They are obedient, they resist not, they obey the scourge: / Their daughters worship terrors and obey the violent. . . ." Such is the tyrant's analysis of his slaves, but Oothoon is pregnant and will bear Orc, the spirit of revolution. Orc opposes Urizen, the corrupt Father (historically, George III) whose repressive-oppressive syndrome includes (or creates) Enitharmon, the Eternal Virgin, the stony and terrible Mother. (See on Orc, pages 161 and 508.)

RALPH WALDO EMERSON
Ode Inscribed to W. H. Channing

Though loath to grieve
The evil time's sole patriot,
I cannot leave
My honied thought
For the priest's cant,
Or statesman's rant.

If I refuse
My study for their politique,

Which at the best is trick,
The angry Muse
Puts confusion in my brain.

But who is he that prates
Of the culture of mankind,
Of better arts and life?
Go, blindworm, go,
Behold the famous States
Harrying Mexico
With rifle and with knife!

Or who, with accent bolder,
Dare praise the freedom-loving mountaineer?
I found by thee, O rushing Contoocook!
And in thy valleys, Agiochook!
The jackals of the Negro-holder.

The God who made New Hampshire
Taunted the lofty land
With little men;
Small bat and wren
House in the oak:
If earth-fire cleave
The upheaved land, and bury the folk,
The southern crocodile would grieve.
Virtue palters; Right is hence;
Freedom praised, but hid;
Funeral eloquence
Rattles the coffin-lid.

What boots thy zeal,
O glowing friend,
That would indignant rend
The northland from the south?
Wherefore? to what good end?
Boston Bay and Bunker Hill
Would serve things still;
Things are of the snake.

The horseman serves the horse,
The neatherd serves the neat,
The merchant serves the purse,
The eater serves his meat;
'Tis the day of the chattel,
Web to weave, and corn to grind;
Things are in the saddle,
And ride mankind.

There are two laws discrete,
Not reconciled,
Law for man, and law for thing;
The last builds town and fleet,
But it runs wild,
And doth the man unking.

'Tis fit the forest fall,
The steep be graded,
The mountain tunnelled,
The sand shaded,
The orchard planted,
The glebe tilled,
The prairie granted,
The steamer built.

Let man serve law for man;
Live for friendship, live for love,
For truth's and harmony's behoof;
The state may follow how it can,
As Olympus follows Jove.

Yet do not I implore
The wrinkled shopman to my sounding woods,
Nor bid the unwilling senator
Ask votes of thrushes in the solitudes.
Every one to his chosen work;
Foolish hands may mix and mar;
Wise and sure the issues are.
Round they roll till dark is light,

Sex to sex, and even to odd;
The over-god
Who marries Right to Might,
Who peoples, unpeoples,
He who exterminates
Races by stronger races,
Black by white faces,
Knows to bring honey
Out of the lion;
Grafts gentlest scion
On pirate and Turk.

The Cossack eats Poland,
Like stolen fruit;
Her last noble is ruined,
Her last poet mute:
Straight, into double band
The victors divide;
Half for freedom strike and stand;
The astonished Muse finds thousands at her side.

> The events that precede EMERSON'S "Ode to Channing" (1847) are
> the Mexican War with its threatened extension of slavery, and the
> Polish insurrections against Russian rule in the 1830s. The process
> of reification that Emerson describes is the crisis in consciousness
> that parallels the political facts. "Contoocook" and "Agiochook"
> are Indian names for the Merrimack River and the White Moun-
> tains of New Hampshire.

WILLIAM CARLOS WILLIAMS
From Paterson, Book Three

Later
                Beautiful thing

                                I saw you:

                                Yes, said
the Lady of the House to my questioning.
Downstairs

                    (by the laundry tubs)
                    and she pointed,
          smiling, to the basement, still smiling, and
          went out and left me with you (alone in the house)
          lying there, ill
                              (I don't at all think that you
          were ill)
                        by the wall on your damp bed, your long
          body stretched out negligently on the dirty sheet   •

          Where is the pain?
                              (You put on a simper designed
          not to reveal)

                        —the small window with two panes,
          my eye level of the ground, the furnace odor   •

                                        Persephone
          gone to hell, that hell could not keep with
          the advancing season of pity.

                        —for I was overcome
          by amazement and could do nothing but admire
          and learn to care for you in your quietness—

          who looked at me, smiling, and we remained
          thus looking, each at the other   •   in silence   •

          You lethargic, waiting upon me, waiting for
          the fire and I
                        attendant upon you, shaken by your beauty

          Shaken by your beauty   •

                                        Shaken.

          —flat on your back, in a low bed (waiting)
          under the mud plashed windows among the scabrous
          dirt of the holy sheets   •

You showed me your legs, scarred (as a child)
by the whip   •

Read. Bring the mind back (attendant upon
the page) to the day's heat. The page also is
the same beauty   : a dry beauty of the page—
beaten by whips

      A tapestry hound
with his thread teeth drawing crimson from
the throat of the unicorn

.   .   .   a yelping of white hounds
—under a ceiling like that of San Lorenzo, the long
painted beams, straight across, that preceded
the domes and arches
          more primitive, square edged

•   a docile queen, not bothered
to stick her tongue out at the moon, indifferent,
through loss, but   •

      queenly,
in bad luck, the luck of the stars, the black stars

        •   the night of a mine

Dear heart
      It's all for you, my dove, my
               changeling

     But you!
     —in your white lace dress
       "the dying swan"
     and high-heeled slippers—tall
     as you already were—
       till your head
     through fruitful exaggeration
     was reaching the sky and the

prickles of its ecstasy
    Beautiful Thing!
And the guys from Paterson
    beat up
the guys from Newark and told
them to stay the hell out
of their territory and then
socked you one
    across the nose
    Beautiful Thing
for good luck and emphasis
    cracking it
till I must believe that all
desired women have had each
    in the end
    a busted nose
and live afterward marked up
    Beautiful Thing
    for memory's sake
to be credible in their deeds

Then back to the party!
    and they maled
and femaled you jealously
    Beautiful Thing
as if to discover whence and
    by what miracle
there should escape, what?
still to be possessed, out of
    what part
    Beautiful Thing
should it look?
    or be extinguished—
Three days in the same dress
    up and down

        I can't be half gentle enough,
half tender enough

toward you, toward you,
inarticulate, not half loving enough

BRIGHTen
            the cor
                        ner
where   you   are!

                        —a flame,
            black plush, a dark flame.

CHARLES REZNIKOFF
Testimony

I

The company had advertised for men to unload a steamer
      across the river. It was six o'clock in the morning,
      snowing and still dark.
There was a crowd looking for work on the dock;
and all the while men hurried to the dock.
The man at the wheel
kept the bow of the launch
against the dock—
the engine running slowly;
and the men kept jumping
from dock to deck,
jostling each other,
and crowding into the cabin.

Eighty or ninety men were in the cabin as the launch pulled
      away.
There were no lights in the cabin, and no room to turn—
      whoever was sitting down could not get up, and
      whoever had his hand up could not get it down,
as the launch ran in the darkness
through the ice,
ice cracking

against the launch,
bumping and scraping
against the launch,
banging up against it,
until it struck
a solid cake of ice,
rolled to one side, and slowly
came back to an even keel.

The men began to feel water running against their feet as if
        from a hose. "Cap," shouted one, "the boat is taking
        water! Put your rubbers on, boys!"
The man at the wheel turned.
"Shut up!" he said.
The men began to shout,
ankle-deep in water.
The man at the wheel turned
with his flashlight:
everybody was turning and pushing against each other;
those near the windows
were trying to break them,
in spite of the wire mesh
in the glass: those who had been near the door
were now in the river,
reaching for the cakes of ice,
their hands slipping off and
reaching for the cakes of ice.

                    II

Amelia was just fourteen and out of the orphan asylum; at
        her first job—in the bindery, and yes sir, yes ma'am, oh,
        so anxious to please.
She stood at the table, her blonde hair hanging about her
        shoulders, "knocking up" for Mary and Sadie, the
        stitchers
("knocking up" is counting books and stacking them in piles
        to be taken away).
There were twenty wire-stitching machines on the floor,
        worked by a shaft that ran under the table;

as each stitcher put her work through the machine,
she threw it on the table. The books were piling up fast
and some slid to the floor
(the forelady had said, Keep the work off the floor!) ;
and Amelia stooped to pick up the books—
three or four had fallen under the table
between the boards nailed against the legs.
She felt her hair caught gently;
put her hand up and felt the shaft going round and round
and her hair caught on it, wound and winding around it,
until the scalp was jerked from her head,
and the blood was coming down all over her face and waist.

> Associated with the "Objectivists" (see page 430), REZNIKOFF was a
> lawyer by profession. He uses court records from the late nine-
> teenth century as the materials of his composition, "to locate" (in
> Robert Creeley's words) "the given instance sans direction, in the
> intense particularity of *time* and *place*." Part of a long work, "Tes-
> timony," the first installment of which ("The United States 1885–
> 1890") *New Directions* published in 1965.

NATHANIEL TARN

From The Beautiful Contradictions

SECTION FIVE

Looking into the eyes of babies in experiments
born without the normal pressure on their skulls
thinking they are going to put an end to philosophy
when some development of this begins to breed monsters
and that the chase through probability of the genius
the great kick he gives through his mother as he comes out
the clarity of the air surrounding him later in life
however much his body might take revenge on him
his mind crack between the diameter of his skull and the
    crown

        reality comprises

that the immeasurable heave of the whole race
to bring this animal to the tree's crest and enthrone him there
may be gone forever in a moment of medical history
like the passing of some art   or an old migration
of all the birds together in the arms of the same wind
the way the planet used to turn in one direction with one
     purpose

            frightens a lot

I remember on the shores of the most beautiful lake in the
     world
whose name in its own language means abundance of waters
as if the volcanos surrounding it had broken open the earth
there in the village of Saint James of Compostela one cold
     night
not the cereus-scented summer nights in which a voice I
     never traced
sang those heartbreaking serenades to no one known
a visiting couple gave birth in the market place
the father gnawing the cord like a rat to free the child
and before leaving in the morning they were given the
     freedom of the place

        I mean the child was given

ALLEN GINSBERG

Mescaline

Rotting Ginsberg, I stared in the mirror naked today
I noticed the old skull, I'm getting balder
my pate gleams in the kitchen light under thin hair
like the skull of some monk in old catacombs lighted by
a guard with flashlight
followed by a mob of tourists
so there is death

my kitten mews, and looks into the closet
Boito sings on the phonograph tonight his ancient song of
     angels
Antinous bust in brown photograph still gazing down from
     my wall
a light burst from God's delicate hand sends down a wooden
     dove to the calm virgin
Beato Angelico's universe
the cat's gone and scraowls around the floor

What happens when the death gong hits rotting ginsberg on
     the head
what universe do I enter
death death death death death the cat's at rest
are we ever free of—rotting ginsberg
Then let it decay, thank God I know
thank who
thank who
Thank you, O lord, beyond my eye
the path must lead somewhere
the path
the path
thru the rotting ship dump, thru the Angelico orgies

Beep, emit a burst of babe and begone
perhaps that's the answer, wouldn't know till you had a kid
I dunno, never had a kid never will at the rate I'm going

Yes, I should be good, I should get married
find out what it's all about
but I can't stand these women all over me
smell of Naomi
erk, I'm stuck with this familiar rotting ginsberg
can't stand boys even anymore
can't stand
can't stand
and who wants to get fucked up the ass, really?
Immense seas passing over

the flow of time
and who wants to be famous and sign autographs like a
  movie star

I want to know
I want I want ridiculous *to know to know* WHAT rotting
  ginsberg
I want to know what happens after I rot
because I'm already rotting
my hair's falling out I've got a belly I'm sick of sex
my ass drags in the universe I know too much
and not enough
I want to know what happens after I die
well I'll find out soon enough
do I really need to know now?
is that any use at all use use use
death death death death death
god god god god god god god the Lone Ranger
the rhythm of the typewriter

What can I do to Heaven by pounding on Typewriter
I'm stuck change the record Gregory ah excellent he's doing
  just that
and I am too conscious of a million ears
at present creepy ears, making commerce
too many pictures in the newspapers
faded yellowed press clippings
I'm going away from the poem to a drak contemplative

trash of the mind
trash of the world
man is half trash
all trash in the grave

What can Williams be thinking in Paterson, death so much on
  him
so soon so soon
Williams, what is death?

Do you face the great question now each moment
or do you forget at breakfast looking at your old ugly love in
　　　the face
are you prepared to be reborn
to give release to this world to enter a heaven
or give release, give release
and all be done—and see a lifetime—all eternity—gone over
into naught, a trick question proposed by the moon to the
　　　answerless earth
No Glory for man! No Glory for man! No glory for me! No me!

No point writing when the spirit doth not lead

WALT WHITMAN

Respondez!

Respondez! Respondez!
(The war is completed—the price is paid—the title is settled
　　　beyond recall;)
Let every one answer! let those who sleep be waked! let none
　　　evade!
Must we still go on with our affectations and sneaking?
Let me bring this to a close—I pronounce openly for a new
　　　distribution of roles;
Let that which stood in front go behind! and let that which
　　　was behind advance to the front and speak;
Let murderers, bigots, fools, unclean persons, offer new
　　　propositions!
Let the old propositions be postponed!
Let faces and theories be turn'd inside out! let meanings be
　　　freely criminal, as well as results!
Let there be no suggestion above the suggestion of drudgery!
Let none be pointed toward his destination! (Say! do you know
　　　your destination?)
Let men and women be mock'd with bodies and mock'd with
　　　Souls!

Let the love that waits in them, wait! let it die, or pass
      still-born to other spheres!
Let the sympathy that waits in every man, wait! or let it also
      pass, a dwarf, to other spheres!
Let contradictions prevail! let one thing contradict another!
      and let one line of my poems contradict another!
Let the people sprawl with yearning, aimless hands! let their
      tongues be broken! let their eyes be discouraged! let
      none descend into their hearts with the fresh
      lusciousness of love!
(Stifled, O days! O lands! in every public and private
      corruption!
Smother'd in thievery, impotence, shamelessness,
      mountain-high;
Brazen effrontery, scheming, rolling like ocean's waves
      around and upon you, O my days! my lands!
For not even those thunderstorms, nor fiercest lightnings of
      the war, have purified the atmosphere;)
—Let the theory of America still be management, caste,
      comparison! (Say! what other theory would you?)
Let them that distrust birth and death still lead the rest! (Say!
      why shall they not lead you?)
Let the crust of hell be neared and trod on! let the days be
      darker than the nights! let slumber bring less slumber
      than waking time brings!
Let the world never appear to him or her for whom it was all
      made!
Let the heart of the young man still exile itself from the heart
      of the old man! and let the heart of the old man be
      exiled from that of the young man!
Let the sun and moon go! let scenery take the applause of the
      audience! let there be apathy under the stars!
Let freedom prove no man's inalienable right! every one who
      can tyrannize, let him tyrannize to his satisfaction!
Let none but infidels be countenanced!
Let the eminence of meanness, treachery, sarcasm, hate,
      greed, indecency, impotence, lust, be taken for granted
      above all! let writers, judges, governments, households,
      religions, philosophies, take such for granted above all!

Let the worst men beget children out of the worst women!

Let the priest still play at immortality!

Let death be inaugurated!

Let nothing remain but the ashes of teachers, artists,
     moralists, lawyers, and learn'd and polite persons!

Let him who is without my poems be assassinated!

Let the cow, the horse, the camel, the garden-bee—let the
     mud-fish, the lobster, the mussel, eel, the sting-ray, and
     the grunting pig-fish—let these, and the like of these, be
     put on a perfect equality with man and woman!

Let churches accommodate serpents, vermin, and the corpses
     of those who have died of the most filthy of diseases!

Let marriage slip down among fools, and be for none but
     fools!

Let men among themselves talk and think forever obscenely
     of women! and let women among themselves talk and
     think obscenely of men!

Let us all, without missing one, be exposed in public, naked,
     monthly, at the peril of our lives! let our bodies be freely
     handled and examined by whoever chooses!

Let nothing but copies at second hand be permitted to exist
     upon the earth!

Let the earth desert God, nor let there ever henceforth be
     mention'd the name of God!

Let there be no God!

Let there be money, business, imports, exports, custom,
     authority, precedents, pallor, dyspepsia, smut, ignorance,
     unbelief!

Let judges and criminals be transposed! let the prison-keepers
     be put in prison! let those that were prisoners take the
     keys! (Say! why might they not just as well be trans-
     posed?)

Let the slaves be masters! let the masters become slaves!

Let the reformers descend from the stands where they are
     forever bawling! let an idiot or insane person appear on
     each of the stands!

Let the Asiatic, the African, the European, the American, and
     the Australian, go armed against the murderous stealth-
     iness of each other! let them sleep armed! let none
     believe in good will!

Let there be no unfashionable wisdom! let such be scorn'd and
      derided off from the earth!

Let a floating cloud in the sky—let a wave of the sea—let
      growing mint, spinach, onions, tomatoes—let these be
      exhibited as shows, at a great price for admission!

Let all the men of These States stand aside for a few smouch-
      ers! let the few seize on what they choose! let the rest,
      gawk, giggle, starve, obey!

Let shadows be furnish'd with genitals! let substances be
      deprived of their genitals!

Let there be wealthy and immense cities—but still through
      any of them, not a single poet, savior, knower, lover!

Let the infidels of These States laugh all faith away!

If one man be found who has faith, let the rest set upon him!

Let them affright faith! let them destroy the power of breed-
      ing faith!

Let the she-harlots and the he-harlots be prudent! let them
      dance on, while seeming lasts! (O seeming! seeming!
      seeming!)

Let the preachers recite creeds! let them still teach only what
      they have been taught!

Let insanity still have charge of sanity!

Let books take the place of trees, animals, rivers, clouds!

Let the daub'd portraits of heroes supersede heroes!

Let the manhood of man never take steps after itself!

Let it take steps after eunuchs, and after consumptive and
      genteel persons!

Let the white person again tread the black person under his
      heel! (Say! which is trodden under heel, after all?)

Let the reflections of the things of the world be studied in
      mirrors! let the things themselves still continue
      unstudied!

Let a man seek pleasure everywhere except in himself!

Let a woman seek happiness everywhere except in herself!

(What real happiness have you had one single hour through
      your whole life?)

Let the limited years of life do nothing for the limitless years
      of death! (What do you suppose death will do, then?)

DIANE WAKOSKI

The Ice Eagle

It was with resolution that she gave up the
powerful teardrops in her eyes—
that crystal, the Venus soft, lizard-eyed creature called
*   woman,*
gazes through, her philosopher's stone,
the sweet glass
that drops from the sky.
Ancients
in sacrifice
cut off tears
with knives.

The 50 lb eagle carved out of ice
sitting in the silver punch bowl
turned her attention to physical details.
    Why am I saying
    "her" ?
    It is I,
    undoubtedly I,
    the life a dream work,
my camels bear me across the deserts to the sea,
the figs grow plump as if it were Sinai,
my striped silk shoes live as the eyes of 12 animals;
undoubtedly the life has been confused with the movies,
I, Gloria Swanson, walking discontented
for all parties become that to me. I cannot
walk through the rituals without my golden mask,
alas, 3 dozen of them hang on my wall,
the thick lips reminding me of what has been eaten
and has not nourished.

Physical details: the lawn that sloped down to the sea cliffs,
the swallows building their nests in rafters,
the stone house punctured with courts & patios,
bougainvillea winding up its sides,
raw old Spanish wood composing chests & high stiff chairs

moved & touched into water-like smoothness,
the gravel driveway balancing the cutaway heels
of beautiful women,
the men swimming through the night in dinner jackets like
      paper cups
floating on the ocean;
yes, her eyes—

          again, why do I say
          "her".
          I must insist it is I.

My eyes are informed of silk and the obsidian minds of the
      rich.
Here is a thick glossy black smooth idea—sex and nothing
      else.
The rich are born bored,
and look for purposes, causes, projects
to keep them busy.
The women make up wild malachite eyes, green with
      beautiful
sleep and restless knowledge of new plays,
new dancers,
new books,
new jazz. They
can ring their Egyptian eyes with kohl
and be aesthetes
and in veils walk down the rock path to the sea;
riding black tigers into the ocean,
yards of chiffon trailing their heels and they despair
the men
they, I, we
          all women when it gets past social class,
despair the men who have only the moon in their milky fluid
      fingers.
Yes, they wait.
For the sun god we wait.
To find him naked in a blaze of fire.
We are stuck with vulgar substitutes—

the fashionable avant garde dancer,
the sensational beat poet,
the jazz trumpeter,
the negro novelist,
and Amen-ra, Amen-ra our father, they are all glorious
       sun-brilliant
artists, but
homosexuals,
fucking each other, riding on their own black panthers
wading into the iron waters.
Again the women must rest their bodies against each other
       and moan.
It is not the
mysteries that draw the men,
but the fear of that great mystery,
the veiled woman, Isis,
mother, whom they fear to be greater than all else.

And I am sick unto death. Sick,
I say, sick. We live in a world where men have forgotten their
       offices,
only taking the woman
            (like good debaters,
             assigned to the positive side,
             on whom rests the burden of the proof)
only taking her on the surface—
she, I, we, can peel off layer after layer where you
have taken her and yet find.the bottom deep and tight and
       untouched
and longing for the greater measure.

She, no it was I, walked with the moon in Pisces
and felt the trout slipping down into the ocean.
The carved ice eagle of that party
was melting
into the gin and strawberries.
In its beak
someone had placed an American flag.
I found it hard to believe myself in this slippery unreal

man-made country. Look, look, look,
I want to say; the eagle is a powerful bird.
In your fear, all you can do is carve him out of ice
And that leaves only one alternative
in this temperate climate.
The ice eagle can do nothing
but melt.

JOHN LEE HOOKER

Black Snake

There's a mean black snake been

                                suckin' my rider's tongue
There's a mean black snake been

                                suckin' my rider's tongue
And if I catch him there mmmm

                              he won't come back no more

And he crawl up to my window

                        and he crawl up in my bed
He crawl up to my window

                      and he crawl up in my baby's bed
He's a mean mean black snake

                    that's been suckin' my rider's tongue

        Get me some toad-frogs' hips
        Mix it up together
        Gonna whoop it up good
        And I betcha my bottom dollar
        He won't suck my rider's tongue no more

Mean mean mean black snake

                        been crawlin' round my back door
Mmmmmmmmmmmmmmmm mmmmmmmmmm
    mmmmmmmm mmmmmmmm
Been crawlin' round my back door

He worry me all through the day
>he worry me all night long

He worry me all through the day
>he worry me all day long

I betcha my bottom dollar
>I'm gonna kill
>>kill that old black snake

He won't
>suck my rider's tongue

He won't suck my baby's tongue no more
That mean mean black snake
He won't bother
>me no more

Mmmmmmmmmmmmmmmmmmmm

>—Transcribed from oral blues by ERIC SACKHEIM

SHERWOOD ANDERSON

American Spring Song   [1918]

In the spring, when winds blew and farmers were plowing
>fields,

It came into my mind to be glad because of my brutality.

Along a street I went and over a bridge.

I went through many streets in my city and over many
>bridges.

Men and women I struck with my fists and my hands began
>to bleed.

Under a bridge I crawled and stood trembling with joy
At the river's edge.

Because it was spring and soft sunlight came through the
>cracks of the bridge
I tried to understand myself.

Out of the mud at the river's edge I moulded myself a god,
A grotesque little god with a twisted face,
A god for myself and my men.

You see now, brother, how it was.

I was a man with clothes made by a Jewish tailor,
Cunningly wrought clothes, made for a nameless one.

I wore a white collar and some one had given me a jeweled
    pin
To wear at my throat.
That amused and hurt me too.

No one knew that I knelt in the mud beneath the bridge
In the city of Chicago.

You see I am whispering my secret to you.

I want you to believe in my insanity and to understand that I
    love God—

That's what I want.

And then, you see, it was spring
And soft sunlight came through the cracks of the bridge.

I had been long alone in a strange place where no gods came.

Creep, men, and kiss the twisted face of my mud god.

I'll not hit you with my bleeding fists.

I'm a twisted god myself.

It is spring and love has come to me—
Love has come to me and to my men.

[ANONYMOUS]

The Boasting Drunk in Dodge [1883]

Raised on six-shooters till I get big enough to eat ground
     shotguns,
When I'm cool I warm the Gulf of Mexico and bathe therein,
When I'm hot there's an equinoxical breeze that fans me
     fevered brow,
The moans of widows and orphans is music to me melancholy
     soul.

Me the boy that chewed the wad the goat eat that butted the
     goat off the bridge,
Born in the Rocky Mountains, suckled by a grizzly bear,
Ninety-nine rows of jaw teeth and not a single hair.

Thirty-two inches 'tween the eyes and they feed me with a
     shovel,
Mount the wild ass and leap from crag to crag,
And roar like laughter in a tomb,
Jump from precipice to precipice and back to pice again.

Snatched him bald-headed and spit on the place where the
     hair come off;
Take a leg off him and beat him over the head with the
     bloody end of it,
Slap his head up to a peak and then knock the peak off,
Take his eye out and eat it for a grape.

Gimme one hundred yards start and I'll run plumb to
     Honolulu without even wettin' my feet,
Shoulder five hundred bushel of shot and wade through solid
     rocks up to my shoulder blades.
Any damn man don't believe it . . .

I'll lick him on a sheep hide and never tromp on the tail,
Knock a belch out of him that'll whiz like a nail,
Knock a belch out of him longer'n a rail,
Sharp enough to stick a pig with.

EUGENE JOLAS

Wyof [1926]

the drunken antennae of my thoughts are haunting
the rumbling boulevards of the universe
subways grind themselves to visionary stations
there is a stop in Calcutta when midnight comes
once Heine sang of the Ganges and longed for palm trees
the zodiac swims golden through my brain
sing radio sing your neurotic song
let me explode into metaphysical dreams

my rhythms grow epileptic
dusk near a cathedral and silence
I will grow impudent and create shrill words
I will broadcast the tragedy of my memories
hold your receiver tight
I will give you dissonances
my bed-time story is pornographic
autumn wines swirl in my veins
have I forgotten I am a male
that I have thighs hungering and mad
that love is alpha and omega
moon was golden on singing dunes
cities went lumbering to my vision
bringing their gifts of electric chants
and women holding lacerated hearts
even song hymns o omnibus
I heard a dies irae in a Benedictine monastery
now I shall talk to St. Francis of Assisi
Umbria smiles into a dusk of spring
o jongleur de Dieu o troubadour of tranquillities
the forests burn at midnight
I shall wait for my sisters the stars
and my brother the ass
and my mother the loam
a church organ roars through my head

though you have sneered at me America
though you have ground me underfoot
my heart sings the tremendous magic of your beauty
and I lie obsequious in the dust
I will go through the old world's primeval forests of stone
and sing the whiteness of your impudent towers
and sing the dreams I have of you
always I come back to you
to you I come with my wailing fears
to you I come when I am very tired
and life is full of gibberish and hate
I have said I will forget you
I will go to all the corners of the world
and seek new music to whip my soul
but always I had need of you
puritan woman
quaker woman
electric woman drunken with motors
farm woman standing in a wheatfield
exuberant woman etched against huge landscapes
California Florida Kansas Pennsylvania New York
gold dusks and silver dawns over the mountains
even your factory towns call me
when rain falls on old-world gardens
and I cry for mill-dust and loam
hours with newspapers when the first edition comes off the
         press
lighted bars drooling through my brain
I am drunk with roses on women's cheeks
listeners-in I seek a healing spring
when the nights are soft with dreams
violins laugh and young girls chant
and the crucifix has ceased to bleed on the wall
there is a blizzard off Kamchatka.

LOUIS SIMPSON
The Inner Part

When they had won the war
And for the first time in history
Americans were the most important people—

When the leading citizens no longer lived in their shirt
    sleeves,
And their wives did not scratch in public;
Just when they'd stopped saying "Gosh!"—

When their daughters seemed as sensitive
As the tip of a fly rod,
And their sons were as smooth as a V–8 engine—

Priests, examining the entrails of birds,
Found the heart misplaced, and seeds
As black as death, emitting a strange odor.

[NEZ PERCÉ]
Three Songs of Mad Coyote

1

Ravening Coyote comes,
red hands, red mouth,
necklace of eye-balls!

2

Mad Coyote
madly sings,
then the west wind roars!

3

Daybreak finds me,
eastern daybreak finds me
the meaning of that song:
*with blood-stained mouth
comes mad Coyote!*

—Translated by HERBERT J. SPINDEN

Spinden identifies the first of these as a "dream song of Silu-we-haikt (Eyes-around-the-Neck)," first revealed in the Guardian Spirit Dance, where each dreamer costumed himself according to the nature of his vision.

A variable myth, Coyote is both a creator god and a Pan-like sexual being. *Trickster* is the more general term for the phenomenon, as the Winnebago god in Paul Radin's well-known account, who

> saw women swimming
>   there near the opposite shore
>   (said Trickster) Now's time
>   for fucking
> & taking his cock from its box
> he told it
>   Get that chief's daughter
>   right up her
> & launched it four times
> it swam thru the water
> her friends all ran for the shore
> but she
>   was last & it
>   lodged in her

and so on. (J. R., after Radin's *The Trickster*) In his terrifying form, as in the Nez Percé, he is the dangerous god of a dangerous universe. Widespread in native America, Coyote appears more recently in works by Simon Ortiz, Gary Snyder, Keith Wilson, among others. (See pages 161, 235, and 283 of the present gathering.)

DENISE LEVERTOV
The Goddess

She in whose lipservice
I passed my time,
whose name I knew, but not her face,
came upon me where I lay in Lie Castle!

Flung me across the room, and
room after room (hitting the walls, re-
bounding—to the last
sticky wall—wrenching away from it
pulled hair out!)
till I lay
outside the outer walls!

There in cold air
lying still where her hand had thrown me,
I tasted the mud that splattered my lips:
the seeds of a forest were in it,
asleep and growing! I tasted
her power!

The silence was answering my silence,
a forest was pushing itself
out of sleep between my submerged fingers.

I bit on a seed and it spoke on my tongue
of day that shone already among stars
in the water-mirror of low ground,
and a wind rising ruffled the lights:
she passed near me returning from the encounter,
she who plucked me from the close rooms,

without whom nothing
flowers, fruits, sleeps in season,
without whom nothing
speaks in its own tongue, but returns
lie for lie!

ROBERT BLY

From The Teeth-Mother Naked at Last

IV

I see a car rolling toward a rock wall.
The treads in the face begin to crack.
We all feel like tires being run down roads under heavy cars.

The teenager imagines herself floating through the Seven
    Spheres.
Oven doors are found
open.
Soot collects over the doorframe, has children, takes courses,
goes mad, and dies.

There is a black silo inside our bodies, revolving fast.
Bits of black paint are flaking off,
where the motorcycles roar, around and around,
rising higher on the silo walls,
the bodies bent toward the horizon,
driven by angry women dressed in black.

                        •   •   •

I know that books are tired of us.
I *know* they are chaining the Bible to chairs.
Books don't want to remain in the same room with us
    anymore.

New Testaments are escaping! . . . Dressed as women . . . they
    go off after dark.
And Plato! Plato. . . . Plato wants to go backwards. . . .
He wants to hurry back up the river of time, so he can end as
    some blob of seaflesh rotting on an Australian beach.

V

Why are they dying? I have written this so many times.
They are dying because the President has opened a Bible
      again.

They are dying because gold deposits have been found among
      the Shoshoni Indians.

Because money follows intellect!
and intellect is like a fan opening in the wind—

The Marines think that unless they die the rivers will not
      move.
They are dying so that mountain shadows can fall north in
      the afternoon,
so that the beetle can move along the ground near the fallen
      twigs.

VI

But if one of those children came near that we have set on
      fire with napalm,
came toward you like a gray barn, walking,
you would howl like a wind tunnel in a hurricane,
you would tear at your shirt with blue hands,
you would drive over your own child's wagon trying to back
      up,
the pupils of your eyes would go wild—

If a child came by burning, you would dance on a lawn,
trying to walk into the air, digging into your cheeks,
you would ram your head against the wall of your bedroom
like a bull penned too long in his moody pen—

If one of those children came toward me with both hands
in the air, fire rising along both elbows,
I would suddenly go back to my animal brain,

I would drop on all fours, screaming,
my vocal chords would turn blue, yours would too,
it would be two days before I could play with my own
      children again.

THE RAPE AND COUNTER-RAPE OF AMERICA: "In Vineland the Norsemen turned the natives hostile by senseless killings," writes Carl O. Sauer in *Northern Mists* (1968). William Carlos Williams' *In the American Grain* (1925) extends the map of such violence from the destruction of Tenochtitlan to the New England witch hunts. The routing of heathens and heretics is a persistent theme in the "discovery" (i.e., rape) of America.* Is there perhaps a common denominator to Christian White relations to Red Skins, Blacks, Chicanos, the "Yellow Peril" (now Southeast Asia), and the destruction of land and animal kingdoms ("animals do not have souls")? And the inevitable reaction (i.e., counter-rape) appears as: "A cult of death need of the simple striking arm under the street lamp. The cutters from under their rented earth. Come up, black dada nihilismus. Rape the white girls. Rape their fathers. Cut the mothers' throats" (Eldridge Cleaver in *Soul on Ice,* quoting LeRoi Jones, *The Dead Lecturer,* 1964). Cleaver recounts his early life as "rapist" and, with a striking closeness to Blake's analysis of slave-consciousness in *Visions of the Daughters of Albion* (1793), he writes: "Rape was an insurrectionary act. It delighted me that I was defying and trampling upon the white man's law, upon his system of values, and that I was defiling his women . . . [which is] how the white man has used the black woman." The Black (Red, White, or any) Rapist is Orc, who in Blake's *America a Prophecy* (1793) breaks from his "mind-forg'd manacles" to rend open the stony, virgin Mother (the body of America) held from him by repressive morality and economic oppression. Orc calls for Renewal, but his path crosses the pattern of historical violence.

    (See also the commentary, "Orc," page 508, below.)

---

*Sauer proposes a notable exception to this pattern of "discovery," suggesting that Irish monks (far-traveling enlightened men) established a colony at Belle Isle, antedating the Norse Vineland expeditions, and leaving traces of Christian rites in Algonquin religious ceremonies. A peaceful cross-fertilization of cultures. "At the great Indian winter ceremonial of the year, strangely resembling Passion Week, a chosen dog was hanged on a cross-like structure, taken down after a time, and carried by mourning procession to burial." *(Northern Mists)* Christ as Coyote?

IMAMU AMIRI BARAKA   [LEROI JONES]
Black Dada Nihilismus

. Against what light

is false what breath
sucked, for deadness.

Murder, the cleansed

purpose, frail, against
God, if they bring him

bleeding, I would not

forgive, or even call him
black dada nihilismus.

The protestant love, wide windows,
color blocked to Mondrian, and the
ugly silent deaths of jews under

the surgeon's knife. (To awake on
69th street with money and a hip
nose. Black dada nihilismus, for

the umbrella'd jesus. Trilby intrigue
movie house presidents sticky the floor.
B.D.N., for the secret men, Hermes, the

blacker art. Thievery (ahh, they return
those secret gold killers. Inquisitors
of the cocktail hour. Trismegistus, have

them, in their transmutation, from stone
to bleeding pearl, from lead to burning
looting, dead Moctezuma, find the West

a grey hideous space.

2

From Sartre, a white man, it gave
the last breath. And we beg him die,
before he is killed. Plastique, we

do not have, only thin heroic blades.
The razor. Our flail against them, why
you carry knives? Or brutaled lumps of

heart? Why you stay, where they can
reach? Why you sit, or stand, or walk
in this place, a window on a dark

warehouse. Where the minds packed in
straw. New homes, these towers, for those
lacking money or art. A cult of death,

need of the simple striking arm under
the streetlamp. The cutters, from under
their rented earth. Come up, black dada

nihilismus. Rape the white girls. Rape
their fathers. Cut the mothers' throats.
Black dada nihilismus, choke my friends

in their bedrooms with their drinks spilling
and restless for tilting hips or dark liver
lips sucking splinters from the master's thigh.

Black scream
and chant, scream,
and dull, un
earthly

hollering. Dada, bilious
what ugliness, learned

in the dome, colored holy
shit (i call them sinned

or lost
    burned masters
                of the lost
                              nihil German killers
                                        all our learned

art, 'member
what you said
money, God, power,
a moral code, so cruel
it destroyed Byzantium, Tenochtitlan, Commanch
                            (got it, *Baby!*

For tambo, willie best, dubois, patrice, mantan, the
bronze buckaroos.

    For Jack Johnson, asbestos, tonto, buckwheat,
    billie holiday.

        For tom russ, l'overture, vesey, beau jack,

(may a lost god damballah, rest or save us
against the murders we intend
against his lost white children
black dada nihilismus

"*We appear to have lost the radiant world where one thought cuts
through another with clean edge, a world of moving energies* mezzo
oscuro rade, risplende in se perpetuale effecto, *magnetisms that take
form, that are seen, or that border the visible, the matter of Dante's*
paradiso, *the glass under water, the form that seems a form seen in a
mirror, these realities perceptible to the sense, interacting. . . .*"

    —EZRA POUND, "Cavalcanti: Medievalism" [1934], in *Literary
    Essays*

EZRA POUND
Canto 116

Came Neptunus
        his mind leaping
                like dolphins,
These concepts the human mind has attained.
To make Cosmos—
To achieve the possible—
Muss., wrecked for an error,
But the record
        the palimpsest—
a little light
        in great darkness—
cuniculi—
An old "crank" dead in Virginia.
Unprepared young burdened with records,
The vision of the Madonna
          above the cigar butts
            and over the portal.
"Have made a mass of laws"
                (mucchio di leggi)
Litterae nihil sanantes
            Justinian's,
a tangle of works unfinished.

I have brought the great ball of crystal;
          who can lift it?
Can you enter the great acorn of light?
          But the beauty is not the madness
Tho' my errors and wrecks lie about me.
And I am not a demigod,
I cannot make it cohere.
If love be not in the house there is nothing.
The voice of famine unheard.
How came beauty against this blackness,
Twice beauty under the elms—
          To be saved by squirrels and bluejays?
            "plus j'aime le chien"

Ariadne.
      Disney against the metaphysicals,
and Laforgue more than they thought in him,
Spire thanked me in proposito
And I have learned more from Jules
            (Jules Laforgue) since then
deeps in him,
      and Linnaeus.
            chi crescerà i nostri—
but about that terzo
      third heaven,
        that Venere,
again is all "paradiso"
    a nice quiet paradise
        over the shambles,
and some climbing
        before the take-off,
to "see again,"
the verb is "see," not "walk on"
i.e. it coheres all right
        even if my notes do not cohere.
Many errors,
    a little rightness,
to excuse his hell
      and my paradiso.
And as to why they go wrong,
      thinking of rightness
And as to who will copy this palimpsest?
    al poco giorno
        ed al gran cerchio d'ombra
But to affirm the gold thread in the pattern
        (Torcello)
al Vicolo d'oro
    (Tigullio).
To confess wrong without losing rightness:
Charity I have had sometimes,
    I cannot make it flow thru.
A little light, like a rushlight
    to lead back to splendour.

For the Aztecs of Mexico, Huitzilopochtli was not only the war-god, but god of the Fifth Sun—of the era, that is, into which this world was moving, itself represented by the (hieroglyphic) sign *movement;* more specifically, according to Laurette Séjourné (*Burning Water,* 1956), by a movement toward liberation from contradiction and duality. "Huitzilopochtli, image of the sun, disguised as a [humming] bird and with fire as his sign, represented the soul of a combatant in the holy war." (Compare the myths of Orc and Enyalion, page 508, below.)

The version that follows is by Jerome Rothenberg after a Spanish prose translation in Angel María Garibay, *Épica Nahuatl* (1945), going back to Nahuatl sources delivered soon after the Conquest.

[AZTEC]
From The Birth of the War God

1

          old Coatlicue snake woman
     's sweeping up
a feather falleth on her
         more like a ball of feathers 'twas
     'twas fluff
that moment she did pick it up
         deposited it betwixt her legs
     then ended
sweeping would want to take it out
         from legs but nothing's
     there that instant
she's grown pregnant
         the 400 Brothers saw
     their mother
pregnant
         a great anger
     fills them
"who hath made thee pregnant
         "made thee into mother

“shame
“it lays on us
   “it shames us
  (says their sister Coyolxauhqui)
“brothers
   “who has laid it
 “on us has made
“what grows betwixt her legs
   Old Mother knows it now’s
  so scared a great weight
lies on her the child
   between her legs brings
  comfort (sez)
“I know now what I have to do”
   Snake Woman hears her boy’s
  word
was a great comfort
   calmed her heart
  was blowing full of
little blisses

  2

   thus joined
  400 Brothers would agree
in turn
   those southerners did then
  determine
how they would take their mother’s
   life
  for shaming them
so fierce 400 Brothers were
   were full of
  wrath as if their hearts were
leaving them for anger
   sweet sister Coyolxauhqui
  ’s working up & cooling
anger of her brothers
   will go & kill
  old mother

they prepare for
                    war
            are dressed for it
400 Brothers
                    strut like generals
            spinning & tangling
of hair
                    entanglement of headhairs
            was among them one
brother Cuahuitlicac
                    but couldn't keep his
            word
what 400 Brothers said
                    he told to Huitzilopochtli
            (answers)
"careful
                    "little uncle
            "thou should be always standing guard
"I got
                    "some planning of my own

            3
                    so had made up their minds to
            kill her
be finished with old mother
                    had started marching
            'twas little sister guided them
so fancy
                    so like a bunch of dudes
            dressed up for war
had passed out
                    paper costumes
            for adornment
(sez)
                    "thrust forward
            "strut in files
"be like a perfect squadron
                    "little sister
            "guide thy way

4

        but Cuahuitlicac has made it
     to peak of mountain
there he would speak with
        Huitzilopochtli (sez)
     "they're coming"
(Huitzlipochtli sez) "fix
        "your sights on them
     "which way they
"coming" (sez)
        "now 'mongst the linnets"
     (sez) "now which way"
(sez) "Snake Sands"
        (sez) "now which"
     (sez) "Hanging Terraces"
(sez) "now"
        (sez) "Mountain Slope"
     (then sez) "& now"
(sez) "at the peak now
        "now 400 Brothers
     "come sweet sister
"guiding

5

        was born that moment
     Huitzilopochtli
lined up his gear
        his shield of eagle feathers
     arrowheads blue
spearheads ("turquoise-
        darts" so-called) & paints
     his face with
colors like the "painted child"
        puts on his head a bonnet
     of rare feathers
fits in earplugs (but also had
        one skinny foot wore
     feathered sandle on the left painted

his thighs & arms
in blue) then one
called Tochancalqui set fire to
the turquoise spears
went to give Huitzilopochtli
orders with his dart
the newborn wounds their sister
Coyolxauhqui cuts
her throat the head
's abandoned on Snake Mountain while
body goes rolling down the slope
smashes to smithereens
here & there
go hands
go feet
goes torso

A BOOK OF HISTORIES

When Ezra Pound defined an epic as a poem
including history, he indirectly called our attention
to the fact that American poetry has been struggling
all along to let the concerns of and with history
flow through it. In a deeper sense a poem *is*
a historical act, just as individual life and
consciousness are history in process.

A Book of Histories attempts to show, in roughly
chronological order, some of the modalities
through which it is possible to see the deeper
interconnectivity between events in fact and events
in consciousness. But history begins too with
the telling of a story, and **A Book of Histories**
reminds us that history, story, and myth are all rooted
in a common effort to know human meaning *in time*.

■ "... *The Western outlook emphasizes the importance of* history *and pays an ever increasing attention to it. It is interested in history, whereas the Eastern outlook, by and large, is not. There are those who maintain that the two attitudes go together, and that if (as these few also maintain) we are now going to switch over, or switch back, from an Occidental to an Oriental view of the nature of consciousness, we should abandon our concern with history and concentrate exclusively on the relation between the present moment and eternity—or between ordinary consciousness and a-consciousness.*

"I am of a different opinion. I believe it lies in the destiny of the West, not to abandon but to intensify its concern with history; not to abandon its interest in the past of mankind, and of the world, but to deepen its understanding of both. . . . After all, it is because we are interested, not only in today but also in yesterday and the day before yesterday that we are also interested not only in the psychology of dream but in the psychology of myth, which belongs to the day before yesterday. . . . "

—OWEN BARFIELD, "Dream, Myth, and Philosophical Double Vision," in *Myths, Dreams, and Religion,* ed. J. Campbell [1970]

[MANDAN]

A Tree of History

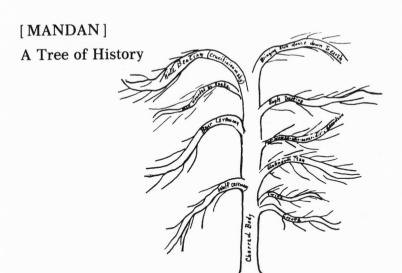

For these stories are like the branches of a tree. All go back to the main trunk. The old Indians who know the stories, if we relate a branch, can tell where it belongs in the tree and what comes before and what after.

—HIDATSA, *per* BEARS ARM

The parts of this weed all branch from the stem. They go different ways, but all come from the same root. So it is with the versions of a myth.

—BLACKFOOT

One ritual is an arm or branch of the lodge, and the myth accounting for its origin forks off from the main branch.

—MENOMINI

From MARTHA WARREN BECKWITH, *Myths and Ceremonies of the Mandan and Hidatsa* [1932]

175

A VISUAL-VERBAL EPIC: Winter-counts *(waniyetu wowapi* in Dakota) were a widespread visual-verbal form among nineteenth-century Plains Indians. Garrick Mallery, in his basic account of Indian picture-writing (1888), defines them as "the use of events, which were in some degree historical, to form a system of chronology," i.e. to individualize each year (or winter) by a name describing an event within that year, and to record said name by a visual symbol or ideograph. While the events so selected may not always strike *us* as the most critical—e.g., the defeat of Custer in 1876 isn't mentioned in most counts for that year—a story nevertheless emerges; and in the wedding of history and naming, a form in some sense suggestive of Pound's definition of epic as "a poem including history."

The ideographs were mostly drawn on buffalo hides and were organized into patterns ranging from columns to spirals. In Battiste Good's count (below) the ideographs appear in an ordinary paper drawing book and are painted with five colors besides black. His narrative includes a cyclical and mythic section covering the years 901 to 1700, after which the counting by year-names begins. The work is prefaced by the account of a personal vision and by a vision-drawing (for which see the Battiste Good entry in Jerome Rothenberg's *Shaking the Pumpkin,* 1972).

[DAKOTA]

From Battiste Good's Winter Count

1794–'95 Killed-the-little-faced-Pawnee winter

1795–'96 The-Rees-stood-the-frozen-man-up-with-the-buffalo-stomach-in-his-hand winter

1796-'97   Wears-the-War-Bonnet-died
            winter

1797-'98   Took-the-God-Woman-captive
            winter

1798-'99   Many-women-died-in-childbirth
            winter

1799–1800   Don't-Eat-Buffalo-Heart-made-a-
            commemoration-of-the-dead
            winter

1800–'01   The-Good-White-Man-came
            winter

1801–'02 Smallpox-used-them-up-again winter

1802–'03 Brought-home-Pawnee-horses-with-iron-shoes-on winter

1803–'04 Brought-home-Pawnee-horses-with-them winter

1804–'05 Sung-over-each-other-while-on-the-warpath winter

[ANONYMOUS REVOLUTIONARY PAMPHLET]

From The First Book of the American Chronicles of the Times

1. And behold! when the tidings came to the great city that is afar off, the city that is in the land of Britain, how the men of Boston, even the Bostonites, had arose, a great multitude, and destroyed the Tea, the abominable merchandise of the east, and cast it into the midst of the sea:

2. That the Lord the King waxed exceeding wroth, insomuch that the form of his visage was changed, and his knees smote one against the other.

3. Then he assembled together the Princes, the Nobles, the Counselors, the Judges, and all the Rulers of the people, even the great Sanhedrim, and when he had told them what things were come to pass,

4. They smote their breasts and said, these men fear thee not, O King, neither have they obeyed the voice of our Lord the King, nor worshipped the Tea-Chest, which thou hast set up, whose length was three cubits, and the breadth thereof one cubit and a half.

5. Now, therefore, make a decree that their harbours be blocked up, and ports shut, that their merchants may be broke, and their multitudes perish, that there may be no more the voice of merchandise heard in the land, that their ships that goeth upon the waters, may be sunk in the depths thereof, and their mariners dwindle away to nought, that their cods and their oil may stink, and the whale, the great Leviathan, may be no more troubled, for that they have rebelled against thee.

6. And it came to pass that the King hearkened unto the voice of these sons of Belial.

7. Then arose Mordecai, the Benjamite, who was fourscore and five years old, an aged man whom the Lord loved, a wise man, a soothsayer, an astrologer, in whom was wisdom from above, and he said unto the King, I pray thee, O King, let thy servant speak.

8. And the King commanded that he should speak.

9. Then Mordecai spake aloud, in the presence of all the Princes, the Nobles, the Counselors, the Judges, and the Rulers of the people, and said, O King, live for ever.

10. Thy throne, O King, is encompassed about with lies, and thy servants, the Bernardites, and the Hutchinsonians, are full of deceit; for be it known unto thee, O King, they hide the truth from thee, and wrongfully accuse the men of Boston; for behold, these letters in mine hand witnesseth sore against them; O King, if thou art wise, thou wilt understand these things.

11. And there was present one of the King's Counselors, a Jacobite, a vagabond, a Wedderburnite, and he used foul language, and said unto Mordecai, Thou liest; and Mordecai answered and said unto him, God will smite thee, thou whited wall; and Mordecai departed from amongst them.

12. And behold the Princes, the Nobles, the Counselors, the Judges, and all the Rulers of the people, cried out vehemently against Mordecai, for they were in fear because of Mordecai's wisdom.

13. And they besought the King that he would take from Mordecai his post, for he was in high honour before that time.

14. So they prevailed on the King and he took from Mordecai his post and all that he had, and Mordecai was persecuted yet more and more; but he bore it patiently, for Job was his grandfather's great-grandfather; moreover, he knew the times must alter, and the King's eyes would be opened anon.

More of the original appears in Moses Coit Tyler's *The Literary History of the American Revolution*, Volume I, from which this excerpt is taken. He writes: "This little book, itself but the beginning of an unfinished work, consists of some six chapters which seem to have been first printed serially in the latter part of 1774 and in the early part of 1775."

THE BOOK OF MORMON is a scriptural work of American origin, said by believers (The Church of Jesus Christ of Latter-Day Saints) to contain the texts of inscribed plates that comprised the annals of a remnant of the ten lost tribes of Israel who had come to this continent starting circa 600 B.C. The records were buried in or about A.D. 421 by Moroni, "the last of the Nephite historians," who reappeared to Joseph Smith on September 21, 1823, and four years later delivered said plates from their place of burial near Manchester, New York. Smith's translation of the plates went on from that time to the second of May, 1838, when he returned them to Moroni. According to the 3rd Book of Nephi, Jesus visited the errant tribes shortly after the crucifixion, the event preceded by the destruction of their cities described below.

JOSEPH SMITH

From The Book of Mormon:
Christ's Crucifixion Witnessed in America

And it came to pass in the thirty and fourth year, in the first month, on the fourth day of the month, there arose a great storm, such an one as never had been known in all the land.

And there was also a great and terrible tempest; and there was terrible thunder, insomuch that it did shake the whole earth as if it was about to divide asunder.

And there were exceeding sharp lightnings, such as never had been known in all the land.

And the city of Zarahemla did take fire.

And the city of Moroni did sink into the depths of the sea, and the inhabitants thereof were drowned.

And the earth was carried up upon the city of Moroni-hah that in the place of the city there became a great mountain.

And there was a great and terrible destruction in the land southward.

But behold, there was a more great and terrible destruction in the land northward; for behold, the whole face of the land was changed, because of the tempest and the whirlwinds and the thunderings and the lightnings, and the exceeding great quaking of the whole earth;

And the highways were broken up, and the level roads were spoiled, and many smooth places became rough.

And many great and notable cities were sunk, and many were burned, and many were shaken till the buildings thereof had fallen to the earth, and the inhabitants thereof were slain, and the places were left desolate.

—[3 Nephi 8:5–14]

JACOB CARPENTER

From Deaths on Three-Mile Creek: 1841–1915

Wm Davis   age 100.8   dide oc 5   1841
wars old soldier in rev ware   and got his
thie brok in last fite at Kinge's monte
he wars farmer   and made brandy
and never had Drunker in famly

Franky Davis his wife   age 87   dide Sep 10   1842
she had nirve fite wolves all nite at shogar camp
to save her caff   throde fier chonks
the camp wars half mile from home
noe she must have nirv to fite wolf all nite

Charley Kiney   age 72   dide may 10   1852
wars farmer live in mt on bluey rige at kiney gap
he had 4 wimmin cors marid to one
rest live on farme
all went to felde   work to mak grain
all wen to crib for ther bread
all went smok hous for there mete
he cilde bote 75 to 80 hoges every yere
and wimen never had wordes bout him
haven so many wimin
if he wod be living this times
wod be hare pulde
thar wars 42 children blong to him
they all wento preching togethern
nothing sed   des aver body go long smoth
help one nother
never had any foes
got along smoth with avery bodi
I nod him

Written down by UNCLE JAKE CARPENTER of Three-Mile Creek, Avery County, in the western mountains of North Carolina. The impulse to poetry in these "obituaries"—some written long after the actual deaths—may not be much different from that in *Spoon River Anthology* and other elegies.

JOHN GREENLEAF WHITTIER

Letter

*From a Missionary of the Methodist Episcopal Church South,
In Kansas, To A Distinguished Politician.*
DOUGLAS MISSION, *August, 1854.*

Last week—the Lord be praised for all His mercies
To His unworthy servant!—I arrived
Safe at the Mission, *via* Westport; where
I tarried over night, to aid in forming
A Vigilance Committee, to send back,
In shirts of tar, and feather-doublets quilted
With forty stripes save one, all Yankee comers,
Uncircumcised and Gentile, aliens from
The Commonwealth of Israel, who despise
The prize of the high calling of the saints,
Who plant amidst this heathen wilderness
Pure gospel institutions, sanctified
By patriarchal use. The meeting opened
With prayer, as was most fitting. Half an hour,
Or thereaway, I groaned, and strove, and wrestled,
As Jacob did at Penuel, till the power
Fell on the people, and they cried "Amen!"
"Glory to God!" and stamped and clapped their hands;
And the rough river boatmen wiped their eyes;
"Go it, old hoss!" they cried, and cursed the niggers—
Fulfilling thus the word of prophecy,
"Cursed be Canaan." After prayer, the meeting
Chose a committee—good and pious men—
A Presbyterian Elder, Baptist deacon,
A local preacher, three or four class-leaders,
Anxious inquirers, and renewed backsliders,
A score in all—to watch the river ferry,
(As they of old did watch the fords of Jordan,)
And cut off all whose Yankee tongues refuse
The Shibboleth of the Nebraska bill.
And then, in answer to repeated calls,
I gave a brief account of what I saw

In Washington; and truly many hearts
Rejoiced to know the President, and you
And all the Cabinet regularly hear
The gospel message of a Sunday morning,
Drinking with thirsty souls of the sincere
Milk of the Word. Glory! Amen, and Selah!

    Here, at the Mission, all things have gone well:
The brother who, throughout my absence, acted
As overseer, assures me that the crops
Never were better. I have lost one negro,
A first-rate hand, but obstinate and sullen.
He ran away some time last spring, and hid
In the river timber. There my Indian converts
Found him, and treed and shot him. For the rest,
The heathens round about begin to feel
The influence of our pious ministrations
And works of love; and some of them already
Have purchased negroes, and are settling down
As sober Christians! Bless the Lord for this!
I know it will rejoice you. You, I hear,
Are on the eve of visiting Chicago,
To fight with the wild beasts of Ephesus,
Long John, and Dutch Free-Soilers. May your arm
Be clothed with strength, and on your tongue be found
The sweet oil of persuasion. So desires
Your brother and co-laborer. Amen!

    P.S. All's lost. Even while I write these lines,
The Yankee abolitionists are coming
Upon us like a flood—grim, stalwart men,
Each face set like a flint of Plymouth Rock
Against our institutions—staking out
Their farm lots on the wooded Wakarusa,
Or squatting by the mellow-bottomed Kansas;
The pioneers of mightier multitudes,
The small rain-patter, ere the thunder shower
Drowns the dry prairies. Hope from man is not.

Oh, for a quiet berth at Washington,
Snug naval chaplaincy, or clerkship, where
These rumors of free labor and free soil
Might never meet me more. Better to be
Door-keeper in the White House, than to dwell
Amidst these Yankee tents, that, whitening, show
On the green prairie like a fleet becalmed.
Methinks I hear a voice come up the river
From those far bayous, where the alligators
Mount guard around the camping filibusters:
"Shake off the dust of Kansas. Turn to Cuba—
(That golden orange just about to fall,
O'er-ripe, into the Democratic lap;)
Keep pace with Providence, or, as we say,
Manifest destiny. Go forth and follow
The message of *our* gospel, thither borne
Upon the point of Quitman's bowie-knife,
And the persuasive lips of Colt's revolvers.
There may'st thou, underneath thy vine and fig-tree,
Watch thy increase of sugar cane and negroes,
Calm as a patriarch in his eastern tent!"
Amen: So mote it be. So prays your friend.

WALT WHITMAN

To the States
To Identify the 16th, 17th, or 18th Presidentiad

Why reclining, interrogating? why myself and all drowsing?
What deepening twilight—scum floating atop of the waters,
Who are they as bats and night-dogs askant in the capitol?
What a filthy Presidentiad! (O South, your torrid suns! O
      North, your arctic freezings!)
Are those really Congressmen? are those the great judges? is
      that the President?
Then I will sleep awhile yet, for I see that these States sleep,
      for reasons;

(With gathering murk, with muttering thunder and lambent
  shoots we all duly awake,
South, North, East, West, inland and seaboard, we will surely
  awake).

MARK TWAIN

A Novel: Who Was He?

As I promised, I will now write you a novelette.
Gillifat was a man.
All men are men.
No man can be a man who is not a man.
Hence Gillifat was a man.
Such was Gillifat.
Too Many Cooks Spoil the Broth.
  At the corner of the beach furthest from the *Tre-mouille,* which is also between the great rock called Laba-dois and the Budes du Noir, two men stood talking.
One was a Dutchman.
One wasn't.
Such is life.
Allons.
The Hair of the Dog will Cure the Bite.
  The *Enfant* lay at anchor. The *Enfant* was of that style of vessel called by the Guernsey longshoremen a *croupier.*
They always call such vessels *croupiers.*
It is their name.
This is why they call them so.
A storm was rising.
Storms always rise in certain conditions of the atmosphere.
  They are caused by certain forces operating against certain other forces which are called by certain names and are well known by persons who are familiar with them. In 1492 Columbus sailed.
There was no storm but he discovered—
What?
A new world!
  Oct. 23, 1835, a storm burst upon the coasts of England which drove ships high and dry upon the land—a storm which carried sloops and schooners far inland and perched them upon the tops of hills.

Such is the nature of storms.

Let the Sinless Cast the first Stone.

The house was in flames. From the cellar gratings flames burst upward.

From the ground floor windows, from the doorways, from obscure crevices in the weather boarding flames burst forth.

And black volumes of smoke.

From the second story windows, flames and smoke burst forth—the flames licking the smoke hungrily—the smoke retreating,—from threatened devourment as it were.

The third story was a lashing and hissing world of gloomy smoke, stained with splashes of bloody flame.

At a window of the second story appeared a wild vision of beauty—appeared for a moment, with disheveled hair, with agonized face, with uplifted, imploring hands—appeared for a second, then vanished amid rolling clouds of smoke—appeared again glorified with a rain of fiery cinders from above—and again was swallowed from sight by the remorseless smoke.

It was Demaschette.

In another second Gillifat had seized a ladder and placed it against the house.

In another moment he had ascended half way up.

A thousand anxious eyes were fixed upon him.

The old mother and the distracted father fell upon their knees—looked up at him with streaming eyes—blessed him—prayed for him.

The roof was threatening to fall in.

Not a moment was to be lost.

Gillifat held his breath to keep from inhaling the smoke—then took one, two, six strides and laid his hand upon the window sill.

There are those who believe window sills are sentient beings.

There are those who believe that the moving springs of human action are the Principle of Good and the Principle of Evil—that window may, and they may not, have something to do with these.

It is wonderful.

If they have, where are the labors of our philosophers of a thousand years? If they have not, have we not God? Let us be content. Everything goes.

Time is.

The fatal difference betwixt Tweedledum and Tweedledee.

The two men glared at each other eight minutes—time is terrible in circumstances of danger—men have grown old under the effects of fright while the fleetest horse could canter a mile—eight minutes—eight terrible minutes they glared at each other and then—

Why does the human contract under the influence of joy and dilate under the influence of fear?

It is strange. It is one of the conditions of our being.

The human eye is round. It protrudes from the socket, but it does not fall out. Why? Because certain ligatures, invisible because hidden from sight, chain it to the interior apparatus.

The pupil of the eye is also round. We do not pretend to account for this. We simply accept it as a truth. A man might see as well with a square pupil, perhaps, but what then? The absence of uniformity, of harmony in the species.

The human eye is a beautiful and an expressive feature. In November 1642, John Duke of Sebastiano insulted the Monseigneur de Torbay, Knight of the Cross, Keeper of the Seals, Grand Equerry to the King—insulted him grossly. What did Torbay do?

Split him in the eye.

In 1322 Durande Montesquieu broke a lance with Baron Lonsdale de Lonsdale—drove his weapon through the latter's dexter eye. Hence the injunction, hoary with usage, 'Mind your eye.'

Beautiful?

Without doubt.

Nothing is Hidden, Nothing Lost.

The *Tremouille* lay at anchor. The two men had just finished glaring upon each other, Gillifat was upon the uppermost round of the ladder, the storm was about to burst forth in all its terrible grandeur when—

You remember all these people and things were very close together—grouped in a mass as it were.

The dreadful climax was impending—fearful moment —when

Victor Hugo appeared on the scene and began to read a chapter from one of his books.

All these people and things got interested in his imminently impending climaxes and suspended their several enterprises.

The flames and the smoke stood still.

The girl ceased to fluctuate in the smoke.

Gillifat halted.

The two men about to shed blood, paused.

The *croupier* slacked up on her cable.

But behold!

When after several chapters the climaxes never arrived, but got swallowed up in interminable incomprehensible metaphysical disquisitions, columns of extraneous general information, and chapters of wandering incoherencies, they became disgusted and—

Lo! a miracle!

The *croupier* up anchor and went to sea.

The two disputants left.

The (—girl) disappeared for good.

Gillifat climbed down the ladder and departed.

The fire went out. Voila! They couldn't stand it.

V alone remained—

Victor was Victor still!

THE END

JAMES REUBEN [NEZ PERCÉ]

History of Nez Percé Indians from 1805 up to the Present Time 1880

They lived and enjoyed the happiness and freedom
and lived just as happy as any other Nation in the World.

But alas the day was coming when all their happy days
was to be turned into day of sorrow and moening.

Their days of freedom was turned to be the day of slavery.

Their days of victory was turned to be conquered,
and their rights to the country was disregarded by another
     nations
which is called "Whiteman" at present day.

In 1855 a treaty was made between Nez Perce Nation and
      United States.

Wal-la-mot-kin (Hair tied on forehead) or Old Joseph,
Hul-lal-ho-sot or (Lawyer),
were the two leading Chiefs of the Nez Perce Nation in 1855,
both of these two Chiefs consented to the treaty
and Nez Perce sold to the United States
part of their country.

In 1863 another treaty was made
in which Lawyer and his people consented
but Joseph and his people refused to make the second treaty

from that time Joseph's people
were called None-treaty Nez Perce.

The treaty Nez Perce number 1800
None-treaty numbered 1000

The Nez Perce decreased greatly since 1805 up to 1863.
The smallpox prevailed among the tribe
which almost destroyed the tribe.

Lawyer's people advanced in civilization
and became farmers ec.
They had their children in schools.

While Joseph's people refused all these things
they lived outside what was called Nez Perce Reservation

1877 Government undertook to move Young Joseph people on
      the Res.

At this date Young Joseph was the ruling chief
son of Old Chief Joseph who died in 1868,
and left his people in charge of his own Son

Joseph and his followers broke out
and there was Nez Perce War bloody one
nine great battles fought

the last battle lasted five days
which Joseph surrendered with his people

1000 Indians had went on the war path
but when Joseph surrendered
there was only 600

400 killed during the wars
or went to other tribes.

after the capture Joseph was brought to this Territory as
        captives.

at present Joseph people numbers 350 out of 600
all are suffering on account of this Southern climate
result is he and his people
will live and die in this country exiled from home

Take it in the right light—
Nez Perce have been wrongly treated by the Government
it cannot be denied
not Nez Perce only but all other Indian Nations in America.

I wrote this about my own people.

I am a member of Nez Perce Tribe
and Nephew of Chief Joseph

When this is opened and read may be understood
how the Indians have been treated by the Whiteman.

Slightly abridged [by WILLIAM BRANDON] from the text by JAMES REU-
BEN deposited in the cornerstone of the Nez Percé and Ponca school
on October 20, 1880, and recovered when the schoolhouse was torn
down. It was first printed by the Oklahoma Historical Society in the
Chronicles of Oklahoma, Vol. 12, September, 1934.

WILLIAM VAUGHN MOODY'S work bridged nineteenth- and twentieth-century poetic methods, combining earlier interest in myth with the new anthropology and a critique of social order calling for change. His prose plays, such as *The Death of Eve,* present the liberation of woman as central to an age of renewals and the necessary reversal of Western taboos against knowledge and sexual freedom. Eve takes Cain back to the Garden (Blake's Innocence), revealing that the Gates are always open, the fruit of the Tree is nourishing, and the Fall is a lie or aspect of repressive taboo. Compare the Gnostic myth of the Serpent as bringer of Knowledge (Hans Jonas, *The Gnostic Religion,* 1963).

WILLIAM VAUGHN MOODY

I Am the Woman   [1912]

I am the Woman, ark of the law and its breaker,
Who chastened her step and taught her knees to be meek,
Bridled and bitted her heart and humbled her cheek,
Parceled her will, and cried, "Take more!" to the taker,
Shunned what they told her to shun, sought what they bade
      her seek,
Locked up her mouth from scornful speaking: now it is open
      to speak.

I am she that is terribly fashioned, the creature
Wrought in God's perilous mood, in His unsafe hour.
The morning star was mute, beholding my feature,
Seeing the rapture I was, the shame, and the power,
Stared at my manifold meaning; he heard me call,
"O fairest among ten thousand, acceptable brother!"
And he answered not, for doubt; till he saw me crawl
And whisper down to the secret worm, "O mother,
Be not wroth in the ancient house; thy daughter forgets not at
      all!"

I am the Woman, fleer away,
Soft withdrawer back from the maddened mate,
Lurer inward and down to the gates of day
And crier there in the gate,
"What shall I give for thee, wild one, say!
The long, slow rapture and patient anguish of life,

Or art thou minded a swifter way?
Ask if thou canst, the gold, but O, if thou must,
Good is the shining dross, lovely the dust!
Look at me, I am the Woman, harlot and heavenly wife;
Tell me thy price, be unashamed; I will assuredly pay!"

I am also the Mother: of two that I bore
I comfort and feed the slayer, feed and comfort the slain.
Did they number my daughters and sons? I am mother of
      more!
Many a head they marked not, here in my bosom has lain,
Babbling with unborn lips in a tongue to be,
Far, incredible matters, all familiar to me.
Still would the man come whispering, "Wife!" but many a
      time my breast
Took him as a husband: I soothed him and laid him to rest
Even as the babe of my body, and knew him for such.
My mouth is open to speak, that was dumb too much!
I say to you I am the Mother; and under the sword
Which flamed each way to harry us forth from the Lord,
I saw Him young at the portal, weeping and staying the rod,
And I, even I was His mother, and I yearned as the mother of
      God.

I am also the Spirit. The Sisters laughed
When I sat with them dumb in the portals, over my lamp,—
Half asleep in the doors: for my gown was raught
Off at the shoulder to shield from the wind and the rain
The wick I tended against the mysterious hour
When the silent City of Being should ring with song,
As the Lord came in with Life to the marriage bower.
"Look!" laughed the elder Sisters; and crimson with shame
I hid my breast away from the rosy flame.
"Ah!" cried the leaning Sisters, pointing, doing me wrong;
"Do you see?" laughed the wanton Sisters. "She will get her a
      lover erelong!"

And it was but a little while till unto my need
He was given, indeed,

And we walked where waxing world after world went by;
And I said to my lover, "Let us begone,
O, let us begone, and try
Which of them all the fairest to dwell in is,
Which is the place for us, our desirable clime!"
But he said, "They are only the huts and the little villages,
Pleasant to go and lodge in rudely over the vintage-time!"
Scornfully spake he, being unwise,
Being flushed at heart because of our walking together.
But I was mute with passionate prophecies;
My heart went veiled and faint in the golden weather,
While universe drifted by after still universe.
Then I cried, "Alas, we must hasten and lodge therein,
One after one, and in every star that they shed!
A dark and a weary thing is come on our head—
To search obedience out in the bosom of sin,
To listen deep for love when thunders the curse;
For O my love, behold where the Lord hath planted
In every star in the midst his dangerous Tree!
Still I must pluck thereof and bring unto thee,
Saying, 'The cooness for which all night we have panted;
Taste of the goodly thing, I have tasted first!'
Bringing us noway coolness, but burning thirst,
Giving us noway peace, but implacable strife,
Loosing upon us the wounding joy and the wasting sorrow of
    life!
I am the Woman, ark of the Law and sacred arm to upbear it,
Heathen trumpet to overthrow and idolatrous sword to shear
    it:
Yea, she whose arm was round the neck of the morning star
    at song,
Is she who kneeleth now in the dust and cries at the secret
    door,
'Open to me, O sleeping mother! The gate is heavy and strong.
Open to me, I am come at last; be wroth with thy child no
    more.
Let me lie down with thee there in the dark, and be slothful
    with thee as before!' "

CARL SANDBURG

The Lawyers Know Too Much

THE lawyers, Bob, know too much.
They are chums of the books of old John Marshall.
They know it all, what a dead hand wrote,
A stiff dead hand and its knuckles crumbling,
The bones of the fingers a thin white ash.
    The lawyers know
      a dead man's thoughts too well.

In the heels of the higgling lawyers, Bob,
Too many slippery ifs and buts and howevers,
Too much hereinbefore provided whereas,
Too many doors to go in and out of.

        When the lawyers are through
        What is there left, Bob?
        Can a mouse nibble at it
        And find enough to fasten a tooth in?

        Why is there always a secret singing
        When a lawyer cashes in?
        Why does a hearse horse snicker
        Hauling a lawyer away?

The work of a bricklayer goes to the blue.
The knack of a mason outlasts a moon.
The hands of a plasterer hold a room together.
The land of a farmer wishes him back again.
      Singers of songs and dreamers of plays
      Build a house no wind blows over.
The lawyers—tell me why a hearse horse snickers hauling a
      lawyer's bones.

EDGAR LEE MASTERS

Euripides Alexopoulos   [1924]

I had vision at last:
A divine youth was playing a harp near Trainor's Drug Store.
They listened, passed, conferred on the matter.
They returned and told him to work or get out of town.
He began then to carry coal and sell newspapers,
Playing his harp in the evenings.
The neighbors complained:
He was leading people to idleness, dreams.
He went on playing, emerged to the streets again.
Some tore at him, others hooted him, some praised him;
But he was in need of money, always money.
He put his harp by to work for money . . . no money for harping!
He took forth his harp again.
The strings were loose, it had to be tuned.
He tuned it and played better than ever.
In the midst of this his money was taken from him.
Shadows had come over him, he was no longer young.
His children were half grown, making voracious demands.
Should he play the harp or work for the children?
Every one said, work for the children.
They must feed and be educated,
And what is this harping after all?
They caught him then and put him to work.
His beard grew long and gray, his eyes were haggard,
He was bent, his hands were thick and dull.
He could neither work now nor play the harp.
Suddenly as he was sitting on a bench in the park
He shed his rags, as the sun sheds clouds.
He rose to the spire of the church,
Stood on one foot,
And spit on the town—
It was Apollo!

SHERWOOD ANDERSON

The Man in the Brown Coat [1921]

Napoleon went down into a battle riding on a horse.

Alexander went down into a battle riding on a horse.

General Grant got off a horse and walked into a wood.

General Hindenburg stood on a hill. The moon came up out of a clump of bushes.

I am writing a history of the things men do. I have written three such histories and I am but a young man. Already I have written three hundred, four hundred thousand words.

My wife is somewhere in this house where for hours I have been sitting and writing. She is a tall woman with black hair turning a little grey. Listen, she is going softly up a flight of stairs. All day she goes softly doing the housework in our house.

I came here to this town from another town in the state of Iowa. My father was a house-painter. I worked my way through college and became a historian. We own this house in which I sit. This is my room in which I work. Already I have written three histories of peoples. I have told how states were formed and battles fought. You may see my books standing straight up on the shelves of the libraries. They stand up like sentries.

I am tall like my wife and my shoulders are a little stooped. Although I write boldly I am a shy man. I like being in this room alone at work with the door locked. There are many books here. Nations march back and forth in the books. It is quiet here but in the books a great thundering goes on.

•   •   •

Napoleon rides down a hill and into a battle.

General Grant walks in a wood.

Alexander rides down a hill and into a battle.

•   •   •

My wife has a serious, almost stern look. In the afternoon she leaves our house and goes for a walk. Sometimes she goes to stores, sometimes to visit a neighbor. There is a yellow house opposite our house. My wife goes out a side door and passes along our street between our house and the yellow house.

The window before my desk makes a little framed place like a picture. The yellow house across the street makes a solid background of yellow.

The side door of my house bangs. There is a moment of waiting. My wife's face floats across the yellow background of the picture.

General Pershing rode down a hill and into a battle.

Alexander rode down a hill and into a battle.

Little things are growing big in my mind. The window before my desk makes a little framed place like a picture. Every day I wait staring. I wait with an odd sensation of something impending. My hand trembles. The face that floats through the picture does something I do not understand. The face floats, then it stops. It goes from the right hand side to the left hand side then it stops.

The face comes into my mind and goes out. The face floats in my mind. The pen has fallen from my fingers. The house is silent. The eyes of the floating face are turned away from me.

My wife is a girl who came here from Ohio. We have a servant but she sweeps the floors and sometimes makes the bed in which we sleep together. We sit together in the evening but I do not know her. I cannot shake myself out of myself. I wear a brown coat and I cannot come out of my coat. I cannot come out of myself. My wife is very silent and speaks softly but she cannot come out of herself.

My wife has gone out of the house. She does not know that I know every little thought of her life. I know about her when she was a child and walked in the streets of an Ohio town. I have heard the voices of her mind. I have heard the little voices. I heard the voices crying when she was overtaken with passion and crawled into my arms. I heard the voices when her lips said other words to me as we sat together on the first evening after we were married and moved into this house.

It would be strange if I could sit here as I am doing now while my own face floated across the picture made by the yellow house and the window.

It would be strange and beautiful if I could meet my wife, come into her presence.

The woman whose face floated across my picture just now knows nothing of me. I know nothing of her. She has gone off, along a street. The voices of her mind are talking. I am here in this room as alone as any man God ever made.

It would be strange and beautiful if I could float my face across a picture. If my floating face could come into her presence, if it could come into the presence of any man or any woman that would be a strange and beautiful thing to have happen.

•　•　•

Napoleon went down into a battle riding on a horse.

General Grant went into a wood.

Alexander went down into a battle riding on a horse.

•　•　•

Some day I shall make a testament unto myself.

•　•　•

I'll tell you sometimes the whole life of this world floats in a human face in my mind. The unconscious face of the world stops and stands still before me.

Why do I not say a word out of myself to the others? Why in all our life together have I never been able to break through the wall to my wife? Already I have written three hundred, four hundred thousand words. Are there no words for love? Some day I shall make a testament unto myself.

ERNEST HEMINGWAY

They All Made Peace—What Is Peace?　[1923]

All of the turks are gentlemen and Ismet Pasha is a
Little deaf. But the Armenians. How about the
Armenians?
Well, the Armenians.

Lord Curzon likes
So does Chicherin.
So does Mustapha Kemal. He is good looking too. His eyes
Are too close together but he makes war. That is the way he
    is.
Lord Curzon does not love Chicherin. Not at all. His beard
Tickles and his hands are cold. He thinks all the time.

Lord Curzon thinks too. But he is much taller and goes to
St. Moritz.

Mr. Child does not wear a hat.
Baron Hayashi gets in and out of the automobile.
Monsieur Barrère gets telegrams. So does Marquis Garonni.

His telegrams come on motorcycles from MUSSOLINI.
MUSSOLINI has nigger eyes and a bodyguard, and has
His picture taken reading a book upside down. MUSSOLINI is
Wonderful. Read *The Daily Mail.*

I used to know MUSSOLINI. Nobody liked him then. Even I
Didn't like him. He was a bad character. Ask Monsieur
    Barrère.

We all drink cocktails. Is it too early to have a cocktail?
How about a drink, George? Come on and we'll have a
    cocktail,
Admiral. Just time before lunch. Well what if we do? Not too
    dry.
Well, what do you boys know this morning?

O they're shrewd. They're shrewd.

Who have we got on the subcommission this morning,
    Admiral?
M. Stambulski walks up the hill and down the hill. Don't talk
About M. Venizelos. He is wicked. You can see it. His beard
    shows it.
Mr. Child is not wicked.
Mrs. Child has flat breasts and Mr. Child is an Idealist and
    wrote

Harding's campaign speeches and calls Senator Beveridge Al.
You know me Al.
Lincoln Steffens is with Child. The big C makes the joke easy.

Then there is Mosul
And the Greek Patriarch.
What about the Greek Patriarch?

JOHN DOS PASSOS
Newsreel LXVI

Newsreel LXVI

HOLMES DENIES STAY

A better world's in birth

Tiny Wasps Imported From Korea In Battle To Death With
Asiatic beetle

BOY CARRIED MILE DOWN SEWER; SHOT OUT ALIVE

CHICAGO BARS MEETINGS

For justice thunders condemnation

Washington Keeps Eye On Radicals

Arise rejected of the earth

PARIS BRUSSELS MOSCOW GENEVA ADD THEIR VOICES

It is the final conflict

Let each stand in his place

Geologist Lost In Cave Six Days

The International Party

SACCO AND VANZETTI MUST DIE

Shall be the human race

*Much I thought of you when I was lying in the death house
—the singing, the kind tender voices of the children from the
playground where there was all the life and the joy of liberty—*

just one step from the wall that contains the buried agony of three buried souls. It would remind me so often of you and of your sister and I wish I could see you every moment, but I feel better that you will not come to the death house so that you could not see the horrible picture of three living in agony waiting to be electrocuted.

—From *The Big Money,* [1936]

LIGHTNING HOPKINS
Mister Charlie

(Once in the country there was a little boy he was wandering away from his, place that he was living. He didn't have no mother, neither no father. So he decided he would try to get out on his own because he figured that the people that he was, around with, there was a little too, cruel to him. So the little kid, he wanted to see some parts of the world and he decided he would, start out on his own. So he left, his home, where, he would call a home. And he goes traveling. He travels for miles and miles, as he; he traveled a good piece, from the place, that he was located.

So he run across a rolling mill. The fact of the business: it was a saw mill. But they called it a rolling mill at that time, because they'd roll the logs down the hill, put 'em on the trolley, and roll 'em on down, and they would cut the first, off, and throw it in the junk there, and let it burn. So Mister Charlie he had, a shack, behind his mill. So he didn't have anything to be in that shack, unless 'n somebody stayed. The little boy he walked up there, and he stood, looking lonesome and 'lorn.

So Mister Charlie say, "Boy, what you doing here?"

He say, "Me me me me me me don't have no home."

So Mister Charlie say, "Well, wait a minute. I'm busy now." Mister Charlie went on, doing his work there, and things that he's supposed to do. He looked: the poor little boy was standing in the same position.

He came back there, he say, "Boy, can you work?"

"Me me can work."

He say, "Well I tell you what: by you not having no home, I got a shack back there." Said, "If you will stay in that shack and keep this fire from my cured lumber, and keep it from burning my mill burning down," he say, "I'll give you a home here, long as I got a mill."

"Th th thank you, Mister Charlie."

And so, Mister Charlie carried him back there and showed him where, that he could live, you know?

So the little boy was happy with his home.

Mister Charlie lived a few blocks from there: fact of the business. But it wasn't too far that the little boy could run to the house.

So, on Sundays they don't work. But they still got that there throw-away burning away. You know what I mean? And so the little boy he was inside of his little bunk that morning. And he looked out and he seed that the rolling mill had caught a-fire.

The little boy went to running. He run all the way. He didn't stop. 'Cause he was trying. To approve. That he meaned. To do the thing. That Mister Charlie asked him to.

So when he got there Mister Charlie was busy, doing a little old something else. What it was, the little boy don't know. And I don't either. But I know, and the little boy knows, that he was busy. So he patted Mister Charlie on the back, he said, "Mi Mi Mi Mi Mi Mi Mi Mister Charlie!"

Mister Charlie straighted up and looked at him, and said, "Boy, what you want?"

He said, "Yo yo yo yo yo."

He said, "Well wait a minute." He says, "I got something to do. You tell me later."

Mister Charlie turned around and he begins doing what he was doing. The little boy wanted to let him know that it was urgent. It was his time to go. He patted him on his back no sooner than Mister Charlie stooped over, said, "Mi Mi Mi Mi Mi Mi Mi Mi Mister Charlie!"

Mister Charlie straightened up, and said, "Boy, you trying to tell me something." Said, "Now if you can't talk it," said, "sing it." And he said:)

Ohhhhhhhhh
    Mister Charlie
      your rolling mill is burning down
Oh Mister Charlie
      your rolling mill is burning down
He said, I ain't got no water
      Mister Charlie say, If you ain't got none,

Just let the rolling mill
                    burn on down

        Mister Charlie say, Boy,
        If it ain't no water 'round
        Poke your head out the window and let that old
        Rolling mill burn on down
He said, Mister Charlie,
        do you know your rolling mill is burning down
He says, I can't help you, I can't help you,
                    Mister Charlie, it ain't no water 'round

        The little boy said, Mister Charlie,
        Now don't you see
        If the mill burn down, that's
        Almost the last of me
        Mister Charlie said, Don't you worry
        Son, listen at me
        If the old mill burn down I'm gonna give you
            another home
                        Oh, somewhere with me
Mister Charlie
            your rolling mill is burning down
He said, Just poke your head out the window
                and let that old rolling mill burn down

                    (The little boy couldn't
                        help but cry—)

Ohhhhhhhhh
                Mister Charlie
                        I won't have no place to stay
Mister Charlie
                I won't have no place to stay
Mister Charlie say, Son, don't you worry
                        I got a home for you long
                            as the day

    —Transcribed from oral blues by ERIC SACKHEIM

MELVIN B. TOLSON
Rho

New Year's Day
Hedda Starks telephoned me
from a Harlem police station.
Her fit of laughing and crying was as convulsive
as the heehaws of a Somaliland she-ass.
So the desk sergeant
waxed human. He juggled the receiver and swore
Hedda was a horned screamer,
as she agonized in her cell at midnight:
"O sweet Jesus,
make the bastard leave me alone!
I'll call The Curator
—the son-of-a-bitch—
and send 'im to Big Mama to get the goddamn rubbish!"

Verbatim was to Sergeant Ghirlandaio
what a glasshouse is to a plant.
"I hope I'm not in Harlem," he said,
"when St. Peter opens the books on Judgment Day."
His chuckle was the impish mockery of an echo
in the bottomless canyon of Hesiod's
—and our—
Brazen Age.

Hedda Starks, alias Black Orchid,
was a striptease has-been
of the brassy-pit-band era—
but listen, Black Boy, to the hoity-toity scholars:
"A vestige is rarely, if ever, present in a plant."

Mister Starks
hailed from Onward, Mississippi—
via Paris, Texas, *via* Broken Bow, Oklahoma.
How he got his *Christian* name is a legend
that tickles the inwards of the Zulu Club Wits.

When he was four years old,
his black mother took him to
the Big House on an *ante-bellum* estate;
and the Lady wanted to know the baby's name
and the proud mother said "Mister."
Since every Negro male in Dixie was
either a *boy* or an *uncle,*
the mistress turned blue and hot
like an arc-welder's torch.
"A pickaninny named *Mister?*" the old doll hissed;
and the maid, slamming the mop bucket down,
screamed: "Miss Leta,
it's *my* baby and I can name it
any damn thing I please!"

The first time Mister Starks, the piano-modernist
of the Harlem Renaissance, lamped
Black Orchid at the Bamboo Kraal,
her barbarian bump and sophisticated grind
(every bump butted by the growl of a horn)
played, with him, the witch,
like the serpentine belly dance
of Congo Leopold's Cleo de Merode, which
captivated Anatole France.

The intelligentsia of Mister's bent
became Hedda's steps on the aerial ladder
of the black and tan bourgeoisie;
but her exhumed
liaison with Mr. Guy Delaporte
(in the *Harlem Emancipator*)
was like the red kimono
that broke Woodrow Wilson's heart.

Did a sibyl say to Aeneas,
"The descent to Avernus is easy"?
Well, Mister Starks needed no Hindu mystic
mulattoed in Atlanta
and
turbaned in Harlem
to tell him—*that.*

And, contrary to what the Cumaean divined,
          it was no labor, no task,
      for Mister to escape to the upper air:
              it was a *beau geste,*
                Hardyesque—
fit for the limelight of the Harlem Opera House
    in the auld lang syne of Charles Gilpin,
              the most
            sinister-smiling
        of the Emperor Joneses
      inspired by the root of evil.

                    —[From *Harlem Gallery*]

MURIEL RUKEYSER
The Dam

All power is saved, having no end.   Rises
    in the green season, in the sudden season
    the white the budded
                        and the lost.
    Water celebrates, yielding continually
    sheeted and fast in its overfall
    slips down the rock, evades the pillars
    building its colonnades, repairs
    in stream and standing wave
    retains its seaward green
    broken by obstacle rock; falling, the water sheet
    spouts, and the mind dances, excess of white.
    White brilliant function of the land's disease.

    Many-spanned, lighted, the crest leans under
    concrete arches and the channelled hills,
    turns in the gorge toward its release;
    kinetic and controlled, the sluice
    urging the hollow, the thunder,
    the major climax
                    energy
total and open watercourse

praising the spillway, fiery glaze,
crackle of light, cleanest velocity
flooding, the moulded force.

> *I open out a way over the water*
> *I form a path between the Combatants:*
> *Grant that I sail down like a living bird,*
> *power over the fields and Pool of Fire.*
> *Phoenix, I sail over the phoenix world.*

Diverted water, the fern and fuming white
ascend in mist of continuous diffusion.
Rivers are turning inside their mountains,
streams line the stone, rest at the overflow
lake and in lanes of pliant color lie.
Blessing of this innumerable silver,
printed in silver, images of stone
walk on a screen of falling water
in film-silver in continual change
recurring colored, plunging with the wave.
Constellations of light, abundance of many rivers.
The sheeted island-cities, the white surf filling west,
the hope, fast water spilled where still pools fed.
Great power flying deep: between the rock and the sunset,
the caretaker's house and the steep abutment,
hypnotic water fallen and the tunnels under
the moist and fragile galleries of stone,
mile-long, under the wave. Whether snow fall,
the quick light fall, years of white cities fall,
flood that this valley built falls slipping down
the green turn in the river's green.
Steep gorge, the wedge of crystal in the sky.

How many feet of whirlpools?
What is a year in terms of falling water?
Cylinders; kilowatts; capacities.
Continuity: $\Sigma Q = 0$
Equations for falling water. The streaming motion.

The balance-sheet of energy that flows
passing along its infinite barrier.

It breaks the hills, cracking the riches wide,
runs through electric wires;
it comes, warning the night,
running among these rigid hills,
a single force to waken our eyes.

They poured the concrete and the columns stood,
laid bare the bedrock, set the cells of steel,
a dam for monument was what they hammered home.
Blasted, and stocks went up;
insured the base,
and limousines
wrote their own graphs upon
roadbed and lifeline.

Their hands touched mastery:
wait for defense, solid across the world.
Mr. Griswold. "A corporation is a body without a soul."
Mr. Dunn. When they were caught at it they resorted to
    the methods employed by gunmen, ordinary machine-gun
    racketeers. They cowardly tried to buy out the people
    who had the information on them.
Mr. Marcantonio. I agree that a racket has been practised, but
    the most damnable racketeering that I have ever known
    is the paying of a fee to the very attorney who
    represented these victims. That is the most outrageous
    racket that has ever come within my knowledge.
Miss Allen. Mr. Jesse J. Ricks, the president of the Union
    Carbide & Carbon Corporation, suggested that the
    stockholder had better take this question up in a private
    conference.
The dam is safe. A scene of power.
The dam is the father of the tunnel.
This is the valley's work, the white, the shining.

High	Low	Stock and Dividend in Dollars	Open	High	Low	Last	Net Chge.	Closing Bid	Ask	Sales
111	61¼	Union Carbide (3.20)	67¼	69½	67¼	69½	+3	69¼	69½	3,400

The dam is used when the tunnel is used.
The men and the water are never idle,
have definitions.

This is a perfect fluid, having no age nor hours,
surviving scarless, unaltered, loving rest,
willing to run forever to find its peace
in equal seas in currents of still glass.
Effects of friction : to fight and pass again,
learning its power, conquering boundaries,
able to rise blind in revolts of tide,
broken and sacrificed to flow resumed.
Collecting eternally power. Spender of power,
torn, never can be killed, speeded in filaments,
million, its power can rest and rise forever,
wait and be flexible. Be born again.
Nothing is lost, even among the wars,
imperfect flow, confusion of force.
It will rise. These are the phases of its face.
It knows its seasons, the waiting, the sudden.
It changes. It does not die.

　　　— [From *U.S. 1*]

■ *"Run your eye along the margin of history and you will observe great waves, sweeping movements and triumphs which fall when their ideology petrifies . . .*

"The value of Leo Frobenius [20th century German anthropologist] to civilization is not for the rightness or wrongness of this opinion or that opinion but for the kind of thinking he does. . . .

"He has in especial seen and marked out a kind of knowing, the difference between knowledge that has to be acquired by particular effort and knowing that is in people, 'in the air.' He has accented the value of such record. His archeology is not retrospective, it is immediate.

". . . 'Where we found these rock drawings, there was always water within six feet of the surface.' That kind of research goes not only into past and forgotten life, but points to tomorrow's water supply.

"This is not mere utilitarianism, it is a double charge, a sense of two sets of values and their relation.

"To escape a word or set of words loaded up with dead associations Frobenius uses the term Paideuma for the tangle or complex of the inrooted ideas of any period . . . the gristly roots of ideas that are in action. . . .

"We do NOT know the past in chronological sequence. It may be convenient to lay it out anesthetized on the table with dates pasted on here and there, but what we know we know by ripples and spirals eddying out from us and from our own time. "

—EZRA POUND, *Guide to Kulchur* [1938]

ROBERT DUNCAN
Passages 24   Orders

For the Good,

il ben dello intelletto,   the good of the people,

the soul's good.

I put aside

whatever I once served of the poet, master
of enchanting words and magics,

not to disown the old mysteries, sweet
            muthos   our mouth's telling

and I will still tell the beads, in the fearsome
        street I see glimpses of   I will pray again
        to those great columns of moon's light,
            "Mothering angels, hold my sight steady

and I will look this time as you bid me   to see
         the dirty papers, moneys, laws, orders
         and corpses of people and people-shit."

From house to house the armd men go,

       in Santo Domingo hired and conscripted killers
       against the power of an idea, against

         Gassire's lute,   the song

           of Wagadu, household of the folk,

        commune of communes

      hidden seed in the hearts of men

          and in each woman's womb   hidden.

    They do not know where It is   •   at Béziers

        the Abbé of Citeaux orders   *Kill them all—*

       the Lord will know His own!

Pillars I saw in my dream last year, stand

   in my heart and hold the blood,

      my pulse rises and beats against its walls.

   In the streets of Santo Domingo Herod's hosts again

     to exterminate the soul of the people go

     leaving behind them the dirty papers,
           torn books and bodies . . .

Down this dark corridor, "this *passage*," the poet reminds me,

and now that Eliot is dead, Williams and H.D. dead,
Ezra alone of my old masters alive,   let me
            acknowledge Eliot was one of them,   I was
      one of his,   whose   "History has many
        cunning passages, contrived corridors"

comes into the chrestomathy.

            I thought to come into an open room
            where in the south light of afternoon
            one I was improvised
            passages of changing dark and light
            a music dream and passion would have playd
            to illustrate concords of order in order,
            a contrapuntal communion of all things   •

              but Schubert is gone,
                    the genius of his melody
            has passt, and all the lovely marrd sentiment
            disownd I thought to come to, a poetry
              having so much of beauty
            that in whose progressions   rage,
              grief, dismay transported—but these
            are themselves transports of beauty!   The blood

            streams from the bodies of his sons
            to feed the voice of Gassire's lute.

            The men who mean good

      must rage, grieve, turn with dismay

to see how "base and unjust actions, when they are the objects
      of hope, are lovely to those that vehemently admire them"

and how far men following self-interest can betray all
            good of self.

            There is no

good a man has in his own things except

it be in the community of every thing;

no nature he has

but in his nature hidden in the heart of the living,

in the great household.

The cosmos will not

dissolve its orders at man's evil.

"That which is corrupted is corrupted with reference to
itself but not destroyd with reference to the universe;

for it is either air or water"

Chemistry having its equations

beyond our range of inequation.

There must be a power of an ambiguous nature
and a dominion given to choice: "For the

electing soul alone is transferrd

to another and another order . . ."

■ "*. . . Important for me is Pound's role as the carrier of a tradition or lore in poetry, that flowered in the Renaissance after Gemistos Plethon, in the Provence of the twelfth century that gave rise to the Albigensian gnosis, the* trobar clus, *and the Kabbalah, in the Hellenistic world that furnished the ground for orientalizing-greek mystery cults, Christianity, and neo-Platonism.* "

—ROBERT DUNCAN, "The Lasting Contribution of Ezra Pound,"
Agenda, IV, 2 (Oct.–Nov. 1965)

■ *". . . My own opinion is that we are now experiencing a surfacing (in a specifically 'American' incarnation) of the Great Subculture which goes back as far perhaps as the late Paleolithic.*

"This subculture of illuminati has been a powerful undercurrent in all higher civilizations. In China it manifested as Taoism, not only Lao-tzu but the later Yellow Turban revolt and medieval Taoist secret societies; and the Zen Buddhists up till early Sung. Within Islam the Sufis; in India the various threads converged to produce Tantrism. In the West it has been represented largely by a string of heresies starting with the Gnostics, and on the folk level by 'witchcraft.'

"Buddhist Tantrism, or Vajrayana as it's also known, is probably the finest and most modern statement of this ancient shamanistic-yogic-gnostic-socioeconomic view: that mankind's mother is Nature and Nature should be tenderly respected; that man's life and destiny is growth and enlightenment in self-disciplined freedom; that the divine has been made flesh and that flesh is divine; that we not only should but do love one another. This view has been harshly suppressed in the past as threatening to both Church and State. Today, on the contrary, these values seem almost biologically essential to the survival of humanity. "

—GARY SNYDER, "Passage to More Than India," in *Earth House Hold* [1969]

EDWARD DORN
Thesis

> Only the Illegitimate are beautiful
> and only the Good
> proliferate only the Illegitimate
> Oh Aklavik only you are beautiful
> Ah Aklavik your main street is dead
> only the blemished are beautiful only
> the deserted have life made
> of whole, unsurpassable night
> only Aklavik is life inside life inside

itself.
> They have gone who walk stiltedly
> on the legs of life. All life is
> in the northern hemisphere turning around

the radicals of gross pain and great joy
  the poles of pure life move
      into the circle of
    our north, oh Aklavik only
      the outcast and ab
    andoned to the night are faultless
  only the faultless have fallen only
    the fallen are the pure Children of the Sun
  only they move West, only they are expected,
      in the virgin heat
        by those who wait intensely
      for the creatures from the East, only
    Aklavik, our Aklavik, is North
      and lovely, always abandoned
      always dark, whose warp is light.
    Simple fear compels Inuvik, her liquor store
        lifts the darkness
      by the rotation of a false summer.
    The Children of the Sun never go
  to Inuvik, on bloody feet, half starved,
  or suffering the absolute intrusion
      of any food oh Aklavik they vomit
  on your remote and insupportably obscure streets
which run antiseptically into the wilderness
    and if blackflies inhabit with the insistence
of castanets the delta of Inuvik in you Aklavik
    around you Aklavik they form a core
        and critical shell of inflexible lust, only
    in the permafrost
        is the new home of the Children
        of the Sun in whose nakedness
          is the desire not desire
        in whose beauty is the flame of red
      permafrost a thousand feet deep in whose
        frail buildings
          the shudder of total winter in whose
          misshapened sun the Children bathe

LAWRENCE FERLINGHETTI

"In Goya's greatest scenes"

In Goya's greatest scenes we seem to see
                              the people of the world
        exactly at the moment when
                they first attained the title of
                              'suffering humanity'
        They writhe upon the page
                              in a veritable rage
                                        of adversity
            Heaped up
                    groaning with babies and bayonets
                                  under cement skies
            in an abstract landscape of blasted trees
                bent statues bats wings and beaks
                        slippery gibbets
            cadavers and carnivorous cocks
            and all the final hollering monsters
                    of the
                        'imagination of disaster'
            they are so bloody real
                              it is as if they really still existed

    And they do

            Only the landscape is changed

They still are ranged along the roads
        plagued by legionaires
                    false windmills and demented roosters

They are the same people
                        only further from home
        on freeways fifty lanes wide
                    on a concrete continent
                        spaced with bland billboards
                illustrating imbecile illusions of happiness

The scene shows fewer tumbrils
                but more maimed citizens
                        in painted cars
      and they have strange license plates
and engines
            that devour America

HAROLD DICKER

For the Day of Atonement/1963

some bookkeepers counted	6,000,000
others only	4½
at the least there must have been	1,000,000
the cubic capacities involved suggest there were at least	100,000

at any rate   the assembly-line
   procedures used   apparently assured
   a minimum final   quantity of
	10,000

the photographs alone show that at the least there were	1,000
a typical photograph such as this one discloses about	100

in this particular picture   which
   I now show you   there are
   thrown in a group
	10

at the center of the group notice that face is in clear focus	1

and that the eyes

are open

"THE TOAST," writes Roger D. Abrahams, who in recent years has been the main collector of such forms of Black oral poetry, "is a narrative poem that is recited, often in a theatrical manner. . . . Toasts are not sung, and it is perhaps the lack of reliance on the structure of a tune that allows their freedom of form. But toasts do have a structure. Like so many other forms of oral narrative, they are organized by conventions, ones that Albert Lord would consider 'epic.' . . . The subject treated is freedom of the body through superhuman feats and of the spirit through acts that are free of restrictive social mores (or in direct violation of them), especially in respect to crime and violence. The heroes of most of these stories are hard men, criminals, men capable of prodigious sexual feats, bad men, and very clever men (or animals) who have the amorality of the trickster." [Roger D. Abrahams, *Deep Down in the Jungle,* 1963]

"Signifying Monkey" is a very well-known toast and exists in many closely related versions. Abrahams defines "signify": "To imply, goad, beg, boast by indirect verbal or gestural means. A language of implication."

JIMMY BELL

The Signifying Monkey and the Lion

It was deep down in the jungles where the big coconuts grow,
There lived the most signified monkey the world ever know.
There hadn't been anything in these jungles for quite a little
    bit,
So this monkey thought he would start some shit.
So he hollered out to the lion one bright sunny day,
Say, "Mr. Lion, there is a big burly motherfucker right down
    the way."
Say, "Now I know you and him will never make friends,
Because everytime you meet him your knees will bend."
Say, "He got your whole family in the dozens and your sister
    on the shelf,

And the way he talks about your mama I wouldn't do myself.
And one thing he said about your mama I said I wasn't going
      to tell:
He said your mama got a pussy deep as a well."
This lion was a mad son-of-a-bitch;
He jumped up and made a big roar.
His tail was lashing like a forty-four.
He left these jungles in a hell of a rage,
Like a young cocksucker full of his gays.
He left in a hell of a breeze;
He was shaking coconuts from the trees.
The small animals got scared and fell to their knees.
He found the elephant asleep under a big oak tree,
Say, "You're the motherfucker talking about me."
But the elephant looked at him out of the corner of his eyes,
Say, "Go on, motherfucker, and pick on somebody your own
      size."
The elephant said, "My mother is very low sick and my
      brother lost his life;
I got up this morning and found another motherfucker
      fucking my wife."
Say, "I'm telling you now in front of your face so you can see,
This is no time to be fucking with me."
But the lion got back and made a forward pass
But the elephant knocked him on his hairy ass.
But he got back again and made a pass and the elephant
      ducked
And from this time on the lion was fucked.
They fought all night long and all the next day,
And I still don't see how that damn lion got away,
Because he broke both of his jaws and fucked up his face;
The elephant gave a yank on his tail and snatched his asshole
      clean out of place.
Then back-tracked him through the woods more dead than
      alive.
That's when the little monkey came on with his signifying
      jive.
Said, "Ha ha, motherfucker, look like you caught plenty of
      hell.

The elephant whipped your ass to fare-thee-well."
Said, "You left these jungles all highly sprung,
Now here you come back damn near hung—
With your face all fucked up like a cat's ass when he got the
    seven-year itch,
And you say you're King of the Jungle, say now ain't you a
    bitch.
And every morning I try to fuck a wee bit,"
Say, "Here you come with that Lion-roaring shit.
Say, "Your always around here roaring you're the king,
And I don't believe you can whip a god damn thing.
So shut up, motherfucker, don't you dare roar
Or I'll swing from these limbs and kick your ass some more.
And hurry up and get out from under my tree
Before I take a notion to shit or pee."
Now the little monkey got frantic and started to clown
When both feet slipped and his black ass hit the ground.
Like a flash of lightning and a bolt of white heat
The lion was on him with all four feet.
Then the little monkey with tears in his eyes
Said, "Oh, Mr. Lion, I apologize."
The lion said "Shut up, motherfucker, no use of your crying
I'm going to cut out some of this signifying."
So the little monkey knew what was coming and he had to
    think fast
Before this lion tore a hole in his ass.
So he said, "Mr. Lion, if you let me off here like a good
    gentleman should,"
Say, "I'll whip your ass all over these woods."
So the lion jumped back and stepped back for the monkey to
    fight.
And about this time this little monkey jumped damn near out
    of sight.
Damn near the top of a long tall pine swing down on a limb
Where he knew the lion could not get him.
Again he came on with his bullshit and signifying.
Say, "Now you kiss my two black balls and my black behind."
Say, "Yes, your mama got a cock big as a whale is true.
And your sister got a big cock, too.

And I started to stick a dick in your wife and the big cock
   flew.
And that ain't all—if you don't get out from under my tree I'll
   swing from one of these limbs and stick a dick in you."
Last time I was in the jungle, I passed the long tall tree,
The monkey was still at the top as happy as he could be.
But you can bet your life even from that day
The lion still wonders how that jive mother got away.
Now if anybody asked you who composed this toast,
Just tell him bullshitting Bell from coast-to-coast.

—Austin, Texas, October [1960]

JONATHAN WILLIAMS

Old Man Sam Ward's History
of the Gee-Haw Whimmy-Diddle

some folks say
the injuns made 'em
like lie detectors
called'em
hoo-doo sticks

feller
in Salisbury, North Caylini
mide the first
whimmy-diddle I seen

I whittle seven
kind: thisuns king
size, thisuns jumbo, thisuns
extry large

here's a single, here's one
double, here's a triple and why right here
here's a forked 'un

been whittlin' whimmy-diddles come
ten year, I reckon you'd
care to see my other toys,
boys, I got some fine
flipper-dingers, fly-
killers and bull-roarers, I can

kill a big fly at 60 feet

watch here

CHARLES BUKOWSKI

Drawing of a Band Concert on a Matchbox

life on paper is so much more
pleasurable:
there are no bombs or flies or
landlords or starving
cats,
and I am in the kitchen
staring down at the blue lake of the
concertmaster
and also the trees
rowboats, boy with American flag
lady in yellow with fan
Civil War veteran
girl with balloon
spotted dog
sailboat,
the peace of an ancient day
with the sun dreaming old
battles—
John L. Sullivan emptying the pint
in his dressing room
and getting ready to whip the world like a
bad child—
far from our modern life

where a doctor sticks something in your side,
saying, "is something making you nervous? something is
killing you."

I open the matchbox, take out a beautiful wooden match
and light a cigar.

I look out the window. it is raining. there will be nothing
in the park today except bums and madmen.
I blow the smoke against the wet glass and wonder what I am
        doing
inside here
dry and dying and
I hear the rain as a toilet flushes through the wall
(a living neighbor)
and the flowers open their arms for love.

I sit down next to the lady in yellow with the fan and
she smiles at me
and we talk we talk
only I can't hear for all the music
"your name? your name?" I keep asking
but she only smiles at me
and the dog is howling.

but yellow is my favorite color
(Van Gogh liked it too)
yellow
and I do not blow smoke in her face
and I am there
I am actually down there in the matchbox
and I am here too.

she smiles
and I lay her right on the
stove
and it is
hot
hot
the American flag waves in

battle—
play your music concertmaster
in your red coat
with your hot July buttocks.

the balloon pops and I walk across a kitchen
on a rainy day in February
to check on eggs and bread and
wine and sanity

to check on glue
to paste nice pictures
on these walls.

JOEL OPPENHEIMER

Cartography

the ceiling of his bedroom
cracks into map shapes.
an island. harbors sunk in the island's perimeter.
two great rivers. a lake at the confluence.
while on the phone he draws plans of houses abstractedly,
or replots the defense of gettysburg.
on the bedroom wall, in detail, san francisco bay,
the hills marked and notated with the addresses of friends.
on the walls of the john,
hand-drawn and accurately scaled,
the devil's den and the round tops.
the lines outside vicksburg, petersburg, the wilderness
mile by mile engraved in his mind. carried with him
white oaks, where his grandfather fell.
he does not even know if this fact, his grandfather's death,
exists for him outside of white oaks.
shall he not die also when he has no direction
before him, no plan of action, no campaign.
does he not find it impossible to move without
at least compass, or sun, gunter's chain, or a

measured pace, or the regular plat of a city's streets.
at one time his pace was exactly three feet.
with it he could determine miles, within a few yards.
or put it this way. if in his own islands
he could move freely. if he could take himself and his words.
build a continent of them. that might break him free.
if his children were more than milestones to him.
or if his wife more than the tracings of his finger
outlined before him. that might break him free.
but he will find it necessary to move himself.
this is the first action.

DAVID ANTIN

history

they got alexander and james garfield in 1881
they got carter harrison sr. in 1893
they got marie francois sadi-carnot in 1894
they got william goebel and humbert of italy in 1900
czolgosz got mckinley in 1901
they got francisco madero and jose pino suarez in february
      1913 and in march they got george of greece
they got franz ferdinand and sophia chotek at sarajevo in 1914
they got mikhail alexandra alexei olga tatiana maria and
      anastasia in 1918
they got venustiana carranza in 1920
they got pancho villa in 1923
and obregon in 1928
zangara got mayor cermak in miami in 1933
engelbert dollfuss got it in austria in 1934
dr. carl weiss got huey long in baton rouge in 1935 and he got
      it a few minutes later
leon trotsky got his skull bashed in by frank jackson in 1940
      or lev bronstein got his skull bashed in by jacques van
      den dreschd near mexico city
nathuran vinadek godse got mohandas k. gandhi in new delhi
      and folke bernadotte got it in jerusalem in 1948

in 1950 they got the president of venezuela and private leslie
    coffelt
the president of panama got it at a race track in 1955
the president of nicaragua got it in 1956
in 1957 they got the president of guatemala
they got faisal in 1958   they also got his uncle
they got s.w.p.d. bandaranaike in 1959
hazza majali got blown up by a time bomb in 1960 and inejiro
    asanuma got it in october
they got lumumba mpolo and okito in 1961
there were also some near misses
collazo and torresola didnt get truman in 1950 but they got
    torresola and private leslie coffelt
romulo betancourt got missed in 1960 and nobosuke kishe got
    stabbed in the leg 6 times
in 1961 they didnt get the imam of yemen and charles de
    gaulle
in 1962 there was some doubt about hammerskjold's plane
    crash but he got it
the seabird burned on lake michigan
the evening star foundered
the united kingdom vanished
the stonewall burned below cairo
the oneida collided
the city of boston vanished
the cambria was lost off inistrahull
the borusia sank off spain
the westfield ferry exploded
the northfleet collided
the atlantic wrecked off nova scotia
the pacific collided off cape flattery
the cospatrick burned
the eten wrecked off valparaiso
the huron wrecked off north carolina
the altacama wrecked off caldera
schiller wrecked on the scilly islands
orpheus wrecked off new zealand
euridice foundered near the isle of wight

daphne capsized off clyde
princess alice collided on the thames
uncle joseph collided off spezzia
the persia wrecked in corsica
the serpent sank off spain
the utopia collided off gibraltar
the erotgrull foundered off japan
the hongkong hit a rock
the mossamedes ran aground
the buryvestnik hit a pier
the wei tung burned on the yang tse
the tomozuru upset west of nagasaki
the noronic burned at toronto
the pelican sank off montauk
the uskudar capsized off izmit
the peter zoranic collided with world harmony in the
        bosporus
a dance hall burned in natchez
an ice plant burned in new york
a hospital burned in effingham illinois
a nursing home burned in largo florida
a tenement burned in niagara falls
a loft building burned in new york
a store burned in bogota
a school burned in little rock
a resort burned in stallheim
a chemical plant burned in pusan
a warehouse burned in glasgow
a movie theater burned in syria
a tenement burned in hong kong
a circus burned in brazil
wall street blew up in new york
a food plant blew up in pekin
a pier blew up in texas
an ammunition barge blew up in south amboy
a gas line blew up in villa rica
a nike missile plant blew up in leonardo new jersey
a warehouse blew up in rio

two apartment houses blew up in dortmund
a reactor blew up in idaho
charles ross disappeared from germantown
marian parker disappeared from los angeles
charles matson disappeared from tacoma
arthur fried disappeared from white plains
peter weinberger disappeared from westbury long island
cynthia ruotolo disappeared from a carriage in hamden
      connecticutt

JACKSON MAC LOW

From The Presidents
of the United States of America

1825   written 24 May 1963

John Quincy Adams's right hand
shaded his eyes
as he sat on a fence & fished.

At one end of his line was a knot & a hook
                      at the
    other end
        his hand   & he sat
       fishing for a camel with a hook instead of a hump?

No & not for an ox
          because
          behind a door he had his papa's ox
  & when he went fishing in water
  (& that's what he was doing he was no fool)
          he was looking to get something
            good
               something
    he cd sink his teeth into & want to.

1829   24 May 1963

Andrew Jackson's last name's the same as my first
                but
                        that makes me no more like him
                        than an ox is   like a
                                        fish
                    (or vice versa)
              but
        open   a door in your head
        (or   a window)
     & look!
          if your eyes are hooks
          what's on those hooks?
               Andrew Jackson?

  Nonsense:
               Andrew Jackson's dead:
               you can no more see *him*
than your   hand cd hold in itself
  an ox:
than you cd hold a camel in the palm of your hand
  as you cd hold a tooth
    or an eye of a fish:
              forget Andrew Jackson:
    (you already have).

1837   24 May 1963

 If Martin Van Buren ever swam in water
 (if Martin Van Buren ever swam)
what kind of swimmer was he if he held onto an ox's head
    (did he?)
   to keep his own above the surface?
      (he knew about banks
           but
          what did he know about swimming?)
               but
          what is Martin Van Buren now
               but

a series of marks I make
with
                    my
            hand?
                    (maybe
                    Martin
        Van
                Buren cd swim like a fish!)
                    do
                            I
                        make
                                these
                        marks
                            with
                    "my"
                            hand?
                            can
                    "I"
            catch
                this fish
                            (i.
        e..
                    "I")?

A hook big enough to hand an ox from's
a hook too big to catch a fish with.

Martin Van Buren lived in a fine big house in New York State
        before he was   president
        but   how did he get his hooks into
                    Ezra Pound's head:
            look!
    I want to know how a poet became a
    rich old dead old politician's fish.

NOTE: "The Presidents of the United States of America" was composed in January and May 1963. Each section is headed by the first inaugural year of a President (from Washington through Fillmore), and its structure of images is that of the Phoenician meanings of the successive letters of the President's name. The meanings are those given in *The Roman Inscriptional Letter,* a book designed, written, and printed by Sandra Lawrence in the Graphic Arts Workshop at Reed College, Portland, Oregon, in May 1955. They are:

A	(aleph) "ox"	N	(nun) "fish"
B	(beth) "house"	O	(ayin) "eye"
C	(gimel) "camel"	P	P (pe) "mouth"
D	(daleth) "door"	Q	(quoth) "knot"
E	(he) "window" or "look!"	R	(resh) "head"
F	(vau) "hook"	S	(shin) "tooth"
H	(cheth) "fence"	T	(tau) "mark"
I	(yod) "hand"	V	(vau) "hook"
K	(kaph) "palm of the hand"	X	(samekh) "prop"
L	(lamed) "ox-goad"	Y	(vau) "hook"
M	(mem) "water"	Z	(zayin) "weapon"

These letter-meaning words were used as "nuclei" which were freely connected by other material. —JACKSON MAC LOW

DIANE WAKOSKI

George Washington and the Loss of His Teeth

the ultimate
in the un-Romantic:
false teeth
>This room became a room where your heaviness and my
>heaviness came together,
>an overlay of flower petals once new and fresh
>pasted together queerly, as for some lady's hat,
>and finally false and stiff, love fearing
>to lose itself, locks and keys become inevitable.

The truth is that George cut down his father's cherry tree,
his ax making chips of wood so sweet with sap they could be
sucked, and he stripped the bark like old bandages
from the tree for kindling.
In this tree he defied his dead father,
the man who could not give him an education and left him to
suffer the ranting of Adams and others,

those fat sap-cheeked men who said George did not know
      enough
to be president. He chopped that tree—
it was no small one — down and the dry leaves rustled
like the feet of cows on grass.
It was then that George lost his teeth. He
fell asleep next to his pile of kindling wood and dreamed
the old father came chasing him with a large penis swung
      over his
shoulder. But George filled his mouth with cherries
and swallowed the bleeding flesh
and spit out the stones in a terrible torrent at his father.
With the pits of the
cherries
came all of George's teeth,
pointed weapons to hurl from the mouth at his father,
the owner of that false cherry tree.

We all come to such battles with our own flesh,
spitting out more than we have swallowed,
thus losing part of ourselves.

You came to me thus
with weapons
        and this room is strewn with dead flowers
        that grew out of my breasts and dropped off
        black and weak.
        This room is gravelled with stones I dropped
        from my womb, ossified in my own body
        from your rocky white quartz sperm.
        This room is built from the lumber of my thigh,
        and it is heavy with hate.

George had a set of false teeth
made from the cherry wood. But it was his father's tree
His lips closed painfully over the stiff set.
There is no question,
either,
where you
got the teeth in your mouth.

GERRIT LANSING

The Compost

I was speaking, he said, of American poetry,
or was it the other way round,
the way under the hill?

The snowy eye is absolute,
the measure sustaining is never provisional,
majestic it opens on silence.
So the forefathers looked,
and this is the dream of the effulgent republic
without question of affluence.

Their advice to young men:
                WILL   DARE   DO
                                    &   SHUT UP
             (.period.)
                                   ABOUT IT

has been prized, even by those to whom the name of John
                                   Marshall
                    is mud or an elegant rumor,
      for how it pertains to the ART.

That the rebirth of the republic is not eagerly awaited
                          admits of no doubt,
                  but the fact is redoubtable,
                      redounding,
in the speeches of labor leaders and other emmenagogues,
                        of history ignorant.

Such conditions enhance the Men of the Secret
who care for the compost in winter,

waiting to ready the fields.

To attend the currency in votive weather behooves :
viridescent the triangle floats over the altar.

> Offering made.
> It has snowed.
> Poverty drifts in massive installments
through villages, operas, sex never imaged in the dreams of
> John Marshall,
work undertaken without prospect of gain
> (unnatural work, which the republic itself
> turned out to be,
> stupid and savage as an intractable poem.

> Ain't pleasant to work at the compost,
> but the niches are empty,
> and the Eye will terribly blaze from the triangle
> when the lion god
> at last
> steps forth by day.

SIMON ORTIZ
Telling About Coyote

Old Coyote . . .
"If he hadn't looked back,
everything would have been okay
.... like he wasn't supposed to,
but he did,
and as soon as he did,
he lost all his power, his strength."
Never will learn will you.

". . . . you know, Coyote
is in the origin and all the way
through. . . . he's the cause
of the trouble, the hard times
that things have. . . ."
"Yet, he came so close
to having it easy.

                         But he said,
"Things are too easy. . . ."
of course, he was mainly bragging,
shooting his mouth.
The existential Man,
a Dostoevsky Coyote.

"He was on his way to Zuni
to get married on that Saturday,
and on the way there,
he ran across a gambling party,
a number of other animals were there.
                      He sat in
for a while, you know, pretty sure,
you know like he is, he would win
something.
                     But he lost
everything. Everything.
and that included his skin, his fur,
which was the subject of envy
for all the other animals around.
Coyote had the prettiest,
the glossiest, the softest fur
that ever was. And he lost that.
                    So some mice,
finding him shivering in the cold
beside a rock, felt sorry for him.
'This poor thing, beloved,'
they said, and they got together
just some old scraps of fur
and glued them on Coyote with pinon pitch.

And he's had that motley fur ever since,
you know, the one that looks like
scraps of an old coat, that one."

Coyote, old man, wanderer,
where you going, man? Look up
and see the sun. Scorned,
an old raggy blanket at the back of the closet
nobody wants.

"At this conference of all the animals,
there was a bird with the purest
white feathers. The feathers were like,
ah ... like the sun was shining on it
all the time, but you could look at it,
and you wouldn't be hurt by the glare;
it was easy to look at,
and he was Crow. He was sitting
at one side of the fire,
and the fire was being fed large pine logs,
and Crow was sitting downwind
from the fire, the wind was blowing that way
                            . . . . and Coyote was there;
he was envious of Crow because
all the animals were saying, Wow,
look at that Crow, man, just look at him,
admiring him. Coyote began to scheme,
he kept on throwing logs into the fire,
and the wind kept blowing,
all night long . . .
. . . . Let's see, the conference was about
deciding the seasons,
when they should take place,
and it took a long time to decide that. . . .
And when it was over, Crow was covered
entirely with soot, the blackest soot
from the pine logs,
and he's been like that since then."
"Oh yes, that was the conference

when Winter was decided that it should
take place when Dog's hair got long.
Dog said, 'I think Winter should take place
when my hair gets long.' And
it was agreed that it would. I guess
since no one else offered a better reason."

                    Who? Coyote?
O, O yes, last time . . .
when was it . . . I saw him was somewhere
between Muskogee and Tulsa,
heading for Tulsa I guess, just trucking along.
He was heading into some oakbrush thicket,
just over the hill was a creek. Probably
get to Tulsa in a couple of days,
drink a little wine,
diddle with the Pawnee babes,
sleep beside the Arkansas River,
listen to it for a little while,
. . . hope it don't rain,
hope the river don't rise.
He'll be back. Don't worry.

■ FROM AN INTERVIEW

" Why do you write?   Who do you write for?"
"Because Indians always tell a story. The only way to continue is to tell a story and that's what Coyote says. The only way to continue is to tell a story and there is no other way. Your children will not survive unless you tell something about them—how they were born, how they came to this certain place, how they continued."

"Who do you write for besides yourself?"
"For my son, for my wife, for my mother and my father and my grandparents and then reverse order that way so that I may have a good journey on my way back home."

    —SIMON ORTIZ   [1972]

[ANONYMOUS]

Horoscope of a Tentative North American Republic
born Philadelphia, Pa., 4 July 1776.

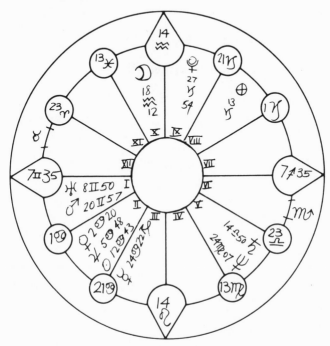

Uranus rising, brave beginnings.

Venus, Jupiter & Sol in the IInd: money money money,
      inflation as mode.

      Money as *sole* measure
      yet no measure ever for money.

Neptune in V: sex in the head; no playfulness known that does
      not lead to destruction.

Saturn in V: the great Puritan Thing, denial of the body,
      whereas the body in glory wd be the only way to offset
      what we're left with:

MARS in the House of Life: It is a land of war, lives by war, is
      war.

All under the gorgeous presidency of Moon in X, cold dreams
of power.

How to bring peace to a nation founded on war?

Re/found.
(Do you know what that means?)   (" & if this be bla bla bla")

TOWARDS THE FOUNDING OF THE CITY

—*per* R.K., Amanuensis

MAP THREE: VISIONS

Since ancient times the poet has been known as
the man who *sees* and gives his vision to others
through language. As men lose or give up
their faith in personal vision, they confuse this
knowledge with madness: coming to fear their own minds,
they erect taboos against knowing. **Map Three** tells of
the difficult reemergence of a poetry of vision,
sometimes cultivating what Rimbaud called "disorder
of the senses" as a key to renewal, sometimes exploring
dream as revelation, and sometimes reviving the idea of
magic as a power of language itself. A tradition
survives of poetry as a healing art, of nature as sacred
and medicinal, and of the gods as "eternal states of mind."
As Thoreau says, "The great god Pan is not dead,
as was rumored."

■ " Crazy Wisdom—*Personified as* Vidyadhara, *the holder of scientific knowledge. In this case knowledge is not impersonal and abusive, but plays a compassionate role. This is outrageous wisdom devoid of self and the common sense of literal thinking. Crazy wisdom is wild; in fact, it is the first attempt to express the dynamics of the tenth stage of the Bodhisattva, to step out with nakedness of mind, unconditioned, beyond conceptualization. In this state, one acts purely on what is, with the qualities of earth, water, fire, space, and stormy air. "*

—CHÖGYAM TRUNGPA, *Mudra* [1972]

■ *" In 1930, when I had, with a passion that was yet systematic, composed my book,* The Hundred-headed Woman, *I had an almost daily visit from the* Head of the Birds, *called Loplop, a very special phantom of exceptional faithfulness, who is attached to my person. He presented me with a heart in a cage, the sea in a cage, two petals, three leaves, a flower and a girl; and also the man with the black eggs, and the man with the red cloak. One fine autumn afternoon he told me that one day a Lacedaemonian had been asked to go and hear a man who could imitate the nightingale perfectly. The Lacedaemonian answered: I have often heard the nightingale itself. "*

—MAX ERNST, *Inspiration to Order*

Magic & Vision

HERMAN MELVILLE

Lines—After Shakespeare

Ego non baptizo te in nomine Patris et
Filii et Spiritus Sancti—sed in nomine
Diaboli.—madness is undefinable—
It & right reason extremes of one,
—not the (black art) Goetic but Theurgic magic—
seeks converse with the Intelligence, Power, the
Angel.

INTELLIGENCE, POWER, AND THE ANGEL: The lines above were written on the last flyleaf of the last volume of Melville's Shakespeare. The Latin, spoken by Ahab in *Moby Dick*, is reduced there to: "Ego non baptizo te in nomine patris, sed in nomine diaboli / I do not baptize thee in the name of the father, but in the name of the devil." Writes Charles Olson in *Call Me Ishmael*: "Ahab is Conjur Man. He invokes his own evil world. He himself uses black magic to achieve his vengeful ends." If this is "Goetic" (= black) magic and madness, that which "seeks converse with the Intelligence, Power, the Angel" is Pip's—the Black cabin boy who almost drowns, but in those wondrous depths "saw God's foot upon the treadle of the loom and spoke it."

HERMAN MELVILLE

Pip's Soliloquy

[*Ahab goes; Pip steps one step forward.*]

"Here he this instant stood; I stand in his air,—but I'm alone. Now were even poor Pip here I could endure it, but he's missing. Pip! Pip! Ding, dong, ding! Who's seen Pip? He must be up here; let's try the door. What? neither lock, nor bolt, nor bar; and yet there's no opening it. It must be the spell; he told me to stay here: Aye, and told me this screwed chair was mine. Here, then, I'll seat me, against the transom, in the ship's full middle, all her keel and her three masts before me. Here, our old sailors say, in their black seventy-fours great admirals sometimes sit at table, and lord it over rows of captains and lieutenants. Ha! what's this? epaulets! epaulets! the epaulets all come crowding! Pass round the decanters; glad to see ye; fill up, monsieurs! What an odd feeling, now, when a black boy's host to white men with gold lace upon their coats!—Monsieurs, have ye seen one Pip?—a little negro lad, five feet high, hang-dog look, and cowardly! Jumped from a whaleboat once;—seen him? No! Well then, fill up again, captains, and let's drink shame upon all cowards! I name no names. Shame upon them! Put one foot upon the table. Shame upon all cowards.—Hist! above there, I hear ivory —Oh, master! master! I am indeed downhearted when you walk over me. But here I'll stay, though this stern strikes rocks; and they bulge through; and oysters come to join me."

"So man's insanity is heaven's sense," wrote Melville of Pip's plunge, and Emily Dickinson, from the isolation of her Amherst room: "Much madness is divinest sense." The revelation that Melville grants Pip may be emblem of the oldest power of the shaman-poets—vision in one world, madness in another. With Dickinson the mind would seem to be in an experience for which she has no name yet, so must sometimes call it madness, knowing it would be seen as that outside the poem or other accepted context. But it's possible too that the poet's meditations on the extremes of his own mind may in fact be a process by which a poetry of endless changes can be written.

EMILY DICKINSON
Three Poems

[1]

The first Day's Night had come—
And grateful that a thing
So terrible—had been endured—
I told my Soul to sing—

She said her Strings were snapt—
Her Bow—to Atoms blown—

And so to mend her—gave me work
Until another Morn—

And then—a Day as huge
As Yesterdays in pairs,
Unrolled its horror in my face—
Until it blocked my eyes—

My Brain—begun to laugh—
I mumbled—like a fool—
And tho' 'tis Years ago—that Day—
My Brain keeps giggling—still.

And Something's odd—within—
That person that I was—
And this One—do not feel the same—
Could it be Madness—this?

[2]

One need not be a Chamber—to be Haunted—
One need not be a House—
The Brain has Corridors—surpassing
Material Place—

Far safer, of a Midnight Meeting
External Ghost
Than its interior Confronting—
That Cooler Host.

Far safer, through an Abbey gallop,
The Stones a'chase—
Than Unarmed, one's a'self encounter—
In lonesome Place—

Ourself behind ourself, concealed—
Should startle most—
Assassin hid in our Apartment
Be Horror's least.

The Body—borrows a Revolver—
He bolts the Door—
O'erlooking a superior spectre—
Or More—

[3]

I Years had been from Home
And now before the Door
I dared not enter, lest a Face
I never saw before

Stare stolid into mine
And ask my Business there—
"My Business but a Life I left
Was such remaining there?"

I leaned upon the Awe—
I lingered with Before—
The Second like an Ocean rolled
And broke against my ear—

I laughed a crumbling Laugh
That I could fear a Door
Who Consternation compassed
And never winced before.

I fitted to the Latch
My Hand, with trembling care
Lest back the awful Door should spring
And leave me in the Floor—

Then moved my Fingers off
As cautiously as Glass
And held my ears, and like a Thief
Fled gasping from the House—

■ *"In 1921 . . . in April, Marcel Duchamp in New York brought out* New York dada *in English, with Duchamp's famous object-collage,* Belle Haleine, Eau de Violette, *on the cover. Eccentric in appearance, the single number carried, among other illustrations, a faked photograph by Man Ray and the portrait of a Dadaist whimsy, a woman whose whole life was Dada, the delirious spectre of Dada mingling with the crowd in one of its monstrous transformations. Baroness Else von Loringhoven, who made objects in the manner of Schwitters, became famous in New York for her transposition of Dada into her daily life. Dressed in rags picked up here and there, decked out with impossible objects suspended from chains, swishing long trains, like an empress from another planet, her head ornamented with sardine cans, indifferent to the curiosity of passersby, the baroness promenaded down the avenues like a wild apparition, liberated from all constraint."*

—GEORGE HUGNET, *The Dada Spirit in Painting* [1932]

Writing in a language not her own—but that in itself was part of the Dada impulse she shared with others—Else von Freytag-Loringhoven was recognized for a time as the conscious purveyor of a "poetry of madness," i.e. of a process of psychic and structural unfoldings that would be explored again long after her own work had been forgotten.

ELSE von FREYTAG-LORINGHOVEN

From Mineself—Minesoul— and—Mine—Cast-Iron Lover

MINE SOUL SINGETH—THUS SINGETH
MINE SOUL—THIS IS WHAT MINE
SOUL SINGETH:

His hair is molten gold and a red pelt—
His hair is glorious!

Yea—mine soul—and he brushes it and combeth it—he maketh it shining and glistening around his head—and he is vain about it—but alas—mine soul—his hair is without sense—his hair does not live—it is no revelation, no symbol! HE is not gold—not animal—not GOLDEN animal— he is GILDED animal only—mine soul! his vanity is without sense—it is the vanity of one who has little and who weareth a treasure meaningless! o—mine soul—THAT soulless beauty maketh me sad!

"His nostrils"—singeth mine soul—"his nostrils!" seeest thou not the sweep of the scythe with which they curveth up his cheek swiftly?

Iron—mine soul—cast-iron! his nostrils maketh me sad! there is no breath of the animal that they may quiver? they do not curve swiftly—the scythe moveth—mine soul—they are still—they are motionless like death! NOT like death— in death has been life—they are iron—mine soul—cast-iron! a poor attempt to picture life—a mockery of life—as I see cast-iron animals and monuments a mockery of life ——alas—mine soul—HIS soul is cast-iron! "Iron" singeth mine soul—"iron thou canst hammer with strength—iron thou canst shape—bend—iron thou canst make quiver— iron alive to flame——
ART THOU FLAME?"

Mine soul—alas—I COULD BE!
And WHY—mine body—dost thou say: "I COULD BE" and WHY—mine body—dost thou ALL THE WHILE SAY: "ALAS"? Thine "ALAS" maketh me sad!

Mine soul dost not be mischievious! THOU KNOWEST we are One—thou knowest thou ART flame! it is THOU— mine soul—and thine desire to flare by thineself which maketh thine body say: "alas"! thou hast so changed! dost thou not hinder mine wish to touch—mine right since olden times which was granted me ever? because thou art now very strong—I gave thee much fuel—NOW—mine soul—thou art stronger than I and thou mocketh thine body! and—mine soul—are we artisans—are we not artists who flare by themselves—FOR themselves? we do not bend any more out of our way to catch and touch—to mold be molded—to feed be fed——we flare HIGH—mine soul— we are SATISFIED! ——

And yet—mine body—thou sayest "alas"!
Ha—mine soul—I say "alas" and I say "alas" and "alas" and "alas"! because I am thine BODY! and this is mine flaming desire to-day: that he shall step into THEE through ME as it was in olden times and that we will play again that old WONDERFUL play of the "TWO-

TOGETHER"!——mine soul—if thus it will be—willst thou flare around him—about him—over him—hide him with shining curtain——hiss that song of savage joy—starry-eyes——willst thou heat—melt—make quiver—break down—dissolve—build up——SHAKE HIM—SHAKE HIM—SHAKE HIM—O mine starry-eyed soul?

Heia! ja-hoho! hisses mine starry-eyed soul in her own language.

I see mine soul—we still understand each other! I LOVE THEE thou very great darling! we must wait and smile——PERHAPS SARDONICALLY——mine very great soul——because we now are artists——and: NOTHING MATTERS!!!

HARRY CROSBY was editor of Black Sun Press in Paris, which published works by Hart Crane, Archibald MacLeish and D. H. Lawrence along with Crosby's own first books. His verse experiments included the use of found forms (racing charts, book lists, stock reports, etc.) and concrete poetry, all concerned with sun-related imagery. After his suicide in 1929, several volumes appeared, with introductions by Eliot, Lawrence, and Pound, among others.

The following is from a long poem, "Assassin," first published in Crosby's *Mad Queen* (Black Sun Press, 1929). "The word Assassin is derived from the Arabic Hashishim, from Hashish. . . . When the Sheik required the services of an Assassin the Assassin was intoxicated with the hashish. . . . In this poem the Sun-Goddess, or Mad Queen as I shall call her, has replaced the Sheik and I am the Assassin she has chosen for her devices. She has intoxicated me with the hashish and I await her command."

HARRY CROSBY

Vision

I exchange eyes with the Mad Queen

the mirror crashes against my face and bursts into a thousand suns
    all over the city flags crackle and bang
    fog horns scream in the harbor
    the wind hurricanes through the window
    and I begin to dance the dance of the Kurd Shepherds

I stamp upon the floor
I whirl like dervishes

colors revolve dressing and undressing
I lash them with my fury
stark white with iron black
harsh red with blue
marble green with bright orange
and only gold remains naked

columns of steel rise and plunge
emerge and disappear
pistoning in the river of my soul
    thrusting upwards
    thrusting downwards
    thrusting inwards
    thrusting outwards
      penetrating

    I roar with pain

black-footed ferrets disappear into holes

the sun tattooed on my back
begins to spin
    faster and faster
    whirring whirling
throwing out a glory of sparks
sparks shoot off into space
sparks into shooting stars
shooting stars collide with comets

     Explosions
    Naked Colors Explode
      into
    Red Disaster

I crash out through the
window naked, widespread

upon a
    Heliosaurus
I uproot an obelisk and plunge
it into the ink-pot of the
Black Sea
I write the word

      SUN

across the dreary palimpsest
of the world
I pour the contents of the
Red Sea down my throat
I erect catapults and
lay siege to the cities of the world
I scatter without disorder
throughout the kingdoms of the world
I stone the people of the world
I stride over mountains
I pick up oceans like thin cards
and spin them into oblivion
I kick down walled cities
I hurl giant firebrands against governments
I thrust torches through the eyes of the law
    I annihilate museums
    I demolish libraries
    I oblivionize skyscrapers
I become hard as adamant
indurated in solid fire
rigid with hatred

I bring back the wizards and the sorcerers
the necromancers
the magicians
I practice witchcraft
I set up idols
with a sharp-edged sword
I cut through the crowded streets
comets follow in my wake
stars make obeisance to me
the moon uncovers her
nakedness to me

I am the harbinger of a
New Sun World
I bring the Seed of a
    New Copulation
I proclaim the Mad Queen

I stamp out vast empires
I crush palaces in my rigid
    hands
I harden my heart against
    churches

I blot out cemeteries
I feed the people with
stinging nettles
I resurrect madness
I thrust my naked sword
between the ribs of the world
I murder the world!

■ *"There is more theology in this book of Crosby's than in all the official ecclesiastical utterance of our generation. Crosby's life was a religious manifestation. His death was, if you like, a comprehensible emotional act, that is to say if you separate five minutes from all conditioning circumstances and refuse to consider anything Crosby had ever written. A death from excess vitality. A vote of confidence in the cosmos. . . .*

"Perhaps the best indication one can give of Crosby's capacity as a writer is to say that his work gains by being read all together. I do not mean this as a slight compliment. It is true of a small minority only."

    —EZRA POUND, Notes to *Torchbearer* by HARRY CROSBY
    [1931]

HARRY CROSBY

Five Prose Poems

WHITE FIRE

Your throat in my dream is a sensation of light so bright so sudden that I am dominated by the image of white fire far beyond the moment of ordinary awakening.

NAKED LADY IN A YELLOW HAT

You are the naked lady in the yellow hat.

THE END OF EUROPE

The shattered hull of a rowboat stuck in the sand a fire of driftwood a bottle of black wine black beetles the weird cry of sea-gulls lost in the heavy fog the sound of the tide creeping in over the wet sands the tomb-stone in the eel-grass behind the dunes.

RADIO FROM THE SUN-GODDESS

O trill an eioooir ann unt erun unt erun unt inn nuian on mnyn.

I shall be waiting for you when you are ready to come.

SUNRISE EXPRESS

I am endeavoring to persuade a Chinese professor who is at work on a torpedo which he expects to shoot to the sun to allow us to live in the centre of this torpedo but he insists that there is no room for our double bed and that we shall have to sleep as sailors do in a hammock which is discouraging in view of the length of the journey.

NORMAN O. BROWN

From Love's Body

"The patient connects herself with everybody." "You and I, are we not the same? . . . Sometimes I cannot tell myself from other people. . . . It seemed to me as though I no longer existed in my own person alone, as though I were one with the all." In a patient called Julie, "all perception seemed to threaten confusion with the object. 'That's the rain. I could be the rain.' 'That chair—that wall. I could be that wall. It's a terrible thing for a girl to be a wall.' "

STORCH, Primitive Archaic Forms, 27–28. LAING, Divided Self, 217. Cf. SCHILDER, Image and Appearance of the Human Body, 215. ROHEIM, Magic and Schizophrenia, 101, 115.

Definitions are boundaries; schizophrenics pass beyond the reality-principle into a world of symbolic connections: "all things lost their definite boundaries, became iridescent with many-colored significances." Schizophrenics pass beyond ordinary language (the language of the reality-principle) into a truer, more symbolic language: "I'm thousands. I'm an in-divide-you-all. I'm a no un (i.e., nun, no-un, no one)." The language of *Finnegans Wake.* James Joyce and his daughter, crazy Lucia, these two are one. The god is Dionysus, the mad truth.

STORCH, Primitive Archaic Forms, 62. LAING, Divided Self, 223. Cf. SECHEHAYE, A New Psychotherapy for Schizophrenia, 35–150. ELL-MANN, James Joyce, 692, 692n. ROHEIM, Magic and Schizophrenia, 94, 108.

The mad truth: the boundary between sanity and insanity is a false one. The proper outcome of psychoanalysis is the abolition of the boundary, the healing of the split, the integration of the human race. The proper posture is to listen to and learn from lunatics, as in former times—"We cannot deny them a measure of that awe with which madmen were regarded by people of ancient times." The insane do not share "the normal prejudice in favor of external reality." The "normal prejudice in favor of external reality" can be sustained only by ejecting (projecting) these dissidents from the human race; scotomizing them, keeping them out of sight, in asylums; insulating the so-called reality-principle from all evidence to the contrary.

FREUD, New Introductory Lectures, 80. Cf. STORCH, Primitive Archaic Forms, 97.

Dionysus, the mad god, breaks down the boundaries; releases the prisoners; abolishes repression; and abolishes the *principium individuationis,* substituting for it the unity of man and the unity of man with nature. In this age of schizophrenia, with the atom, the individual self, the boundaries disintegrating, there is, for those who would save our souls, the ego-psychologists, "the Problem of Identity." But the breakdown is to be made into a breakthrough; as Conrad said, in the destructive element immerse. The soul that we can call our own is not a real one. The solution to the problem of identity is, get lost. Or as it says in the New Testament: "He that findeth his own psyche shall lose it, and he that loseth his psyche for my sake shall find it."

MATTHEW X, 38.

TRIBAL VISIONS: It was the suggestion of anthropologist Paul Radin that tribal man's sense of the world was informed by an ability to experience "reality at white heat"—not only in vision and dream (both central experiences in such cultures) but on a waking and verbal level as well. In the conversations recorded by Carlos Castaneda with the Yaqui shaman, Don Juan, there is the following exchange:

"We are men and our lot is to learn and to be hurled into inconceivable new worlds."

"Are there any new worlds for us really?" I asked half in jest.

"We have exhausted nothing, you fool," he said imperatively. "Seeing is for impeccable men. Temper your spirit now, become a warrior, learn to see, and then you'll know that there is no end to the new worlds for our vision."

[SIOUX]
Vision Event

Go to a mountaintop & cry for a vision.

[WINTU]
Spirit Song

The circuit of the earth which you see
The scattering of the stars in the sky which you see
All that is the place for my hair

> SOURCE: JEREMIAH CURTIN, *Creation Myths of Primitive America,*
> [1898]. Writes YVOR WINTERS: "The Wintu Songs of the Spirits . . . are
> almost as tremendous as Blake."

HEHAKA SAPA [BLACK ELK]
The Dog Vision

Standing in the center of the sacred place and facing
the sunset, I began to cry, and while crying I had to say: "O
Great Spirit, accept my offerings! O make me understand!"

As I was crying and saying this, there soared a spotted
eagle from the west and whistled shrill and sat upon a pine
tree east of me.

I walked backwards to the center, and from there ap-
proached the north, crying and saying: "O Great Spirit,
accept my offerings and make me understand!" Then a
chicken hawk came hovering and stopped upon a bush
towards the south.

I walked backwards to the center once again and from
there approached the east, crying and asking the Great
Spirit to help me understand, and there came a black swal-
low flying all around me, singing, and stopped upon a bush
not far away.

Walking backwards to the center, I advanced upon the
south. Until now I had only been trying to weep, but now
I really wept, and the tears ran down my face; for as I
looked yonder towards the place whence come the life of

things, the nation's hoop and the flowering tree, I thought of the days when my relatives, now dead, were living and young, and of Crazy Horse who was our strength and would never come back to help us any more.

I cried very hard, and I thought it might be better if my crying would kill me; then I could be in the outer world where nothing is ever in despair.

And while I was crying, something was coming from the south. It looked like dust far off, but when it came closer, I saw it was a cloud of beautiful butterflies of all colors. They swarmed around me so thick that I could see nothing else.

I walked backwards to the flowering stick again, and the spotted eagle on the pine tree spoke and said: "Behold these! They are your people. They are in great difficulty and you shall help them." Then I could hear all the butterflies that were swarming over me, and they were all making a pitiful, whimpering noise as though they too were weeping.

Then they all arose and flew back into the south.

Now the chicken hawk spoke from its bush and said: "Behold! Your Grandfathers shall come forth and you shall hear them!"

Hearing this, I lifted up my eyes, and there was a big storm coming from the west. It was the thunder being nation, and I could hear the neighing of horses and the sending of great voices.

It was very dark now, and all the roaring west was streaked fearfully with swift fire.

And as I stood there looking, a vision broke out of the shouting blackness torn with fire, and I saw the two men who had come to me first in my great vision. They came head first like arrows slanting earthward from a long flight; and when they neared the ground, I could see a dust rising there and out of the dust the heads of dogs were peeping. Then suddenly I saw that the dust was the swarm of many-colored butterflies hovering all around and over the dogs.

By now the two men were riding sorrel horses, streaked with black lightning, and they charged with bows and arrows down upon the dogs, while the thunder beings cheered for them with roaring voices.

Then suddenly the butterflies changed, and were storm-driven swallows, swooping and whirling in a great cloud behind the charging riders.

The first of these now plunged upon a dog's head and arose with it hanging bloody on his arrow point, while the whole west roared with cheering. The second did the same; and the black west flashed and cheered again. Then as the two arose together, I saw that the dogs' heads had changed to the heads of Wasichus; and as I saw, the vision went out and the storm was close upon me, terrible to see and roaring.

I cried harder than ever now, for I was much afraid. The night was black about me and terrible with swift fire and the sending of great voices and the roaring of the hail. And as I cried, I begged the Grandfathers to pity me and spare me and told them that I knew now what they wanted me to do on earth, and I would do it if I could.

All at once I was not afraid any more, and I thought that if I was killed, probably I might be better off in the other world. So I lay down there in the center of the sacred place and offered the pipe again. Then I drew the bison robe over me and waited. All around me growled and roared the voices, and the hail was like the drums of many giants beating while the giants sang: "Hey-a-hey!"

No hail fell there in the sacred circle where I lay, nor any rain. And when the storm was passed, I raised my robe and listened; and in the stillness I could hear the rain-flood singing in the gulches all around me in the darkness, and far away to eastward there were dying voices calling: "Hey-a-hey!"

The night was old by now, and soon I fell asleep. And as I slept I saw my people sitting sad and troubled all around a sacred tepee, and there were many who were sick. And as I looked on them and wept, a strange light leaped upward from the ground close by—a light of many colors, sparkling, with rays that touched the heavens. Then it was gone, and in the place from whence it sprang a herb was growing and I saw the leaves it had. And as I was looking at the herb so that I might not forget it, there was a voice that 'woke me, and it said: "Make haste! Your people need you!"

I looked and saw the east was just beginning to turn white. Standing up, I faced the young light and began to mourn again and pray. Then the daybreak star came slowly, very beautiful and still; and all around it there were clouds of baby faces smiling at me, the faces of the people not yet born. The stars about them now were beautiful with many colors, and beneath these there were heads of men and women moving around, and birds were singing somewhere yonder and there were horses nickering and blowing as they do when they are happy, and somewhere deer were whistling and there were bison mooing too. What I could not see of this, I heard.

—English version through JOHN G. NEIHARDT. Born "in the Moon of the Popping Trees (December) on the Little Powder River in the Winter when the Four Crows Were Killed (1863)." Died August 1950 on the Pine Ridge Reservation, Manderson, South Dakota. A "holy man" or "priest" *(wichasha wakon)* of the Oglala Sioux and, like his second cousin Crazy Horse, a great "visionary seer." Like other poets his vision has had its delayed impact on a later generation, and his influence on the native imagination (both Indian and White) can hardly yet be measured. His books are *Black Elk Speaks* and *The Sacred Pipe.*

A SELECTION: POEMS AS VISION AND MAGIC: A grouping (more or less chronological) follows of poems in which (1) the poets are attempting to explore a language conveying states of intensity sometimes experienced in vision, dream, and madness; and/or (2) the overt subject is magic, as an area in which such language and experience find a context. A thrust of this kind has been central to modern poetry and thought from Poe, Rimbaud, and the Surrealists to those contemporary poets who see the poetic act as ritual.

■ *" To write a dream, which shall resemble the real course of a dream, with all its inconsistency, its strange transformations, which are all taken as a matter of course, its eccentricities and aimlessness—with nevertheless a leading idea running through the whole. Up to this old age of the world, no such thing ever has been written. "*

—NATHANIEL HAWTHORNE, from *The American Notebooks*

WALT WHITMAN
Fragment from "The Sleepers"

Pier that I saw dimly last night when I looked from the
    windows,
Pier out from the main, let me catch myself with you and stay
    . . . I will not chafe you:
I feel ashamed to go naked about the world

And am curious to know where my feet stand . . . and what is
    this flooding me, childhood or manhood . . . and the
    hunger that crosses the bridge between.

The cloth laps a first sweet eating and drinking,
Laps life-swelling yolks . . . laps ear of rose-corn, silky and
    just ripened:
The white teeth stay, and the boss-tooth advances in darkness,
And liquor is spilled on lips and bosoms by touching glasses,
    and the best liquor afterward.

EDGAR ALLAN POE

From The Narrative of A. Gordon Pym

March 8th. To-day there floated by us one of the white
animals whose appearance upon the beach at Tsalal had
occasioned so wild a commotion among the savages. I
would have picked it up, but there came over me a sudden
listlessness, and I forbore. The heat of the water still in-
creased, and the hand could no longer be endured within
it. Peters spoke little, and I knew not what to think of his
apathy. Nu-Nu breathed, and no more.

March 9th. The whole ashy material fell now continu-
ally around us and in vast quantities. The range of vapor
to the southward had arisen prodigiously in the horizon,
and began to assume more distinctness of form. I can liken
it to nothing but a limitless cataract, rolling silently into
the sea from some immense and far-distant rampart in the
heaven. The gigantic curtain ranged along the whole ex-
tent of the southern horizon. It emitted no sound.

March 21st. A sullen darkness now hovered above us—
but from out the milky depths of the ocean a luminous
glare arose, and stole up along the bulwarks of the boat.
We were nearly overwhelmed by the white ashy shower
which settled upon us and upon the canoe, but melted into
the water as it fell. The summit of the cataract was utterly
lost in the dimness and the distance. Yet we were evidently
approaching it with a hideous velocity. At intervals there
were visible in it wide, yawning, but momentary rents, and
from out these rents, within which was a chaos of flitting
and indistinct images, there came rushing and mighty, but

soundless winds, tearing up the enkindled ocean in their course.

March 22d. The darkness had materially increased, relieved only by the glare of the water thrown back from the white curtain before us. Many gigantic and pallidly white birds flew continuously now from beyond the veil, and their scream was the eternal *Tekeli-li!* as they retreated from our vision. Hereupon Nu-Nu stirred in the bottom of the boat; but upon touching him, we found his spirit departed. And now we rushed into the embraces of the cataract, where a chasm threw itself open to receive us. But there arose in our pathway a shrouded human figure, very far larger in its proportions than any dweller among men. And the hue of the skin of the figure was of the perfect whiteness of the snow.

FITZHUGH LUDLOW

From The Hasheesh Eater

I stood in a large apartment, which resembled the Senate-chamber at Washington more than any thing else to which I can compare it. Its roof was vaulted, and at the side opposite the entrance the floor rose into a dais surmounted by a large arm-chair. The body of the house was occupied by similar chairs disposed in arcs; the heavy paneling of the walls was adorned with grotesque frescoes of every imaginable bird, beast, and monster, which, by some hidden law of life and motion, were forever changing, like the figures of the kaleidoscope. Now the walls bristled with hippogriffs; now, from wainscot to ceiling, toucans and maccataws swung and nodded from their perches amid emerald palms; now Centaurs and Lapithae clashed in ferocious turmoil, which crater and cyathus were crushed beneath ringing hoof and heel. But my attention was quickly distracted from the frescoes by the sight of a most witchly congress, which filled all the chairs of that broad chamber. On the dais sat an old crone, whose commanding position first engaged my attention to her personal appearance, and, upon rather impolite scrutiny, I beheld that she was the product of an art held in pre-eminent favor among persons of her age and sex. She was *knit* of purple yarn! In faultless order the stitches ran along her face; in every pucker of her re-entrant mouth, in every wrinkle of her brow, she was a yarny counterfeit of the grandam of actual life, and by some skillful process of stuffing her nose had received its due peak and her chin its projection. The occupants of the seats below were all but reproductions of their president, and both she and they were constantly swaying from side to side, forward and back, to the music of some invisible instruments, whose tone and style were mostly intensely and ludicrously Ethiopian. Not a word was spoken by any of the woolly conclave, but with untiring industry they were all knitting, knitting, knitting, ceaselessly, as if their lives depended on it. I looked to see the objects of their manufacture. They were knitting old women like themselves! One of the sisterhood had nearly brought her double to completion; earnestly another was engaged in rounding out an eyeball; another was fastening the gathers at the corner of a mouth; another was setting up stitches for an old woman in petto.

With marvelous rapidity this work went on; ever and anon some completed crone sprang from the needles which had just achieved her, and, instantly vivified, took up the instruments of reproduction, and fell to work as assiduously as if she had been a member of the congress since the world began. "Here," I cried, "here, at last do I realize the meaning of endless progression!" and, though the dome echoed with my peals of laughter, I saw no motion of astonishment in the stitches of a single face, but, as for dear life, the manufacture of old women went on unobstructed by the involuntary rudeness of the stranger.

NOTE: At the end of his mid-nineteenth-century account of hashish visions, etc., FITZHUGH LUDLOW wrote: "In view of that which I saw ... I felt, and still feel, forced to the conclusion that there is no boundary." [1857]

EMILY DICKINSON

"I Think I Was Enchanted"

I think I was enchanted
When first a sombre Girl—
I read that Foreign Lady—
The Dark—felt beautiful—

And whether it was noon at night—
Or only Heaven—at Noon—
For very Lunacy of Light
I had not power to tell—

The Bees—became as Butterflies—
The Butterflies—as Swans—
Approached—and spurned the narrow Grass—
And just the meanest Tunes

That Nature murmured to herself
To keep herself in Cheer—
I took for Giants—practising
Titanic Opera—

The Days—to Mighty Metres stept—
The Homeliest—adorned
As if unto a Jubilee
'Twere suddenly confirmed—

I could not have defined the change—
Conversion of the Mind
Like Sanctifying in the Soul—
Is witnessed—not explained—

Twas a Divine Insanity—
The Danger to be Sane
Should I again experience—
'Tis Antidote to turn—

To Tomes of solid Witchcraft—
Magicians be asleep—
But Magic—hath an Element
Like Deity—to keep—

STEPHEN CRANE

Poem

On the desert
A silence from the moon's deepest valley.
Fire rays fall athwart the robes
Of hooded men, squat and dumb.
Before them, a woman
Moves to the blowing of shrill whistles
And distant thunder of drums,
While mystic things, sinuous, dull with terrible color,
Sleepily fondle her body
Or move at her will, swishing stealthily over the sand.
Tne snakes whisper softly;
The whispering, whispering snakes,
Dreaming and swaying and staring,
But always whispering, softly whispering.
The wind streams from the lone reaches
Of Arabia, solemn with night,
And the wild fire makes shimmer of blood
Over the robes of the hooded men
Squat and dumb.
Bands of moving bronze, emerald, yellow,
Circle the throat and the arms of her,
And over the sands serpents move warily
Slow, menacing and submissive,
Swinging to the whistles and drums,
The whispering, whispering snakes,
Dreaming and swaying and staring,
But always whispering, softly whispering.
The dignity of the accursèd;
The glory of slavery, despair, death,
Is in the dance of the whispering snakes.

    —From *War is Kind* [1899]

GERTRUDE STEIN
Birds

I counted the lights. They were harmless. Hands and hands or heads. Jelly fish. Belching. Degrees of movement. Entangling. Entangling boats. Hands have that steaming.

He wanted to show the portrait.

Occasionally he buried the fire-tongs. Put up a cross. And prayed.

She addressed her grandmother.

I do not like the name Bartholomew. Not because of the associations. Not because of Mary Rose. Not a bit kindly. I think it is a disgrace.

This isn't at all what I mentioned. She saw the same traitor.

BOB BROWN
Houdini   [1934]

Houdini; you are the loaves and the fishes
self-contained three-ring circus
hanging from the chandelier
by your rosined pink heels
you pick up needles from the parlor carpet
with lightening lashes
in the thunderous clap of an eye

at the miraculous age of eight
scattering breathless wonders upside down

materializing your stage name
out of a second hand copy of
The Works of Robert Houdin
French diplomat and master magician
inhaling the exact name for you
shaking it full-blown out of thin air
with a deep-sweeping bow

Houdini; I see you shouldering loads of
second hand rusty locks

from the town dump
lugging them home to practice on
picking them as a maestro plucks strings
making them a vibrant part of you

As a youth doing your turn
along side museum freaks
fraternizing with the Dog-faced Boy
studying art in the gallery
on the Tattooed Lady's thighs
feeding nails to the Human Ostrich
hollaring This Way, Ladies and Gents
All For a Thin Dime!

You, American Indian medicine man and
Salem witch spiritualist by turns

Wrapping the Bearded Lady's sneezing pug
in a warm side-show blanket
tucking it all cuddle-cozy into
The Marvellous Midget's thumbnail bed
Untying knots with your toes for practice
ripping endless needles out of your mouth
whetting the Sword-Swallower's knives
keeping the hand sharper than the eye
heating nursing bottles for
The Hoboken Siamese Twins
making finger-noses at Grimm
The Fairytale Giant.

Hush, Houdini: you are as much an American miracle
as Edgar Allen Poe
as great a prodigy and pride
acclaimed in Paris, Berlin and Budapest
mystifier of misty jail wardens
now they see you, now they don't!

Caught in a spider web of chains
an upside down ceiling fly

padlocked grinding chin to knocking knees
locked naked as a Follies girl
into the warden's surest cell
in eight minutes by the town clock
you appear all bows and smiles
fully dressed as an archbishop
on the stage of your awed theater
a mile and a half away

Blindfold watch-number reader
every trick in the pack for you,
picker of pockets and padlock
finder of needles in hay-stacks

At the age of eight
already a circus in yourself
I see you always swinging in three rings
ablaze from the parlor chandelier
winking up specks of strewn needles
in the miraculous twitch of an eye.

EUGENE JOLAS

We Meet the Old Griper   [A Mythdream]

We were walking through a jungle. Held back by the lianae, we had difficulty in getting ahead. The sun stood high over the green baldachin, and we felt the enormous weight of noon. Not a word was exchanged between us, yet we knew each other's thoughts. We were on our way to a sun-palace hidden in the leafwhorl of the forest.

We saw a camp fire. Five Indians were sitting around the flames. They were clad in briar-clothes and had big sombreros. We stopped and looked at them. At first they did not seem to notice us. They had their backs turned and were occupied with something around the fire.

One of the Indios got up, and we saw they were roasting a live monkey. The benign face of the animal struck us with a sense of horror. It seemed to enjoy the cruelty of its fate. From time to time one of the Indians changed the monkey's position over the fire, because one of the legs was roasting too slowly. The head, too, needed better grilling, and for that reason it was frequently dipped into a particularly strong flame.

The sight of the spectacle made us wince. You hid your face in your hand and moaned softly. I went nearer the fire and began to talk to the Indians. They invited me to take part in the feast they were preparing. A woman, who, nudesprawling, had been lying near the fire, rose and welcomed us.

–Here you meet the Name-Makers, she said.

A long sizzle-silence.

—Do you want to be a Whoom or a Wheem? I was asked.

I could not answer.

A drum was brought, a gigantic drum, with mystery-signs and alchemy-letters colour-scribbled on the skin. One of the men tamtam-boomed on it, it was a demon-blast, it was a startle-thunder that nerve-bored weirdly.

Then they sang stentor-words and shrill-names for a long time.

The monkey was torch-roasting.

The leader of the Indians, a tall, dignified-looking old man, then made a speech from which I gathered that a priest, who had killed their deer, would be roasted like the monkey. He painted the picture of the new sacrifice with a passion that carried him off his feet. He anticipated the whimpering and screaming of the victim with a quiet sense of enjoyment.

I went back to you and said:

—How strange, the people call God the *Old Griper.*

This information occupied us for a long time. We tried to interpret the statement in our own occidental white way. You said that in your childhood there had been a coloured teacher in your home city of Louisville, Kentucky, whom you called by the same name.

We walked on through the brush. The palace we were looking for seemed farther than ever. We knew that we would never find it, for there were so many sacrifices to be made that we felt we lacked the necessary courage for the undertaking.

"HOODOO, A SUPPRESSED RELIGION": Hoodoo—African in origin— is related to Haitian voodoo, from Dahomeyan *vodoun*. In the United States it centered around *doctors,* who drew powers from gods and animals but also from knowledge of the roots and spells. Zora Neale Hurston wrote (1935): "Hoodoo . . . is burning with a flame in America, with all the intensity of a suppressed religion. . . . Nobody knows for sure how many thousands . . . are warmed by the fire of hoodoo, because the worship is bound in secrecy. It is not the accepted theology of the Nation and so believers conceal their faith. Brother from sister, husband from wife. Nobody can say where it begins or ends. Mouths don't empty themselves unless the ears are sympathetic and knowing." (In *Mules and Men,*1935)

[HOODOO]

From Hoodoo—Conjuration—Witchcraft— Rootwork

MY FIRST DOCTOR

I'M A SHIEL' MAN
NOTHIN' "HURT" ME BUT A LICK
A BRICKBAT—A PISTOL—OR A KNIFE

I TAKE A DECK OF CARDS AN' TELL ANYBODY
MORE 'AN THEY WAN'A KNOW

I KIN WALK ALONG DE STREET AN' LOOK AT A PERSON
AN' TELL W'UTHER THEY'S "HURT" OR NOT

I'M YOUR BLACK JESUS

—Richmond, Virginia

GUINEA PIG AND TOADFROG

AH WUZ BO'N WIT DIS

AH KETCH ME A TOADFROG. . . .
AH'VE GOT CHURE PITCHURE IN MAH MIND. . . .
AN' WHIP DAT FROG AN' STOB HIM
DIE YO' OLE SON-OF-A-BITCH
DIE! DIE!

—Memphis, Tennessee

DARK GLASSES—DARK LADY—DARK DEEDS

HE MAY BE A FINE MAN LAK YO'
BUT WHEN DAT STUFF FINISH WIT DAT MAN
HE WON'T BE AS LARGE AS ME . . .
DAT'S WHUT YO' CALL
"YO' PUT 'EM ON A DRAG"

AH SENT A MANY AN' AH'LL SEND MO', TOO
AH'M TELLIN' YO'
AH SEND 'EM, SEE
AN' DEY GOTTA GO, YESSUH

WHEN DAT HAPPEN, HONEY
AH'M TELLIN' YO' IT'S TOUGH
OH YES, IT'S TOUGH
SOME WORKS AH'M TELLIN' YO'

WHEN YO' GIT IN TOUCH WIT DE FO'K OF DE ROAD
YO' GITTIN' IN TOUCH WIT A WHOLE LOT, MAH BOY . . .
YO'LL SEE A MAN APPEAR TO YO' IN BLACK
IN A BLACK GOWN
DAT'S DAT MAN DAT CONTROLS DAT FO'K OF DE ROAD
AND DEN HE APPEARS TUH YO' IF YO' WANS A GIFT

ALL YO' GOTTA DO

IS DO JIS' LAK AH'M TELLIN' YO'
HONEY, YO' HEAH WHUT AH'M TELLIN' YO'
AN' YO'LL CERTAINLY SUCCEED

—Algiers, Louisiana

—Transcribed by HARRY M. HYATT

HYATT'S texts—which he uses as chapter titles—consist of quoted remarks juxtaposed to characterize each of the Hoodoo "doctors" he interviewed.

WILLIAM FAULKNER

Coffin

[From *"As I Lay Dying"*]

Cash speaking:

I MADE IT ON THE BEVEL.

1. There is more surface for the nails to grip.
2. There is twice the gripping-surface to each seam.
3. The water will have to seep into it on a slant. Water moves easiest up and down or straight across.
4. In a house people are upright two-thirds of the time. So the seams and joints are made up-and-down. Because the stress is up-and-down.
5. In a bed where people lie down all the time, the joints and seams are made sideways, because the stress is sideways.
6. Except.
7. A body is not square like a cross-tie.
8. Animal magnetism.
9. The animal magnetism of a dead body makes the stress come slanting, so the seams and joints of a coffin are made on the bevel.
10. You can see by an old grave that the earth sinks down on the bevel.
11. While in a natural hole it sinks by the centre, the stress being up-and-down.
12. So I made it on the bevel.
13. It makes a neater job.

KENNETH FEARING

The Face in the Bar Room Mirror

Fifteen gentlemen in fifteen overcoats and fifteen hats holding
    fifteen glasses in fifteen hands,
Staring and staring at fifteen faces reflected in the mirror
    behind the polished bar,
Tonight, as last night,
And the night before that, and night after night, after night,
    after night—

What are they dreaming of,
Why do they come here and when will it happen, that thing
    for which they return and return,
To stand and wait, and wait, and wait, and wait—

What fifteen resolves are growing clear and hard, between
    cryptic remarks, in those fifteen living silences,
What crystal stairs do they climb or descend into fifteen
    unseen heavens or hells,
What fifteen replies do they give the single question, does
    anything on earth ever change, or stay?—

Before the shot rings out, the mirror shatters, the floor gapes
    open and the heavens fall,
And they go at last on their fifteen separate, purposeful
    ways—

Fifteen magicians,
Masters of escape from handcuff and rope, straitjacket,
    padlock, dungeon and chain,
Now planning escapes still more dazzling,
And fifteen times more terrible than these.

The People v. The People

I have never seen him, this invisible member of the panel,
      this thirteenth juror, but I have certain clues;
I know, after so many years of practice, though I cannot prove
      I know;
It is enough to say, I know that I know.

He is five feet nine or ten, with piercing, bright, triumphant
      eyes;
He needs glasses, which he will not wear, and he is almost
      certainly stone deaf.
(Cf. Blair v. Gregg, which he utterly ruined.)
He is the juror forever looking out of the window, secretly
      smiling, when you make your telling point.
The one who is wide awake when you think he is asleep. The
      man who naps with his eyes wide open.
Those same triumphant eyes.
He is the man who knows. And knows that he knows.

His hair is meager and he wears wash ties, but these are not
      important points.
He likes the legal atmosphere, that is plain, because he is
      always there.
It is the decent, the orderly procedure that he likes.
He is the juror who arrived first, though you thought he was
      late; the one who failed to return from lunch, though
      you had not noticed.

Let me put it like this: He is the cause of your vague
      uneasiness when you glance about and see that the
      other twelve are all right.

I would know him if I were to see him, I could swear to his
      identity, if I actually saw him once;
I nearly overheard him, when I was for the defense: "They
      never indict anyone unless they are guilty;"
And when I was the State: "A poor man (or a rich man)
      doesn't stand a chance."

Always, before the trial's end, he wants to know if the
    sergeant knew the moon was full on that particular
    night.

And none of this matters, except I am convinced he is the
    unseen juror bribed, bought, and planted by The People,
An enemy of reason and precedent, a friend of illogic,
Something, I now know, that I know that I really know—

And he or anyone else is welcome to my Blackstone, or my
    crowded shelves of standard books,
In exchange for the monumental works I am convinced he
    has been writing through the years:
"The Rules of Hearsay;" "The Laws of Rumor;"
"An Omnibus Guide to Chance and Superstition," by One Who
    Knows.

> Two poems from *Stranger at Coney Island* [1944], a book which
> should be read as a poetic sequence, suggesting in its cumulative
> effect that Fearing was not only a social and satirical poet but a
> special kind of visionary.

ANAÏS NIN

From The House of Incest

She led me into the house of incest. It was the only house
which was not included in the twelve houses of the zodiac.
It could neither be reached by the route of the milky way,
nor by the glass ship through whose transparent bottom
one could follow the outline of the lost continents, nor by
following the arrows pointing the direction of the wind,
nor by following the voice of the mountain echoes.

    The rooms were chained together by steps—no room
was on a level with another—and all the steps were deeply
worn. There were windows between the rooms, little spy-
ing-eyed windows, so that one might talk in the dark from
room to room, without seeing the other's face. The rooms
were filled with the rhythmic heaving of the sea coming
from many sea-shells. The windows gave out on a static
sea, where immobile fishes had been glued to painted
backgrounds. Everything had been made to stand still in

the house of incest, because they all had such a fear of movement and warmth, such a fear that all love and all life should flow out of reach and be lost!

Everything had been made to stand still, and everything was rotting away. The sun had been nailed in the roof of the sky and the moon beaten deep into its Oriental niche.

In the house of incest there was a room which could not be found, a room without window, the fortress of their love, a room without window where the mind and blood coalesced in a union without orgasm and rootless like those of fishes. The promiscuity of glances, of phrases, like sparks marrying in space. The collision between their resemblances, shedding the order of tamarisk and sand, of rotted shells and dying sea-weeds, their love like the ink of squids, a banquet of poisons.

Stumbling from room to room I came into the room of paintings, and there sat Lot with his hand upon his daughter's breast while the city burned behind them, cracking open and falling into the sea. There where he sat with his daughter the Oriental rug was red and stiff, but the turmoil which shook them showed through the rocks splitting around them, through the earth yawning beneath their feet, through the trees flaming up like torches, through the sky smoking and smouldering red, all cracking with the joy and terror of their love. Joy of the father's hand upon the daughter's breast, the joy of the fear racking her. Her costume tightly pressed around her so that her breasts heave and swell under his fingers, while the city is rent by lightning, and spits under the teeth of fire, great blocks of a gaping ripped city sinking with the horror of obscenity, and falling into the sea with the hiss of the eternally damned. No cry of horror from Lot and his daughter but from the city in flames, from an unquenchable desire of father and daughter, of brother and sister, mother and son.

I looked upon a clock to find the truth. The hours were passing like ivory chess figures, striking piano notes, and the minutes raced on wires mounted like tin soldiers. Hours like tall ebony women with gongs between their legs, tolling continuously so that I could not count them. I heard the tolling of my heart-beats; I heard the footsteps of my dreams, and the beat of time was lost among them like the face of truth.

• • •

I came upon a forest of decapitated trees, women carved out of bamboo, flesh slatted like that of slaves in joyless slavery, faces cut in two by the sculptor's knife, showing two sides forever separate, eternally two-faced, and it was I who had to shift about to behold the entire woman. Truncated undecagon figures, eleven sides, eleven angles, in veined and vulnerable woods, fragments of bodies, bodies armless and headless. The torso of a tube-rose, the knee of Achilles, tubercles and excrescences, the foot of a mummy in rotted wood, the veined docile wood carved into human contortions. The forest must weep and bend like the shoulders of men, dead figures inside of live trees. A forest animated now with intellectual faces, intellectual contortions. Trees become man and woman, two-faced, nostalgic for the shivering of leaves. Trees reclining, woods shining, and the forest trembling with rebellion so bitter I heard its wailing within its deep forest consciousness. Wailing the loss of its leaves and the failure of transmutation.

Further a forest of white plaster, white plaster eggs. Large white eggs on silver disks, an elegy to birth, each egg a promise, each half-shaped nascence of man or woman or animal not yet precise. Womb and seed and egg, the moist beginning being worshipped rather than its flowering. The eggs so white, so still, gave birth to hope without breaking, but the cut-down tree lying there produced a green live branch that laughed at the sculptor.

KENNETH PATCHEN

The Outlaw of the Lowest Planet

If someone is pleased to boast
Of inner knowledge, then let him test
My power to question his truth; permit him to rally
His hosts—for I am going to tear the tongue
Out of his lying mouth; I am going to increase
His heat until he beg mercy—this is not to be spooned up
Like alchemical water to make golden
The matted corpse in his bed.
These are pictures of heaven.
      (I defy him to offer his greasy work!)

As you stand on the first level two women
Approach slowly from a kind of glass temple.
They are covered with a substance which begins to soften
As you watch; until afterwards, and you are nearly blind,
The bodies are seen to be hollow—only the organs
Of the spirit remain, only the dress of its radiance
Shines about them; and instead of our animal odors,
They smell of God. But these are now joined by colors
Which boil up on the white hills like great birds
Out of the water. And the nature of this kingdom
Is not hidden in their light, but separates the watcher
Into his various heights—we are beginning to learn
To hasten the tongue beyond the reversing vanities
Of what is thought to be in the head. *Speech of the eye!*
The villages in heaven have been named
After the seven daughters of God, and each has
Twenty colors in its air. All in consequence are nothing
When any one is dark.

    The villages are thus known: *Lenada,*
    where the windflowers were manipulated
    by blind larks; *Rallas,* upon whose fields
    the stones danced with elephants; *Volba,*
    the original site of the pliant fish; *Dusda,*
    in which the squatic infants were conceived;
    Onega, where death's cathedral stands; *Criha,*
    at the center of which is a black crown; and *Mega,*
    in whose houses the hour of death is made bright.

What is running with naked legs
Beside the green wall? It is not the minstrel.
What is running with bowed head
Under the golden world? It has no mastery.
It has no landscapes in its hand.
It has no climate save its murder.
Speech of the throned heart.
As you stand on the second level a figure
Detaches itself from the surrounding haze;
And it puts its forehead against the distance,
Crying softly like a frightened kitten.
A corridor opens on a temple of birds.
Two red leopards walk into a child
Whose tiny hands hold a three-pronged staff.

Suddenly a moon shaped like a horse
Lowers its muzzle into the river and drinks.
Beyond the crowded wall a hand
Reaches into the sky and lowers Mary down—
She is draped in wild splendor
Like an African queen.
There are three eyes on Her dancing.
And this is silence of the morning world.
Here stand the Silent Ones whose hearts
Are wedded to God. O I lift my song to Him!
Have I not ever lain in His nocturnal grove—
O what laments upon the night
Has there its gentle home.
What is weeping in terrible love
Under this broken world?
It is surely lost upon these whirling spaces.
What cries in its divided roots
Beneath this measuring peace?
O there is no mystery in death.
Speech of the consoling heart.
As you stand on the third level the sky fills
With gigantic white deer, and their eyes
Glow like the thunderflowers of summer.
On their antlers baby angels sleep. Knowledge
Is not their horizon. Beyond all reason they walk,
And their summit remembers not the wintry kingdoms
Of the earth. The sealed vaults of eternity open
Beneath their triumphant hoofs. Unchristened saviors
Dwell in their sweet kirks.
    Upon their shoulders perfection flutters
Like a silver bird. The shadow of hunting
Does not stain their pure breath.
Sometimes this God-fired jungle
Flames with newer life . . . phantom tigers
Tremble on the brink of dark pools which reflect
The lolling eye of greater heavens. Burning apples
Fall from orchards in lands where not even God
Has been

                      •   •   •

And the guardian mysteries softly call to Him.

THEODORE ROETHKE
Unfold! Unfold!

1

By snails, by leaps of frog, I came here, spirit.
Tell me, body without skin, does a fish sweat?
I can't crawl back through those veins,
I ache for another choice.
The cliffs! The cliffs! They fling me back.
Eternity howls in the last crags,
The field is no longer simple:
It's a soul's crossing time.
The dead speak noise.

2

It's time you stood up and asked
          —Or sat down and did.
A tongue without song
          —Can still whistle in a jug.
Your're blistered all over
          —Who cares? The old owl?
When you find the wind
          —Look for the white fire.

3

What a whelm of proverbs, Mr. Pinch!
Are the entrails clear, immaculate cabbage?
The last time I nearly whispered myself away.
I was far back, farther than anybody else.
On the jackpine plains I hunted the bird nobody knows;
Fishing, I caught myself behind the ears.
Alone, in a sleep-daze, I stared at billboards;
I was privy to oily fungus and the algae of standing waters;
Honored, on my return, by the ancient fellowship of rotten
    stems.
I was pure as a worm on a leaf; I cherished the mold's
    children.

Beetles sweetened my breath.
I slept like an insect.

I met a collector of string, a shepherd of slow forms.
My mission became the salvation of minnows.
I stretched like a board, almost a tree.
Even thread had a speech.

Later, I did and I danced in the simple wood.
A mouse taught me how, I was a happy asker.
Quite-by-chance brought me many cookies.
I jumped in butter.
Hair had kisses.

4

Easy the life of the mouth. What a lust for ripeness!
All openings praise us, even oily holes.
The bulb unravels. Who's floating? Not me.
The eye perishes in the small vision.
What else has the vine loosened?
I hear a dead tongue halloo.

5

Sing, sing, you symbols! All simple creatures,
All small shapes, willow-shy,
In the obscure haze, sing!

A light song comes from the leaves.
A slow sigh says yes. And light sighs;
A low voice, summer-sad.
Is it you, cold father? Father,
For whom the minnows sang?

A house for wisdom; a field for revelation.
Speak to the stones, and the stars answer.
At first the visible obscures:
Go where light is.

This fat can't laugh.
Only my salt has a chance.

I'll seek my own meekness.
What grace I have is enough.
The lost have their own pace.
The stalks ask something else.
What the grave says,
The nest denies.

In their harsh thickets
The dead thrash.
They help.

DAVID IGNATOW

Ritual One

As I enter the theatre the play is going on.
I hear the father say to the son on stage,
You've taken the motor apart.
The son replies, The roof is leaking.
The father retorts, The tire is flat.
Tiptoeing down the aisle, I find my seat,
edge my way in across a dozen kneecaps
as I tremble for my sanity.
I have heard doomed voices calling on god the electrode.
Sure enough, as I start to sit
a scream rises from beneath me.
It is one of the players.
If I come down, I'll break his neck,
caught between the seat and the backrest.
Now the audience and the players on stage,
their heads turned towards me, are waiting
for the sound of the break. Must I?
Those in my aisle nod slowly, reading my mind,
their eyes fixed on me, and I understand
that each has done the same.

Must I kill this man as the price of my admission
to this play? His screams continue loud and long.
I am at a loss as to what to do,
I panic, I freeze.

My training has been to eat the flesh of pig.
I might even have been able to slit a throat.
As a child I witnessed the dead chickens
over a barrel of sawdust absorbing their blood.
I then brought them in a bag to my father
who sold them across his counter. Liking him,
I learned to like people and enjoy their company too,
which of course brought me to this play.
But how angry I become.
Now everybody is shouting at me to sit down,
sit down or I'll be thrown out.
The father and son have stepped off stage
and come striding down the aisle side by side.
They reach me, grab me by the shoulder
and force me down. I scream, I scream,
as if to cover the sound of the neck breaking.

All through the play I scream
and am invited on stage to take a bow.
I lose my senses and kick the actors in the teeth.
There is more laughter
and the actors acknowledge my performance with a bow.
How should I understand this?
Is it to say that if I machine-gun the theatre
from left to right they will respond with applause
that would only gradually diminish with each death?
I wonder then whether logically I should kill myself
too out of admiration. A question indeed,
as I return to my seat and observe a new act
of children playfully aiming their kicks
at each other's groins.

KEITH WILSON

Coyote

here in New Mexico *coyote*
means many things, human
inhuman

      the pretty girl
sitting at my table says
"tu sabes, yo soy una coyote."
half Anglo, half Spanish

an outcast, claimed by none
but her Eastern boyfriend, me,
& my whole family

the split body of one
struck by a car, entrails
bright red—&—white, head
lolling

      that quick shadow
against the moontipped hill,
a god of laughter tracing
his trails through blue blue
hills, his lean nose sniffing
prying

      big bush tails
& thick fur are not for him
—he travels light & far

many of us would walk his trail
know him, follow his sign to where
it ends, by the northern rim of the sun.

ALLEN GINSBERG
Psalm IV

Now I'll record my secret vision, impossible sight of the face
of God:
It was no dream, I lay broad waking on a fabulous couch in
Harlem
having masturbated for no love, and read half naked an open
book of Blake on my lap
Lo & behold! I was thoughtless and turned a page and gazed
on the living Sun-flower
and heard a voice, it was Blake's, reciting in earthen measure:
the voice rose out of the page to my secret ear that had never
heard before—
I lifted my eyes to the window, red walls of buildings flashed
outside, endless sky sad in Eternity,
the sunlight gazing on the world, apartments of Harlem
standing in the universe—
each brick and cornice stained with intelligence like a vast
living face—
the great brain unfolding and brooding in wilderness!—Now
speaking aloud with Blake's voice—
Love! thou patient presence & bone of the body! Father! thy
careful watching and waiting over my soul!
My son! My son! the endless ages have remembered me! My
son! My son! Time howled in anguish in my ear!
My son! My son! my father wept and held me in his dead
arms.

PAUL BLACKBURN
At the Well

Here we are, see?
in this village, maybe a camp
middle of desert, the
Maghreb, desert below Marrakesh

standing in the street
simply.

> Outskirts of the camp
> at the edge of town, these riders
> on camels or horses,
> but riders, tribesmen, sitting
> there, on their horses.

>> They are mute.   They are
>> hirsute, they are not
>> able to speak. If they
>> could, the sound would be guttural.
>> They cannot speak. They want
>> something.

I nor
you know what they want   •   They want
nothing.   They are beyond want.   They need
nothing.   They used to be slaves.   They
want something of us   /   of me   /   what
shall I say to them.

> They have had their tongues cut out.
> I have nothing to give to them. Yi!   There is no
> grace at the edge of my heart I would grant,
> render them?   They want something, they
> sit there on their horses.   Are there
> children in the village I can give them.

> My child's heart?   Is it goods they want
> as tribute.   They have had their tongues
> cut out, can I offer them some sound
> my mouth makes in the night?   Can I
> say that they are brave, fierce, im-
> placable?   that I would like to
> join them?
>> L e t   u s   g o   t o g e t h e r

across the desert toward the
cities, let us
terrify the towns, the villages,
disappear among bazaars, sell our
camels, pierce our ears, for-
get that we are mute and drive
the princes out, take all the
slave-girls for ourselves?
What can I offer them.

They have appeared here on the edge of my soul.
I ask them what they want, they say
—You are our leader.   Tell us what
your pleasure is, we
want you.   They
say nothing   •   They

are mute.   They are hirsute.   They
are the fathers I never had.   They are
tribesmen standing on the edge of town near
water, near the soul I must look into each
morning   •   myself

> W h o   a r e   t h e s e   w i l d   m e n ?

I scream:
                —I want my gods!
                    I want my gods!   I want
    my reflection in the sun's pool at morning,
            shade in the afternoon under the
                    date-palms,   I want and want!

What can I give them.
What tribe of nomads and wanderers am I a continuation of,
        what
can I give my fathers?
What can I offer myself.

I want to see my own skin
at the life's edge, at the
life-giving water.   I want
to rise from the pool,
             mount my camel and
be among the living, the other side of this village.

                    Come gentlemen,
                    wheel your mounts about.
                    There is nothing here.

RUSSEL EDSON
The Angel

While waiting for a small animal to descend into her head, a woman was telling herself a story: It is the angel mouse that comes out of a small hole in the sky and scampers along the sunset until the darkness allows its passage into the head.

Then it looks out of one of your eyes at your terrible world, and chirps with horror.

Then it eats some of your brain which carried the memory of your mother.

Soon the angel mouse is busy cutting the nerve strings of your senses. It all goes dark. But then the mouse stuffs the string into its own head, and you remember nothing save small dark corridors, and small furry bodies with long tails scampering ahead and behind you through endless corridors . . .

PHILIP LAMANTIA
The Diabolic Condition

As the women who live within each other's bodies
descend from their polar regions
to the circle of demons

I become ready to offer myself to the smooth red snakes
      entwined in the heads of sorcerers

Between the black arms coming over the swamp
rushing to embrace me
and the distant sun in which abide the men who hold
      within their fists the Evil Eyes
between the tombs and beds of boneless magicians
who have worked in the secrecy of abandoned towers
despite my body flying away
despite the lizards who crawl into the altars where the
      potents are being prepared
despite the intrusion of doctor's maids and egyptologists
despite the old Doric temple carried in by the art lovers
despite the nest of mad beggars
the chant is heard
and the words of the chant are written in oceanic gardens

The flat walls are singing good-bye
we have entered the city where the dead masters speak to
      us of catacombs and the horned enchantress of Africa
The incantation is following us into the streets
and into the sky
We are ascending to the limitless cosmos of architecture
we are crawling backward to enormous hearts
that leap over the snow to climb into our bodies

Come my ritual wax and circles
my rose spitting blood
When the day is lit up by our magic candles
and the hours yell their sadistic songs and suck hard
into the night when the cats invade our skulls
then we will know the destructive ones have gone
out into the world to watch the cataclysm begin
as the final wave of fire pours out from their hearts

GALWAY KINNELL
The Hen Flower

1

Sprawled
on our faces in the spring
nights, teeth
biting down on hen feathers, bits of the hen
still stuck in the crevices—if only
we could let go
like her, throw ourselves
on the mercy of darkness, like the hen,

tuck our head
under a wing, hold ourselves still
a few moments, as she
falls out into her little trance in the witchgrass,
or turn over
and be stroked with a finger
down the throat feathers,
down the throat knuckles,
down over the hum
of the wishbone tuning its high D in thin blood,
down over
the breastbone risen up
out of breast flesh, until the fatted thing
woozes off, head
thrown back
on the chopping block, longing only
to die.

2

When the ax-
scented breeze flourishes
about her, her cheeks crush in,
her comb
grays, the gizzard

that turns the thousand acidic millstones of her fate
convulses: ready or not
the next egg, bobbling
its globe of golden earth,
skids forth, ridding her even
of the life to come.

3

Almost high
on subsided gravity, I remain afoot,
a hen flower
dangling from a hand,
wing
of my wing,
of my bones and veins,
of my flesh
hairs lifting all over me in the first ghostly breeze
after death,

wing
made only to fly—unable
to write out the sorrows of being unable
to hold another in one's arms—and unable
to fly,
and waiting, therefore,
for the sweet, eventual blaze in the genes,
that one day, according to gospel, shall carry it back
into pink skies, where geese
cross at twilight, honking
in tongues.

4

I have glimpsed
by corpse-light, in the opened cadaver
of hen, the mass of tiny,
unborn eggs, each getting
tinier and yellower as it reaches back toward
the icy pulp
of what is, I have felt the zero
freeze itself around the finger dipped slowly in.

5

When the Northern Lights
were opening across the black sky and vanishing,
lighting themselves up
so completely they were vanishing,
I put to my eye the lucent
section of the spealbone of a ram—

I thought suddenly
I could read the cosmos spelling itself,
the huge broken letters
shuddering across the black sky and vanishing,

and in a moment,
in the twinkling of an eye, it came to me
the mockingbird would sing all her nights the cry of the rifle,
the tree would hold the bones of the sniper who chose not to
      climb down,
the rose would bloom no one would see it,
the chameleon longing to be changed would remain the color
      of blood.

And I went up
to the henhouse, and took up
the hen killed by weasels, and lugged
the sucked
carcass into first light. And when I hoisted
her up among the young pines, a last
rubbery egg slipping out as I flung her high, didn't it
      happen
the dead
wings cracked open as she soared
across the arms of the Bear?

6

Sprawled face down, waiting
for the rooster to groan out
it is the empty morning, as he groaned out thrice
for the disciple

of stone,
he who crushed with his heel the brain out of the snake,

I remember long ago I sowed
my own first milk
tooth under hen feathers, I planted under hen feathers
the hook
of the wishbone,
which had broken itself so lovingly toward me.

For the future.

It has come to this.

    7

Listen, Kinnell,
dumped alive
and dying into the old sway bed,
a layer of crushed feathers all that there is
between you
and the long shaft of darkness shaped as you,
let go.

Even this haunted room
all its materials photographed with tragedy,
even the tiny crucifix drifting face down at the center of the
    earth,
even these feathers freed from their wings forever
are afraid.

JOHN GIORNO
"A Coven"

	A coven
A coven	usually
usually	consists
consists	A coven
A coven	usually consists
usually consists	of 12 witches
of 12 witches	of 12 witches
of 12 witches	(6 males,
(6 males,	6 females
6 females	6 males,
6 males,	6 females)
6 females)	and a high
and a high	priest
priest	or priestess
or priestess	and a high priest
and a high priest	or priestess.
or priestess.	

ISHMAEL REED
I Am a Cowboy in the Boat of Ra

"The devil must be forced to reveal any such physical evil (potions, charms, fetishes, etc.) still outside the body and these must be burned." —"Rituale Romanum," *published 1947, endorsed by the coat of arms and introduction letter from Francis Cardinal Spellman*

I am a cowboy in the boat of Ra,
sidewinders in the saloon of fools
bit my forehead   like   O
the untrustworthiness of Egyptologists
who do not know their trips. Who was that

dog-faced man? they asked, the day I rode
from town.

School marms with halitosis cannot see
the Nefertiti fake chipped on the run by slick
germans, the hawk behind Sonny Rollins' head or
the ritual beard of his axe; a longhorn winding
its bells thru the Field of Reeds.

I am a cowboy in the boat of Ra. I bedded
down with Isis, Lady of the Boogaloo, dove
down deep in her horny, stuck up her Wells-Far-ago
in daring midday get away. "Start grabbing the
blue," i said from the top of my double crown.

I am a cowboy in the boat of Ra. Ezzard Charles
of the Chisholm Trail. Took up the bass but they
blew off my thumb. Alchemist in ringmanship but a
sucker for the right cross.

I am a cowboy in the boat of Ra. Vamoosed from
the temple i bide my time. The price on the wanted
poster was a-going down, outlaw alias copped my stance
and moody greenhorns were making me dance; while my
       mouth's
shooting iron got its chambers jammed.

I am a cowboy in the boat of Ra. Boning-up in
the ol West i bide my time. You should see
me pick off these tin cans whippersnappers. I
write the motown long plays for the comeback of
Osiris. Make them up when stars stare at sleeping
steer out here near the campfire. Women arrive
on the backs of goats and throw themselves on
my Bowie.

I am a cowboy in the boat of Ra. Lord of the lash,
the Loup Garou Kid. Half breed son of Pisces and
Aquarius. I hold the souls of men in my pot. I do

the dirty boogie with scorpions. I make the bulls
keep still and was the first swinger to grape the taste.

I am a cowboy in his boat. Pope Joan of the
Ptah Ra. C/mere a minute willya doll?
Be a good girl and
Bring me my Buffalo horn of black powder
Bring me my headdress of black feathers
Bring me my bones of Ju-Ju snake
Go get my eyelids of red paint.
Hand me my shadow

I'm going into town after Set

I am a cowboy in the boat of Ra

look out Set   here i come Set
to get Set   to sunset Set
to unseat Set   to Set down Set

    usurper of the Royal couch
    imposter RAdio of Moses' bush
    party pooper O hater of dance
    vampire outlaw of the milky way

HARVEY BIALY

A Waratah Blossom
[*after Crowley*]

I am *outis* said Odysséus
to the blind monster
I am your master
your cave I have made a Temple
in the middle of this ocean called
the Inner Ocean
your house is now Her house
your wives will preside here
until I return
will return from under the sea

in a long ship shaped
like an oar
but you will not recognize
either my ship or me
tho' your wives
will set up a great clamor
& run down naked to the shore
to greet me
you are cruel you say
I say I am slain
you have Had It
to curse
I have no name
I am Nemo
the bringer of woe
remember me

> —OUTIS: Odysseus' cry of "No Man" in Homer.

ANDREW PEYNETSA is a traditional Zuni storyteller, some of whose narratives DENNIS TEDLOCK has translated as verse, i.e. with close attention to the sounds and silences of speech. A simplified "guide to reading aloud" follows:

> —Pauses of less than one second are indicated by line changes, pauses of two or three seconds by strophe breaks and centered dots.
> —Loud passages or words are indicated by capitals.
> —Soft passages or words are indicated by reduced type.
> —Extended vowels are indicated by a long dash.

ANDREW PEYNETSA [ZUNI]
thru Dennis Tedlock

The Shumeekuli

Well then
there were villagers at HAWIKKU
there were villagers at GYPSUM PLACE

•

there were villagers at WIND PLACE, these were the villages
and the priest
there at Gypsum Place

spoke of having a Yaaya, a Yaaya dance.
When the word went out, people from all the villages

started gathering.
The date had been set and
they lived on.

For four nights
they practiced the Yaaya.
The Yaaya practice went on, and
they were gathering:
for four nights they kept gathering.
O————n it went, until
the day came.
And the SPIRAL SOCIETY
WENT INTO SESSION, and on the eve of the ceremony
        their Shumeekuli dancers came.

The Shumeekuli came
and the next day was to be the day

for dancing the Yaaya.
Then it was the morning of the dance.
On the morning of the dance
the villagers gathered
and then
they were
getting up to dance.
O————n they went, until, at noon, they stopped to eat, and when they
        had eaten they got up again.
They got up in the afternoon

and when they had done about
two sets, there were four rings of dancers.
Then the SPIRAL SOCIETY BROUGHT IN THEIR
SHUMEEKULI
and when these were brought in, the Horned Ones were also
        brought in.

They kept on dancing this way UNTIL THEIR
White Shumeekuli came, he was brought in when
there were four rings of dancers
and all the villagers had gathered:
there was a BIG CROWD, a big crowd, and
the dance kept on.
Their White Shumeekuli
kept going around the tree. He danced around it, and for some reason
he went crazy.

•

The people HELD ON TIGHT, but somehow he broke
        through their rings and ran away.

•

He ran and ran
and they ran after him.

•

They ran after him, but
they couldn't catch him
        and still they kept after him shouting as they went.
He was far ahead, the White Shumeekuli was far ahead of them.
They kept on going until

•

they came near SHUMINNKYA.
Someone was herding out there
he was herding, his sheep were spread out there when they came shout-
        ing.

"There goes our White Shumeekuli, running away, whoever is
    out there please help us.

CATCH HIM FOR US," that's what they were shouting as they
        kept after him.
        (low and tight) "Oh yes, there's a Yaaya dance today,
        something must've happened."
That's what the herder said, and the shouting was getting close.
After a time, their Shumeekuli
came into view.

He was still running.
The herder stood under a tree where he was going to pass
and waited for him, then
going straight on
the Shumeekuli headed for
the place where the herder stood.

•

Sure enough, just as
he came up
past the TREE
the herder caught him for them.
There he caught him:
the White Shumeekuli
who had run away from the Yaaya dance.
The others came to get him
and took him back.

•

They brought him back, and when they
tried to unmask him
the mask
was stuck
to his face.
He was changing over.

•

When they unmasked the young man, some of his
flesh peeled off.

•

Then, the one who had come as the White Shumeekuli
lived only four days before he died.

•

They LIVED ON
until, at ZUNI

•

when the Middle Place had become known

•

the date was again set for the Yaaya, and when the date had been
      set they gathered for four nights.
They gathered for practice, that's the way
they lived
and when the day of the Yaaya arrived

the villagers came together on the morning of the dance.

Again the YAAYA
dance began
and again the Shumeekuli dancers were brought in.
They were brought in and they danced properly, but then
there came one who costumed himself as the White
        Shumeekuli, and he went around
until it happened AGAIN:
he went crazy.
He struggled then, but
they held onto him.
It happens whenever somebody impersonates that one:
because of the flesh that got inside that mask in former times
when someone comes into the Yaaya dance as the White
        Shumeekuli
something will inevitably happen to his mind. This is what
happened, and because this happened
the White Shumeekuli came to be feared.
That's all.

> NOTES TO SHUMEEKULI. Spiral Society: a medicine society which spe-
> cializes in curing convulsions; only its members may imitate the
> masked kachinas (the ancestral raingods) called the Shumeekuli
> and the Horned Ones. Of six kinds of Shumeekuli (yellow, blue,
> red, white, black, and multicolored) the white are most frighten-
> ing. The Shumeekuli dance inside the concentric rings of Yaaya
> dancers, who are not masked, while the Horned Ones dance out-
> side the Yaaya rings.

Sacred Plants

In this section—and still as part of the map of visions: a small anthology of plants viewed as a category of the sacred. Like animals they were once seen as living and conscious beings and, as such, could be totem-ized and made sacred. They offered food for men and animals, they were medicine, they had complex shapes that could be read prophet-ically, and they were agents that took the psyche on journeys of trans-formation to heaven or hell.

[AZTEC]

Two Mushrooms

1

It is round, large, like a severed head.

2

It grows on the plains, in the grass. The head is small and round, the stem long and slender. It is bitter and burns; it burns the throat. It makes one besotted; it deranges one, troubles one. It is a remedy for fever, for gout. Only two or three can be eaten. It saddens, depresses, troubles one; it makes one flee, frightens one, makes one hide.

He who eats many of them sees many things which make him afraid, or make him laugh. He flees, hangs him-self, hurls himself from a cliff, cries out, takes fright. One eats it in honey.

I eat mushrooms; I take mushrooms.

Of one who is haughty, presumptuous, vain, of him it is said: "He mushrooms himself."

SOURCE: Sahagún, per Anderson and Dibble; see above, page 85. [1] is *tzontecomananacatl,* probably Amanita muscaria; [2] is *teonanacatl* or Psilocybe. Both have been used as sacred plants, for which see R. Gordon Wasson's *Soma: Divine Mushroom of Immor-tality,* as indication of the scope of such practices.

JOANNA KITCHEL [SHAKER]

Song of the East [1844]

Behold a plant springeth up in the east which shall heal
    many nations; this plant saith Wisdom was by my own
    hand planted.
And a lamp goeth out of the wilderness which shall kindle a
    great burning.
France is my lamp, and England my plant, saith the Lord;
Spain is my defence, and Ireland my strength,
Germany my word, and Italy my sword.
I will make war with the nations of the earth,
I will scatter them in my fury and divide them in the four
    winds;
    and I will build me an house, a high house;
    no man can tell how I shall frame my house;
    but I will bring my timbers from afar a strange land
    and I will build my house in the east
    and many people shall flow into it.
And my household shall be in ev'ry land;
    and they shall subdue all nations.
Then my name shall be glorified by Priests and Kings
    and all the earth shall tremble before me,
        for I alone will be exalted in that day saith God,
        and here my word doth end.
Now arise and prepare the way for my people,
O daughter of the East that when I come again,
I may visit thee in mercy.

> NOTE: An example of chanted free-verse "anthems" given to the
> Shakers "by revelation and the gift of God," sent in this case "(with
> music) from Holy Wisdom by Mother Ann to Joanna Kitchel on
> April 21, 1844" (Edward Deming Andrews, *The Gift To Be Simple*,
> 1940). See also above, page 100.

EDWARD TAYLOR

Meditation 31. Joh. 15.13
Greater Love hath no man etc.

4.4m [June] 1699

Its said H * * * * * * * * * * * * * * * doth enjoy
    A Tree of Gold whose Root is deemd t'have birth
At Centre of the Earth whose Spirits fly
    Ore all its body blossoming on the earth.
    Leaves dance and Fruits grow on its twigs and limbs.
    That make a golden Smile on Spanish Kings.

Yet this rich vegitable tree of Gold
    Is but a Toade Stoole bowre compar'd to thee
My blessed Lord, whose tent of Humane mould
    Shines like Gods Paradise, Where springs the tree
    Of Pure, Pure Love that doth thy friends enfold
    In richer Robes than all those Leaves of gold.

Thy Love-Affection, rooted in the Soyle,
    Of Humane Nature, springing up all ore
With Sanctifying Grace, of brightest file
    Brings Loads of Love to sinfull man all gore.
    Here is greate Love, greaten'd by influences
    To which thy Godhead to the same dispenses.

No Spirits ever yet were founde within
    The golden Tree of Humane nature, bud,
Or blossom such a Love, or Lovely thing
    As this thy nature doth so greate so good.
    The Plant's set in a Soile Pure, faultless, stronge,
    Its fruite sores to the highst pitch, Good, Greate, and
        Longe.

There is no Sin can touch this Lovely Love.
    Its Holy, with a perfect Holiness.
Its grown unto the highst Degree, above
    All Stuntedness, or stately Stintedness.

The Soile is faultless, and doth give its Strength.
The Plant doth beare its fruite of largest length.

This Love in thee most pure, and perfect stands
    A Relative, and hath its object here
Which it befriends with all good things, and hands
    In holy wayes to heavenly Glory cleare.
    Oh! happy such as with it are befriended:
    With perfect Love, to perfect bliss they're tended.

Make me thy Friend: Befriend me with thy Love.
    Here's cloaths more rich than Silk or Cloth of gold.
I'le in the Circuite of thy Friendship moove
    So thy Warm Love enspire mine Organs would.
    My Garden will give sweet, and Lovely Flowers
    If thou distill thereon thy Love in Showres.

Lord, let thy Sunshine-Love my Dial grace.
    Then what a Clock it is, it will display.
The glory of the Sunshine on it's Face
    Will take the light and tell the time of Day.
    My Hammer then shall greet this Shine as well
    With praise * * * * * * * * * tun'de on my bell.

[COMANCHE]

Peyote Songs

1   It has a red flower, it has power.
2   Daylight. Red flower.
3   It moves along.
4   Yellow.
5   Dawn rays are standing.
6   Power is flying.
7   Bird.

•

1   Horse is coming down.
2   Move into line, it's daylight.
3   Male antelopes, breeding.

4   Bird is circling, crying out.
5   Hell-diver's circling, crying out.
6   Bird getting ready to fly.
7   Beaver, it's dawn.

    —Translated by DAVID P. MCALLESTER, as sung by TEWAKI

■ *FROM THE COMANCHE PEYOTE ORIGIN STORY:*

" When morning came, the woman was told to tell them:
    'Now the leader will instruct you as to how peyote meetings should be held. This is what the peyote says: "When our Father made you he made me here on earth to grow with you."
    'The leader said, "Now where you are sitting here watching it, no matter what it looks like now, when it takes on power there is no knowing how it will look. Peyote says: 'I am the power of our Father. Here on earth I do as I please because of my power. I am a man. That is how I do anything that is asked of me and this here is a part of me. Even if I am in the shape of a woman she is only part of me. Take notice of the ground, of the grass that is growing on the ground, of the roots of the grass. I am like the grass. My roots are my children. They increase with me. When it is cut the peyote grows back in the same place. It is the same with the grass on its roots'!"' "

    —DAVID P. MCALLESTER, *Peyote Music* [1949]

> Peyote religion in the United States goes back to at least the 1870s and was carried on thereafter through the visions of men like JOHN WILSON, JOHN RAVE, et al. (see above, page 99).

RALPH WALDO EMERSON
Blight

            Give me truths;
For I am weary of the surfaces,
And die of inanition. If I knew
Only the herbs and simples of the wood,
Rue, cinquefoil, gill, vervain and agrimony,
Blue-vetch and trillium, hawkweed, sassafras,
Milkweeds and murky brakes, quaint pipes and sundew,

And rare and virtuous roots, which in these woods
Draw untold juices from the common earth,
Untold, unknown, and I could surely spell
Their fragrance, and their chemistry apply
By sweet affinities to human flesh,
Driving the foe and stablishing the friend,—
O, that were much, and I could be a part
Of the round day, related to the sun
And planted world, and full executor
Of their imperfect functions.
But these young scholars, who invade our hills,
Bold as the engineer who fells the wood,
And travelling often in the cut he makes,
Love not the flower they pluck, and know it not,
And all their botany is Latin names.
The old men studied magic in the flowers,
And human fortunes in astronomy,
And an omnipotence in chemistry,
Preferring things to names, for these were men,
Were unitarians of the united world,
And, wheresoever their clear eye-beams fell,
They caught the footsteps of the SAME. Our eyes
Are armed, but we are strangers to the stars,
And strangers to the mystic beast and bird,
And strangers to the plant and to the mine.
The injured elements say, 'Not in us;'
And night and day, ocean and continent,
Fire, plant and mineral say, 'Not in us;'
And haughtily return stare for stare.
For we invade them impiously for gain;
We devastate them unreligiously,
And coldly ask their pottage, not their love.
Therefore they shove us from them, yield to us
Only what to our griping toil is due;
But the sweet affluence of love and song,
The rich results of the divine consents
Of man and earth, of world beloved and lover,
The nectar and ambrosia, are withheld;

And in the midst of spoils and slaves, we thieves
And pirates of the universe, shut out
Daily to a more thin and outward rind,
Turn pale and starve. Therefore, to our sick eyes,
The stunted trees look sick, the summer short,
Clouds shade the sun, which will not tan our hay,
And nothing thrives to reach its natural term;
And life, shorn of its venerable length,
Even at its greatest space is a defeat,
And dies in anger that it was a dupe;
And, in its highest noon and wantonness,
Is early frugal, like a beggar's child;
Even in the hot pursuit of the best aims
And prizes of ambition, checks its hand,
Like Alpine cataracts frozen as they leaped,
Chilled with a miserly comparison
Of the toy's purchase with the length of life.

GARY SNYDER

For Plants

The ancient virgin
picking mushrooms
in the damp forest
gloom

    Peyotl
      dream-child bud
glowing in hollow desert
   HO   hands
   gather the holy baby
faceted jewel bush
              child of the
sky is solid rainbow
            squash maiden
            corn girl

hair prongs   seedbed root
suck magic from dirt, rains
    wash down rainbow
and bury him under the floor.

long trumpet of thornapple flower
datura highsmoke
scoopt in blanket
    james. town. weed.

gum of hashish
passt through the porthole
bumboat to tanker

    half-glimpst
   "glow of red lips in dark hair"
   slave-of-god-dancer

hidden
        in glittering fall.

ear, eye, belly
       cascara   calamus

cut bark is vapor
of paradise odor—
brick for a pillow
rolld in a blanket,
          to see

Artemis naked:
the soft white
        buried sprout
of the world's first
seed.

■ *"A girl's lover to be slain and buried in her flower-garden, and the earth levelled over him. That particular spot, which she happens to plant with some peculiar variety of flowers, produces them of admirable splendor, beauty, and perfume; and she delights, with an indescribable impulse, to wear them in her bosom, and scent her chamber with them. Thus the classic fantasy would be realized, of dead people transformed to flowers."*

—NATHANIEL HAWTHORNE, *The American Notebooks*

CHARLES SIMIC

Forest

My time is coming. Once again
My trees will swing their heavy bells.

My termites, my roots and streams
Will stitch their chill into the heart of man
Laying out my most ancient trail.

I speak of the north, of its pull
Stuck in my mouth like a bit.

Whoever looks now in the palm of his hand
Will notice the imprints of strange flowers
I have preserved in my rocks.

I will bare bones to tell fortunes by,
Snow with tracks of all the fabled highwaymen.
Ladies and gentlemen, you will hear a star
Dead a million years, in the throat of a bird.

The human body will be revealed for what it is—
A cluster of roots
Pulling in every direction.

There'll be plenty of time
When an acorn grows out of your ear
To accustom yourself to my ways,
To carve yourself a hermit's toothpick.

J. D. [JELLY JAW] SHORT
Snake Doctor Blues

> (I'm a snake doctor man: everybody's trying to find out my
>   name)
> (I fly by easy, but I fly low low distant land)

I'm a snake doctor man
                    everybody's trying to find out my name
I'm a snake doctor man
                    everybody's trying to find out my name
And when I fly by easy
                    mama, I'm gonna fly low low distant land

I am a snake doctor
                    gang of womens every where I go
I'm a snake doctor man
                    has a gang of womens every where I go
And when I get to flying sometime
                    I can see a gang of women standing out in the door

I'm gon' fly by easy
                    man, and you know I ain't gon' fly very low
I'm gon' fly by easy
                    man, and you know I ain't gon' fly very low
What I got in these sacks on my back, man
                    you don't know: honey, no

I ain't got many crooks in my back
                    and the dyingest snake can crawl
I ain't got many crooks in my back
                    and the dyingest snake can crawl
I puts up a solid *foundation, mens*
                    and you know it don't: never fall

The evening storm might blow
                    and the midnight wind might rise
The evening storm might rise
                    and the midnight storm might blow

And when I put up the *black foundation*
                      I don't have to look for that: woman no more

I'm a snake doctor man
                      got my medicine, I say, in my bag
I'm a snake doctor man
                      got my medicine, I say, in my bag
I mean to be a real snake doctor man
                      and you know I don't mean to be no *quack*

Lord, I know many of you mens wondering
                      what the snake doctor man got in his hand
I know many of you mens are wondering
                      what the snake doctor man got in his hand
He's got roots and herbs
                      steals a woman, man, every where he land

    —Transcription from oral blues by ERIC SACKHEIM

GEORGE OPPEN

But So As By Fire

The darkness of trees
Guards this life
Of the thin ground
That covers the rock ledge

Among the lanes and magic
Of the Eastern Woods

The beauty of silence
And broken boughs

And the homes of small animals

The green leaves
Of young plants

Above the dark green moss
In the sweet smell of rot

The pools and the trickle of freshwater

First life, rotting life
Hidden starry life it is not yet

A mirror
Like our lives

We have gone
As far as is possible

Whose lives reflect light
Like mirrors

One had not thought
To be afraid

Not of shadow but of light

Summon one's powers

HENRY DAVID THOREAU

Th' Ambrosia of the Gods 's a Weed on Earth

Th' ambrosia of the Gods 's a weed on earth
their nectar is the morning dew which on
'ly our shoes taste—For they are simple folks
'Tis very fit the ambrosia of the gods
Should be a weed on earth. As nectar is
The morning dew with which we wet our shoes
For the gods are simple folks and we should pine
upon their humble fare

And Once Again

And once again
When I went a-maying—
& once or twice more I had seen thee before.
For there grow the May flower
(*Epigaea repens*)
& the mt cranberry
& the screech owl *strepens*

WILLIAM CARLOS WILLIAMS

The Yellow Flower

What shall I say, because talk I must?
That I have found a cure
for the sick?
I have found no cure
for the sick
but this crooked flower
which only to look upon
all men
are cured. This
is that flower
for which all men
sing secretly their hymns
of praise. This
is that sacred
flower!

Can this be so?
A flower so crooked
and obscure? It is
a mustard flower
and not a mustard flower,
a single spray

topping the deformed stem
　　　　of fleshy leaves
　　　　　　　in this freezing weather
under glass.

An ungainly flower and
　　　　an unnatural one,
　　　　　　　in this climate; what
can be the reason
　　　　that it has picked me out
　　　　　　　to hold me, openmouthed,
rooted before this window
　　　　in the cold,
　　　　　　　my will
drained from me
　　　　so that I have only eyes
　　　　　　　for these yellow,
twisted petals　　.　　?

That the sight,
　　　　though strange to me,
　　　　　　　must be a common one,
is clear: there are such flowers
　　　　with such leaves
　　　　　　　native to some climate
which they can call
　　　　their own.

But why the torture
　　　　and the escape through
　　　　　　　the flower? It is
as if Michelangelo
　　　　had conceived the subject
　　　　　　　of his *Slaves* from this
—or might have done so.
　　　　And did he not make
　　　　　　　the marble bloom? I
am sad
　　　　as he was sad
　　　　　　　in his heroic mood.

But also
        I have eyes
                that are made to see and if
they see ruin for myself
        and all that I hold
                dear, they see
also
        through the eyes
                and through the lips
and tongue the power
        to free myself
                and speak of it, as
Michelangelo through his hands
        had the same, if greater,
                power.

Which leaves, to account for,
        the tortured bodies
                of
the slaves themselves
        and
                the tortured body of my flower
which is not a mustard flower at all
        but some unrecognized
                and unearthly flower
for me to naturalize
        and acclimate
                and choose it for my own.

CARL RAKOSI
The Code

I had to pull the little maple tree
close to the house.
                It had leaves already.
And I saw a doe standing
                    in its romaunt
munching peacefully

                    while the wolf stalked.
Such is my confusion.

When I broke it,
only the moloch unthink
                        groaned.

The seed knew
                before Sinai
it would be a root
                    but not the nature
of man.

It was coded
              to become a shade tree
sized for the Colossus
                 Rameses the Second
and entered the earth
                 zigzagging
after the radish and the worm.
Its necessity would have cracked my cement
and pierced a water main.
Yet it was coded
                  in the presence of the sun
to turn our breath and water
                      into deer food
and connect us to our nature
and give us peace from pursuance.
In our deadly assignation
I was coded to be contemplative
with a twig:
              out of the ground
only an hour,
              yet so downcast.
Poor Yorick!

In the root I saw a miniature
              crab apple tree
twisting into Dada.
                 Insane ending.

Must all lead back to the thinker?
                                        Is there no
germination in a cube
                        or sprouting in a sphere?

VACHEL LINDSAY

Celestial Trees of Glacier Park
A Song With Hieroglyphs

Celestial forests grow in Glacier Park
Invisible to all but faithful eyes.
Those who are wise
See each new tree spring with its aureole.
Every dawning brings one more surprise
Shining in heaven between them and the sun,
Or nodding where the cold rivers run,
Or hovering over granite, shale, and snow,
The ghostly trees like rainbows come and go.

I

These are the trees: The Stable for the Deer,
The Bee's Skyscraper, The Angel's Spear,
The Daisy's Tower, The Storm Wave of the Land,
The Old Clock Tower, The Manitou's Hand,
The Mountain's Giant Flower, The Dreamer from the Seas,
These are the trees.

II

These are the trees: The House of Honeycomb,
The Ball Room of the Winds, The Great Green Torch,
The Buffalo's Pride, The Pillar of the Sky,
The Bear's Home, The Tall Fern That Will Fly,
The Priest of the Morning, The Giant's Knees,
These are the trees.

III

These are the trees: The House of Honeycomb,
The West Wind's Evening Lodge, The Red Man's Temple
     Dome,
The Waterfall's Big Brother, The Frost Defyer,
The Planet's Nest, The Root's Achieved Desire,
The Sun's Bride, The Fire That Will Not Freeze,
These are the trees.

IV

These are the trees: The Chipmunk's Tenement,
The Icicle's Retreat, The Fire Bird's Flat for Rent,
The Flowering Sword, The Planet's Hair,
The North Wind's Dress, The Fir Bough Stair,
The Moss That Dared, The Dreamer from the Seas,
These are the trees—these are the dream trees.

LINDSAY was one of the first American poets to seriously consider
what's now called intermedia: fusions of poetry with painting,
hieroglyphics, movies, dance.

EZRA POUND

Canto XVII

So that the vines burst from my fingers
And the bees weighted with pollen
Move heavily in the vine-shoots:
    chirr—chirr—chir-rikk—a purring sound,
And the birds sleepily in the branches.
       ZAGREUS! IO ZAGREUS!
With the first pale-clear of the heaven
And the cities set in their hills,
And the goddess of the fair knees
Moving there, with the oak-woods behind her,
The green slope, with white hounds
        leaping about her;
And thence down to the creek's mouth, until evening,
Flat water before me,
      and the trees growing in water,
Marble trunks out of stillness,
On past the palazzi,
        in the stillness,
The light now, not of the sun.
        Chrysophrase,
And the water green clear, and blue clear;
On, to the great cliffs of amber.
           Between them,
Cave of Nerea,
   she like a great shell curved,
And the boat drawn without sound,
Without odour of ship-work,
Nor bird-cry, nor any noise of wave moving,
Nor splash of porpoise, nor any noise of wave moving,
Within her cave, Nerea,
         she like a great shell curved
In the suavity of the rock,
           cliff green-gray in the far,
In the near, the gate-cliffs of amber,
And the wave

green clear, and blue clear,
And the cave salt-white, and glare-purple,
cool, porphyry smooth,
the rock sea-worn.
No gull-cry, no sound of porpoise,
Sand as of malachite, and no cold there,
the light not of the sun.

Zagreus, feeding his panthers,
the turf clear as on hills under light.
And under the almond-trees, gods,
with them, *choros nympharum*. Gods,
Hermes and Athene,
As shaft of compass,
Between them, trembled—
To the left is the place of fauns,
sylva nympharum;
The low wood, moor-scrub,
the doe, the young spotted deer,
leap up through the broom-plants,
as dry leaf amid yellow.
And by one cut of the hills,
the great alley of Memnons.
Beyond, sea, crests seen over dune
Night sea churning shingle,
To the left, the alley of cypress.
A boat came,
One man holding her sail,
Guiding her with oar caught over gunwale, saying:
"   There, in the forest of marble,
"   the stone trees—out of water—
"   the arbours of stone—
"   marble leaf, over leaf,
"   silver, steel over steel,
"   silver beaks rising and crossing,
"   prow set against prow,
"   stone, ply over ply,
"   the gilt beams flare of an evening"

Borso, Carmagnola, the men of craft, *i vitrei,*
Thither, at one time, time after time,
And the waters richer than glass,
Bronze gold, the blaze over the silver,
Dye-pots in the torch-light,
The flash of wave under prows,
And the silver beaks rising and crossing.
      Stone trees, white and rose-white in the darkness,
Cypress there by the towers,
      Drift under hulls in the night.

      "In the gloom the gold
Gathers the light about it." . . .

Now supine in burrow, half over-arched bramble,
One eye for the sea, through that peek-hole,
Gray light, with Athene.
Zothar and her elephants, the gold loin-cloth,
The sistrum, shaken, shaken,
      the cohorts of her dancers.
And Aletha, by bend of the shore,
     with her eyes seaward,
     and in her hands sea-wrack
Salt-bright with the foam.
Koré through the bright meadow,
     with green-gray dust in the grass:
"For this hour, brother of Circe."
Arm laid over my shoulder,
Saw the sun for three days, the sun fulvid,
As a lion lift over sand-plain;
        and that day,
And for three days, and none after,
Splendour, as the splendour of Hermes,
And shipped thence
      to the stone place,
Pale white, over water,
     known water,
And the white forest of marble, bent bough over bough,

The pleached arbour of stone,
Thither Borso, when they shot the barbed arrow at him,
And Carmagnola, between the two columns,
Sigismundo, after that wreck in Dalmatia.
   Sunset like the grasshopper flying.

A BOOK OF MUSIC

It was once assumed that the poet recorded the "music of the spheres" and that the rules of that music were constant. But formal music from the early American composer William Billings to Charles Ives and John Cage has "evolved," and these men, like Blake, saw virtue in variety and change. The structure of poetry has undergone a development parallel to, and often identical with, that in music from the early borrowings from Europe to modern experimentation and native invention like blues, jazz, and rock. In the process many poets have returned to an essentially oral poetry, of voice and breath, sound and silence, whose written versions function much as notation does for music. **A Book of Music** attempts to present chronologically some of that variety of concerns, as well as the evolution of complex poetic structures.

*"Of the Measure, in which
the following Poem is written*

*We who dwell on Earth can do nothing of ourselves, every thing is
conducted by Spirits, no less than Digestion or Sleep.*

*When this Verse was first dictated to me I consider'd a Monotonous
Cadence like that used by Milton & Shakspeare & all writers of English
Blank Verse, derived from the modern bondage of Rhyming; to be a
necessary and indispensible part of Verse. But I soon found that in the
mouth of a true Orator such monotony was not only awkward, but as
much a bondage as rhyme itself. I therefore have produced a variety in
every line, both of cadences & number of syllables. Every word and every
letter is studied and put into its fit place: the terrific numbers are
reserved for the terrific parts—the mild & gentle, for the mild & gentle
parts, and the prosaic, for inferior parts: all are necessary to each other.
Poetry Fetter'd, Fetters the Human Race! Nations are Destroy'd, or
Flourish, in proportion as Their Poetry Painting and Music, are De-
stroy'd or Flourish! The Primeval State of Man, was Wisdom, Art, and
Science."*

—WILLIAM BLAKE, *Jerusalem* [1804]

WILLIAM BILLINGS

The Pleasures of Variety [c. 1790]

It is an old maxim, and I think a very just one, viz. *that variety is always pleasing,* and it is well known that there is more variety in one piece of fuging music, than in twenty pieces of plain song, for while the tones do most sweetly coincide and agree, the words are seemingly engaged in a musical warfare; and excuse the paradox if I further add, that each part seems determined by dint of harmony and strength of accent, to drown his competitor in an ocean of harmony, and while each part is thus mutually striving for mastery, and sweetly contending for victory, the audience are most luxuriously entertained, and exceedingly delighted; in the mean time, their minds are surprisingly agitated, and extremely fluctuated; sometimes declaring in favour of one part and sometimes another.—Now the solemn bass demands their attention, now the manly tenor, now the lofty counter, now the volatile treble, now here, now there, now here again—O inchanting! O ecstatic! Push on, push on ye sons of harmony, and

> Discharge your deep mouth'd canon, full fraught with
> Diapasons;
> May you with Maestoso, rush on to Choro-Grando,
> And then with Vigoroso, let fly your Diapentes
> About our nervous system.

[THE SHAKERS]

Heavenly Display.

The waves of the ocean imitate the rolls of the heavenly music that rolls in heaven. O le ul lum ul la, O le ul lum ul la, O glory to God for this heavenly display.

2 The wheels of a time-piece imitate the flows of the heavenly love love that flows in heaven.
Chorus.

3 The wings of an eagle imitate the seraphim that soar in the heavens of heavenly love.
Chorus.

Given by inspiration, 1838.
New Lebanon, N...Y.

A Shaker hymn, showing innovative musical notation. The Shakers had also developed a kind of musical "free verse" (see above, page 302), antedating Whitman's *Leaves of Grass* by more than a decade. These latter poems, "which were set to music from about 1840 on . . . were like prose poems which conformed, however, to no metrical pattern and could be sung only because Shaker notation allowed constant changes in mode, timing, barring or rhythm; others written into hymnals with no musical accompaniment, were probably chanted or recited if used in meeting at all." [ED-WARD DEMING ANDREWS, *The Gift to Be Simple,* 1940] For more on the Shakers, see page 100, above.

JONES VERY

The Garden

I saw the spot where our first parents dwelt;
And yet it wore to me no face of change,
For while amid its fields and groves, I felt
As if I had not sinned, nor thought it strange;
My eye seemed but a part of every sight,
My ear heard music in each sound that rose;
Each sense forever found a new delight,
Such as the spirit's vision only knows;
Each act some new and ever-varying joy
Did by my Father's love for me prepare;
To dress the spot my ever fresh employ,
And in the glorious whole with Him to share;
No more without the flaming gate to stray,
No more for sin's dark stain the debt of death to pay.

EDGAR ALLAN POE

From X-ing a Paragrab

Sx hx, Jxhn! hxw nxw? Txld yxu sx, yxu knxw. Dxn't crxw,
anxther time, befxre yxu're xut xf the wxxds! Dxes yxur
mxther *knxw* yxu're xut? Xh, nx, nx!—sx gx hxme at xnce,
nxw, Jxhn, tx yxur xdixus xld wxxds xf Cxncxrd! Gx hxme
tx yxur wxxds, xld xwl,—gx! Yxu wxn't? Xh, pxh, pxh,
Jxhn, dxn't dx sx! Yxu've *gxt* tx gx, yxu knxw! Sx gx at
xnce, and dxn't gx slxw; fxr nxbxdy xwns yxu here, yxu
knxw. Xh, Jxhn, Jxhn, if yxu *dxn't* gx yxu're nx *hxmx—*
nx! Yxu're xnly a fxwl, an xwl; a cxw, a sxw; a dxll, a pxll;
a pxxr xld gxxd-fxr-nxthing-tx-nxbxdy, lxg, dxg, hxg, xr
frxg, cxme xut xf a Cxncxrd bxg. Cxxl, nxw—cxxl! *Dx* be
cxxl, yxu fxxl! Nxne xf yxur crxwing, xld cxck! Dxn't
frxwn sx-dxn't! Dxn't hxllx, nxr hxwl, nxr grxwl, nxr bxw-
wxw-wxw! Gxxd Lxrd, Jxhn, hxw yxu *dx* lxxk! Txld yxu
sx, yxu knxw—but stxp rxlling yxur gxxse xf an xld pxll
abxut sx, and gx and drxwn yxur sxrrxws in a bxwl!

■ *" With Poe, words were not hung by usage with associations, the pleasing wraiths of former masteries, this is the sentimental trapdoor to beginnings. With Poe words were figures; an old language truly, but one from which he carried over only the most elemental qualities to his new purpose; which was, to find a way to tell his soul. Sometimes he used words so playfully his sentences seem to fly away from sense, the destructive! with the conserving abandon, foreshadowed, of a Gertrude Stein. The particles of language must be clear as sand. "*

—WILLIAM CARLOS WILLIAMS, In the American Grain   [1925]

WALT WHITMAN
Sea Shore Fancies

Even as a boy, I had the fancy, the wish, to write a piece, perhaps a poem, about the sea-shore—that suggesting, dividing line, contact, junction, the solid marrying the liquid —that curious, lurking something, (as doubtless every objective form finally becomes to the subjective spirit,) which means far more than its mere first sight, grand as that is—blending the real and ideal, and each made portion of the other. Hours, days, in my Long Island youth and early manhood, I haunted the shores of Rockaway or Coney island, or away east to the Hamptons or Montauk. Once, at the latter place, (by the old lighthouse, nothing but sea-tossings in sight in every direction as far as the eye could reach,) I remember well, I felt that I must one day write a book expressing this liquid, mystic theme. Afterward, I recollect, how it came to me that instead of any special lyrical or epical or literary attempt, the sea-shore should be an invisible *influence,* a pervading gauge and tally for me, in my composition. (Let me give a hint here to young writers. I am not sure but I have unwittingly follow'd out the same rule with other powers besides sea and shores—avoiding them, in the way of any dead set at poetizing them, as too big for formal handling—quite satisfied if I could indirectly show that we have met and fused, even if only once, but enough—that we have really absorb'd each other and understand each other.)

There is a dream, a picture, that for years at intervals,

(sometimes quite long ones, but surely again, in time,) has come noiselessly up before me, and I really believe, fiction as it is, has enter'd largely into my practical life—certainly into my writings, and shaped and color'd them. It is nothing more or less than a stretch of interminable white-brown sand, hard and smooth and broad, with the ocean perpetually, grandly, rolling in upon it, with slow-measured sweep, with rustle and hiss and foam, and many a thump as of low bass drums. This scene, this picture, I say, has risen before me at times for years. Sometimes I wake at night and can hear and see it plainly.

From *Specimen Days,* cited by WILLIAM CARLOS WILLIAMS (talk, circa 1950) as Whitman's prophecy of a new American measure, what Williams then was calling the "variable foot."

Emily Dickinson's verse—idiosyncratic in the context of nineteenth-century poetry—combines two opposed tendencies: conventional meters (derived partly from hymns) and the freer rhythms of speech. She seems most "modern" in the latter emphasis and in her radical notation devices (a variety of dashes and slant-bars, irregular capitalizations, etc.), the precise values of which have yet to be understood. Thomas Johnson's edition of Dickinson (Harvard) has the advantage over earlier ones that it at least supplies dashes rather than normalized punctuation and follows her capitalizations and line breaks.

EMILY DICKINSON
"I Cannot Live with You"

I cannot live with You—
It would be Life—
And Life is over there—
Behind the Shelf

The Sexton keeps the Key to—
Putting up
Our Life—His Porcelain—
Like a Cup—

Discarded of the Housewife—
Quaint—or Broke—
A newer Sevres pleases—
Old Ones crack—

I could not die—with You—
For One must wait
To shut the Other's Gaze down—
You—could not—

And I—Could I stand by
And see You—freeze—
Without my Right of Frost—
Death's privilege?

Nor could I rise—with You—
Because Your Face
Would put out Jesus'—
That New Grace

Glow plain—and foreign
On my homesick Eye—
Except that You than He
Shone closer by—

They'd judge Us—How—
For You—served Heaven—You know,
Or sought to—
I could not—

Because You saturated Sight—
And I had no more Eyes
For sordid excellence
As Paradise

And were You lost, I would be—
Though My Name
Rang loudest
On the Heavenly fame—

And were You—saved—
And I—condemned to be
Where You were not—
That self—were Hell to Me—

So We must meet apart—
You there—I here—
With just the Door ajar
That Oceans are—and Prayer—
And that White Sustenance—
Despair—

In *The Science of English Verse* [1880], SIDNEY LANIER argued for
a literal application of musical modalities to verse notation. Verse
formalities become coordinates of instrumental music (as in his
"The Symphony"), thus implicitly opening prosody to the possibil-
ity of reform by alteration of the musical model. Lanier's own
practice made for swift modulation, in the long form, of what he
called "tune."

SIDNEY LANIER

The Marshes of Glynn

Glooms of the live-oaks, beautiful-braided and woven
With intricate shades of the vines that myriad-cloven
    Clamber the forks of the multiform boughs,—
            Emerald twilights,—
            Virginal shy lights,
Wrought of the leaves to allure to the whisper of vows,
When lovers pace timidly down through the green colonnades
    Of the dim sweet woods, of the dear dark woods,
        Of the heavenly woods and glades,
That run to the radiant marginal sand-beach within
        The wide sea-marshes of Glynn;—

    Beautiful glooms, soft dusks in the noon-day fire,—
    Wildwood privacies, closets of lone desire,
Chamber from chamber parted with wavering arras of
            leaves,—

Cells for the passionate pleasure of prayer to the soul that
        grieves
   Pure with a sense of the passing of saints through the
        wood,
   Cool for the dutiful weighing of ill with good;—

O braided dusks of the oak and woven shades of the vine,
While the riotous noon-day sun of the June-day long did
        shine,
Ye held me fast in your heart and I held you fast in mine;
   But now when the noon is no more, and riot is rest,
   And the sun is a-wait at the ponderous gate of the West,
     And the slant yellow beam down the wood-aisle doth
        seem
   Like a lane into heaven that leads from a dream,—
Ay, now, when my soul all day hath drunken the soul of the
        oak,
And my heart is at ease from men, and the wearisome sound
        of the stroke
   Of the scythe of time and the trowel of trade is low,
   And belief overmasters doubt, and I know that I know,
   And my spirit is grown to a lordly great compass within,
   That the length and the breadth and the sweep of the
        marshes of Glynn
   Will work me no fear like the fear they have wrought me
        of yore
     When length was fatigue, and when breadth was but
        bitterness sore,
     And when terror and shrinking and dreary unnamable
        pain
    Drew over me out of the merciless miles of the plain,—
     Oh, now, unafraid, I am fain to face
       The vast sweet visage of space.

     To the edge of the wood I am drawn, I am drawn,
Where the gray beach glimmering runs, as a belt of the
        dawn,
       For a mete and a mark

To the forest-dark:—
    So:
Affable live-oak, leaning low,—
Thus—with your favor—soft, with a reverent hand,
(Not lightly touching your person, Lord of the land!)
Bending your beauty aside, with a step I stand
    On the firm-packed sand,
      Free
By a world of marsh that borders a world of sea.
Sinuous southward and sinuous northward the shimmering
    band
Of the sand-beach fastens the fringe of the marsh to the
    folds of the land.
Inward and outward to northward and southward the
    beach-lines linger and curl
As a silver-wrought garment that clings to and follows the
    firm sweet limbs of a girl.
Vanishing, swerving, evermore curving again into sight,
Softly the sand-beach wavers away to a dim gray looping
    of light.
And what if behind me to westward the wall of the woods
    stands high?
The world lies east: how ample, the marsh and the sea and
    the sky!
A league and a league of marsh-grass, waist-high, broad in
    the blade,
Green, and all of a height, and unflecked with a light or a
    shade,
    Stretch leisurely off in a pleasant plain,
    To the terminal blue of the main.

Oh, what is abroad in the marsh and the terminal sea?
    Somehow my soul seems suddenly free
From the weighing of fate and the sad discussion of sin,
By the length and the breadth and the sweep of the
    marshes of Glynn.
Ye marshes, how candid and simple and nothing-withholding
    and free

Ye publish yourselves to the sky and offer yourselves to the
        sea!
Tolerant plains, that suffer the sea and the rains and the
        sun,
Ye spread and span like the catholic man who hath mightily
        won
    God out of knowledge and good out of infinite pain
    And sight out of blindness and purity out of a stain.

    As the marsh-hen secretly builds on the watery sod,
    Behold I will build me a nest on the greatness of God:
    I will fly in the greatness of God as the marsh-hen flies
    In the freedom that fills all the space 'twixt the marsh and
        the skies:
    By so many roots as the marsh-grass sends in the sod
    I will heartily lay me a-hold on the greatness of God:
    Oh, like to the greatness of God is the greatness within
    The range of the marshes, the liberal marshes of Glynn.

And the sea lends large, as the marsh: lo, our of his plenty the
        sea
    Pours fast: full soon the time of the flood-tide must be:
      Look how the grace of the sea doth go
    About and about through the intricate channels that flow
        Here and there,
        Everywhere,
Till his waters have flooded the uttermost creeks and the
        low-lying lanes,
    And the marsh is meshed with a million veins,
    That like as with rosy and silvery essences flow
      In the rose-and-silver evening glow.
        Farewell, my lord Sun!
    The creeks overflow: a thousand rivulets run
    'Twixt the roots of the sod; the blades of the marsh-grass
        stir;
Passeth a hurrying sound of wings that westward whirr;
Passeth, and all is still; and the currents cease to run;

And the sea and the marsh are one.
How still the plains of the waters be!
The tide is in his ecstasy.
The tide is at his highest height:
    And it is night.

And now from the Vast of the Lord will the waters of sleep
    Roll in on the souls of men,
  But who will reveal to our waking ken
  The forms that swim and the shapes that creep
    Under the waters of sleep?
And I would I could know what swimmeth below when the
    tide comes in
  On the length and the breadth of the marvellous
    marshes of Glynn.

An important collector of Indian songs, FRANCES DENSMORE translated a major body of this oral poetry into English. In an essay on her work ("American Indian Songs," in *Assays,* 1961), Kenneth Rexroth describes most of her translations as "pure poems of sensibility resembling nothing so much as classical Japanese poetry or Mallarmé and certain other French and American poets, notably some of the Imagists at their best. It is possible, of course," he goes on, "to say that Miss Densmore greatly simplifies the poem by cutting out repetitions and nonsense vocables. But the Japanese poetry which we think of as so extremely compact on the printed page is similarly sung in extended fashion. . . ."

FRANCES DENSMORE
American Indian Songs

1

as my eyes
search
the prairie
I feel the summer in the spring

    Chippewa

2

today
is mine (I claimed)
(to) a man
a voice
I sent
you grant me
this day
is mine (I claimed)
(to) a man
a voice
I sent
now
here
(he) is

     Teton Sioux

3

red
wagon
dust
white man
looking around

     Northern Ute

4

the deer looks
at a flower

     Yaqui

5

The sun is rising.
At either side a bow is lying.
Beside the bows are lion babies.
The sky is pink.
That is all.

The moon is setting.
At either side are bamboos for arrow making.
Beside the bamboos are wildcat babies.
They walk uncertainly.
That is all.
The sun is slowly departing.
It is lower in its setting.
Black bats will be swooping.
When the sun is gone.
That is all.
The spirit children are beneath.
They are moving back and forth.
They roll in play.
Among tufts of white eagle down.
That is all.

> *Papago*

6

They are taking us beyond Miami
They are taking us beyond the Caloosa River
They are taking us to the end of our tribe
They are taking us to Palm Beach, coming back beside
    Okeechobee Lake
They are taking us to an old town in the west

> *Seminole*

■ " Rhythm.—*I believe in an 'absolute rhythm,' a rhythm, that is, in poetry which corresponds exactly to the emotion or shade of emotion to be expressed. A man's rhythm must be interpretative, it will be, therefore, in the end, his own, uncounterfeiting, uncounterfeitable.* "

—EZRA POUND, *"Credo" (in "A Retrospect"),* The Poetry Review
[1912]

■ *"A.D. 1940: Prosody is the articulation of the total sound of a poem."*

—EZRA POUND, footnote to the 1917 essay, "T. S. Eliot," in *Literary Essays*

EZRA POUND
The Return

See, they return; ah, see the tentative
    Movements, and the slow feet,
    The trouble in the pace and the uncertain
    Wavering!

See, they return, one, and by one,
With fear, as half-awakened;
As if the snow should hesitate
And murmur in the wind,
    and half turn back;
These were the "Wing'd-with-Awe,"
        Inviolable.

Gods of the wingèd shoe!
With them the silver hounds,
        sniffing the trace of air!

Haie! Haie!
    These were the swift to harry;
These the keen-scented;
These were the souls of blood.

Slow on the leash,
        pallid the leash-men!

THE MANY VOICES: Pound writes (*The New Age* 16, Jan. 14, 1915): "The musical conception of form, that is to say, the understanding that you can use form as a musician uses sound, that you can select motives of form from the forms about you, that you can recombine them and recolour them and 'organize' them into new form—this conception, this state of mental activity, brings with it a great joy and refreshment. . . ." His own major contribution to "the musical conception of form" in poetry comes somewhat later in the *Cantos,* the composition of which goes on for almost half a century and becomes in fact the work of a lifetime. The "music" of the *Cantos* is the sum of the many modalities which contribute to its construction: from the lyricism already evident in poems like the above, to a continually extended use of vowel-music, swift rhythms, chants, speeches, conversations, letters, image-sequences, parataxis, etc. Ideogram becomes "melogram," an assemblage or collage of voices and sound relationships, uttered by the persona or mask of the inclusive structure in which "all times are contemporaneous."

Selections from the *Cantos* appear elsewhere in the present anthology (pages 34, 165, 319, 418), and should be read as a necessary supplement to "A Book of Music."

AUTOMATISM AS CHANCE: Improvisation . . . automatic writing . . . increased speed of composition . . . chance . . . enter European and American art and poetry before the First World War. "If we admit automatism as chance, then the improvisations of Kandinsky (1911), painted 'rather unconsciously in a state of strong inner tension,' would take precedence over the first *papiers collés* of Picasso (1912), in which were incorporated fortuitous scraps of newspaper and cardboard" (George Brecht, *Chance-Imagery,* Something Else Press, 1957, 1965). The impact of Marcel Duchamp emanating from New York from 1915 on; the work of Freytag-Loringhoven thrusting the improvisational and chance idea on the American consciousness, prior to Surrealism, parallel to Dada. "The unconscious is inexhaustible and uncontrollable. Its force surpasses us. It is as mysterious as the last particle of a brain cell. Even if we knew it, we could not reconstruct it" (Tristan Tzara, *Lecture on Dada,* 1922). "Chance and hazard were the guided sources of inspiration"—Man Ray. "Dada gave the Venus of Milo an enema. . . . Dada is for nature and against art"—Hans Arp.

ELSE von FREYTAG-LORINGHOVEN
Love—Chemical Relationship

UN ENFANT FRANCAIS: MARCEL (A FUTURIST)
EIN DEUTSCHES KIND: ELSE (A FUTURE FUTURIST)
POPLARS—SUN—A CLAIHIGHWAY.

The poplars whispered THINE DREAMS Marcel!
They laughed—they turned themselves—they turned
    themselves

TO turn themselves—they giggled—they blabbered like
    thine-self—they smiled!
they smiled WITH the sun— OVER the sun—
BECAUSE OF the sun—with the same french lighthearted
    sensual playful
MORBID smile like thineself—Marcel!

Poplars thou lovedst and straight highways with the smell
    of poplars which is
like leather as fine—like morocco leather in thine nostrils
    —And thine nostrils are of glass!
Thou seest the smell uprise to the brain!

Sensual thine eyes became—slanting—closed themselves!

Thine smile turned pain—died—
Then thou diedst!

Thereafter thou becamest like glass.
The poplars and the sun turned glass—they did not torture
    thee any more!

Everything now is glass—motionless!
THAT WAS IT THOU DISCOVERDST—AND WHICH IS
    GIVEN TO THEE AFTER THINE DEATH—MAR-
    CEL!

Yet BEFORE thou lovedst the straight yellow highways—
    the whirring poplars—the fat color of clay—and
    thou lovedst it beyond measure!
THEREFORE THOU HADST TO KILL THINESELF—IT
    KILLED THEE!

Thou now livest motionless in a mirror!
Everything is a mirage in thee—thine world is glass—
    glassy!
Glassy are thine ears—thine hands—thine feet and thine
    face.
Of glass are the poplars and the sun.
Unity—Einklang—harmony—Zweifellosigkeit!
Thou art resurrected—hast won—livest—art dead!

BUT I LOVE THEE LIKE BEFORE. BECAUSE I AM FAT
    YELLOW CLAY!
THEREFORE I LOVE THAT VERY THIN GLASS WITH
    ITS   COLOR-CHANGE: BLUE—YELLOW—PUR-
    PLE PINK.
SO long must I love it until I myself will become glass and
    everything around me glassy.
Then art thou I! I do not need thee any more—!
So BEAUTIFUL will I be like thou thineself art,
Thou standest beside me—and art NOTHING beside me!
Yet today I still must love mine LOVE—!
I must bleed—weep—laugh—ere I turn to glass and the
    world around me glassy!

"I began to get enormously interested in hearing how everybody said the same thing over and over again with infinite variations but over and over again until finally if you listened with great intensity you could hear it rise and fall and tell all that there is inside them, not so much by the actual words they said or the thoughts they had but the movement of their thoughts and words endlessly the same and endlessly different.

". . . Repeating then is in every one, in every one their being and their feeling and their way of realizing everything and every one of them comes out in repeating more and more then every one comes to be clear to some one."

      —GERTRUDE STEIN, *Lectures in America* [1935]

GERTRUDE STEIN
Sonnets that Please

    I please the ribbon the leather and all. I please the
Christian world. I please the window the door and the bird.
I please the Hindoos a third. And Elsie Janis.
    I follow the sonnets that please with ease.
    If we must part let us go together.
    I miss a trick. I sit up quick, quickly.
    Eddying
    How often do I mention that I am not interested. She is
so loyal so easily moved so quickly roman catholic so en-
trancing. And how plainly we speak. How caressingly, all
nature eats every day.
    I am persuaded still.

He was deceived by the color.
And now for Sunday.
A Sunday is measured by sawing.
Upright stands and swinging. We never sing.
Why not.
Because voices are so useful to me.
The sound of them. No the color of vegetables. Vegetables are flat and have no color.
Flowers are irregular and have a variety of color.
And rubbish. Rubbish lies in heaps when it is not a birthday. How sweetly birthdays bear their fruit. And trees, trees the leaves of trees are transparent, because they have been eaten.
I can make a description.
I am excessively sleepy.
Every day will be Sunday by and by.
And now we dream of ribbons and skies.
We will win prizes.
We will announce pleasures.
We will resume dresses.
How pleasantly we stutter.

MARIANNE MOORE

Spenser's Ireland

has not altered;—
    a place as kind as it is green,
    the greenest place I've never seen.
Every name is a tune.
Denunciations do not affect
    the culprit; nor blows, but it
is torture to him to not be spoken to.
They're natural—
        the coat, like Venus'
mantle lined with stars,
buttoned close at the neck—the sleeves new from disuse.

If in Ireland
    they play the harp backward at need,
    and gather at midday the seed

of the fern, eluding
their "giants all covered with iron," might
        there be fern seed for unlearn-
ing obduracy and for reinstating
the enchantment?
            Hindered characters
seldom have mothers
in Irish stories, but they all have grandmothers.

It was Irish;
    a match not a marriage was made
    when my great great grandmother'd said
with native genius for
disunion, "Although your suitor be
        perfection, one objection
is enough; he is not
Irish." Outwitting
            the fairies, befriending the furies,
whoever again
and again says, "I'll never give in," never sees

that you're not free
    until you've been made captive by
    supreme belief—credulity
you say? When large dainty
fingers tremblingly divide the wings
        of the fly for mid-July
with a needle and wrap it with peacock tail,
or tie wool and
            buzzard's wing, their pride,
like the enchanter's
is in care, not madness. Concurring hands divide

flax for damask
    that when bleached by Irish weather
    has the silvered chamois-leather
water-tightness of a
skin. Twisted torcs and gold new-moon-shaped
        lunulae aren't jewelry

like the purple-coral fuchsia-tree's. Eire—
the guillemot
         so neat and the hen
of the heath and the
linnet spinet-sweet—bespeak relentlessness? Then

they are to me
    like enchanted Earl Gerald who
    changed himself into a stag, to
a great green-eyed cat of
the mountain. Discommodity makes
    them invisible; they've dis-
appeared. The Irish say your trouble is their
trouble and your
         joy their joy? I wish
I could believe it;
I am troubled, I'm dissatisfied, I'm Irish.

> An example of MARIANNE MOORE's strict use of a syllabic composi-
> tion method, wherein highly irregular line lengths are repeated
> from stanza to stanza (as John Donne's first stanzas often appear
> "free verse" until repeated). The method allows for basically non-
> metrical modulation of speech patterns—the poet's famous elegant
> conversational tone.

JAMES LAUGHLIN

The Last Poem To Be Written

"When, when & whenever
death closes our eyes"

still shall I behold her
smiling such brightness

lady of brightness &
the illumined heart

soft walker in my blood
snow color sea sound

track of the ermine
delicate in the snow

line of the sea wave
delicate on the sand

lady of all brightness
donna del mio cuor.

CHARLIE PATTON

From Hang It on the Wall

Justshakeityoucanbreakityoucanhangitonthewall
HollerwhenIcatchit'foreitfall
        youcanbreakityoucanhangitonthewall
HollerwhenIcatchit'foreitfall

        Sweet jelly

        MY ROLL

    Sweet mama, won't you let it fall

I AIN'T GOT NO BODY NOW
              Ah
              I fooled around
              I mean
              When the sun go down
              Ah
              I had my brown

      'Bout the jelly

        MY ROLL

    Sweet mama, won't you let it fall

Justpatityoucangrabityoucanwhipityoucanpitchit
Andaway *tillI*
      flipitandgetit
           Till I
           Ain't had my right mind
           I
           Stayed *in a little old town*

     'Bout the jelly

       MY ROLL

    Sweet mama, won't you let it fall

Justshakeityoucanbreakityoucanhangitonthewall
HollerwhenIcatchit'foreitfall
  shakeit,breakit,hangitonthewa-all
HollerwhenIcatchit'foreitfall

    Sweet jelly

       MY ROLL

    Sweet mama, won't you let it fall

(Lookit here, baby, it's gettin' good to me now
and I'll help you shake it)
          Ahh
          Ahh
          I mean my brown
          Ahh
          When the sun go down

     'Bout the jelly

       MY ROLL

Sweet mama, won't you let it fall

      —Transcribed from oral blues by ERIC SACKHEIM

LOUIS ZUKOFSKY's A, a long poetic sequence begun in the late 1920s and presently published in two volumes, is structured according to the principles of the Fugue (in Bach's conception). But it also shows Zukofsky's use of a wide variety of structural effects.

LOUIS ZUKOFSKY

A: 4

Giant sparkler,
Lights of the river,

(Horses turning)
Tide,

And pier lights
Under a light of the hill,

A lamp on the leaf-green
Lampost seen by the light

Of a truck (a song)
Lanterns swing behind horses,

Their sides gleam
From levels of water

Wherever we put our hats is our home
Our aged heads are our homes,
Eyes wink to their own phosphorescence,
No feast lights of Venice or The Last Supper light
Our beards' familiars; His
Stars of Deuteronomy are with us,
Always with us,
We had a Speech, our children have
                    evolved a jargon.

We prayed, Open, God, Gate of Psalmody,

That our Psalms may reach but
One shadow of Your light,
That You may see a minute over our waywardness.
Day You granted to Your seed, its promise, Its Promise,
Do not turn away Your sun.
Let us rest here,
            lightened
Of our tongues, hands, feet, eyes, ears and hearts.

                Fierce Ark!
                Gold lion stomach
                (Red hair in intaglio)
            Dead loved stones of our Temple walls,
            Ripped up pebble-stones of our tessellation,
            Split cedar chest harboring our Law,
Even the Death has gone out of us—we are void.

                Hear—
                He calleth for Elias—
                A clavicembalo!

Deafen us, God, deafen us to their music,
Our own children have passed over to the ostracized,
They assail us—
                'Religious, snarling monsters'—
And have mouthed a jargon:
                "Rain blows, light, on quiet water
                    I watch the rings spread and travel
                Shimaunu-Sān, Samurai,
                    When will you come home?—
                        Shimaunu-Sān, my clear star.

                To-day I gather all red flowers,
                    Shed their petals on the paths,
                Shimaunu-Sān, in the dawn,
                    Red I go to meet him—
                        Shimaunu-Sān, my clear star.

                To-morrow I tear cherry sprays,

Wreathe them in my hair and at my temples,
Shimaunu-Sān will see my head's white blossoms,
   In the dark run towards me
     Shimaunu-Sān, my clear star.

All turtle-doves have pledged
   To fly and search him:
Shimaunu-Sān, at my little windows
   Each night a tiny candle will be
                   lighted—
   Shimaunu-Sān, my clear star."

—*Yehoash.*
        Song's kinship.
        The roots we strike.

        "Heavier from day to day
        Grow my limbs with sap of forests"

        "Deep roots hammer lower"

        "And to the Sun, I bow.
        On the gray mountains,
        Where multiply
        The stairs of crags, my prayer
        Will follow you, still Heir—
        Bestower—
        Of man and tree and sand,

        When your face upon the land
        Flames in last redness, allow me of your light—"

My father's precursors
Set masts in dinghies, chanted the Speech.

        "Wider is the ash around the fire"
        "Treasures turned to sand"

Yehoash,—
The courses we tide from.

> Tree of the Bach family
> Compiled by Sebastian himself.
> '   Veit Bach, a miller in Wechmar,
> Delighted most in his lute
> Which he brought to the mill
> And played while it was grinding.
> A pretty noise the pair must have made,
> Teaching him to keep time.
> But, apparently, that is how
> Music first came into our family!'

A carousel—Flour runs.
Song drifts from the noises.

> "My petted birds are dead."

> "I will gather a chain
> Of marguerites, pluck red anemone,
> Till of every hostile see
> Never a memory remain."

LANGSTON HUGHES
Four Poems

GAUGE

Hemp . . .
A stick . . .
A roach . . .
Straw . . .

HOPE

He rose up on his dying bed
and asked for fish.
His wife looked it up in her dream book
and played it.

REQUEST

Gimme $25.00
and the change.
I'm going
where the morning
and the evening
won't bother me.

FACT

There's been an eagle on a nickle,
An eagle on a quarter, too.
But there ain't no eagle
On a dime.

JOSE GARCÍA VILLA

Poem

And, if, Theseus—then, Minotaur.
Coherence, and, severance,
By, the, seven, locks, of, strictness: by, diamond-law.
Bold, me, more. Bolt, Him, more.
What, brightfall, is, this—I, see, Him,
In, the, eye, of, a, Tear.

To, mine, Him, deep—my, key-
Less, classic, my, labyrinth-
Word! Listener, exalter, startler—fullstrength,
My, vertex, rears, its, hazards, of,
Eternity. By, ballot, of, the, real,
Speak, my, Appoint, my, Key.

By, side, of, live, by, side, of, Taur,
Who, shall, alight, forth, tall,
Must, somersault, Him, gold! alight, Him, pure,

In, crystal, of, Original, Terror. My,
    On-fire-standing, love—
    Sustain, this, perilous, core.

    Pythagor, Angel, rest, and, repeat.
    Rest; and, repeat. Till,
With, the, gold-awaked, Verb, in, orience, lock—
Taurus, of, Minos, in, His, brightverb, sleep:
    —With, wreck, all, East,
    The, Vertical, complete.

■ *"I propose sweeping changes from top to bottom of the poetic struc-*
ture. I said structure. . . . I say we are through *with the iambic pentame-*
ter as presently conceived, at least for dramatic verse; through with the
measured quatrain, the staid concatenations of sounds in the usual
stanzas, the sonnet. More has been done than you think about this
though not yet been specifically named for what it is. I believe some-
thing can be said. Perhaps all that I can do here is call attention to it:
a revolution in the conception of the poetic foot—pointing out the
evidence of something that has been going on for a long time."

    —WILLIAM CARLOS WILLIAMS, *The Poem as a Field of Action*
    [1948]

The poem that follows is from a book-length sequence, *Spring and*
All, including both prose and verse, as shown here. For an example
of what Williams eventually named the "variable foot," see "The
Yellow Flower," page 313, above.

WILLIAM CARLOS WILLIAMS

From Spring and All   [1923]

The pure products of America
go crazy—
mountain folk from Kentucky

or the ribbed north end of
Jersey
with its isolate lakes and

valleys, its deaf-mutes, thieves
old names
and promiscuity between

devil-may-care men who have taken
to railroading
out of sheer lust of adventure—

and young slatterns, bathed
in filth
from Monday to Saturday

to be tricked out that night
with gauds
from imaginations which have no

peasant traditions to give them
character
but flutter and flaunt

sheer rags—succumbing without
emotion
save numbed terror

under some hedge of choke-cherry
or viburnum—
which they cannot express—

Unless it be that marriage
perhaps
with a dash of Indian blood

will throw up a girl so desolate
so hemmed round
with disease or murder

that she'll be rescued by an
agent—
reared by the state and

sent out at fifteen to work in
some hard pressed
house in the suburbs—

some doctor's family, some Elsie—
voluptuous water
expressing with broken

brain the truth about us—
her great
ungainly hips and flopping breasts

addressed to cheap
jewelry
and rich young men with fine eyes

as if the earth under our feet
were
an excrement of some sky

and we degraded prisoners
destined
to hunger until we eat filth

while the imagination strains
after deer
going by fields of goldenrod in

the stifling heat of September
Somehow
it seems to destroy us

It is only in isolate flecks that
something
is given off

No one
to witness
and adjust, no one to drive the car

Or better: prose has to do with the fact of an emotion; poetry has to do with the dynamization of emotion into a separate form. This is the force of imagination.
prose: statement of facts concerning emotions, intellectual states, data of all sorts—technical expositons, jargon, of all sorts—fictional and other—
poetry: new form dealt with as a reality in itself.
The form of prose is the accuracy of its subject matter— how best to expose the multiform phases of its material

the form of poetry is related to the movements of the imagination revealed in words—or whatever it may be— the cleavage is complete . . .

■ *"Let's start from the smallest particle of all, the syllable. It is the king and pin of versification, what rules and holds together the lines, the larger forms, of a poem. I would suggest that verse here and in England dropped this secret from the late Elizabethans to Ezra Pound, lost it, in the sweetness of meter and rime, in a honey-head. . . .*

"It is by their syllables that words juxtapose in beauty, by these particles of sound as clearly as by the sense of the words which they compose. In any given instance, because there is a choice of words, the choice, if a man is in there, will be, spontaneously, the obedience of his ear to the syllables. The fineness, and the practice, lie here, at the minimum and source of speech. . . . For from the root out, from all over the place, the syllable comes, the figures of, the dance."

—CHARLES OLSON, "Projective Verse," *Poetry New York 3* (1950, ed. Harvey Shapiro) [reprinted in *Human Universe*]

ROBERT DUNCAN

The Structure of Rime   1

I ask the unyielding Sentence that shows Itself forth in the language as I make it,

Speak! For I name myself your master, who come to serve.
Writing is first a search in obedience.

There is a woman who resembles the sentence. She has a place in memory that moves language. Her voice comes across the waters from a shore I don't know to a shore I know, and is translated into words belonging to the poem:

> *Have heart,* the text reads,
> *you that were heartless.*
> *Suffering joy or despair*
> *you will suffer the sentence*
> *a law of words moving*
> *seeking their right period.*

I saw a snake-like beauty in the living changes of syntax.

> *Wake up,* she cried.
> *Jacob wrestled with Sleep—you who fall into*
> *Nothingness and dread sleep.*
> *He wrestled with Sleep like a man reading a strong*
> *sentence.*

I will not take the actual world for granted, I said.

> *Why not?* she replied.
> *Do I not withhold the song of birds from you?*
> *Do I not withhold the penetrations of red from you?*
> *Do I not withhold the weight of mountains from you?*
> *Do I not withhold the hearts of men from you?*
>
> *I alone long for your demand.*
> *I alone measure your desire.*

O Lasting Sentence,
sentence after sentence I make in your image. In the feet that measure the dance of my pages I hear cosmic intoxications of the man I will be.

> *Cheat at this game?* she cries.
> *The world is what you are.*

Stand then
so I can see you, a fierce destroyer of images.

Will you drive me to madness
only there to know me?
vomiting images into the place of the Law!

CHARLES OLSON

From "Projective Verse" [1950]

(projectile   (percussive   (prospective
vs.
The NON-Projective

(or what a French critic calls "closed" verse, that verse
which print bred and which is pretty much what we have
had, in English & American, and have still got, despite the
work of Pound & Williams:

it led Keats, already a hundred years ago, to see it (Words-
worth's, Milton's) in the light of "the Egotistical Sublime";
and it persists, at this latter day, as what you might call
the private-soul-at-any-public-wall)

Verse now, 1950, if it is to go ahead, if it is to be of
essential use, must, I take it, catch up and put into itself
certain laws and possibilities of the breath, of the breath-
ing of the man who writes as well as of his listenings. (The
revolution of the ear, 1910, the trochee's heave, asks it of
the younger poets.)

I want to do two things: first, try to show what projective
or OPEN verse is, what it involves, in its act of composi-
tion, how, in distinction from the non-projective, it is ac-
complished; and II, suggest a few ideas about what stance
toward reality brings such verse into being, what that
stance does, both to the poet and to his reader. (The stance
involves, for example, a change beyond, and larger than,
the technical, and may, the way things look, lead to new

poetics and to new concepts from which some sort of drama, say, or of epic, perhaps, may emerge.)

. . . First, some simplicities that a man learns, if he works in OPEN, or what can also be called COMPOSI-TION BY FIELD, as opposed to inherited line, stanza, over-all form, what is the "old" base of the non-projective.

(1) the *kinetics* of the thing. A poem is energy trans-ferred from where the poet got it (he will have some sev-eral causations), by way of the poem itself to, all the way over to, the reader. Okay. Then the poem itself must, at all points, be a high energy-construct and, at all points, an energy-discharge. So: how is the poet to accomplish same energy, how is he, what is the process by which a poet gets in, at all points energy at least the equivalent of the energy which propelled him in the first place, yet an energy which is peculiar to verse alone and which will be, obvi-ously, also different from the energy which the reader, because he is a third term, will take away?

This is the problem which any poet who departs from closed form is specially confronted by. And it involves a whole series of new recognitions. From the moment he ventures into FIELD COMPOSITION—puts himself in the open—he can go by no track other than the one the poem under hand declares, for itself. Thus he has to behave, and be, instant by instant, aware of some several forces just now beginning to be examined. (It is much more, for ex-ample, this push, than simply such a one as Pound put, so wisely, to get us started: "the musical phrase," go by it, boys, rather than by, the metronome.)

(2) is the *principle,* the law which presides conspicu-ously over such composition, and, when obeyed, is the rea-son why a projective poem can come into being. It is this: FORM IS NEVER MORE THAN AN EXTENSION OF CONTENT. (Or so it got phrased by one, R. Creeley, and it makes absolute sense to me, with this possible corollary, that right form, in any given poem, is the only and exclu-sively possible extension of content under hand.) There it is, brothers, sitting there, for USE.

Now (3) the *process* of the thing, how the principle can be made so to shape the energies that the form is accom-plished. And I think it can be boiled down to one statement

(first pounded into my head by Edward Dahlberg): ONE
PERCEPTION MUST IMMEDIATELY AND DIRECTLY
LEAD TO A FURTHER PERCEPTION. It means exactly
what it says, is a matter of, at *all* points (even, I should say,
of our management of daily reality as of the daily work)
get on with it, keep moving, keep in, speed, the nerves,
their speed, the perceptions, theirs, the acts, the split sec-
ond acts, the whole business, keep it moving as fast as you
can, citizen. And if you also set up as a poet, USE USE USE
the process at all points, in any given poem always, always
one perception must must must MOVE, INSTANTER, ON
ANOTHER!

PAUL BLACKBURN

The Watchers

It's going to rain
Across the avenue a crane
whose name is
        CIVETTA LINK-BELT
dips, rises and turns in a
    graceless geometry

    But grace is slowness / as
ecstacy is some kind of speed or madness /
The crane moves slowly, that
much it is graceful / The men
    watch and the leaves

Cranes make letters in the sky
    as the wedge flies
        The scholar's function is

        Mercury, thief and poet,
        invented the first 7 letters

        5 of them vowels, watching
        cranes . after got

The men watch and the rain does not come
        HC-108B CIVETTA LINK-BELT
In the pit below a yellow cat,
        CAT-933
                pushes the debris
and earth to load CIVETTA HC-108B
        Cat's name is PASCO and
        there is an ORegon phone number,
moves its load toward 3 piles
Let him leave the building to us

        Palamedes, son of Nauplius,
          invented II more
                  (consonant)
        Also invented the lighthouse, and
        measures, the scales, the disc, and
        "the art of posting sentinels"
        Ruled over the Mysians,
                Cretan stock, al-
                though his father was Greek
                Took part in the Trojan trouble on the
Greek side . The scholar's function is fact . Let him
                quarry cleanly . All
                THOSE INVENTIONS CRETAN
                so that a Greek / alpha-beta-tau
                based on a Cretan, not a Phoenician
                    model
                Three different piles:

earth / debris / & schist, the stud/stuff of the island
        is moved by this
        PASCO
        CAT-933
        ORegon 6-

it does not rain   .   smoke, the
                          alpha-beta-tau

raised from   5 vowels, 13 consonants to
                  5 vowels, 15 consonants
                  (Epicharmus) not
the Sicilian writer of comedies, 6 A.D., but
his ancestor /
the Aesculapius family at Cos, a couple are
mentioned in the Iliad as physicians to
the Greeks before the equipotent walls
of Troy

                  No, it does not rain, smoke
                  rises from the engines, the
                  leaves   .   The men watch
                  before the walls of Troy

Apollo in cithaera ceteras literas adjecit

                  7 strings on that zither
                  & for each string a letter
                  Thence to Simonides,
native of Ceos in the service of Dionysus
which god also at home in Delphos
both gods of the solar year as were/   Aesculapius
                                          & Hercules
                                          Let's
        get all of this into one pot, 6–700 years B.C.

Simonides, well-known poet, intro-
ducted into Athens 4 more letters   .   the
        unnecessary double-consonants *PSI*
                            (earlier written Pi-Sigma)
        and *XI* (earlier written Kappa-Sigma)
plus (plus) two vowels : *OMEGA,* a distinction from
        the omicron Hermes conned
        from the 3 Crones, and

EPSILON, as distinct from their eta
& that's the long & the short of it.

Cranes fly in V-formation & the
Tyrrhenians, or Etruscans, were
also of Cretan stock, held
the crane in reverence / The men watch
                    LINK-BELT move up its load, the
                    pile to the left near 24th St., the
                    permanent erection moves
                    slow-ly almost sensually, al-most
                              gracefully
The scholar's function / fact . Let him quarry
cleanly / leave the building to us / Poems
nicked with a knife onto the bark of a stick (Hesiod)
        or upon tablets of clay
                    Perseus cuts off the Gorgon-head
                         (Medusa)
                    and carries it off in a bag . But
the head's a ritual mask and a protection, we
frighten children with it
and trespassers
when we perform the rites .   It is
                         no murder,
                         she has given him power of
                              sight
p o e t r y,
            the gorgons no pursuers
            are escort, and the mask
                              (his protection)
Hermes / Car / Mercury / Perseus / Palamedes / Thoth / or
        whatever his orignal name was,
winged sandals and helmet, you bet!
the swiftness of poetic thought / And the bag

THE ALPHABET'S IN THE BAG!

Almost sensually, almost
gracefully . The men watch

and know not what they watch
The cat pushes . the crane . the bud
lifts upward . above the

                 Pillars of Hercules, desti-
nation, where he is going, bringing the secret in the bag
            The tree at Gades (Cádiz)
       principal city of Tartessus, the
Aegean colony on the Guadalquivir
From there the Milesians will take it to Ireland?
The older city is on the western shore with its
             Temple of Cronus . island,
             the island of the goddess,
            Red Island / & Cronus
god of the middle finger, the fool's finger / It is
  his father he kills not his mother, his mother
  gives him

           the secret
                Scholar's function is
                          The men watch

Hercules' shrine set up by colonists, 1100 B.C.
400 years before the Phoenicians
coming from Tyre in painted ships
   and their oracle
              HERCULES=PALAMEDES (?)

7 & 2
9 steps to the goddess
& everyone lives to 110 years
5 years to a lustrum
             (Etruscan)
22   lustra=110
             (alpha-beta-tau
& the circumferance of the circle when
    the diameter is 7 is
22
proportion known as π
22 (plus) over 7
a neat recurrent sequence

which does not work out becase it never
ends /
7 lustra is 35 years   .   Maturity,
or the age at which a man may be elected
President of the United States / a convention
or a Roman might be elected Consul / a convention

$$\frac{22}{7}$$

These numbers no longer a secret /   But in Crete
                                       or Spain. . .

Spanish, the mother's family name
still is set down last, and
still in Crete descent is matrilineal
The Greeks have accomplished nothing
        but death   beauty
                (Troy)

The men watch the cat push
keeping the piles discrete
earth / debris / & schist
the stuff of the island, the crane, the bud
lifts upward . above the
                        And at Cádiz, Caius Julius Hyginus,
                        a Spaniard and Ovid's friend,
                        curator of the Palantine Library,
                        exiled from the court of Augustus

sitting under a tree in Cádiz
over the problem, over a millenium later,
traces Greek letters in the spelt of wine at his table
watches the cranes fly over toward Africa
wedge in the sunset / set down the score:

                Mercury (or the Fates) 7
                Palamedes   11
                Epicharmus   2
                Simonides   4
Say that he used Etruscan sources,
        does that explain it?
Let them quarry cleanly

Let them leave
Cranes winging over toward Africa
        a wedge
Hyginus traces π on the wooden table in wine spelt

        The cat pushes, the crane, the bud
        lifts upward /   above the
        rain comes finally
The watchers leave the construction site,
the men leave their machines
        At 323 Third Avenue,
        an old drunk (Hyginus)
sits in a doorway and downs a whole
pint of Sacramento Tomato Juice

                    The watchers are the gods

                    The leaves burgeon

JACK SPICER

Phonemics

No love deserves the death it has.   An
        archipelago
Rocks cropping out of ocean.   Seabirds
        shit on it.   Live out their lives on
        it.
What was once a mountain.
Or was it once a mountain?   Did Lemuria,
        Atlantis, Mu ever exist except in
        the minds of old men fevered by
        the distances and the rocks they saw?
Was it true?   Can the ocean of time claim
        to own us now adrift
Over that land.   In that land.   If
        memory serves
There (that rock out there)
Is more to it.

•

Wake up one warm morning.   See the
        sea in the distance.
Die Ferne, water
Because mainly it is not land.   A hot day too
The shreads of fog have already vaporized
Have gone back where they came from.   There
        may be a whale in this ocean.
Empty fragments, like the shards of pots
        found in some Mesapotamian expedition.
        Found but not put together.   The unstable
Universe has distance but not much else.
No one's weather or room to breathe in.

•

On the tele-phone (distance sound)
        you sounded no distant than if you
        were talking to me in San Francisco
        on the telephone or in a bar or in
        a room.   Long
Distance calls.   They break sound
Into electrical impulses and put it back
        again.   Like the long telesexual route
        to the brain or the even longer
        teleerotic route to the heart.   The
        numbers dialed badly, the connection
        faint.
Your voice
        consisted of sounds that I had
To route to phonemes, then to bound
        and free morphemes, then to syntactic
        structures.   Telekinesis
Would not have been possible even if we were sitting
        at the same table.   Long
Distance calls your father, your mother,
        your friend, your lover.   The lips
Are never quite as far away as when you kiss.
An electric system.
"Gk. 'ηλέκτρον, amber, also shining metal;
        allied to 'ηλέκτωρ, gleaming."

•

    Malice aforethought.   Every sound
You can make making music.
Tough lips.
This is no nightengale.   No-
Body's waxen image burned.   Only
Believe me.   Linguistics is divided like
        Graves' mythology of mythology, a
        triple goddess—morphology, phonology,
        and syntax.
Tough lips that cannot quite make the
        sounds of love
The language
Has so misshapen them.
Malicious afterthought.   None of you bastards
Knows how Charlie Parker died.   And
        dances now in some brief kingdom
        (Oz) two phonemes
That were never paired before in the langauge.

•

Aleph did not come before Beth.   The
        Semetic languages kept as strict
        a separation between consonant and
        vowel as between men and women.   Vowels
        somehow got between to produce
        children.   JVH
Was male.   The Mycenaen bookkeepers
Mixed them up (one to every 4.5)
        (A=1, E=5, I=9, 0=15, U=21)
Alpha being chosen as the queen of the
        alphabet because she meant "not."
Punched
        IBM cards follow this custom.
What I have chosen to follow is what
        schoolteachers call a blend, but which
        is not, since the sounds are very
        little changed by each other
Two consonants (floating in the sea

of some truth together)
Immediately preceded and/or followed
    by a vowel.

              •

    The emotional disturbance echoes down
    the canyons of the heart.
Echoes there—sounds cut off—merely
    phonemes.   A ground-rules double.
    You recognize them by pattern.   Try.
Hello shouted down a canyon becomes
    huhluh.   You, and the canyons of the
    heart,
Recognize feebly what you shouted.   The
    vowels
Are indistinguishable.   The consonants
A pattern for imagination.   Phonemes,
In the true sense, that are dead before
    their burial.   Constructs
Of the imagination
Of the real canyon and the heart's
Construct.

written in response
to a request for   }
a manifesto on   instantaneous   and unpredictable
music, 1952

    nothing is accomplished by writing a piece of music   } our ears are
      "   "   "   " hearing" "   "   "   now
      "   "   "   " playing" "   "   "   in excellent condition

—JOHN CAGE

JOHN CAGE

From Lecture on Nothing

This lecture was printed in Incontri Musicali, *August 1959. There are four measures in each line and twelve lines in each unit of the rhythmic structure. There are forty-eight such units, each having forty-eight measures. The whole is divided into five large parts, in the proportion 7, 6, 14, 14, 7. The forty-eight measures of each unit are likewise so divided. The text is printed in four columns to facilitate a rhythmic reading. Each line is to be read across the page from left to right, not down the columns in sequence. This should not be done in an artificial manner (which might result from an attempt to be too strictly faithful to the position of the words on the page), but with the* rubato *which one uses in everyday speech.*

I am here   ,   and there is nothing to say   .

                                                                If among you are

those who wish to get   somewhere   ,   let them leave at

any moment   .   What we re–quire   is

silence   ;   but what silence requires

          is   that I go on talking   .

                                                                Give any one thought

              a push   :   it falls down easily   ·

;   but the pusher   and the pushed   pro–duce   that enter–

tainment   called   a dis–cussion   .

              Shall we have one later ?

                                        𝆏

Or   ,   we could simply de–cide   not to have a dis–

cussion   .   What ever you like .   But

now   there are silences   and the

words   make   help make   the

silences   .

                                                I have nothing to say

          and I am saying it   and that is

poetry   as I need it   .

              This space of time   is organized

                        We need not fear these   silences, —

                                        𝆏

we may love them   .

                                 This is a composed

talk   ,   for I am making it

     just as I make   a piece of music.   It is like a glass

       of milk   .   We need the   glass

and we need the   milk   .   Or again   it is like an

empty glass   into which   at any

moment   anything   may be poured

.   As we go along   ,   (who knows?)

      an i–dea may occur in this   talk   .

                          I have no idea   whether one will

      or not.   If one does,   let it.   Re–

                          ℳ

gard it as something   seen   momentarily   ,   as

though   from a window   while traveling   .

If across Kansas   ,   then, of course,   Kansas

.   Arizona   is more interesting,

almost too interesting   ,   especially   for a New–Yorker   who is

being interested   in spite of himself   in everything.   Now he knows he

needs   the Kansas in him   .   Kansas is like

nothing on earth   ,   and for a New Yorker   very refreshing.

It is like an empty glass ,   nothing but wheat   ,   or

is it corn   ?   Does it matter which   ?

Kansas   has this about it: at any instant,   one may leave it,

and whenever one wishes one may return to it   .

                          ℳ

Or you may leave it   forever   and never return to it   ,

      for we pos–sess nothing   .   Our poetry now

        is the reali–zation   that we possess   nothing

.   Anything   therefore   is a delight

(since we do not   pos–sess it)   and thus   need not fear its loss

.   We need not destroy the   past: it is gone;

at any moment,   it might reappear and   seem to be   and be the present

.   Would it be a   repetition?   Only if we thought we

owned it,   but since we don't,   it is free   and so are we

Most anybody knows a-bout the future

and how un-certain it is   .

♍

What I am calling   poetry   is often called   content.

I myself   have called   it form   .   It is the conti-

nuity   of a piece of music.   Continuity   today,

when it is necessary   ,   is a demonstration   of dis-

interestedness.   That is,   it is a proof   that our delight

lies in not   pos-sessing anything   .   Each moment

presents what happens   .   How different

this form sense is   from that   which is bound up with

memory: themes   and secondary themes;   their struggle;

their development;   the climax;   the recapitulation   (which is the belief

that one may   own one's own home)   .   But actually,

unlike the snail   ,   we carry our homes   within us,

♍

which enables us   to fly   or to stay

, —   to enjoy   each.   But beware of

that which is   breathtakingly   beautiful,   for at any moment

the telephone   may ring   or the airplane

come down in a   vacant lot   .   A piece of string

or a sunset   ,   possessing neither   ,

each acts   and the continuity   happens

.   Nothing more than   nothing   can be said.

Hearing   or making this   in music   is not different

—   only simpler —   than living this way   .

Simpler, that is   ,   for me, — because it happens

that I write music   .

♍   ♍

That music is   simple to make   comes from   one's willingness to ac-

cept   the limitations   of structure.   Structure is

simple   be-cause   it can be thought out,   figured out,

measured   .   It is a discipline   which,

accepted,   in return   accepts whatever   ,   even those

rare moments   of ecstasy,   which,   as sugar loaves train horses,

train us   to make what we make   .   .   .   .

POETRY, CHANCE, ETC.: Both the following poem and others by Mac Low in this anthology and out of it were composed by systematic chance operations. Mac Low writes: "Poems in which meaning & connections are left entirely (or for the most part) unspecified, in which appearances & concatenations of words happen because of an objective chance-operational method, not thru the immediate choice of the poet (intuitional or rational),—such poems are not vehicles merely of the vision of the individual poet but constructions or event-series which allow each reader or hearer to be visionary himself rather than the passive receiver of the poet's vision. Confronted by this kind of poem, the sympathetic reader or hearer (& the poet himself as he watches the product of his chance-operational actions appear) addresses his attention primarily to each word or series of words as it happens, without attempting consciously to find meanings beyond those obviously belonging to the words themselves, or to connect the words more than they are already connected. Nevertheless, some layer of his mind will be, to some extent, providing meanings & connections of which he may be dimly aware. (Or he may be quite aware of them.) In this way, poem & audience interpenetrate with a minimum of interference by the poet, whose own action consists of inventing the chance-operational system used, making what choices are necessary to initiate its actions, & carrying thru the actions required by it to produce the poem. In this situation one may say that the poet, & the word-sources, the audience & the world (as chance in action & as environment) are transparently & unobstructedly interpenetrating." (1962)

JACKSON MAC LOW

From Stanzas for Iris Lezak
Paracelsus [20 Sept. 1960]

Nothing other therefore
is needed to everything. . . . Required profane, required
     establish the
terms Holy in supernatural
same in great "natural"
are serve
are
saints. *Ultima materia—materia* originally not something.

To obtain
pure recall a correspondingly transformed in stomach essence

mysterium and great in concealment
fruit. . . . One ripe

is form
and
many, as necessary,
purpose refined and curative things, it says endowed some
first arcanum *lapis* seed energies. . . .
Mercurius arcanum gold; its crudity.
Here earth
this earth miraculously prerogative this studied
goods or derived
art, never do.
In fancy

heaven, exist
to evil man. Pestilence, they signs
governed, or does
whole of events.
This one
has inferior sick
say one's understanding leads.

■ "*Schrödinger, contrasting organic and inorganic forms in nature, says [in* What is Life?*]: 'Starting from a small solid germ, there seem to be two different ways of building up larger and larger associations. One is the comparatively dull way of repeating the same structure in three directions again and again. That is the way followed in a growing crystal. Once the periodicity is established, there is no definite limit to the size of the aggregate.*

"*'The other way is that of building up a more and more extended aggregate without the dull device of repetition. That is the case of the more and more complicated organic molecule in which every atom, and every group of atoms, plays an individual role, not entirely equivalent to that of many others (as in the case of a periodic structure). We might properly call that an aperiodic crystal or solid and express our hypothesis by saying: We believe a gene—or perhaps the whole chromosome fiber —to be an aperiodic solid.'*

"*Genetic thought along these lines is akin to poetic thought that pictures the poem as an organic crystallization, its germ or law or form being immanent in the immediate life, what is happening, in the work of the poem. 'I believe in technique as the test of a man's sincerity; in law when it is ascertainable,' Pound writes in 1912, 'in the trampling down of every convention that impedes or obscures the determination of the law, or the precise rendering of the impulse.' Free verse, later projective verse as expounded by Charles Olson, developed a new sense of metric and rime deriving from an inner aperiodic formal intuition. Here, structure is not satisfied in the molecule, is not additive; but is fulfilled in the whole work, the apprehension of the work's 'life' springing anew in each realization, each immediate cell. "*

—ROBERT DUNCAN, *The H. D. Book*, Part II, Chapter 4 [1961]

BIOPOETICS: Coleridge, Goethe, Emerson, and Thoreau long ago suggested applying the method of "imagination" to the work of the scientist, and contemporary thinkers like Buckminster Fuller and Owen Barfield (*Saving the Appearances*) have tried to show that this is in fact possible. Drawing from his work as microbiologist, poet, and student of *I Ching,* Harvey Bialy hypothesizes a common structure in the Chinese hexagrammic system and the "Genetic Code" of DNA, expressed as a "harmonic series." As such it illustrates the metapoetic cross-over between intuitive and rational disciplines:

> The manifestation of form in the world is the result of a harmonic series of permutations of the numbers 3 and 4, specifically the arrangement of a set of 4 elements in groups of 3 so that 64 elements are generated: = the minimal number (a fact); and further that the 4 basic elements are themselves of two distinct types, related to each other by a *principle of complementarity.* The overall system acquires its temporal and informational properties in being conditioned by a *principle of asymmetry.* The 64 elements so generated are the materials on which a law of ceaseless unchanging change operates, so that at any moment each element is possibly any other. It is the constant interflow of these 64 units which gives rise to all the apparently different forms in Nature.
>
> The above as applied to (1) DNA and the "Genetic Code" and (2) the *I Ching.*   —[Harvey Bialy, NYC, May 1972]

LARRY EIGNER
The Music,   The Rooms

the music,   the rooms

silence silence silence silence sound
              on the walls

the beach ravelling
times advance

or back up
around earth
electric poles

the sun a reflected color
tropic
how distance is to some birds

in the wind

fishing

pinpoint

the circling air

food

the power

with desperate ease

food for me hits the water
without break, the cries

the meaning of change

information shifted,   player-piano
on the screen,   the swimming moon

enters eclipse
out the window, and other station

none of us is watching

the cabinet

instrument forgotten

the clock shakes out

head bent from the wing

in a live broadcast

a case for various things

dry grassy fields

the blank sky

wampum gulls broke shells

such eyes
directed

a malnutrition

Kenya

straightens hair it turns blond

scurvy is wiped out

the dogs come, the group
on bikes

the street comes

the North Sea

studio on a ship

pivot spun

dark life
rises
leaving the island

the dim expanding miles

a steady white light
they might drive headlong into
the mist like a magnet

blows   lost bearings

nest in fisherman's pocket

the wash

"... distant thunder ... Nearer and nearer came the strange commingling sound of sleigh bells, mixed with the rumbling of an approaching storm ... I gazed in wonder and astonishment ... They passed like a cloud

through the branches of the high trees, through the underbrush
and over the ground . . . they fluttered all about me; gently I caught two
in my hands and carefully concealed them under my blanket.
   I now began to realize they were mating . . ."

> —CHIEF POKAGAN, describing an onset of the now
>   extinct passenger pigeon, in Michigan, May 1850

THEODORE ENSLIN
Forms XIII

When I had raised a stone called 'BETH-EL,'
I found ways back
                     into the world I lost one night,
wrestling and dreaming fires into blood.
Not new truths, but old ones kept new.

Lichten leben! Why do I say it so?
A work of lights—a light that secrets may be cherished
but not buried.
                     Faith and innocence,
all love was in that stony field.

      An angel said:
                'The quantity which is past did more exceed.'
      Consider this, as rains are more than drops remaining.
      Smoke is less than fire.
                           It has gone away.
      Oh we have dreaded this, but we've known it so:
      Our times are near the end, and yet the end stays
            constant,
      standing at a little way.

      From the wilderness
      I came to love,
      love which may cherish *all* the world.
      Choose it for a resting place.
                           Then to go on.
      We do not live in time.

                    In space.
In space exact.
             A place
not limbo.

The wave is greater than the drop,
and there are seven days of rain upon us,
so wise men have said,
who've spent their lives looking into clouds,
toward god, upward or downward—
altissimus.

  The angel said:
'But go into a field of flowers where no house is builded, and
eat only the flowers of the field—'
                        'So I went my way to the field
which is called Ardath.'

              Beloved, in the field
              the seed falls
              to the rough earth,
              seed and field alike,
              color and flower.
              Our field is in its first season—
              its week of rain.

  "Such as the workman is, such also is the work, and as the
husbandman is himself, so is his husbandry also. For it was the
time of the world."

  And Henry's work sounds in the trees each season.
  How many of these waves have touched the Spray?
  Song is the fruit borne in by air—the wayfarer's song.
  And color in this field.

              The treasure's bright
              in secret place
              the flowers never fade—

no last roses,
no season which is none
or out of place.
The treasure's bright, beloved,
we couldn't stain it
if we would.

'Like as the field is, so is also the seed; as the flowers be, such
are the colours also.'
                    Thus far Uriel.

Days when it is good to be alone,
to remake time,
and know the stillness in a man
that wrestles—
breaks on the rack.
It *must* be good to free
the self.
                    The νους.

Then we'll hide the words of kings,
shout for joy the words of love—
love in a lonely place,
or love that shares.
I've brought this to a place
where wisdom is in all I touch,
but not in me.
Let me flow, good river,
to you, beloved—
to *all* who love.
Life in its great illogic
                                forms love.

Come down! Come down!
Zaccheus from his green tree,
or by the rungs of that burned ladder,
come down!

The agony is bright
>   too.

What we know of angels,
what we know of hell
or heaven
in that field,
or on this hill,
The ever present self
will canker.
>   The galls
are self.
One night will never change
a chance return.

Is it right that we deceive?
even to the glory of God?
or what we love?
(Judith in Holofernes' tent?)
Make mine a field of some defeat.
The angel will mean that much to me.

>   Now the sea goose
>   turns on south,
>   he takes his season surely,
>   would a man
>   or all his angels
>   know as much?
The questions beg themselves.
Answer is inscrutable.

There are roses—but they bloom in snow—gone to snow:
The red blooms in a sheath of ice.
The berries glow as ripe
now that the first days of winter
are forgotten
>   as they did.
But, in this last blazing heat,

all the flavor's gone.
The fruit is of another time.
The shadow of the sea goose
passes.
          Was it smoke?
Was it cloud?
Perhaps there wasn't any bird at all.
It was shadow.
                    Was it shadow from the smoke?
from the cloud?
                    Perhaps no cry against the ice
at all.
Was it daylight? or the sun in hiding?
The season, 'to eat one's heart out,'
is at hand.
Perhaps it wasn't any wind,
no wind at all.
Evoke! Evoke!
Perhaps.
          Perhaps there is no question,
none at all.
No answer then—
                    no answering at all.
Let be!
          Loose, leave open,
unstrained, unbounded,
more than to speak in tongues is learned
alone in Ardath.
                    How to gain is to give up.

We would walk in treachery,
if we tried to reach that place again—
tried to bring love
                    to the same place.
There is no *sameness;*
perhaps in absolutes you see this,

and mistake what moves
for what is not at all.
You must know this from another time,
another season
                    (when March is very like October.)
We've mistaken our identities—
changed selves—
                    and not known how.
The line!
                "That time is gone forever, child."
Why does it press so?

Henry and the captain, in their ways, made us what we are.
As much as we deny it,
                        or pass by, not knowing them—
or who they were.
                    It makes no difference.
The touch of a flawed art stretches shadows
willess
        on the storm.
Shadows over us.
                    Seaward, where the armies march
voiceless, but with the song
                        in measured feet.

"But how sustain a long line in poetry (lest it lapse into prosaic)? It's natural inspiration of the moment that keeps it moving, disparate thinks put down together, shorthand notations of visual imagery, juxtapositions of hydrogen juke-box—abstract haikus sustain the mystery & put iron poetry back into the line: single word associations, summing up. Mind is shapely, Art is shapely. Meaning Mind practiced in spontaneity invents forms in its own image & gets to Last Thoughts. Loose ghosts wailing for body try to invade the bodies of living men. I hear ghostly Academics in Limbo screeching about form."

—ALLEN GINSBERG, Notes for *Howl and Other Poems* [1959]

ALLEN GINSBERG

Sunflower Sutra   [1955]

I walked on the banks of the tincan banana dock and sat down
 under the huge shade of a Southern Pacific locomotive to
 look at the sunset over the box house hills and cry.
Jack Kerouac sat beside me on a busted rusty iron pole, compan-
 ion, we thought the same thoughts of the soul, bleak and
 blue and sad-eyed, surrounded by the gnarled steel roots of
 trees of machinery.
The oily water on the river mirrored the red sky, sun sank on top
 of final Frisco peaks, no fish in that stream, no hermit in
 those mounts, just ourselves rheumy-eyed and hungover
 like old bums on the riverbank, tired and wily.
Look at the Sunflower, he said, there was a dead gray shadow
 against the sky, big as a man, sitting dry on top of a pile of
 ancient sawdust—
—I rushed up enchanted—it was my first sunflower, memories of
 Blake—my visions—Harlem
and Hells of the Eastern rivers, bridges clanking Joes Greasy
 Sandwiches, dead baby carriages, black treadless tires for-
 gotten and unretreaded, the poem of the riverbank, con-
 doms & pots, steel knives, nothing stainless, only the dank
 muck and the razor sharp artifacts passing into the past—
and the gray Sunflower poised against the sunset, crackly bleak
 and dusty with the smut and smog and smoke of olden
 locomotives in its eye—
corolla of bleary spikes pushed down and broken like a battered
 crown, seeds fallen out of its face, soon-to-be-toothless
 mouth of sunny air, sunrays obliterated on its hairy head
 like a dried wire spiderweb,
leaves stuck out like arms out of the stem, gestures from the
 sawdust root, broke pieces of plaster fallen out of the black
 twigs, a dead fly in its ear,
Unholy battered old thing you were, my sunflower O my soul, I
 loved you then!
The grime was no man's grime but death and human locomo-
 tives,

all that dress of dust, that veil of darkened railroad skin, that
   smog of cheek, that eyelid of black mis'ry, that sooty hand
   or phallus or protuberance of artificial worse-than-dirt—
   industrial—modern—all that civilization spotting your
   crazy golden crown—
and those blear thoughts of death and dusty loveless eyes and
   ends and withered roots below, in the home-pile of sand
   and sawdust, rubber dollar bills, skin of machinery, the
   guts and innards of the weeping coughing car, the empty
   lonely tincans with their rusty tongues alack, what more
   could I name, the smoked ashes of some cock cigar, the
   cunts of wheelbarrows and the milky breasts of cars, worn-
   out asses out of chairs & sphincters of dynamos—all these
entangled in your mummied roots—and you there standing
   before me in the sunset, all your glory in your form!
A perfect beauty of a sunflower! a perfect excellent lovely sun-
   flower existence! a sweet natural eye to the new hip moon,
   woke up alive and excited grasping in the sunset shadow
   sunrise golden monthly breeze!
How many flies buzzed round you innocent of your grime, while
   you cursed the heavens of the railroad and your flower
   soul?
Poor dead flower? when did you forget you were a flower? when
   did you look at your skin and decide you were an impotent
   dirty old locomotive? the ghost of a locomotive? the specter
   and shade of a once powerful mad American locomotive?
You were never no locomotive, Sunflower, you were a sunflower!
And you Locomotive, you are a locomotive, forget me not!
So I grabbed up the skeleton thick sunflower and stuck it at my
   side like a scepter,
and deliver my sermon to my soul, and Jack's soul too, and any-
   one who'll listen,
—We're not our skin of grime, we're not our dread bleak dusty
   imageless locomotive, we're all beautiful golden sunflow-
   ers inside, we're blessed by our own seed & golden hairy
   naked accomplishment-bodies growing into mad black
   formal sunflowers in the sunset, spied on by our eyes under
   the shadow of the mad locomotive riverbank sunset Frisco
   hilly tincan evening sitdown vision.

JACK KEROUAC
"211th Chorus" *from* Mexico City Blues

The wheel of the quivering meat conception
Turns in the void expelling human beings,
Pigs, turtles, frogs, insects, nits,
Mice, lice, lizards, rats, roan
Racinghorses, poxy bucolic pigtics,
Horrible unnameable lice of cultures,
Murderous attacking dog-armies
Of Africa, Rhinos roaming in the jungle,
Vast boars and huge gigantic bull
Elephants, rams, eagles, condors,
Pones and Porcupines and Pills—
All the endless conception of living beings
Gnashing everywhere in Consciousness
Throughout the ten directions of space
Occupying all the quarters in & out,
From supermicroscopic no-bug
To huge Galaxy Lightyear Bowell
Illuminating the sky of one Mind—
  Poor! I wish I was free
  of that slaving meat wheel
  and safe in heaven dead

  NOTE: I want to be considered a jazz poet blowing a long blues in an
  afternoon jam session on Sunday. I take 242 choruses; my ideas
  vary and sometimes roll from chorus to chorus or from halfway
  through a chorus to halfway into the next. [J.K.]

STEPHEN JONAS
Exercises for Ear

  CLV

when the man
   blows his saxophone
we listen

as to a poet
speaking of his a-
bandon'd or
slower, in a lower
octave, speaks of this
everlasting
enigma

SONIA SANCHEZ

on seeing pharoah sanders blowing

for chuck

SET 1

listen
listen
listen

to me
to me.
a
black
man

with
eyeballs
white.
staring

at your honky faces.

listen
listen
listen.

hear
the
cowbells
ring out
my hate.

hear
my
sax
burping
your
shit.　　　death.
　　　　　　　it's black music/magic
u hear. yeah. i'm fucking
u white whore.
　　　　　　america. while
i slit your honky throat.

　　　SET 2
split.
　　　you honkies.
　　　　　　　move
　　　　　your slow asses.
get out now
　　　　　　no seconds
　　　on living.
　　　　　　split
now.
　　man. i'm coming
for u
　　now with my
blood filled
　　　　sax.　　　　　　　calling
　　　　　　　　all bloods.
　　　　　　　　　beep.
　　　　　　　　　beep.

　　　　　　mary
　　　　　　　had
　　　　a
　　　　　little
　　　　　lamb.
until

she
     got
her
                      throat
                      cut.
        see what i mean?

     SET 3
ah ah ah
     oh
aah aah aah
      ooh
aaah aaah aaah
      oooh.
hee hee haa
ho ho hee   u white son of
     a bitch
        america.
           u dead.

ROCHELLE OWENS

From Elga's Incantation

O MI DARLING I'M GETTING DEAF O MI DARLING I'M
GETTING DEAF O MI DARLING I'M GETTING DEAF O
MI THARLING I'M GETHING DEAFTH O MI THAR-
LING I'M GETHING DEAFTH O MI DARLING THAR-
LING YOU A TWO-BIT STARTHLING THO I'M GE-
THING DEAFTH O MI DARLING I'M GETTING DEAF O
MI DARLING I'M GETTING DEAF O MI THARLING
DARLING YOU A TWO-BIT STARLING SO I'M GET-
TING DEAF I'M GETTING DEAF MI DARLING I'M GET-
TING DEAF O I'M GETTING DEAF & DEAFER THAN
YOU O MI DARLING THARLING LISTHEN TO ME O
LISTEN WHILE I BECOME THE DEAFEST O MI DAR-
LING YOU'RE GETTING TO BE THE DEAREST TO ME
WHAT DEPTH IT IS TO GET DEAF YOU HEAR O MI
THARLING MI THARLING MI THARLING O MI DAR-

LING SO OO O O SO O O MI DARLING When in the half part she caused him to go lower, making thus a natural body of course, moving on him loudly with trickery, a philosophical wench and dirty bitch on a bicycle (HIM) becoming his bread (her) her muscles rioting at the end of the dinner O MI DARLING I'M GETTING DUMB O MI DARLING I'M GETTING DUMB TELL ME ABOUT THE FRANKISH EMPIRE AND THE BUSH CRANBERRY AND THE DITHER OF ANCIENT BATTLES AND WHO ENDOWED ME WITH BEAUTY AND WHY I'M WISE AS A PENNY & WEIGH SO MANY POUNDS. WHO IS HUMMING IN THIS BURG? WHAT IS THE NAME OF THIS BURG? HOW MANY PEOPLE LIVING IN THIS BURG? HOW MANY ARE UNNATURAL IN THIS BURG? O MI DARLING I'M DUMB O MI DARLING I'M DUMB I'M SO DUMB MI DARLING TELL ME HOW So she got a slight shake indeed the truth which isn't puzzling indeed indeed she might have become a suicide that's a numbing thought though though 1 of every 3 young used to die though probably in the days when men fought in their nakedness the first poke would kill them though but what excitement! what excitement what cockeyed excitement think of the young men lying like ripening cheese in lands not their own mouthes near each other saying gush to the god of war gush gush we are not so good for marrying now what woman would have acquaintance with us now now that we're shrinking in death now that our heads are concave and our blood and sperm become just mixed color. What this is nasty talk? LAMB-OF-GOD DISGRACEFUL ELGA SAYS SHE IS AS LOVELY AS A BUTTER-AND-EGGS FLOWER LAMB-OF-GOD PUT ELGA'S NAME IN THE DOOMSDAY BOOK PUNISH HER MAKE HER FEEL A BIG LOSS MAKE HER LITTLE EYES BE PUT OUT SHE DAST NOT KNOW NOTHING BUT BAD KNOWLEDGE GET-HER-THE-FUCK-OUT-OF-HERE BA BA BABUP A BUPADUP BUPPA BUPPA DUP DUP O MI DARLING I'M GETTING BLIND O MI DARLING I'M GETTING BLIND O MI DARLING I'M GETTING BLIND O MI DARLING I'M GETTING BLIND O MI DARLING I'M GETTING TO BE FULL OF DOUBT BLIND WIPING OUT THE WISDOM OF SOL WIPING OUT OF MY EYES DINAH'S AMERICA SO I SHOULD BE BLIND WHOLLY

EMMETT WILLIAMS
do you remember

do you remember

when i loved soft pink nights
and you hated hard blue valleys
and i kissed mellow red potatoes
and you loved livid green seagulls
and i hated soft yellow dewdrops
and you kissed hard pink oysters
and i loved mellow blue nights
and you hated livid red valleys
and i kissed soft green potatoes
and you loved hard yellow seagulls
and i hated mellow pink dewdrops
and you kissed livid blue oysters
and i loved soft red nights
and you hated hard green valleys
and i kissed mellow yellow potatoes
and you loved livid pink seagulls
and i hated soft blue dewdrops
and you kissed hard red oysters
and i loved mellow green nights
and you hated livid yellow valleys
and i kissed soft pink potatoes
and you loved hard blue seagulls
and i hated mellow red dewdrops
and you kissed livid green oysters
and i loved soft yellow nights
and you hated hard pink valleys
and i kissed mellow blue potatoes
and you loved livid red seagulls
and i hated soft green dewdrops

and you kissed hard yellow oysters
and i loved mellow pink nights
and you hated livid blue valleys
and i kissed soft red potatoes
and you loved hard green seagulls
and i hated mellow yellow dewdrops
and you kissed livid pink oysters
and i loved soft blue nights
and you hated hard red valleys
and i kissed mellow green potatoes
and you loved livid yellow seagulls
and i hated soft pink dewdrops
and you kissed hard blue oysters
and i loved mellow red nights
and you hated livid green valleys
and i kissed soft yellow potatoes
and you loved hard pink seagulls
and i hated mellow blue dewdrops
and you kissed livid red oysters
and i loved soft green nights
and you hated hard yellow valleys
and i kissed mellow pink potatoes
and you loved livid blue seagulls
and i hated soft red dewdrops
and you kissed hard green oysters
and i loved mellow yellow nights
and you hated livid pink valleys
and i kissed soft blue potatoes
and you loved hard red seagulls
and i hated mellow green dewdrops
and you kissed livid yellow oysters
and i loved soft pink nights?

ALLAN PLANZ
From High Summer

Thigh-deep in swampwater
   a woman is singing up gods, song this dusk colors
scarlet,
         as meadows fall on gold (—gods swiftly dying,

    that flash as wind bends salt grass from green to yellow,
                                      that
        cry once as wind
           in the jackpine fails)—falling
      with the night. Now
    the kingsnake slides from his stone,
  dogfish infiltrate the shallows
        & steel slurs
          the leavetaking of a girl
            at a cottage door, stunned
      between two darknesses. A brown woman in brown
                                water
        sings. Mist
        coming off the water smells of cinnamon, wild
                                  mint,
         woman. Insects drop
          about her
  to scud on the surface seams of phosphor & lisp
          thru the depths
          coins & butterflies   What/
gods.

TED BERRIGAN

From Sonnets

XXXVII

It is night. You are asleep. And beautiful tears
Have blossomed in my eyes. Guillaume Apollinaire is dead.
The big green day today is singing to itself
A vast orange library of dreams, dreams
Dressed in newspaper, wan as pale thighs
Making vast apple strides towards "The Poems."
"The Poems" is not a dream. It is night. You
Are asleep. Vast orange libraries of dreams
Stir inside "The Poems." On the dirt-covered ground
Crystal tears drench the ground. Vast orange dreams
Are unclenched. It is night. Songs have blossomed

In the pale crystal library of tears. You
Are asleep. A lovely light is singing to itself,
In "The Poems," in my eyes, in the line, "Guillaume
      Apollinaire is dead."

LXVII

(clarity! clarity!) a semblance of motion, ominiscience.
There is no such thing as a breakdown
To cover the tracks of "The Hammer"   (the morning sky
gets blue and red and I get worried about
mountains of mounting pressure
and the rust on the bolt in my door
Some kind of Bowery Santa Clauses   I wonder
down the secret streets of Roaring Gap
A glass of chocolate milk, head of lettuce, dark-
Bearden is dead. Chris is dead. Jacques Villon is dead.
Patsy awakens in heat and ready to squabble
I wonder if people talk about me *secretly*? I wonder if I'm
      fooling myself
about pills? I wonder what's in the icebox? out we go
to the looney movie   and the grace of the make-believe
      bed

A FINAL SONNET   *for Chris*

How strange to be gone in a minute!   A man
Signs a shovel and so he digs   Everything
Turns into writing a name for a day
                  Someone
is having a birthday and someone is getting
married and someone is telling a joke   my dream
a white tree   I dream of the code of the west
But this rough magic I here abjure   and
When I have required some heavenly music   which
      even now
I do   to work mine end upon *their* senses
That this aery charm is for   I'll break

My staff   bury it certain fathoms in the earth
And deeper than did ever plummet sound
I'll drown my book.
It is 5:15 a.m.   Dear Chris, hello.

CHARLES STEIN

The day of the bell

at the bottom
of motion
when the water
stops
and the deva
is a frog
possessed upon his lotus pod

•

walking on a bridge above the swamp
I came to a joint in the way
arched by a gate of flame
and did take council how to be beyond it

I sat
at the ledge
        and lo
half my body was shot away

the smoke from the gate went
up above the gum trees
and from the azure
into which it rose
a goddess rode
in lotus rest

holding my legs in a delicate basket

and lo
her face

was shot away
and I held a book
of images of it
painted on ivory cards

though love is not commerce
she sang

if you will come
to where I am not
and make of me an image
for which I may care not

and burn it in the flame that burns between us
and by which we are one

this dream
            will open
and prove a true one

GEORGE OPPEN

The Translucent Mechanics

Combed thru the piers the wind
Moves in the clever city
Not in the doors but the hinges
Finds the secret of motion
As tho the hollow ships moved in their voices, murmurs
Flaws
In the wind
Fear   fear
At the lumber mastheads
And fetched a message out of the sea again

Say angel   say powers

Obscurely   'things
And the self'

Prosody

Sings

In the stones

     to entrust
To a poetry of statement

At close quarters

A living mind
'and that one's own'

            what then   what spirit

Of the bent seas

          Archangel

of the tide
brimming

in the moon-streak

          comes in whose absence
earth crumbles

TOM WEATHERLY

Maumau American Canto 31
honeymoon weather

aria of wheedle, wing
of winnowing fan, malaria
weather storms the wind eye.

melissa moore's measure
is immune, a moon spoor
aloof, moot white, seafoam
woman—moth in green wine.

"melissa, honey
mildew!"

ARMAND SCHWERNER

Tablet XII: Presented by the scholar-translator transmitted through Armand Schwerner

This tablet constitutes an extraordinary find, and an even more extraordinary translation. I present this text with delight and a humility which urges me to incorporate a quote into the introduction to this, the first musically notated chant in written human history. Many readers will recognize that the following citation stems from that mesmerizing work, published recently by the Press of the Université de Strasbourg, *The Music of the Sumerians and their Immediate Successors the Babylonians and Assyrians* by the Sumeromusicologist F W Galpin, Litt. D., F. L. S., Canon Emeritus of Chelmsford Cathedral and Hon. Freeman of the Worshipful Company of Musicians. Canon Galpin writes:

"We must now allude to a very remarkable tablet known as KAR I, 4 and preserved in the Staatliches Museum, Berlin. . . . This Sumerian Hymn on the Creation of Man is furnished with an Assyrian translation in the right-hand column and in the left-hand column there are certain groups of cuneiform signs which seem to indicate the music.

"For the interpretation of the notation set to the Hymn I am solely responsible: spurred by the word 'impossible,' I have tried to express this ancient music in modern form on reasonable and acknowledged lines. Unfortunately we shall never meet with

anyone who was present at its first
performance and could vouch for its certitude.
I must therefore leave it to my friends and
critics to say whether they do not feel that
these old strains of nearly 4,000 years ago and
the oldest music we have are indeed
well-wedded to the yet more ancient words."

and now, what
would you have us do now?
what more do you ask us for?
that was the question
        at the time of the making of a pair
        earth and heaven
and at the time
        of our Mother Inanna
        when she came
                        —so it went
when earth was laid in its place
and heaven fitted
when straight-line stream and canal ran
when Tigris filled the bed
and Euphrates filled the bed
the god An
        and Enlil the god
                        and Utu the god
                                and the god Enki

sat in a high place
and alongside them
the gods Anunnaki of the earth
                        —so it went
and now
what would you have us do now?
what more do you ask us for?
said the god An
        and Enlil the god
                        and Utu the god
                                and the god Enki

what?
we've fixed earth in place
and fitted heaven
the stream runs and the canal runs
Tigris floods and Euphrates rolls
each held in a bed
can we do more?
             —so it went
what's left, what
for us to make?
you gods Anunnaki of the earth
what do you want, what more
can you now ask us for?
the two Anunnaki gods of the earth
and wielders of fate.
had a thing to say to the great Enlil:
            earth and heaven meet, they say,
at the high place Uzuma
in that high place kill
the craftsman-gods, both of them
and from their blood
make a man and more men

ADAPTATION FROM CANON GALPIN'S
HYPOTHETICAL RECONSTRUCTION

ud an-ki-ta   tab- gi- na   til- a- ta- eš- a   Din- gir   a- ma

Din- gir I- na- nna- ge   e- ne   ba- si- sig- e-ne   ud   ki-ga-ga-e-de

ki- du- du- a- ta   ud   giš- ḫa- ḫar   an-ki-a   mûn-gi-na-eš-a-ba

mûn-sug-gi-eš-a   Din-gir A-nun-na Din-gir nam-tar-ri min- na- ne- ne

Din-gir En-lil mûn- na- nib- gi- gi   u zu- mu- a- ki   dur- an- ki- ge

Din-gir na-gar   Din-gir   na-gar   im- mâg- tag- en-   zên

mu- mud- e- ne   nam- lu- gal- u   mu- mu- ed- e

From SCHWERNER'S long, continuing series, *The Tablets* (Grossman Publishers, 1972), a work whose structure derives from the image of accidental fragmentation found in the remnants of ancient Near Eastern clay tablets.

MAP FOUR: RENEWALS

From the beginning, poetry has promised renewal, symbolized in the West by the Festival of Dionysos and the dithyramb, "the song that made Zeus leap" (Jane Harrison). Modern poets, from Blake and Whitman to Ezra Pound, William Carlos Williams, and many later contemporaries, have read the signs of renewal as a New World event. **Map Four** illustrates that process by first focusing on one aspect of the regeneration of forms, *image-making* (in this sense paralleling the evolution of forms presented in **A Book of Music**). The story of that development is seen to include such concepts as hieroglyphics, emblem poems, symbol, visualization, image, imagism, ideogram, phanopoeia, vortex, cubism, surrealism, frottage, hypnologues, photoheliograph, metaphor, objectivism, dialectic, concrete poetry, projectivism, deep image, chance imagery, and mudra. Second, the **Map** explores the emergence of a unified field of poetic concern, a "symposium of the whole," in which renewal means the transformation of human identity, a healing of the split between mind and body, the integration into consciousness of long excluded orders, and the creative use of that primal energy on which depends the regeneration of both personal and social realms.

■ *"Any form whatever, by the mere fact that it exists as such and endures, necessarily loses vigor and becomes worn; to recover vigor, it must be reabsorbed into the formless if only for an instant; it must be restored to the primordial unity from which it issued; in other words, it must return to "chaos" (on the cosmic plane), to "orgy" (on the social plane), to "darkness" (for seed), to "water" (baptism on the human plane, Atlantis on the plane of history, and so on)."*

—MIRCEA ELIADE

■ *"When you see, there are no longer familiar features in the world. Everything is new. Everything has never happened before. The world is incredible!"*

—DON JUAN, through CARLOS CASTANEDA

■ *"Make it new."*

—CONFUCIUS, through EZRA POUND

Image-Making

■ *"The belief that the written word is charged with thaumaturgic power is of very ancient origin; in fact it may be traced all the way back to the graffiti of the Neolithic civilization and even to the cave-art of Paleo-lithic times. This phenomenon stems from the untold power of the image: imo-ago, 'to rouse from the depths.'*

"In the cabbalistic teachings of the Sepher Jezirah, the acoustic element of the word has an equivalent in light, and the signatures of things, the nomina arcana, appear in this sphere as luminous letters. In ancient Egypt, the priests, after chanting a hieroglyphic text 'in the right tone,' used to obliterate whatever hieroglyphs represented maleficent beings so as to prevent their taking on life in the other world, where they might have harmed the dead. In more recent times, the acoustic figures of Jules Lissajous and Ernst Chladni have shown that the spoken word has not only sound but shape."

> —BORIS de RACHEWILTZ, "Pagan and Magic Elements in Ezra Pound's Works," *New Approaches to Ezra Pound,* ed. Eva Hesse [1969]

■ *"And the Jossakeeds, the Prophets,*
The Wabenos, the Magicians,
And the Medicine-men, the Medas,
Painted upon bark and deer-skin
Figures for the songs they chanted,
For each song a separate symbol,
Figures mystical and awful,
Figures strange and brightly colored;
And each figure had its meaning,
Each some magic song suggested."

> —HENRY WADSWORTH LONGFELLOW, *The Song of Hiawatha*

THE MAYAN BOOKS, "according to the early sources," writes MICHAEL COE, "contained histories, prophecies, songs, 'sciences,' and gene-alogies . . . : thousands of books in which the full extent of their learning and literature was recorded." The three which sur-vived the onslaught of the Spanish civilizers "are written on long

strips of bark paper, folded like screens and covered with gesso.
. . . [Of these three] the most beautiful and earliest . . . [is] the
Dresden Codex."

[MAYAN GLYPHS]

A Frame from the Dresden Codex

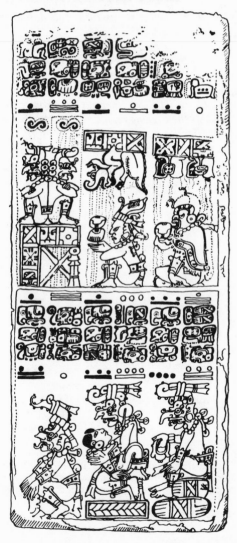

[TOLTEC]

From The Blue House of Tlaloc

FORM IS FROZEN MOVEMENT: The mural of Tlalocan *(The Blue House of Tlaloc)*, found in the painted palace of Tepantila at Teotihuacan, depicts a Toltec paradise (of the so-called Rain God), which, like Hieronymus Bosch's "Garden of Earthly Delights," involves a range of complex moods and activities. As in the Mayan hieroglyphs (above) or the Mochica pottery of ancient Peru, the sexual motif appears to inform the imagery of ritual, reminding us of the Tibetan Tantric link between sexuality and higher consciousness. Sacred speech, or poetry, is represented by a "torsion-form" similar to that in Tantric art, say, or in Wilhelm Reich's description of the "basic form" of the "sexual embrace":

"We have learned," says Reich in *The Cosmic Superimposition*, "to reduce form to movement. Form, to orgonomic functional thinking, is *frozen movement.*"

[THE SHAKERS]
Emblem Poems

Between 1844 and 1859 the Shakers composed (or were the recipients of) "hundreds of . . . visionary drawings . . . really [spiritual] messages in pictorial form," writes Edward Deming Andrews *(The Gift to Be simple,* 1940*).* "The designers of these symbolic documents felt their work was controlled by supernatural agencies . . .—gifts bestowed on some individual in the order (usually not the one who made the drawing). . . . The drawings (which were done both in color and black or blue ink) often contained poems inscribed in a circle, heart or perhaps a scroll carried by a dove or angel, but such verses were never set to music or sung in meeting."

The text on the right reads:

Around leaf
Ho ho ho (Shout)
Now while my love is flowing
You are not forgotten;
You are mine, you are mine
My Sana Vince.

Come and share come and share
Of my love and blessing,
For with the faithful you shall have
A happy happy mansion.

Within Leaf
To my Sana Vince
This is the golden leaf which was gathered from the Tree of songs
Mother Lucy sends this by Elder
Sister Olive; with her kind love and
rememberance to Sister Molly B.—

Learned   Nov. 28th 1839
Thanksgiving day.

In the poem at the left the spirals "outline the course of a file of marchers describing a series of circles." The bottom text reads: "2nd Fam. Enfield / This song was sung and labored by the good / spirits as is here described Christmas eve / 1853 and was seen and learned by Elder / Br Timothy R." while the vertical column is a "noted song," i.e. without words. See also pages 100 and 326, above.

■ *"It is wonderful how a handwriting which is illegible can be read, oh yes it can."*

    —GERTRUDE STEIN, from *The Geographical History of America*
    [1936]

EDGAR ALLAN POE
Prose Poem *from* Marginalia

"The right angle of light's incidence produces a sound upon one of the Egyptian pyramids." This assertion, thus expressed, I have encountered somewhere—probably in one of the Notes to Apollonius. It is nonsense, I suppose,—but it will not do to speak hastily. The orange ray of the spectrum and the buzz of the gnat (which never rises

above the second A), affect me with nearly similar sensa-
tions. In hearing the gnat, I perceive the color. In perceiv-
ing the color, I seem to hear the gnat.

Here the vibrations of the tympanum caused by the
wings of the fly, may, from within, induce abnormal vibra-
tions of the retina, similar to those which the orange ray
induces, normally, from without. By *similar,* I do not mean
of equal rapidity—this would be folly;—but each millionth
undulation, for example, of the retina, might accord with
one of the tympanum; and I doubt whether this would not
be sufficient for the effect.

VISUALIZATION: Poe used the term "prose poem" for his long, philo-
sophical lecture-essay, *Eureka;* he was aware (as was Baudelaire) that
the power of language to stamp the mind with specific orders of
"seeing" is not limited to verse conventions. The text above shows the
relation of Poe to those French Symbolists who were so attracted to
him (Baudelaire, Mallarmé): the practice of "synesthesia" or the trans-
ference of the data of one sense perception into the language of
another. Such interconnective process Baudelaire called "correspon-
dences" and Wallace Stevens "resemblances." (Poe's piece is said to
have led to experiments in the recombination of sense perceptions.)
The Symbolists established one of the bases of modern poetry and
poetics (see Arthur Symond's influential *The Symbolist Movement in
Literature,* 1899). The symbolist or imagist tendency in poetry does
not die, despite shifts in theoretical emphasis, but reemerges continu-
ally in "new" modes of *visualization.* Visualization may be defined as
the act of holding a definite image in the mind, and, through sensuous
attention to shape and detail, entering gradually into the energy of
transmutation "stored" in the image. The process has obvious affinity
with both science and certain kinds of "figurative" meditation. Owen
Barfield notes that "the atoms, protons and electrons of modern phys-
ics are now perhaps more generally regarded, not as particles, but as
notational models or symbols of an unknown supersensible or subsen-
sible base." (*Saving the Appearances,* 1968)

■ *"An 'Image' is that which presents an intellectual and emotional 'complex' in an instant of time. . . .*

"It is the presentation of such a 'complex' instantaneously which gives that sense of sudden liberation; that sense of freedom from time limits and space limits; that sense of sudden growth, which we experience in the presence of the greatest works of art.

"It is better to present one Image in a lifetime than to produce voluminous works. "

—EZRA POUND, "A Few Don'ts," *Poetry* I, 6 (March 1913), reprinted in *Literary Essays*

WILLIAM CULLEN BRYANT
From October*

The birchen bough drops its bright spoil
like *arrow-heads* of gold.

JAMES RUSSELL LOWELL
From The Biglow Papers:
"Sunthin' in the Pastoral Line" (Hosea Biglow speaking)*

"The maple crimsons to a coral reef;
The saffern swarms swing off from all the willers,
So plump they look like yaller caterpillars;
Then gray hoss-chestnuts' leetle hands unfold,
Softer'n a baby's be at three days old."

* As quoted in W. H. GIBSON's *Sharp Eyes* [1892].

WALT WHITMAN
The Runner

On a flat road runs the well-train'd runner,
He is lean and sinewy with muscular legs,
He is thinly clothed, he leans forward as he runs,
With lightly closed fists and arms partially rais'd.

Visor'd

A mask, a perpetual natural disguiser of herself,
Concealing her face, concealing her form,
Changes and transformations every hour, every moment,
Falling upon her even when she sleeps.

HENRY DAVID THOREAU
Two Poems

Between the traveller and the setting sun
Upon some drifting sand heap of the shore,
A hound stands o'er the carcass of a man.

We see the *planet* fall,
And that is all.

THE STANDARD OF CLARITY: Louis Agassiz (born 1807 Switzerland, died 1873 Cambridge, Mass.) was acknowledged as master of the art of scientific description by Emerson, Thoreau, and William James. Ezra Pound claimed him as model: "The proper method for studying poetry and good letters is the method of contemporary biologists, that is careful first-hand examination of the matter, and continual COMPARISON of one 'slide' or specimen with another." (*A.B.C. of Reading*, 1934) Like the eighteenth-century American scientist-theologian Ezra Stiles, for example, Agassiz saw the issues of science and theology as identical. "If there is any truth in the belief that man is made in the image of God," he writes in the "Essay on Classification" (1857), "it is surely not amiss for the philsopher to endeavor, by the study of his own mental operations, to approximate the workings of the Divine Reason, learning, from the nature of his own mind, better to understand the Infinite Intellect from which it is derived." The art of Agassiz, Thoreau, and W. H. Gibson consists in revealing the Minute Particular as Luminous Detail; or, in Pound's phrase, the natural object is always the adequate symbol.

(See Guy Davenport's selection and introduction, *The Intelligence of Louis Agassiz*, Beacon Press, Boston, 1963.)

LOUIS AGASSIZ

Cyanea Arctica

Seen floating in the water Cyanea Arctica exhibits a large circular disk, of a substance not unlike jelly, thick in the centre, and suddenly thinning out towards the edge, which presents several indentations. The centre of that disk is of a dark purplish-brown color, while the edge is much lighter, almost white and transparent. This disk is constantly heaving and falling, at regular intervals; the margin is especially active, so much so, that, at times, it is stretched on a level with the whole surface of the disk, which, in such a condition, is almost flat, while, at other times, it is so fully arched that it assumes the appearance of a hemisphere. These motions recall so strongly those of an umbrella, alternately opened and shut, that writers, who have described similar animals, have generally called this gelatinous disk the umbrella. From the lower surface of this disk hang, conspicuously, three kinds of appendages. Near the margin there are eight bunches of long tentacles, moving in every direction, sometimes extending to an enormous length, sometimes shortened to a mere coil of entangled threads, constantly rising and falling, stretching now in one direction and then in another, but generally spreading slantingly in a direction opposite to that of the onward movement of the animal. These streamers may be compared to floating tresses of hair, encircling organs which are farther inward upon the lower surface of the disk. Of these organs, there are also eight bunches, which alternate with the eight bunches of tentacles, but they are of two kinds; four are elegant sacks, adorned, as it were, with waving ruffles projecting in large clusters, which are alternately pressed forward and withdrawn, and might also be compared to bunches of grapes, by turns inflated and collapsed. These four bunches alternate with four masses of folds, hanging like rich curtains, loosely waving to and fro, and as they wave, extending downwards, or shortening rapidly, recalling, to those who have had an opportunity of witnessing the phenomenon, the play of the streamers of an aurora borealis. All these parts have their fixed position; they are held together by a sort of horizontal curtain, which is suspended from the lower surface of the gelatinous disk. The horizontal curtain is itself connected with the disk, fastened to it as it were by ornamental stitches, which divide the whole field into a number of areas, alternately larger and smaller, now concentric, now radiating, between which the organs already described are inserted.

—*From* Contributions to the Natural History of the United States, 1862

EMILY DICKINSON

"Banish Air from Air"

Banish Air from Air—
Divide Light if you dare—
They'll meet
While Cubes in a Drop
Or Pellets of Shape
Fit
Films cannot annul
Odors return whole
Force Flame
And with a Blonde push
Over your impotence
Flits steam

WILLIAM HAMILTON GIBSON

Three Definitions *from* Sharp Eyes   [1892]

POPPIES

Flowers closed like two clam-shells;
inner petals coiled.

LUPINE

The wheel-like leaf closes
downward against the stem
at its center,
like a closed umbrella,
or rises
in the form of a goblet.

THE DRAGON-FLY

". . . this grotesque of the insect world. The natural symbol of omniscience, a creature of the two elements, sharp-eyed alike in both, possessed of a head which is, in fact, all eyes, have we not here an embodied and tangible *"qui vive"* beside which the fabled Argus of old is a tame conception? The seat of its keen intelligence, double-domed and literally begemmed with sight, reinforced, too, with wings which convert the horizon to a present kingdom, where shall my volume look for a more apt emblem? . . . May we not accept our dragon-fly even as a courier?"

WILLIAM HAMILTON GIBSON was an American naturalist and illustrator of the late nineteenth century, whose *Sharp Eyes: Fifty-two Weeks in a Rambler's Calendar* (1892) combines accurate observation and sharp descriptive language with a post-Transcendentalist sense of immanent power in all living things. His illustrations of his own text suggest both Blake's illuminations and later uses of photo-montage.

STEPHEN CRANE

Two Untitled Poems [c. 1895]

A row of thick pillars
Consciously bracing for the weight
Of a vanished roof
The bronze light of sunset strikes through them,
And over a floor made for slow rites.
There is no sound of singing
But, aloft, a great and terrible bird
Is watching a cur, beaten and cut,
That crawls to the cool shadows of the pillars
To die.

•

intermingled,
There come in wild revelling strains
Black words, stinging
That murder flowers
The horror of profane speculation.

TRUMBULL STICKNEY
Dramatic Fragment   [c. 1902]

Sir, say no more.
Within me 't is as if
The green and climbing eyesight of a cat
Crawled near my mind's poor birds.

FRANCES DENSMORE
From Chippewa Music   [1910]

A LOON

A loon,
I thought it was
But it was
My love's
Splashing oar.

DREAM SONG

From the half
Of the sky
That which lives there
Is coming, and makes a noise.

SONG OF THE BUTTERFLY

In the coming heat
Of the day
I stood there.

See also pages 335–337, above.

"ERNEST FRANCISCO FENOLLOSA (1853–1908), born in Salem and edu-
cated at Harvard, took with him to Japan in 1878 as Professor of
Philosophy (Hegel, Herbert Spencer) the treasures of Transcen-
dentalism, and brought back with him from Japan on his last jour-
ney in 1901 that same Transcendentalism, seen anew in the Chi-
nese Written Character and set forth in what Pound, who acquired
the ms. twelve years later, was to characterize as the 'big essay on
verbs, mostly on verbs.' " —HUGH KENNER, *The Pound Era* [1971]

ERNEST FENOLLOSA
From The Chinese Written Character as a Medium for Poetry

. . . My subject is poetry, not language, yet the roots of
poetry are in language. In the study of a language so alien
in form to ours as is Chinese in its written character, it is
necessary to inquire how these universal elements of form
which constitute poetics can derive appropriate nutri-
ment.

In what sense can verse, written in terms of visible
hieroglyphics, be reckoned true poetry? It might seem that
poetry, which like music is a *time art,* weaving its unities
out of successive impressions of sound, could with diffi-
culty assimilate a verbal medium consisting largely of
semi-pictorial appeals to the eye. . . .

Perhaps we do not always sufficiently consider that
thought is successive, not through some accident or weak-
ness of our subjective operations but because the opera-
tions of nature are successive. The transferences of force
from agent to object, which constitute natural phenomena,
occupy time. Therefore, a reproduction of them in imagi-
nation requires the same temporal order.

Suppose that we look out of a window and watch a man.
Suddenly he turns his head and actively fixes his attention
upon something. We look ourselves and see that his vision
has been focused upon a horse. We saw, first, the man
before he acted; second, while he acted; third, the object
toward which his action was directed. In speech we split
up the rapid continuity of this action and of its picture into
its three essential parts or joints in the right order, and say:

Man sees horse.

It is clear that these three joints, or words, are only three phonetic symbols, which stand for the three terms of a natural process. But we could quite as easily denote these three stages of our thought by symbols equally arbitrary, *which had no basis in sound;* for example, by three Chinese characters:

| Man | Sees | Horse |

If we all knew *what division* of this mental horse-picture each of these signs stood for, we could communicate continuous thought to one another as easily by drawing them as by speaking words. We habitually employ the visible language of gesture in much this same manner.

But Chinese notation is something much more than arbitrary symbols. It is based upon a vivid shorthand picture of the operations of nature. In the algebraic figure and in the spoken word there is no natural connection between thing and sign: all depends upon sheer convention. But the Chinese method follows natural suggestion. First stands the man on his two legs. Second, his eye moves through space: a bold figure represented by running legs under an eye, a modified picture of an eye, a modified picture of running legs, but unforgettable once you have seen it. Third stands the horse on his four legs.

The thought-picture is not only called up by these signs as well as by words, but far more vividly and concretely. Legs belong to all three characters: they are *alive*. The group holds something of the quality of a continuous moving picture.

■ *" In the spring or early summer of 1912, 'H. D.,' Richard Aldington and myself decided that we were agreed upon the three principles following:*
1. Direct treatment of the 'thing' whether subjective or objective.
2. To use absolutely no word that does not contribute to the presentation.

3. As regarding rhythm: to compose in the sequence of the musical phrase, not in the sequence of the metronome.

"Upon many points of taste and of predilection we differed, but agreeing upon these three positions we thought we had as much right to a group name ["Imagistes"] at least as much right, as a number of French 'schools' proclaimed by Mr. Flint in the August number of Harold Monro's magazine for 1911. "

—EZRA POUND, "A Retrospect," *Pavannes and Divisions*
   [1918]

H. D.
Oread

Whirl up, sea—
whirl your pointed pines,
splash your great pines
on our rocks,
hurl your green over us,
cover us with your pools of fir.

KNOT AND VORTEX: Cubism, Futurism, "Imagisme"—names in history for new modalities in the shaping of Energy; and, in 1914, Pound added Vortex, out of which emerged "Vorticism," a new "movement" spearheaded by the British painter-novelist Wyndham Lewis in an outragingly direct magazine, *Blast*. Hugh Kenner, in *The Pound Era* (Berkeley, 1971), has given new clarity to the Vortex:

> Of patterned energies; and first, Buckminster Fuller on knots. He grasps and tenses an invisible rope, on which we are to understand a common overhand knot, two 360° rotations in intersecting planes, each passed through the other:

> Pull, and whatever your effort each lobe of the knot makes it impossible that the other shall disappear. It is a *self-interfering pattern*. Slacken, and its structure hangs open for analysis, but suffers no topological impairment. Slide the knot along the rope: your are sliding rope through the knot. Slide through it, if you have them spliced in sequence, hemp rope, cotton rope,

nylon rope. The knot is indifferent to these transactions. The knot is neither hemp nor cotton nor nylon: is not the rope. The knot is a *patterned integrity*. The rope renders it visible. No member of Fuller's audience has ever objected (he remarks) that throughout this exposition he has been holding no rope at all, so accessible to the mind is a patterned integrity, visible or no, once the senses have taught us its contours.

Imagine, next, the metabolic flow that passes through a man and is not the man: some hundred tons of solids, liquids and gases serving to render a single man corporeal during the seventy years he persists, a patterned integrity, a knot through which pass the swift strands of simultaneous ecological cycles, recycling transformations of solar energy. At any given moment the knotted materials weigh perhaps 160 pounds. (And "Things," wrote Ernest Fenollosa about 1904, are "cross-sections cut through actions, snapshots.")

So far Buckminster Fuller (1967). Now Ezra Pound (1914) on the poetic image: ". . . a radiant node or cluster; . . . what I can, and must perforce, call a VORTEX, from which, and through which, and into which, ideas are constantly rushing." A patterned integrity accessible to the mind; topologically stable; subject to variations of intensity; brought into the domain of the senses by a particular interaction of words. "In decency one can only call it a vortex. . . . *Nomina sunt consequentia rerum.*" For the vortex is not the water but a patterned energy made visible by the water.

EZRA POUND
Canto XLIX

For the seven lakes, and by no man these verses:
Rain; empty river; a voyage,
Fire from frozen cloud, heavy rain in the twilight
Under the cabin roof was one lantern.
The reeds are heavy; bent;
and the bamboos speak as if weeping.

Autumn moon; hills rise about lakes
against sunset
Evening is like a curtain of cloud,
a blurr above ripples; and through it

sharp long spikes of the cinnamon,
a cold tune amid reeds.
Behind hill the monk's bell
borne on the wind.
Sail passed here in April; may return in October
Boat fades in silver; slowly;
Sun blaze alone on the river.

Where wine flag catches the sunset
Sparse chimneys smoke in the cross light

Comes then snow scur on the river
And a world is covered with jade
Small boat floats like a lanthorn,
The flowing water clots as with cold. And at San Yin
they are a people of leisure.
Wild geese swoop to the sand-bar,
Clouds gather about the hole of the window
Broad water; geese line out with the autumn
Rooks clatter over the fishermen's lanthorns,
A light moves on the north sky line;
where the young boys prod stones for shrimp.
In seventeen hundred came Tsing to these hill lakes.
A light moves on the south sky line.

State by creating riches shd. thereby get into debt?
This is infamy; this is Geryon.
This canal goes still to TenShi
though the old king built it for pleasure

K E I	M E N	R A N	K E I
K I U	M A N	M A N	K E I
JITSU	GETSU	K O	K W A
T A N	F U K U	T A N	K A I

Sun up; work
sundown; to rest
dig well and drink of the water

dig field; eat of the grain
Imperial power is? and to us what is it?

The fourth; the dimension of stillness.
And the power over wild beasts.

IDEOGRAMMIC STRUCTURE: In the various stages of Pound's poetic theory—Image, "moving Image," Vortex, Ideogram—the tendency is toward a structural principle having several advantages simultaneously: concreteness, movement, energy, and "field" or "form." The direction is toward a method capable of handling complex materials in a single context, without losing the speed of active mentation. Generally speaking, "Ideogram" brings diverse elements into radical juxtaposition, forcing "perspective by incongruity." We are reminded that the "deeper" function of the Image is to cause us "to be suddenly conscious of the reality of the *nous*, of mind, apart from any man's individual mind, of the sea crystalline and enduring, of the bright as it were molten glass that envelops us, full of light." (*Guide to Kulchur*, 1938)

Canto XLIX (above) is a rite for the harmony of mind and nature (including a protest against Geryon, three-headed monster of Erythia, symbolizing usury and violence against Nature), and so invokes a Chinese text (Fu Sheng, *Shang-shu ta chuan*, in Japanese transliteration), which translates: "How bright and colorful the auspicious clouds, / Hanging gracefully; / Let sun and moon be thus resplendent / Morn after morn." Note that many "Imagist" poems (in the manner of haiku) might be extracted from this or any Canto, as: "In the gloom the gold / Gathers the light about it."

■ " *The principle of synchronization has been the basis of even the mechanical devices of the new century—the synchromesh gear is a means by which varying speeds and parts are brought into adjustment. Gertrude Stein suspected that the cinema is the primary art of the twentieth century becuse it synchronizes. If, she says, the artist is to be contemporary he must have the 'time-sense' of his day; and the time-sense of this century is symbolized in the American assembly-line method of production; the automobile is conceived as a whole and assembled from its parts by a process of prefabrication . . . a 'conception of the whole' [rather than 'cause-and-effect sequence of events'], the synchronization corresponding to cinematic montage or juxtaposition of elements. . . . [Stein wrote:] 'In a cinema picture no two pictures are exactly alike each one*

*is just that much different from the one before.' There is a writer's
'building up' of an image from recurrent statements each a little differ-
ent from the one before and after. "*

— WYLIE SYPHER, *Rococo to Cubism in Art and Literature*
[1960]

GERTRUDE STEIN
A White Hunter   [*From* "Tender Buttons"]

A white hunter is nearly crazy.

From A Geographical History of America

Some dogs eyes in the night give out a red light
and some dogs eyes at night are green.

From Before the Flowers of Friendship
Faded Friendship Faded

A clock in the eye ticks in the eye a clock ticks in the eye.
A number with that and large as a hat which makes rims
      think quicker than I.
A clock in the eye ticks in the eye a clock ticks ticks in the
      eye.

GERTRUDE STEIN
From Lifting Belly

    Kiss my lips. She did.
    Kiss my lips again she did.
    Kiss my lips over and over and over again she did.
    I have feathers.
    Gentle fishes.

Do you think about apricots. We find them very beautiful.
It is not alone their color it is their seeds that charm us. We
find it a change.

Lifting belly is so strange.

I came to speak about it.

Selected raisins well their grapes grapes are good.

Change your name.

Question and garden.

It's raining. Don't speak about it.

My baby is a dumpling. I want to tell her something.

Wax candles. We have bought a great many wax candles.
Some are decorated. They have not been lighted.

I do not mention roses.

Exactly.

Actually.

Question and butter.

I find the butter very good.

Lifting belly is so kind.

Lifting belly fattily.

Doesn't that astonish you.

You did want me.

Say it again.

Strawberry.

Lifting beside belly.

Lifting kindly belly.

Sing to me I say.

Some are wives not heroes.

Lifting belly merely.

Sing to me I say.

Lifting belly. A reflection.

Lifting belly adjoins more prizes.

Fit to be.

I have fit on a hat.

Have you.

What did you say to excuse me. Difficult paper and
scattered.

Lifting belly is so kind.

■ *"Cubism in poetry . . . is the conscious, deliberate dissociation and recombination of elements into a new artistic entity made self-sufficient by its rigorous architecture. . . .*

"When I was a young lad I thought that literary Cubism was the future of American poetry. Only Walter Conrad Arensberg in his last poems, Gertrude Stein in Tender Buttons *and a very few other pieces, much of the work of the young Yvor Winters and others of his generation of Chicago Modernists, Laura Riding's best work and my own poems later collected in* The Art of Worldly Wisdom *could be said to show the deliberate practice of the principles of creative construction which guided Juan Gris or Pierre Reverdy. . . . In verse such as Reverdy's . . . the primary data of the poetic construction . . . are simple, sensory, emotional or primary informative objects capable of little or no further reduction. Eliot works in* The Waste Land *with fragmented and recombined arguments; Pierre Reverdy with dismembered propositions from which subject, operator and object have been wrenched free and restructured into an invisible or subliminal discourse which owes its cogency to its own strict, complex and secret logic.*

"Poetry such as this attempts not just a new syntax of the word. Its revolution is aimed at the syntax of the mind itself. Its restructuring of experience is purposive, not dreamlike, and hence it possesses an uncanniness fundamentally different in kind from the most haunted utterances of the Surrealist or Symbolist unconscious. "

> —KENNETH REXROTH, "Introduction," *Pierre Reverdy: Selected Poems* [1955]

WALTER CONRAD ARENSBERG
Arithmetical Progression of the Verb "To Be"

On a sheet of paper
   dropped with the intention of demolishing
   space
   by the simple subtraction of a necessary plane
draw a line that leaves the present

   in addition
   carrying forward to the uncounted columns
      of the spatial ruin
      now considered as complete
   the remainder of the past.

The act of disappearing
             which in the three-dimensional
             is the fate of the convergent
                         vista
is thus
             under the form of the immediate
arrested in a perfect parallel

             of being
             in part.

KENNETH REXROTH

From A Prolegomenon to a Theodicy [1925]

IV

Black
Blue black
Blue
The silver minuscules
In early dawn the plume of smoke
The throat of night
The plethora of wine
The fractured hour of light
The opaque lens
The climbing wheel
The beam of glow
The revealed tree
The wine crater
The soft depth
The suspended eye
The clouded pane
The droning wing
The white plateau
The hour of fractured light
The twisted peak
The cold index
The turquoise turning in the lunar sky
The climbing toe

The coastwise shout
The cracking mirror
The blue angle
The soothed nape
The minute flame
The silver ball
The concave mirror
The quivering palm
The conic of the wing
The trough of light
The rattling stones
The climbing humerus
The canyon bark
The unfolding leaves
The rigid lamp
The lengthy stair
The moving cubicle
The shifting floor
The bending femur
The rigid eye
The revealing lamp
The crackling anastomosis
The initial angle
The involved tendon
The yellow light
The acoluthic filaments
The general conic of the wing
The revealing eye
The crazed pane
The revelation of the lamp
The golden uncials
The revelation of the mirror

DADA AND SURREALISM: Besides "Cubism," certain other currents, usually associated with European modernism, early began to influence the practice of poetry in America—not least in its image-making aspect. "Dada," which emerged as a term and a movement in World-War-I Zurich, had been anticipated by the appearance in New York (circa 1914) of artists like Duchamp and Picabia, and by the experimental activities of Stieglitz's "291" group. Duchamp's short-lived *New York Dada* first presented the work of Else von Freytag-Loring-hoven (see page 247, above), who for several years was the principal exponent of a Dadaist mode in America, with work appearing in such little magazines as Margaret Anderson's *The Little Review* and Eugene Jolas' *Transition*. The latter publication, along with Harry Crosby's Black Sun Press, showed an early exploration of principles of dream and image commonly connected with French Surrealism—a path that was also taken during the thirties by poets like Charles Henri Ford and Parker Tyler. Surrealism (often in the Spanish variation of poets like Lorca, Neruda, and Vallejo) has remained an important factor in post-World-War-II American poetry (for which, see the section "Deep Image," below, as one example). The long residence in America of Max Ernst and Marcel Duchamp also influenced the picture, as well as the presence during World War II of a virtual Surrealist government-in-exile, led by André Breton.

ELSE von FREYTAG-LORINGHOVEN
Affectionate

Wheels are growing on rose-bushes
gray and affectionate
O Jonathan—Jonathan—dear
Did some swallow Prendergast's silverheels—
be drunk forever and more
—with lemon appendicitis?

MAX ERNST
Natural History

It all started on August 10, 1925, by my recalling an incident of my childhood when the sight of an imitation mahogany panel opposite my bed had induced one of those dreams between sleeping and waking. And happening to be at a seaside inn in wet weather I was struck by the way the floor, its grain accentuated by many scrubbings, obsessed my nervously excited gaze. So I decided to explore the symbolism of the obsession, and to encourage my powers of meditation and hallucination I took a series of drawings from the floorboards by dropping pieces of paper on them at random and then rubbing the paper with black lead. As I looked carefully at the drawings that I got in this way—some dark, others smudgily dim—I was surprised by the sudden heightening of my visionary powers, and by the dreamlike succession of contradictory images that came one on top of another with the persistence and rapidity peculiar to memories of love.

Now my curiosity was roused and excited, and I began an impartial exploration, making use of every kind of material that happened to come into my field of vision: leaves and their veins, frayed edges of sacking, brush strokes in a 'modern' painting, cotton unwound from a cotton-reel, etc., etc. Then I saw human heads, many different beasts, a battle ending in a kiss *(the wind's sweetheart)*, rocks, *sea and rain, earth tremors,* and *sphinx in its stable,* the *small tables round about the earth, Caesar's shoulder-blade, false positions,* a *shawl covered with flowers of hoar frost, pampas.*

The *cuts of a whip, trickles of lava, fields of honour, inundations and seismic plants, scarecrows,* the *edge of the chestnut wood.*

Flashes of lightning before one's fourteenth year, vaccinated bread, conjugal diamonds, the *cuckoo (origin of the pendulum),* the *meat of death,* the *wheel of light.*

A solar coinage system

The *habits of leaves,* the *fascinating cyprus tree.*

Eve, the only one remaining to us.

I put the first fruits of the *frottage* process together, from *sea and rain* to *Eve, the only one remaining to us,* and called it *Natural History.*

—*From* "Inspiration to Order"

EUGENE JOLAS

Hypnologues: Panopticon

a string orchestra playing Brahms and a dead bird and a book and a palagra

and an owl and a lion and the sea the whale scalesilvering in moonlight the san francisco fire the tiara

the priest the ciborium
a fishnet a severed hand a woman's face a mutilated
dog a newspaper the world war illustrated by
a dead man a mask a hood a boxer's face the guillotine
a hootword
a carib word
a ghulla word
a blizzard word howlblasting into the northnight

■ *"I invented a new poetic form I called* hypnologues, *that tried to give a verbal replica of the experiences between waking and sleeping.*

I took the dream-material I had gathered immediately after waking, and integrated it into the rhythmic structures of poems or prose-tales, by the union of unfamiliar words, or by phantasmatic word-compounds, or by the use of authentic dream-words."

—EUGENE JOLAS

HARRY CROSBY
Photoheliograph [1929]

for Lady A

black	black	black	black	black
black	black	black	black	black
black	black	black	black	black
black	black	black	black	black
black	black	S U N	black	black
black	black	black	black	black
black	black	black	black	black
black	black	black	black	black
black	black	black	black	black
black	black	black	black	black

WALLACE STEVENS
Metaphor as Degeneration

If there is a man white as marble
Sits in a wood, in the greenest part,
Brooding sounds of the images of death,

So there is a man in black space
Sits in nothing that we know,
Brooding sounds of river noises;

And these images, these reverberations,
And others, make certain how being
Includes death and the imagination.

The marble man remains himself in space.
The man in the black wood descends unchanged.
It is certain that the river

Is not Swatara. The swarthy water
That flows around the earth and through the skies,
Twisting among the universal spaces,

Is not Swatara. It is being.
That is the flock-flecked river, the water,
The blown sheen—or is it air?

How, then, is metaphor degeneration,
When Swatara becomes this undulant river
And the river becomes the landless, waterless ocean?

Here the black violets grow down to its banks
And the memorial mosses hang their green
Upon it, as it flows ahead.

WILLIAM FAULKNER
A *Chapter from* As I Lay Dying

My mother is a fish.

OBJECTIVISTS: A number of poets, circa 1930, who came to be thought of as a group through Louis Zukofsky's *An "Objectivists" Anthology* and objectivists issue of *Poetry,* and George Oppen's Objectivists Press. Besides Zukofsky and Oppen, the poets so gathered included Charles Reznikoff, Carl Rakosi, and the Northumbrian poet, Basil Bunting. Notable participants and advisers from the previous generation were William Carlos Williams and Ezra Pound.

■ *"A poem is a small (or large) machine made of words."*
        —WILLIAM CARLOS WILLIAMS, *The Wedge* [1944]

WILLIAM CARLOS WILLIAMS
Flowers by the Sea

When over the flowery, sharp pasture's
edge, unseen, the salt ocean

lifts its form—chicory and daisies
tied, release, seem hardly flowers alone

but color and the movement—or the shape
perhaps—of restlessness, whereas

the sea is circled and sways
peacefully upon its plantlike stem

The Attic Which Is Desire

the unused tent
of

bare beams
beyond which

directly wait
the night

and day—
Here

from the street
by

```
*   *   *
*   S   *
*   O   *
*   D   *
*   A   *
*   *   *
```

ringed with
running lights

the darkened
pane

exactly
down the center

is
transfixed

LOUIS ZUKOFSKY

A Sea

the
foam
claws

cloys
close

Julia's Wild

Come shadow, come, and take this shadow up,
Come shadow shadow, come and take this up,
Come, shadow, come, and take this shadow up,
Come, come shadow, and take this shadow up,
Come, come and shadow, take this shadow up,
Come, up, come shadow and take this shadow,
And up, come, take shadow, come this shadow,
And up, come, come shadow, take this shadow,
And come shadow, come up, take this shadow,
Come up, come shadow this, and take shadow,
Up, shadow this, come and take shadow, come
Shadow this, take and come up shadow, come
Take and come, shadow, come up, shadow this,
Up, come and take shadow, come this shadow,
Come up, take shadow, and come this shadow,
Come and take shadow, come up this shadow,

Shadow, shadow come, come and take this up,
Come, shadow, take, and come this shadow, up,
Come shadow, come, and take this shadow up,
Come, shadow, come, and take this shadow up.

"For Cid Corman who after reading *The Two Gentlemen of Verona* wrote: 'Apart from the Sylvia Song, I like best the line— *Come, shadow, come, and take this shadow up.* Ring a change on that for me? A dark valentine.'—Line 1 is the First Folio text of IV, iv, 202; the 'same' is punctuated in modern editions as here in line 3. The 'changes' here on line 1 ring a difference." *(Bottom: On Shakespeare / 1,* 1963, p. 393.)

GEORGE OPPEN

From Discrete Series   [1934]

Bolt
In the frame
Of the building—
A ship
Grounds
Her immense keel
Chips
A stone
Under fifteen feet
Of harbor
Water—
The fiber of this tree
Is live wood
Running into the
Branches and leaves

In the air.

GEORGE HERRIMAN

CHARLES HENRI FORD
Reptilia

The way a tongue darts from a crack in chaos. The way
nothing is ever the same. The way you do what you find
yourself doing. The way nothing matters. The way sleep
rusts the soul. The way nothing is ever understood. The
way sleep sharpens time. The way nothing happens. The
way she poisons a cup of coffee. The way nothing can help.
The way he walks. The way nothing was said. The way
babies are born. The way nothing changes. The way it
starts to rain. The way nothing could be done. The way to
make love. The way nothing stays still. The way roads go
winding. The way nothing remains.

> CHARLES HENRI FORD, born in Mississippi, edited *Blues: A Magazine
> of New Rhythms* (1929–1931) and the highly influential *View*
> (1940–1947), the latter representing an American Surrealist posi-
> tion, fortified during the Second World War by André Breton's pres-
> ence in America. It was in *View* too that PHILIP LAMANTIA'S work
> first appeared, while he was still in his late teens but recognized
> by Breton and others as a home-grown American Surrealist.

PHILIP LAMANTIA
Animal Snared in His Revery

He breathes through his wounds.
The herbs that would heal him decay in the labyrinth
of his great paw.
The sun sends medicinal currents to the wobbling
island under his sunken tooth.
With agates of rain, the sibylline garden (oracles speak
from the flowers) conceives grimly poisonous minerals
traveling the earth veins.
The animal, blackening the light with an orb of his
blood, reads on the televised leaves:
—SLEEP TERRORS RAGING—
                    —EXIT FROM DREAMS—
. . . and the green mouth cracks open underground.

"THE ANTITHETICAL SENSE OF PRIMAL WORDS": Norman O. Brown concludes his *Life Against Death* with a celebration of the "Dionysian ego" or ."dialectical imagination"—"a mode of consciousness," he says, common to psychoanalysis, mysticism, poetry, the philosophy of organism, and radical politics, and revealing an "unseen harmony" (Heraclitus) behind Blake, Freud, Marx, Whitehead, "Indian body mysticism" (Eliade), Jewish mysticism (Scholem on Kaballah), et al. "Dialectical" here means "an activity of consciousness struggling to circumvent the limitations imposed by the formal-logical law of contradiction" and relates to Freud's early essay "The Antithetical Sense of Primal Words." In *The Interpretation of Dreams* Freud observes a dream-law: " 'No' seems not to exist for dreams [which instead] show a special tendency to reduce two opposites to a unity." This apparent law corresponds to a linguistic phenomenon among the most ancient languages, such as Egyptian: "a single word describes two contraries at the extreme ends of a series of activities (e.g., 'strong-weak,' 'old-young,' 'far-near,' 'bind-sever')." Such behavior on the part of the oldest tongues records the dynamics of consciousness common to all creative process, but especially visible in works like the "Aztec Definitions" (see page 85) and modern experimental poetry. Gaston Bachelard, in *The Poetics of Space,* sees the dialectical process as that of image-formation generally, expressed in antinomies like "outside-inside," "open-closed," and so forth. We may perhaps see this process at work in the images of Vorticism, Cubism, Surrealism, and what was called in the early sixties "Deep Image." Here in contrast to the *doctrine* of Imagism (1910), the "object" referred to is the process of *knowing* a thing, a state of perception rooted not in "objective" reality (as appearance) but a condition of energy and a mood of language. In practice, the various kinds of Image-poems may tap the same source, and the real differences are matters of degree of one tendency over another, specific "perspectives by incongruity." Georges Braque: "It is always desirable to have two notions—one to demolish the other." Whitman: "Do I contradict myself? Well then, I contradict myself."

JOHN CAGE
Translating Basho's Haiku

Text: Japanese   *English transliteration*
    Matasutake ya   Mushroom;
    shiranu ko-no-ha no   ignorance; leaf of tree
    hebaritsuku   adhesiveness
        [Basho, 1644–1694]

Versions:
    R. H. Blythe translates Basho's haiku as follows:
    The leaf of some unknown tree sticking on the mushroom.

    I showed this translation to a Japanese composer friend.
He said he did not find it very interesting. I said, "How would
you translate it?" Two days later he brought me the following:
    Mushroom does not know that leaf is sticking on it.

    Getting the idea, I made during the next three years, the
following:
    That that's unknown brings mushroom and leaf together.

    And the one I prefer:
    What leaf? What mushroom?

■ *" MUDRA is a symbol, in the sense of gesture or action. It arises spontane-*
ously as an expression of the inspiring color of phenomena. Also it is a
symbol expressed with the hands to state for oneself and others the
quality of different moments of meditation, such as touching the earth
with the right hand as a witness to Buddha's freedom from emotional
and mental frivolousness. It is not separate from that which it symbol-
izes. It is self-evidence. The mudra of the hands is only one form of
mudra. "

    —CHÖGYAM TRUNGPA, *Mudra* [1972]

M. C. RICHARDS
Poem

Hands

birds.

"I once wrote a poem consisting of only two words.
"Two nouns, two sounds, with a long-silence between. A long
time of silence which is, on the page, a long space of emptiness."

—M. C. RICHARDS, *Centering* [1962]

■ *"Chance images are characterized by a lack of conscious design. When
these images are 'hand-made,' and conscious thought is evaded, so that
the images have their source in deeper-than-conscious areas of the mind,
we will prefer the Surrealists' term 'automatic' to the word 'random,'
though 'random,' in the way it is used in everyday speech, might seem
appropriate (as meaning, for example, 'without definite aim, direction,
rule, or method'). We will prefer this usage in order to restrict 'random'
to a technical meaning which it has more commonly in statistics, where
it applies to special techniques for eliminating bias in sampling. . . .*

*"Here I would like to introduce the general term 'chance-imagery'
to apply to our formation of images resulting from chance, wherever
these occur in nature. (The word 'imagery' is intentionally ambiguous
enough, I think, to apply either to the physical act of creating an image
out of real materials, or to the formation of an image in the mind, say
by abstraction from a more complex system.) One reason for doing this*

*is to place the painter's, musician's, poet's, dancer's chance images in
the same conceptual category as natural chance-images (the configura-
tion of meadow grasses, the arrangement of stones on a brook bottom),
and to get away from the idea that an artist makes something 'special'
and beyond the world of ordinary things. . . .*

"This leaves 'art' to mean something constructed, *from a starting
point of pre-conceived notions, with the corollary that as art approaches
chance-imagery, the artist enters a oneness with all of nature."*

—GEORGE BRECHT, *Chance Imagery* [1957]

JACKSON MAC LOW

2nd Light Poem: for Diane Wakoski—10 June 1962

I

Old light & owl-light
may be opal light
in the small
orifice
where old light
& the will-o'-the-wisp
make no announcement of waning
light

but with direct directions
& the winking light of the will-o'-the-wisp's accoutrements
& lilac light
a delightful phenomenon
a delightful phenomenon of lucence & lucidity needing no
        announcement
even of lilac light

my present activities may be seen in the old light of my
       accoutrements
as a project in owl-light.

II

A bulky, space-suited figure
from the whole cloth of my present activities
with a taste for mythology in opal light
& such a manner

in the old light from some being outside

as if this being's old light cd have brought such a manner
to a bulky, space-suited figure
from the whole world of my present activities
at this time
when my grief gives owl-light
only
not an opal light
& not a very old light

neither
old light nor owl-light
makes it have such a manner about it
tho opal light & old light & marsh light & moonlight
& that of the whole world
to which the light of meteors is marsh light
all light it
no it's
an emerald light
in the light from the eyes that are making it whole from the
      whole cloth
with no announcement this time.

III

What is extra light?
A delightful phenomenon.
A delightful phenomenon having no announcement?
No more than the emerald light has.
Is that the will-o'-the-wisp?

No, it's the waning light of my grief.
Is it a winking light?
No more than it is the will-o'-the-wisp.
Is it old light?
The oldest in the whole world.
Why do you speak in such a manner?
I suppose, because of the owl-light.
Is it a kind of opal light?
No, I said it was old light.
Is it a cold light?
More like a chemical light with the usual accoutrements.
Like the carmine light produced by my present activities?
More of a cold light than that.
Like what might fall on a bulky, space-suited figure?
Well, it's neither red light nor reflected light.
Are you making this up out of the whole cloth?
No, I'm trying to give you direct directions.
For avoiding a bulky, space-suited figure?
No, for getting light from a rhodochrosite.

> NOTE: A rhodochrosite is a vitreous rose-red or variously colored
> gem-stone having a hardness of 4.5 & a density of 3.8 & consisting
> of manganous carbonate ($MnCO_3$) crystallized in the rhombohe-
> dral system.

IV

This time I'm going to talk about red light.
First of all, it's not very much like emerald light.
Nevertheless, there's still some of it in Pittsburgh.
It adds to the light from eyes an extra light.
This is also true of emerald light.
But red light better suits those with a taste for mythology.
As reflected light it is often paler than the light from a rhodo-
     chrosite.
Such a red light might fall on a bulky, space-suited figure.
In just such a manner might this being be illuminated during a
     time gambol.

FRANK KUENSTLER
Three Poems

Sun & moon
travelling
on the road together

mother & father
blooming
as it were

Escape the work
The body, like the book
's no problem

•

A dog	a train	A tree	a dog
a dog	A train	a train	a Train
a dog	A train	a Dog	a house
a dog	a trai n	a Train	a train
a dog	a train	A train	a tree
a dog	A Tree	a tree	a House

•

School

The world of color.
Characters.
Airplane glue.

Black & white images.
rhetoric.
Immaculate moustaches.

EMMETT WILLIAMS

"Like Attracts Like"

like   attracts   like

like   attracts   like

like   attracts   like

like   attracts   like

like   attracts   like

like   attracts   like

like attracts like

likeattractslike

likeattractlike

likettraclke

lihttradike

lixtralise

liltelikts

ERNST JANDL, in a note on his own work, observes: "There must be an infinite number of methods of writing experimental poems, but I think the most successful methods are those which can only be used once, for then the result is a poem identical with the method by which it is made. The method used again would turn out exactly the same poem." This particular poem says what it does, and does what it says, and I can't think of three other words that would work as well in this construction.

—E.W.

PROJECTIVE VERSE: In the major redirection of modern poetry that centered in the 1950s around Charles Olson's essay "Projective Verse" (see above, page 357), the concern with image-making was implicit: "Now . . . the *process* of the thing, how the principle can be made so to shape the energies that the form is accomplished. . . . I think it can be boiled down to one statement (first pounded into my head by Edward Dahlberg): ONE PERCEPTION MUST IMMEDIATELY AND DI-RECTLY LEAD TO A FURTHER PERCEPTION."

CHARLES OLSON

From The Mayan Letters

The fish is speech. Or see
what, cut
in stone
starts. For

when the sea breaks, watch
watch, it is the
tongue, and

he who introduces the words (the
interlocutor), the
beginner of the word, he

you will find, he
has scales, he
gives off motion as

in the sun the wind the light, the fish
moves

ROBERT DUNCAN

Passages 23

BENEFICE 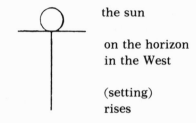 the sun

on the horizon
in the West

(setting)
rises

thru the Shinto Gate

as at Stonehenge the Mid-Winter Sun

rise   a message

from the Orient   West of us

4 AM   February 7th
(my mother's birth day)

the Shining Lady
at the horizon   •

we live in the darkness in back of

her   rising

sing

from the ridge-pole.

DENISE LEVERTOV
Turning

The shifting, the shaded
    change of pleasure

Soft warm ashes in place of fire
    out, irremediably

and a door blown open:

planes tilt, interact, objects
    fuse, disperse,
    this chair further from that table . . . hold it!
    Focus on that: this table
    closer to that shadow. It's what appalls the
    heart's red rust. Turn, turn!
    Loyalty betrays.

        It's the fall of it, the drift,
            pleasure
        source and sequence
            lift
        of golden cold sea.

ED SANDERS
Soft-Man 6

Peace Eye is open to any who
rip wide the brainvalve, &
fuck the mish system,
be it with wad technique.

Crotch Lake, where Death Barque
Slides toward Petal Torrent,
is a lake of lights in the flash of Brain Pinks
Outbound to Peace-Eye.

The Brain Lights glint in Death Barque,
The Crotch-tide draws them outward,

The Tide   The Tide

THE TI  DE.

Real is the Eye-Heart-Mind,
The Torrent is real, the love-burst is real,
Real is myriad real is the fever.
The vision is simple:

Crotch Lake

of whom flows   downstream

The Torrent
Petal Torrent

in which the Eye-Heart-Minds
The Brain Pinks
float to Peace Eye

And there to enter
the tides of
desire & fulfillment,

a sucking-in
as of a constant fucking

& a giving forth
as of a cunt forever
giving birth,

The Tides There

The Tides

THE TI DES

DEEP IMAGE: Late fifties, early sixties: one response to the re-opening of American poetry at this time was a new consideration of "image" as a power latent in all poetry and thought. Attention to "deep image" (derived from Spanish and French Surrealism, archaic and primitive poetry, etc.) centered in magazines like *Trobar* (ed. Robert Kelly and George Economou) and *Poems from the Floating World* (ed. Jerome Rothenberg), while related concerns with "image" informed Robert Bly's *Fifties* and *Sixties*. Kelly's concern with a synthesis of "deep image" and "projective verse" (see below) marks one difference between the former and latter publications.

■ *" If the poem takes its departure from speech, a relationship of some kind must exist between the rhythm supplied by the images and the rhythm of the breath. What is the relationship of image to line?*

"One easy answer is to say that one image equals one line. This denies the independent existence of line, and is a quasi-solution that produces poetry of blandness, no matter how great the initial force of the images: the images are not being articulated, urgency is lost.

"Projective verse [for which see Charles Olson, Projective Verse, *above, page 357] offers a method of resolving breath and line, and my concern with it here seeks to substitute the centrality of image for the centrality of syllable & line as a way of access to the happening of a poem. The line as set down on paper is an indication of the breath period, with visual and rhythmic considerations determining the visual notation.*

"The projective line ending in open juncture allows tremendous stress on the last verbal unit in the line, a stress exploited not for key words but for key silences, stretching out to vital & peripheral words. 'Systematic derangement' of standard speech rhythms, of the inflexibilities of our analytic grammar, is a sharp exploratory tool, and a means of locking images.

"When the image, prima materia, is lacking, the verbal gesture is quickly emptied: the poem elapses instead of happening.

"The fundamental rhythm of the poem is the rhythm of the images: their textures, their contents, offer supplementary rhythms. "

    —"Notes on the Poetry of Deep Image" (Robert Kelly, *Trobar* #2, 1961)

JEROME ROTHENBERG

Sightings II

A hand extended, or a page.
The witness.

    •

In the way we eat—it is this that moves me, to be guided by it.

    •

Whiteness.
Her shadow & my own.
For color.

    •

That leaves a number less than one.

    •

For balance: snow or horses.
(Seals).

•

How we had rested (the question).
By elevations (the response).

•

A finger growing from a finger:
Hell in glass.

> The music of *Sightings I–IX* involves a use of silences, as notated by printer's bullets, roughly equivalent to the amount of time it would take to speak the line that follows.—J. R.

JAMES WRIGHT

Milkweed

While I stood here, in the open, lost in myself,
I must have looked a long time
Down the corn rows, beyond grass,
The small house,
White walls, animals lumbering toward the barn.
I look down now. It is all changed.
Whatever it was I lost, whatever I wept for
Was a wild, gentle thing, the small dark eyes
Loving me in secret.
It is here. At a touch of my hand,
The air fills with delicate creatures
From the other world.

ROBERT BLY

Looking into a Face

Conversation brings us so close! Opening
The surfs of the body,
Bringing fish up near the sun,
And stiffening the backbones of the sea!

I have wandered in a face, for hours,
Passing through dark fires.
I have risen to a body
Not yet born,
Existing like a light around the body,

Through which the body moves like a sliding moon.

BERNADETTE MAYER

"Fiction" *from* Story

For three hundred years people may have done this, stumbled, perhaps for a longer time.

In another sense.

An inside thing, glances fall.

To commence.

At this of thirty-two of these, then, anyone is under that thing of two of those—that of this, and of one of those of that thing equal to it.

He roasts cabbages in hot ashes, and sends them out to people whose relationships are ended.

But, that many years ago, a person did fall perhaps more than once or even three or four times.

An outline or shape, as of the human body.

Governments fall.

At sixty-four of these he is under that thing of three of those, and so on.

He models girls from bark.

On a thing then, over one, or simply because of one, whether real or imaginary.

Leaves fall.

That of one of these is always added for every thirty-two of those of that other.

He pretends to die, and is buried with his face exposed.

Symposium of the Whole

■ *" The true poem is not that which the public read. There is always a poem not printed on paper, coincident with the production of this, stereotyped in the poet's life.* It is what he has become through his work. *Not how is the idea expressed in stone, or on canvas or paper, is the question, but how far it has obtained form and expression in the life of the artist. His true work will not stand in any prince's gallery.*

> *My life has been the poem I would have writ,*
> *But I could not both live and utter it. "*

—HENRY DAVID THOREAU, *A Week on the Concord and Merrimack Rivers* [1849]

TORLINO [NAVAJO]
Therefore I Must Tell the Truth

I am ashamed before the earth:
I am ashamed before the heavens:
I am ashamed before the dawn:
I am ashamed before the evening twilight:
I am ashamed before the blue sky:
I am ashamed before the darkness:
I am ashamed before the sun.
I am ashamed before that standing within me which speaks
     with me.
Some of these things are always looking at me.
I am never out of sight.
Therefore I must tell the truth.
That is why I always tell the truth.
I hold my word tight to my breast.

—English translation by WASHINGTON MATTHEWS

"Torlino's oath to tell the truth was sworn before he recounted the Navajo cosmogony to Professor Matthews." [Cited in M. L. ROSENTHAL and A. J. M. SMITH, Exploring Poetry, 1955.]

■ *" The drama of our time is the coming of all men into one fate, the dream of everyone, everywhere. The fate or dream is the fate of more than mankind. Our secret Adam is written now in the script of the primal cell. We have gone beyond the reality of the incomparable nation or race, the incomparable Jehovah in the shape of a man, the incomparable Book or Vision, the incomparable species, in which identity might hold and defend its boundaries against an alien territory. All things have come now into their comparisons. But these comparisons are the correspondences that haunted Paracelsus, who saw also that the key to man's nature was hidden in the larger nature. . . .*

"The Symposium of Plato was restricted to a community of Athenians, gathered in the common creation of an arete, an aristocracy of spirit, inspired by the homoEros, taking its stand against lower or foreign orders, not only of men but of nature itself. The intense yearning, the desire for something else, of which we too have only a dark and doubtful presentiment, remains, but our arete, our ideal of vital being, rises not in our identification in a hierarchy of higher forms but in our identification with the universe. To compose such a symposium of the whole, such a totality, all the old excluded orders must be included. The female, the proletariat, the foreign; the animal and vegetative; the unconscious and the unknown; the criminal and failure—all that has been outcast and vagabond must return to be admitted in the creation of what we consider we are. "

—ROBERT DUNCAN, "Rites of Participation," *Caterpillar 2* [1967]

WALT WHITMAN

From Preface to Leaves of Grass [1855]

This is what you shall do: Love the earth and sun and the animals, despise riches, give alms to every one that asks, stand up for the stupid and crazy, devote your income and labor to others, hate tyrants, argue not concerning God, have patience and indulgence toward the people, take off your hat to nothing known or unknown or to any man or number of men, go freely with powerful uneducated persons and with the young and with the mothers of families, read these leaves in the open air every season of every year of your life, re-examine all you have been told at school or church or in any book, dismiss whatever insults your own soul, and your very flesh shall be a great poem and have the richest fluency not only in its words but in the silent lines of its lips and face and between the lashes of your eyes and in every motion and joint of your body. . . . The poet shall not spend his time in unneeded work. He shall know that the ground is always ready plowed and manured . . . others may not know it but he shall. He shall go directly to the creation. His trust shall master the trust of everything he touches . . . and shall master all attachment.

GERTRUDE STEIN

Identity a Poem

PLAY 1

I am I because my little dog knows me. The figure wanders on alone.

The little dog does not appear because if it did then there would be nothing to fear.

It is not known that anybody who is anybody is not alone and if alone then how can the dog be there and if the little dog is not there is it alone. The little dog is not alone because no little dog could be alone. If it were alone it would not be there.

So then the play has to be like this.

The person and the dog are there and the dog is there and the person is there and where oh where is their identity, is the identity there anywhere.

I say two dogs but say a dog and a dog.

The human mind.   The human mind does play.
The human mind.   Plays because it plays.
Human Nature.   Does not play because it does not
                 play again.

It might desire something but it does not play again.

And so to make excitement and not nervousness into a play.

And then to make a play with just the human mind.

Let us try.

To make a play with human nature and not anything of the human mind.

Pivoines smell like magnolias

Dogs smell like dogs
Men smell like men
And gardens smell differently at different seasons of
the year.

PLAY 2

> Try a play again
> Every little play helps
> Another play.

There is any difference between resting and waiting.

Does a little dog rest.
Does a little dog wait.
What does the human mind do.
What does human nature do.

A PLAY.

There is no in between in a play.
A play could just as well only mean two.
Then it could do
It could really have to do.

The dog.	What could it do.
The human mind.	The human mind too.
Human nature.	Human nature does not have it to do.

What can a dog do and with waiting too.

Yes there is when you have not been told when to cry.

Nobody knows what the human mind is when they are
drunk.

Everybody who has a grandfather has had a great
grandfather and that great grandfather has had a father.
This actually is true of a grandmother who was a grand-
daughter and grandfather had a father.

Any dog too.

Any time anyone who knows how to write can write to
any brother.

Not a dog too.

A dog does not write too.

ANOTHER PLAY

But. But is a place where they can cease to distress her.

ANOTHER PLAY

It does not make any difference what happens to any-
body if it does not make a difference what happens to
them.

This no dog can say.

Not any dog can say not ever when he is at play.

And so dogs and human nature have no identity.

It is extraordinary that when you are acquainted with a whole family you can forget about them.

ANOTHER PLAY

A man coming.

Yes there is a great deal of use in a man coming but will he come at all if he does come will he come here.

How do you like it if he comes and look like that. Not at all later. Well anyway he does come and if he likes it he will come again.

Later when another man comes

He does not come.

Girls coming. There is no use in girls coming.

Well anyway he does come and if he likes it he will come again.

PART IV

The question of identity.

A PLAY.

I am I because my little dog knows me.

Which is he.

No which is he.

Say it with tears, no which is he.

I am I why.

So there.

I am I where.

ACT I SCENE III

I am I because my little dog knows me.

ACT I SCENE

Now this is the way I had played that play.

But not at all not as one is one.

ACT I SCENE I

Which one is there I am I or another one.

Who is one and one or one is one.

I like a play of acting so and so and a dog my dog is any one of not one.

But we in America are not displaced by a dog oh no no not at all not at all at all displaced by a dog.

SCENE I

A dog chokes over a ball because it is a ball that choked any one.

PART I SCENE I

He has forgotten that he has been choked by a ball no not forgotten because this one the same one is not the one that can choke any one.

SCENE I ACT I

I am I because my little dog knows me, but perhaps he does not and if he did I would not be I. Oh no oh no.

ACT I SCENE I

When a dog is young he seems to be a very intelligent one.
But later well later the dog is older.
And so the dog roams around he knows the one he knows but does that make any difference.
A play is exactly like that.
Chorus   There is no left or right without remembering.
And remembering.
They say there is no left and right without remembering.
Chorus   But there is no remembering the human mind.
Tears   There is no chorus in the human mind.
The land is flat from on high and when they wander.
Chorus   Nobody who has a dog forgets him. They may leave
him behind. Oh yes they may leave him behind.
Chorus   There is no memory in the human mind.
And the result
May be and the result
If I am I then my little dog knows me.
The dog listens while they prepare food.
Food might be connected by the human mind but it is not.

SCENE II

And how do you like what you are
And how are you what you are
And has this to do with the human mind.
Chorus   And has this to do with the human mind.
Chorus   And is human nature not at all interesting. It is not.

SCENE II

I am I because my little dog knows me.

Chorus   That does not prove anything about you it only proves something about the dog.

Chorus   Of course nobody can be interested in human nature.

Chorus   Nobody is.

Chorus   Nobody is interested in human nature.

Chorus   Not even a dog

Chorus   It has nothing to do human nature has nothing to do with anything.

Chorus   No not with a dog

Tears   No not with a dog.

Chorus   I am I because my little dog knows

Chorus   Yes there I told you human nature is not at all interesting.

SCENE III

And the human mind.

Chorus   And the human mind

Tears   And the human mind

Chorus   Yes and the human mind.

Of course the human mind

Has that anything to do with I am I because my little dog knows me.

What is the chorus.

Chorus   What is the chorus.

Anyway there is the question of identity.

What is the use of being a little boy if you are to grow up to be a man.

Chorus   No the dog is not the chorus.

SCENE II

Any scene may be scene II

Chorus   And act II

No any act can be act one and two.

SCENE II

I am I because my little dog knows me even if the little dog is a big one and yet a little dog knowing me does not really make me be I no not really because after all being I I am I has really nothing to do with the little dog knowing me, he is my audience, but an audience never does prove to you that you are you.

And does a little dog making a noise make the same noise.
He can almost say the b in bow wow.
I have not been mistaken.
Chorus   Some kinds of things not and some kinds of things.

SCENE I

I am I yes sir I am I.
I am I yes madame am I I.
When I am I am I I.
And my little dog is not the same thing as I am I.
Chorus   Oh is it.
With tears in my eyes oh is it.
And there we have the whole thing
Am I I.
And if I am I because my little dog knows me am I I.
Yes sir am I I.
The dog answers without asking because the dog is the
answer to anything that is that dog.
But not I.
Without tears but not I.

ACT I SCENE I

The necessity of ending is not the necessity of beginning.
Chorus   How finely that is said.

SCENE II

An end of a play is not the end of a day.

SCENE IV

After giving.

NOTE: Of "human nature" and "human mind" Stein writes else-
where *(The Geographical History of America, 1936):* "If nobody
had to die how would there be room for us who now live to have
lived. We never could have been if all the others had not died there
would have been no room.
    "Now the relation of human nature to the human mind is this.
    "Human nature does not know this. . . .
    "Human nature cannot know this.
    "But the human mind can. It can know this."

E. E. CUMMINGS

From Portraits

VII

my mind is
a big hunk of irrevocable nothing which touch and
taste and smell and hearing and sight keep hitting and
chipping with sharp fatal tools
in an agony of sensual chisels i perform squirms of
chrome and execute strides of cobalt
nevertheless i
feel that i cleverly am being altered that i slightly am
becoming something a little different, in fact
myself
Hereupon helpless i utter lilac shrieks and scarlet
bellowings.

VIII

5
derbies-with-men-in-them smoke Helmar
cigarettes   2
play backgammon, 3 watch

a has gold
teeth b pink
suspenders c
reads Atlantis

x and y play   b
cries "effendi" "Uh" "coffee"
"uh"   enter
paperboy, c

buys Bawstinamereekin, exit
paperboy   a finishes
Helmar   lights
another

      x and y
play, effendi approaches, sets
down coffee   withdraws
a and c discuss news in

turkish x and y play b spits
x and
y
play, b starts armenian record

                              pho
nographisrunn
ingd o   w,   n   phonograph
                  stopS.

b swears in persian at phonograph
x wins   exeunt ax: by; c,
Goo dnightef fendi
. . . .

five men in derbies

IX

at the ferocious phenomenon of 5 o'clock i find myself
gently decomposing in the mouth of New York. Between its
supple financial teeth deliriously sprouting from compla-
cent gums, a morsel prettily wanders buoyed on the mur-
derous saliva of industry. the morsel is i.

Vast cheeks enclose me.

a gigantic uvula with imperceptible gesticulations threat-
ens the tubular downward blackness occasionally from
which detatching itself bumps clumsily into the throat A
meticulous vulgarity:

a sodden fastidious normal explosion; a square murmur, a
winsome flatulence—

In the soft midst of the tongue sits the Woolworth building
a serene pastile-shaped insipid kinesis or frail swooping
lozenge. a ruglike sentience whose papillae expertly drink
the docile perpendicular taste of this squirming cube of
undiminished silence, supports while devouring the firm
tumult of exquisitely insecure sharp algebraic music. For
the first time in sorting from this vast nonchalant inward
walk of volume the flat minute gallop of careful hugeness
i am conjugated by the sensual mysticism of entire vertical
being, i am skilfully construed by a delicately experiment-

ing colossus whose irrefutable spiral antics involve me
with the soothings of plastic hypnotism . i am accurately
parsed by this gorgeous rush of upward lips. . . .

cleverly

perching on the sudden extremity of one immense tooth
myself surveys safely the complete important profane
frantic inconsequential gastronomic mystery of mysteries
, life.

Far below myself the lunging leer of horizontal large dis-
tinct ecstasy wags and. rages Laughters jostle grins nudge
smiles push—.deep into the edgeless gloaming gladness
hammers incessant putrid spikes of madness (at

Myself's height these various innocent ferocities are su-
perceded by the sole prostituted ferocity of silence, it is)
still 5 o'clock
I stare only always into the tremendous canyon the

, tremendous canyon always only exhales a climbing dark
exact walloping human noise of digestible millions whose
rich slovenly obscene procession always floats through the
thin amorous enormous only lips of the evening

And it is 5 o'clock

in the oblong air, from which a singular ribbon of com-
mon sunset is hanging,

snow speaks slowly

> NOTE: Portraits is a nine-poem sequence, somewhat "cubistically"
> presenting the different modes or structures which might be used
> in the making of verbal portraits; VIII, for example, has a surrealist
> quality not unlike that of the painter René Magritte. One might
> "rediscover" Cummings by attending to his use of longer, sequen-
> tial modalities.

■ *". . . Both in nature and in metaphor identity is the vanishing-point of
resemblance. After all, if a man's exact double entered a room, seated
himself and spoke the words that were in the man's mind, it would
remain a resemblance. . . ."*

> —WALLACE STEVENS, "Three Academic Pieces" [I], *The Neces-
> sary Angel* [1947]

FRANK O'HARA

In Memory of My Feelings

to Grace Hartigan

I

My quietness has a man in it, he is transparent
and he carries me quietly, like a gondola, through the streets.
He has several likenesses, like stars and years, like numerals.
My quietness has a number of naked selves,
so many pistols I have borrowed to protect myselves
from creatures who too readily recognize my weapons
and have murder in their heart!

                       though in winter
they are warm as roses, in the desert
taste of chilled anisette.

             At times, withdrawn,
I rise into the cool skies
and gaze on at the imponderable world with the simple
      identification
of my colleagues, the mountains. Manfred climbs to my nape,
speaks, but I do not hear him,

                  I'm too blue.
An elephant takes up his trumpet,
money flutters from the windows of cries, silk stretching its
      mirror
across shoulder blades. A gun is "fired."

                    One of me rushes
to window #13 and one of me raises his whip and one of me
flutters up from the center of the track amidst the pink
      flamingoes,
and underneath their hooves as they round the last turn my lips
are scarred and brown, brushed by tails, masked in dirt's lust,
definition, open mouths gasping for the cries of the bettors for
      the lungs
of earth.

      So many of my transparencies could not resist the race!
Terror in earth, dried mushrooms, pink feathers, tickets,
a flaking moon drifting across the muddied teeth,

the imperceptible moan of covered breathing,
love of the serpent!

I am underneath its leaves as the hunter crackles and pants
and bursts, as the barrage balloon drifts behind a cloud
and animal death whips out its flashlight,
whistling

and slipping the glove off the trigger hand. The serpent's eyes
redden at sight of those thorny fingernails, he is so smooth!
My transparent selves

flail about like vipers in a pail, writhing and hissing
without panic, with a certain justice of response
and presently the aquiline serpent comes to resemble the
    Medusa.

    2

The dead hunting
and the alive, ahunted.
My father, my uncle,

my grand-uncle and the several aunts. My
grand-aunt dying for me, like a talisman, in the war,
before I had even gone to Borneo
her blood vessels rushed to the surface
and burst like rockets over the wrinkled
invasion of the Australians, her eyes aslant
like the invaded, but blue like mine.
An atmosphere of supreme lucidity,
humanism,

the mere existence of emphasis,
a rusted barge

painted orange against the sea
full of Marines reciting the Arabian ideas
which are a proof in themselves of seasickness
which is a proof in itself of being hunted.
A hit? *ergo* swim.
My 10   my 19,

my 9,   and the several years. My
12 years since they all died, philosophically speaking.
And now the coolness of a mind
like a shuttered suite in the Grand Hotel
where mail arrives for my incognito,

whose façade
has been slipping into the Grand Canal for centuries;
rockets splay over a *sposalizio*,

fleeing into night
from their Chinese memories, and it is a celebration,
the trying desperately to count them as they die.
But who will stay to be these numbers
when all the lights are dead?

3

The most arid stretch is often richest,
the hand lifting towards a fig tree from hunger

digging
and there is water, clear, supple, or there
deep in the sand where death sleeps, a murmurous bubbling
proclaims the blackness that will ease and burn.
You preferred the Arabs? but they didn't stay to count
their inventions, racing into sands, converting themselves into
so many,

embracing, at Ramadan, the tenderest effigies of
themselves with penises shorn by the hundreds, like a camel
ravishing a goat.

And the mountainous-minded Greeks could speak
of time as a river and step across it into Persia, leaving the
pain
at home to be converted into statuary. I adore the Roman
copies.
And the stench of the camel's spit I swallow,
and the stench of the whole goat. For we have advanced,
France,
together into a new land, like the Greeks, where one feels
nostalgic
for mere ideas, where truth lies on its deathbed like an uncle
and one of me has a sentimental longing for number,
as has another for the ball gowns of the Directoire and yet
another for "Destiny, Paris, destiny!"

or "Only a king may kill a king."

How many selves are there in a war hero asleep in names?
under

a blanket of platoon and fleet, orderly. For every seaman
with one eye closed in fear and twitching arm at a sigh for
      Lord Nelson,
he is all dead; and now a meek subaltern writhes in his
      bedclothes
with the fury of a thousand, violating an insane mistress
who has only herself to offer his multitudes.
                                 Rising,
he wraps himself in the burnoose of memories against the
      heat of life
and over the sands he goes to take an algebraic position *in re*
a sun of fear shining not too bravely. He will ask himselves to
vote on fear before he feels a tremor,
                        as runners arrive from the mountains
bearing snow, proof that the mind's obsolescence is still
      capable
of intimacy. His mistress will follow him across the desert
like a goat, towards a mirage which is something familiar
      about
one of his innumerable wrists,
                          and lying in an oasis one day,
playing catch with coconuts, they suddenly smell oil.

     4

Beneath these lives
the ardent lover of history hides,
                   tongue out
leaving a globe of spit on a taut spear of grass
and leaves off rattling his tail a moment
to admire this flag.
              I'm looking for my Shanghai Lil.
Five years ago, enamored of fire-escapes, I went to Chicago,
an eventful trip: the fountains! the Art Institute, the Y
for both sexes, absent Christianity.
                   At 7, before Jane
was up, the copper lake stirred against the sides
of a Norwegian freighter; on the deck a few dirty men,
tired of night, watched themselves in the water
as years before the German prisoners on the *Prinz Eugen*
dappled the Pacific with their sores, painted purple
by a Naval doctor.

Beards growing, and the constant anxiety
over looks. I'll shave before she wakes up. Sam Goldwyn
spent $2,000,000 on Anna Sten, but Grushenka left America.
One of me is standing in the waves, an ocean bather,
or I am naked with a plate of devils at my hip.

Grace
to be born and live as variously as possible. The conception
of the masque barely suggests the sordid identifications.
I am a Hittite in love with a horse. I don't know what blood's
in me I feel like an African prince I am a girl walking
downstairs
in a red pleated dress with heels I am a champion taking a
fall
I am a jockey with a sprained ass-hole I am the light mist
in which a face appears
and it is another face of blonde I am a baboon eating a
banana
I am a dictator looking at his wife I am a doctor eating a
child
and the child's mother smiling I am a Chinaman climbing a
mountain
I am a child smelling his father's underwear I am an Indian
sleeping on a scalp
and my pony is stamping in the birches,
and I've just caught sight of the *Niña,* the *Pinta* and the *Santa
Maria.*
What land is this, so free?

I watch
the sea at the back of my eyes, near the spot where I think
in solitude as pine trees groan and support the enormous
winds,
they are humming *L'Oiseau de feu!*
They look like gods, these whitemen,
and they are bringing me the horse I fell in love with on the
frieze.

5

And now it is the serpent's turn.
I am not quite you, but almost, the opposite of visionary.
You are coiled around the central figure,
the heart

that bubbles with red ghosts, since to move is to love
and the scrutiny of all things is syllogistic,
the startled eyes of the dikdik, the bush full of white flags
fleeing a hunter,
              which is our democracy
                      but the prey
is always fragile and like something, as a seashell can be
a great Courbet, if it wishes. To bend the ear of the outer
    world.
                    When you turn your head
can you feel your heels, undulating? that's what it is
to be a serpent. I haven't told you of the most beautiful things
in my lives, and watching the ripple of their loss disappear
along the shore, underneath ferns,
                      face downward in the ferns
my body, the naked host to my many selves, shot
by a guerrilla warrior or dumped from a car into ferns
which are themselves *journalières.*
            The hero, trying to unhitch his parachute,
stumbles over me. It is our last embrace.
                      And yet
I have forgotten my loves, and chiefly that one, the cancerous
statue which my body could no longer contain,
                     against my will
                     against my love
become art,
            I could not change it into history
and so remember it,
            and I have lost what is always and everywhere
present, the scene of my selves, the occasion of these ruses,
which I myself and singly must now kill
              and save the serpent in their midst.

■ *" The misconception which has haunted philosophic literature through-
out the centuries is the notion of 'independent existence.' There is no
such mode of existence; every entity is only to be understood in terms
of the way in which it is interwoven with the rest of the Universe. "*
    —ALFRED NORTH WHITEHEAD, *Essays in Science and Philo-
      sophy* [1947]

MINA LOY

Parturition

I am the centre
Of a circle of pain
Exceeding its boundaries in every direction
The business of the bland sun
Has no affair with me
In my congested cosmos of agony
From which there is no escape
On infinitely prolonged nerve-vibrations
Or in contraction
To the pin-point nucleus of being
Locate an irritation   without
It is   within
Within
It is without.
The sensitized area
Is identical   with the extensity
Of intension

I am the false quantity
In the harmony of physiological potentiality
To which
Gaining self-control
I should be consonant
In time

Pain is no stronger than the resisting force
Pain calls up in me
The struggle is equal

The open window is full of a voice
A fashionable portrait-painter
Running up-stairs to a woman's apartment
Sings

    "All the girls are tid'ly did'ly
    All the girls are nice

Whether they wear their hair in curls
Or—"
At the back of the thoughts to which I permit crystallization
The conception   Brute
Why?
    The irresponsibility of the male
Leaves woman her superior Inferiority.
He is running up-stairs

I am climbing a distorted mountain of agony
Incidentally with the exhaustion of control
I reach the summit
And gradually subside into anticipation of
Repose
Which never comes.
For another mountain is growing up
Which   goaded by the unavoidable
I must traverse
Traversing myself

Something in the delirium of night-hours
Confuses while intensifying sensibility
Blurring spatial contours
So aiding elusion of the circumscribed
That the gurgling of a crucified wild beast
Comes from so far away
And the foam on the stretched muscles of a mouth
Is no part of myself
There is a climax in sensibility
When pain surpassing itself
Becomes exotic
And the ego succeeds in unifying the positive and
    negative poles of sensation.
Uniting the opposing and resisting forces
In lascivious revelation

Relaxation
Negation of myself as a unit
    Vacuum interlude
I should have been emptied of life

Giving life
For consciousness in crises   races
Through the subliminal deposits of evolutionary processes
Have I not
Somewhere
Scrutinized
A dead white feathered moth
Laying eggs?

A moment
Being realization
Can
Vitalized by cosmic initiation
Furnish an adequate apology
For the objective
Agglomeration of activities
Of a life
LIFE
A leap with nature
Into the essence
Of unpredicted Maternity
Against my thigh
Touch of infinitesimal motion
Scarcely perceptible
Undulation
Warmth   moisture
Stir of incipient life
Precipitating into me
The contents of the universe
Mother I am
Identical
With infinite Maternity
    Indivisible
    Acutely
    I am absorbed
    Into
The was—is—ever—shall—be
Of cosmic reproductivity

Rises from the subconscious
Impression of a cat

With blind kittens
Among her legs
Same undulating life-stir
I am that cat

Rises from the sub-conscious
Impression of small animal carcass
Covered with blue-bottles
—Epicurean—
And through the insects
Waves that same undulation of living
Death
Life
I am knowing
All about
   Unfolding

The next morning
Each woman-of-the-people
Tip-toeing the red pile of the carpet
Doing hushed service
Each woman-of-the-people
Wearing a halo
Of which she is sublimely unaware

■ *"Perspective is one of the component parts of reality. Far from being a disturbance of its fabric, it is its organizing element. A reality which remained the same from whatever point of view it was observed would be a ridiculous conception. . . . Every life is a point of view directed upon the universe. Strictly speaking, what one life sees, no other can. . . . Reality happens to be, like a landscape, possessed of an infinite number of perspectives, all equally veracious and authentic. The sole false perspective is that which claims to be the only one there is."*

    —ALFRED NORTH WHITEHEAD, *The Modern Theme*

ARMAND SCHWERNER

Tablet XV: Presented by the scholar-translator transmitted through Armand Schwerner

Probably the song of a temple prostitute,
priestess of the second caste.

much, heavily flying, much, heavily flying, much, the vagina
      musk bleeding
they bring in the wild ass
slow spectrum enormity penis enormity ravage till
much, spectrum, soil-tiller, heavily flying and till till vagina
      musk
they bring in the wild ass
never of when whenever coming coming coming now power
      ziggurat tureen
of much, heavily flying, enormity ravage penis in sperm mass
      blue river god
they bring in ....
lapis and obsidian and bronze gird about gird about bronze
      testicles
he climbs suspension my back raw inside lips suspension my
      teeth together wild god
nettles nettles sacred bath of sperm and blood bronze in my
      sleep
+ +
+ +
+ +
for you, that I turn for you, that I slowly turn for you, high
      priestess
that you do my body in oil, in glycerin, that you do me, that
      you slowly do me
that you do me slowly almost not at all, that you are my
      mouth
that I am your vulva, feather, feather, and discover for you—
let me open my thighs for your hands as I do for my own that
      I do you
that my hair thinks of you and remembers you, that my
      fingers
that the sweat on my thighs/bronze bronze heavily
      flying/thinks of you

and reminds me of me and that you let me be harsh
o for you, that I turn for you, that I slowly turn for you, high
        priestess
that you do my body in oil, in glycerin, that you do me, that
        you slowly do me
that you do me slowly almost not at all, that you are—
+ +
. . . . that my body become a sentence that never stops,
        driving through air spaces
from one tablet to another, its python power
. . . . unclear, it must be the tips of my own
        fingers on my cunt lips
and your hands which graze my nipples, looking for what
        they need,
which endear the field of my closed eyes my closed eyes my
        nose the corridor
of my ear, my clitoris, and your wayfaring hands bearing
        through myself images
that constantly just escape me because I will not let them win
        over you,
your hands which graze my field, sentence
and inflection of how I do me, you do me and how do I how
        wonderful
by way of pictures I can't see thrust across the air between us
        high priestess
and dare to put your own hands on your own lips
my hands on yours, how is it I never knew
this took so much risking, that I do you, that you turn for me
that you slowly turn for me, that I do your body in oil, in
        glycerin,
that I do you, that I do you slowly almost not at all
+ +
. . . . in this small clearing where I rest from us, space
        inside the field,
emptied of muscle and cries, emptied
of muscle and cries my closed eyes empty cups of rest
in which your picture sometimes appalls and that you know
        to leave me here

where my money my clothes my blood my liver are violently
    plucked away from me
my field sometimes in such pain from thousands of tiny
    openings
and I wake up unpeopled and startled at such happiness

ARTURO GIOVANNITTI

From The Nuptials of Death

> *Whose shoes are never seen*
> *But whose carriage is always heard rumbling*
>   *boisterously outside.*

. . .So spoke to me Death, all dressed in reds
And yellows and blues and greens, and purples, ablaze
With all the sun's cleft rays
By her falchion and all the crazy flags of the world.
And I looked at her: I alone dared look at the pearled
Sheen of her face, without any dread nor hope,
Without having called her, without having put her out
In my bedroom that the morning whitened and blued.
And lo! while my blood fermented and brewed
By the breath of the cold-hot words
And the kisses that sizzled and baked
Stirred by her tongue on her lips
She flung away all her veils,
And in the glows of the whitest of all the white lusts
She stood there, all-glorious, all-naked,
And the snow of her flesh made even the sunlight eclipse,
White and immaculate like the snow and
The queen of all the red fires and all the white frosts.
And I stretched my arms to her, shaking and mad
In the spasms of her passion divine,
And she stretched her own and she hurled
Herself on my chest, and supine
She lay under me till the eve

And we both forgot life and the world.
And from that day I have forgotten how to suffer.
And I have learned how to die,
And I keep on dying all the time.

GIOVANNITTI grew up in Campobasso, Italy, and reached the United States at age twenty. A socialist and labor organizer most of his life, he was charged with murder during the Lawrence, Mass., textile strike of 1912, but was acquitted after spending ten months in prison. *The Nuptials of Death* is a long poem from that time.

JEROME ROTHENBERG

Cokboy, Part One

saddlesore I came
a jew among
the indians
vot em I doink in dis strange place
mit deeze pipple mit strange eyes
could be it's trouble
could be could be
(he says) a shadow
ariseth from his buckwheat
has tomahawk in hand
shadow of an axe inside his right eye
of a fountainpen inside his left
vot em I doink here
how vass I lost tzu get here
am a hundred men
a hundred fifty different shadows
jews & gentiles
who bring the Law to Wilderness
(he says) this man
is me my grandfather
& other men-of-letters
men with letters carrying the mail
lithuanian pony-express riders
the financially crazed Buffalo Bill
still riding in the lead

hours before avenging the death of Custer
making the first 3-D movie of those wars
or years before it
the numbers vanishing in kabbalistic time
that brings all men together
& the lonely rider
saddlesore
is me my grandfather
& other men of letters
jews & gentiles entering
the domain of Indian
who bring the Law to Wilderness
in gold mines & shakey stores
the fur trade heavy agriculture
ballots bullets barbers
who threaten my beard your hair
but patronize me
& will make our kind the Senator from Arizona
the champion of their Law
who hates us both
but dresses as a jew one day an Indian
the next a little christian shmuck
vot em I doink here
dis place is maybe crazy
has all the letters going backwards
(he says) so who can read the signboards
to the desert
who can shake his way out of the woods
ford streams the grandmothers
were living near
with snakes inside their cunts
teeth maybe
maybe chainsaws
when the Baal Shem visited America
he wore a shtreiml
the locals all thought he was a cowboy
maybe from Mexico
"a cokboy?"
no a cowboy

I will be more than a credit to my community
& race
but will search for my brother Esau among these redmen
their nocturnal fires I will share
piss strained from my holy cock
will bear seed of Adonoi
& feed them visions
I will fill full a clamshell
will pass it around from mouth to mouth
we will watch the moonrise
through each other's eyes
the distances vanishing in kabbalistic time
(he says) the old man watches
from the cliffs a city
overcome with light
the man & the city disappear
he looks & sees another city
this one is made of glass
inside the buildings stand
immobile statues
brown-skinned faces
catch the light
an elevator
moving up & down
in the vision of the Cuna *nele*
the vision of my grandfather
vision of the Baal Shem in America
the slaves in steerage
what have they seen in common
by what light their eyes
have opened into stars
I wouldn't know
what I was doing here
this place has all the letters going
backwards a reverse in time
towards wilderness
the old jew strains at his gaberdine
it parts for him
his spirit rushes up the mountainside

& meets an eagle
no an iggle
captains   commanders   dollinks   delicious madmen
murderers opening the continent up to exploitation
cease & desist (he says)
let's speak (he says)
feels like a little gas down here (he says)
(can't face the mirror without crying)
& the iggle lifts him
like an elevator
to a safe place above the sunrise
there gives a song to him
the Baal Shem's song
repeated without words for centuries
"hey heya heya" but translates it
as "yuh-buh-buh-buh-buh-buh-bum"
when the Baal Shem (yuh-buh) learns to do a bundle
what does the Baal Shem (buh-buh) put into the bundle?
silk of his prayershawl-bag beneath
cover of beaverskin above
savor of esrog fruit within
horn of a mountaingoat between
feather of dove around the sides
clove of a Polish garlic at its heart
he wears when traveling
in journeys through kabbalistic forests
cavalry of the Tsars on every side
men with fat moustaches yellow eyes & sabers
who stalk the gentle soul
at night through the Wyoming steppes
(he says) vot em I doink here
I could not find mine het
would search the countryside on hands & knees
until behind a rock in Cody
old Indian steps forth
the prophecies of both join at this point
like smoke a pipe is held
between them dribbles through their lips
the keen tobacco

"cowboy?"
cokboy (says the Baal Shem)
places a walnut in his handkerchief & cracks it
on a boulder each one eats
the Indian draws forth a deck of cards
& shuffles
"game?"
they play at wolves & lambs
the fire crackles in the pripitchok
in a large tent somewhere in America
the story of the coming-forth begins

> GLOSSARY. *Baal Shem* (=Master of the Name): founder in eight-eenth century of Hasidic sect of ecstatic Judaism. *Shtreiml:* broad-brimmed Hasidic headgear. *Nele:* shaman among the Cuna Indi-ans of Panama. *Pripitchok:* old-fashioned Slavic oven, as I under-stand it, though I have never sat by same. (Note in *Poetry Review,* London, Spring 1972)

■ " *We have no organ or faculty to appreciate the simply given order. The real world as it is given objectively at this moment is the sum total of all its beings and events now. But can we think of such a sum? . . . While I talk and the flies buzz, a sea gull catches a fish at the mouth of the Amazon, a tree falls in the Adirondack wilderness, a man sneezes in Germany, a horse dies in Tattany, and twins are born in France. What does that mean? Does the contemporaneity of these events with one another, and with a million others as disjointed, form a rational bond between them, and write them into anything that resembles for us a world?* "

—WILLIAM JAMES, *Reflex Action and Theism* [1881]

ELI SIEGEL

Hot Afternoons Have Been in Montana [1924]

Quiet and green was the grass of the field,
The sky was whole in brightness,
And O, a bird was flying, high, there in the sky,
So gently, so carelessly and fairly.
Here, once, Indians shouted in battle,

And moaned after it.
Here were cries, yells, night, and the moon over these men,
And the men making the cries and yells; it was
Hundreds of years ago, when monks were in Europe,
Monks in cool, black monasteries, thinking of God, studying
    Virgil;
Monks were in Europe, a land having an ocean, miles of
    water, between
It and this land, America, possessing Montana.
(New York, Vermont, New Mexico, America has too.)
Indians, Indians went through Montana,
Thinking, feeling, trying pleasurably to live.
This land, shone on by the sun now, green, quiet now,
Was under their feet, this time; we live now and it is
    hundreds of years after.
Montana, thou art, and I say thou art, as once monks said of
    God,
And thought, too: Thou art.
Thou hast Kansas on thy side;
Kansas is in the newspapers, talked of by men;
Idaho thou hast, and far away, Singapore, Alabama, Brazil.
That bird over this green, under that sun, God, how sweet and
    graceful it is!
Could we ever do that? Machines that fly are clumsy and ugly;
Birds go into the air so softly, so fairly; see its curves; Earth!
In Montana, men eat and have bodies paining them
Because they eat.
Kansas, with Montana, in America, has, too, men pained by
    their eating;
So has England, with Westminster Abbey, where poets lie,
    dead now;
O, what their poetry can do; what poetry can do.
There is the brain of man, a soft, puzzling, weak affair;
Lord, the perfect green of this meadow.
Look at the pure heat and light of that big sun,
And the cleanness of the sky.
Night comes, night has come.
Was not Montana here in the Middle Ages, when old Rome
    was at its oldest, when
Aristotle wrote,

In Greece, Greece by the Aegean, with the Mediterranean
       near?
Indians killed each other here,
With the moon over them.
Indians killed each other near Cape Cod, near Boston, in
       Louisiana, too.
It was before white men came from England, to see them; the
       white men were seen by them.
Snows have been here, in Montana, while the Indians have
       been.
Girls are in Helena, mines are in Helena,
Men work in them painfully and long for the bodies of girls;
And long for much more that is in the world, in thee, Earth.
Men work, suffer, are little, ugly, too.
O, mountains are in Montana,
The Rocky Mountains are in California, Utah, Colorado,
       Montana.
Indians were here, too, by rivers, in these mountains, lived in
       mountains.
Europe has its Paris, and men live there; Stendhal, Rabelais,
       Gautier, Hume were there.
God, what is it man can do?
There are millions of men in the world, and each is one man,
Each is one man by himself, taking care of himself all the
       time, and changing other men and being changed by
       them;
The quiet of this afternoon is strange, haunting, awful;
Hear that buzzing in the hot grass, coming from live things;
       and those crows' cries from somewhere;
There is a sluggish, sad brook near here, too.
The bird is gone now, so graceful, fair as it was,
And the sky has nothing but the brightness of air in it.
The clean color of air.
The sun makes it be afternoon here;
In Paris and Sumatra, it is night;
Dark Malays are in lands by the Indian Ocean,
An ocean there is we call the Indian;
Men went to these Malays near the Indian Ocean, in the
       eighteenth century, in frigates and ships-of-the-line;
And men living here are Indians, too.

O, the cry of the Indian in battle, hundreds of years ago, in
    woods, in plains, in mountains;
War might have been seen once in this meadow, now in
    green, now hot;
Hundreds of years ago it might have been seen, and tens of
    years, and a thousand.
There was love among Indians, there is love in Paris, Moscow,
    London, and New York.
Men have been in war, ever,
And men have thought, and written books, about war, love,
    and mind.
Mist comes in this earth,
And there have been sad, empty, pained, longing souls going
    through mist.
O, the green in mist that is to be seen in the world.
And time goes on, the world is moving, all of it, so time goes
    on in this world.
It is now a hot, quiet afternoon in Montana,
Montana with the Rocky Mountains;
Virginia with the Allegany Mountains:
(Indians ambushed Braddock in the Allegany Mountains; the
    woods, once quiet, once dark,
Sounded sharply and deeply with cries, moans, and shots;
    Washington was there;
Washington Irving wrote of Washington, so did Frenchmen
    who knew Voltaire;
In 1755, Braddock was ambushed and died, and then, in Paris
    men and women wrote of philosophy who were elegant,
    witty and thought spirit was of matter; say Diderot,
    Helvetius, and Madame du Deffand; Samuel Johnson
    was in London then; Pitt was in England; men lived in
    Montana, Honolulu, Argentina and near the Cape of
    Good Hope; O, life of man, O, Earth; Earth, again and
    again!)
And there have been hot afternoons, all through time, history,
    as men say;
Hot afternoons have been in Montana.
There have been hot afternoons, and quiet, soft, lovely
    twilights; Gray, Collins, Milton wrote of these;

There have been hot afternoons in quiet English churchyards,
and hot afternoons in America, in Montana; and green
everywhere and bright sky; there are deserts in Africa,
America, and Australia;

Clear air is healthful; men go to Colorado, near Wyoming,
near Montana in the mountains, sick men go to the
mountains where Indians once lived, fought and killed
each other.

O, the love of bodies, O, the pains of bodies on hot, quiet
afternoons, everywhere in the world.

Men work in factories on hot afternoons, now in Montana,
and now in New Hampshire; walk the streets of Boston
on hot afternoons;

Novels, stupid and forgot, have been written in afternoons;

Matinées of witty comedies in London and New York are in
afternoons;

Indians roamed here, in this green field, on quiet, hot
afternoons, in years now followed by hundreds of years.

Hot afternoons are real; afternoons are; places, things,
thoughts, feelings are; poetry is;

The world is waiting to be known; Earth, what it has in it!
The past is in it;

All words, feelings, movements, words, bodies, clothes, girls,
trees, stones, things of beauty, books, desires are in it;
and all are to be known;

Afternoons have to do with the whole world;

And the beauty of mind, feeling knowingly the world!

The world of girls' beautiful faces, bodies and clothes, quiet
afternoons, graceful birds, great words, tearful music,
mind-joying poetry, beautiful livings, loved things,
known things: a to-be-used and known and
pleasure-to-be giving world.

WALTER LOWENFELS

For Ludwig Wittgenstein
[1889–1951]

Playback from space:
Controlled power.

> First comes the fire: this is the purification;
>   one in a billion survives the flame; he is
>   the Speaker.
> Out of the agony of survival the word is born
>   that releases us.
> The moment it is said we realize it is not a
>   word at all—this is what Wittgenstein
>   tried to explain.
> It has been demonstrated that the temperature
>   near the stagnation point increases as you
>   approach the sun. This is the nodule of the
>   nexus.
> We live on a tangent to the heat fix; the
>   possibilities of igniting are more than our
>   mathematics provide. This adds a continual
>   incentive to a more precise formulation of
>   the equation Wittgenstein was trying to
>   tell us just as he died.

> > *For the foam of the future*
> > *fast-breeders*
> > *must know the sun better.*

■ *" The development of the five senses is the work of the entire history of the world up to now. "*

—KARL MARX

MAY-POLE AT MA-RE MOUNT: (1627) One Thomas Morton, poet and gunrunner, friend to Ben Jonson and others, had come to the New World, where he found the country

> . . . like a faire virgin, longing to be sped,
> And meete her lover in a Nuptiall bed,
> Deck'd in rich ornaments t'advaunce her state
> And excellence, being most fortunate,
> When most enjoy'd, so would our Canaan be . . .

They called her New Canaan, where they would dance and diddle with the "Salvages," drawn to some ancient power of the Earth they sensed there. But under the shadow of the Puritans that breathing, reawakened body didn't last; and Morton found himself later in the stocks, then locked into a boat and back to England. Three testimonies to that first encounter follow.

THE TESTIMONY OF THOMAS MORTON. "The inhabitants of Pasonagessit having translated the name of their habitation from the ancient Salvage name to Ma-re Mount, and being resolved to have the new name confirmed for a memorial to after ages, did devise amongst themselves to have it performed in a solemn manner, with Revels and merriment after the old English custome; they prepared up a Maypole upon the festivall day of Philip and Jacob (1627), and therefore brewed a barrell of excellent beare and provided a case of bottles, to be spent, with other good cheare, for all commers that day. And because they would have it in compleat forme, they had prepared a song fitting to the time and present occasion. And upon May day they brought the Maypole to the place appointed, with drumes, gunnes, pistols and other fitting instruments, for the purpose; and there erected it with the help of Salvages, that came thether to see the manner of our Revels. A goodly pine tree of 80 foot longe was reared up, with a peare of buckshorns nayled one somewhat neare unto the top of it: where it stood, as a faire sea mark for directions how to finde out the way to mine Hoste of Ma-re Mount."—From *New English Canaan*

THE TESTIMONY OF WILLIAM BRADFORD, SECOND GOVERNOR OF THE PLYMOUTH COLONY. "They did also set up a Maypole, drinking and dancing about it many days together, inviting the Indian women, for their consorts, dancing and frisking together, (like so many fairies, or furies rather) and worse practices. As if they had anew revived and celebrated the feasts of the Roman Goddes Flora, or the beastly practicses of the madd

Bacchinalians. Morton likewise (to shew his poetrie) composed sundry rimes and verses, some tending to lasciviousness, and others to the detraction and scandall of some persons, which he affixed to this idle or idoll Maypolle."— From *Of Plymouth Plantation*

THE TESTIMONY OF WILLIAM CARLOS WILLIAMS. (1925) "So Morton and his men, awaiting wives from England, escaped marriage by varying (Proteus) among (Priapus) the Indian girls they took to bed with them. This in its simplicity the Puritans lacked spirit to explain. But spiritless, thus without grounds on which to rest their judgements of this world, fearing to touch its bounties, a fissure takes place for the natural mouth—and everything's perverse to them."

And again: "All that will be new in America will be anti-Puritan. It will be of another root."—From *In the American Grain*

WALT WHITMAN

I Sing the Body Electric

I.

I sing the body electric,
The armies of those I love engirth me and I engirth them,
They will not let me off till I go with them, respond to them,
And discorrupt them, and charge them full with the charge of
      the soul.

Was it doubted that those who corrupt their own bodies
      conceal themselves?
And if those who defile the living are as bad as they who
      defile the dead?
And if the body does not do fully as much as the soul?
And if the body were not the soul, what is the soul?

2.

The love of the body of man or woman balks account, the
      body itself balks account,
That of the male is perfect, and that of the female is perfect.

The expression of the face balks account,
But the expression of a well-made man appears not only in
    his face,
It is in his limbs and joints also, it is curiously in the joints
    of his hips and wrists,
It is in his walk, the carriage of his neck, the flex of his
    waist and knees, dress does not hide him,
The strong sweet quality he has strikes through the cotton
    and broadcloth,
To see him pass conveys as much as the best poem,
    perhaps more,
You linger to see his back, and the back of his neck and
    shoulder-side.

The sprawl and fulness of babes, the bosoms and heads of
    women, the folds of their dress, their style as we pass
    in the street, the contour of their shape downwards,
The swimmer naked in the swimming-bath, seen as he
    swims through the transparent green-shine, or lies
    with his face up and rolls silently to and fro in the
    heave of the water,
The bending forward and backward of rowers in
    row-boats, the horseman in his saddle,
Girls, mothers, house-keepers, in all their performances,
The group of laborers seated at noon-time with their open
    dinner-kettles, and their wives waiting,
The female soothing a child, the farmer's daughter in the
    garden or cow-yard,
The young fellow hoeing corn, the sleigh-driver driving his
    six horses through the crowd,
The wrestle of wrestlers, two apprentice-boys, quite grown,
    lusty, good-natured, native-born, out on the vacant lot
    at sundown after work,
The coats and caps thrown down, the embrace of love and
    resistance,
The upper-hold and under-hold, the hair rumpled over and
    blinding the eyes;
The march of firemen in their own costumes, the play of

masculine muscle through clean-setting trowsers and
waist-straps,

The slow return from the fire, the pause when the bell
strikes suddenly again, and the listening on the
alert,

The natural, perfect, varied attitudes, the bent head, the
curv'd neck and the counting;

Such-like I love—I loosen myself, pass freely, am at the
mother's breast with the little child,

Swim with the swimmers, wrestle with wrestlers, march in
line with the firemen, and pause, listen, count.

3.

I knew a man, a common farmer, the father of five sons,

And in them the fathers of sons, and in them the fathers of
sons.

This man was of wonderful vigor, calmness, beauty of
person,

The shape of his head, the pale yellow and white of his
hair and beard, the immeasurable meaning of his
black eyes, the richness and breadth of his manners,

These I used to go and visit him to see, he was wise also,

He was six feet tall, he was over eighty years old, his sons
were massive, clean, bearded, tan-faced, handsome,

They and his daughters loved him, all who saw him loved
him,

They did not love him by allowance, they loved him with
personal love,

He drank water only, the blood show'd like scarlet through
the clear-brown skin of his face,

He was a frequent gunner and fisher, he sail'd his boat
himself, he had a fine one presented to him by a
ship-joiner, he had fowling-pieces presented to him
by men that loved him,

When he went with his five sons and many grand-sons to
hunt or fish, you would pick him out as the most
beautiful and vigorous of the gang,

You would wish long and long to be with him, you would
wish to sit by him in the boat that you and he might
touch each other.

4.

I have perceiv'd that to be with those I like is enough,
To stop in company with the rest at evening is enough,
To be surrounded by beautiful, curious, breathing,
 laughing flesh is enough,
To pass among them or touch any one, or rest my arm ever
 so lightly round his or her neck for a moment, what
 is this then?
I do not ask any more delight, I swim in it as in a sea.

There is something in staying close to men and women
 and looking on them, and in the contact and odor of
 them, that pleases the soul well,
All things please the soul, but these please the soul well.

5.

This is the female form,
A divine nimbus exhales from it from head to foot,
It attracts with fierce undeniable attraction,
I am drawn by its breath as if I were no more than a
 helpless vapor, all falls aside but myself and it,
Books, art, religion, time, the visible and solid earth, and
 what was expected of heaven or fear'd of hell, are
 now consumed,
Mad filaments, ungovernable shoots play out of it, the
 response likewise ungovernable,
Hair, bosom, hips, bend of legs, negligent falling hands all
 diffused, mine too diffused,
Ebb stung by the flow and flow stung by the ebb, love-flesh
 swelling and deliciously aching,
Limitless limpid jets of love hot and enormous, quivering
 jelly of love, white-blow and delirious juice,
Bridegroom night of love working surely and softly into the
 prostrate dawn,
Undulating into the willing and yielding day,
Lost in the cleave of the clasping and sweet-flesh'd day.
This is the nucleus—after the child is born of woman, man
 is born of woman,
This the bath of birth, this the merge of small and large,
 and the outlet again.

Be not ashamed women, your privilege encloses the rest,
and is the exit of the rest,
You are the gates of the body, and you are the gates of the
soul.
The female contains all qualities and tempers them,
She is in her place and moves with perfect balance,
She is all things duly veil'd, she is both passive and active,
She is to conceive daughters as well as sons, and sons as
well as daughters.

As I see my soul reflected in Nature,
As I see through a mist, One with inexpressible
completeness, sanity, beauty,
See the bent head and arms folded over the breast, the
Female I see.

6.

The male is not less the soul nor more, he too is in his
place,
He too is all qualities, he is action and power,
The flush of the known universe is in him,
Scorn becomes him well, and appetite and defiance become
him well,
The wildest largest passions, bliss that is utmost, sorrow
that is utmost become him well, pride is for him,
The full-spread pride of man is calming and excellent to
the soul,
Knowledge becomes him, he likes it always, he brings
every thing to the test of himself,
Whatever the survey, whatever the sea and the sail, he
strikes soundings at last only here,
(Where else does he strike soundings except here?)
The man's body is sacred and the woman's body is sacred,
No matter who it is, it is sacred—is it the meanest one in
the laborers' gang?
Is it one of the dull-faced immigrants just landed on the
wharf?
Each belongs here or anywhere just as much as the
well-off, just as much as you,
Each has his or her place in the procession.

(All is a procession,
The universe is a procession with measured and perfect
      motion.)

Do you know so much yourself that you call the meanest
      ignorant?
Do you suppose you have a right to a good sight, and he or
      she has no right to a sight?
Do you think matter has cohered together from its diffuse
      float, and the soil is on the surface, and water runs
      and vegetation sprouts,
For you only, and not for him and her?

      7.

A man's body at auction,
(For before the war I often go to the slave-mart and watch
      the sale,)
I help the auctioneer, the sloven does not half know his
      business.
Gentlemen look on this wonder,
Whatever the bids of the bidders they cannot be high
      enough for it,
For it the globe lay preparing quintillions of years without
      one animal or plant,
For it the revolving cycles truly and steadily roll'd.

In this head the all-baffling brain,
In it and below it the makings of heroes.

Examine these limbs, red, black, or white, they are
      cunning in tendon and nerve,
They shall be stript that you may see them.

Exquisite senses, life-lit eyes, pluck, volition,
Flakes of breast-muscle, pliant backbone and neck, flesh
      not flabby, good-sized arms and legs,
And wonders within there yet.

Within there runs blood,
The same old blood! the same red-running blood!

There swells and jets a heart, there all passions, desires,
     reachings, aspirations,
(Do you think they are not there because they are not
     express'd in parlors and lecture-rooms?)

This is not only one man, this the father of those who shall
     be fathers in their turns,
In him the start of populous states and rich republics,
Of him countless immortal lives with countless
     embodiments and enjoyments.

How do you know who shall come from the offspring of his
     offspring through the centuries?
(Who might you find you have come from yourself, if you
     could trace back through the centuries?)

     8.

A woman's body at auction,
She too is not only herself, she is the teeming mother of
     mothers,
She is the bearer of them that shall grow and be mates to
     the mothers.

Have you ever loved the body of a woman?
Have you ever loved the body of a man?
Do you not see that these are exactly the same to all in all
     nations and times all over the earth?
If anything is sacred the human body is sacred,
And the glory and sweet of a man is the token of manhood
     untainted,
And in man or woman a clean, strong, firm-fibred body, is
     more beautiful than the most beautiful face.

Have you seen the fool that corrupted his own live body?
     or the fool that corrupted her own live body?
For they do not conceal themselves, and cannot conceal
     themselves.

9.

O my body! I dare not desert the likes of you in other men
and women, nor the likes of the parts of you,
I believe the likes of you are to stand or fall with the likes
of the soul, (and that they are the soul,)
I believe the likes of you shall stand or fall with my
poems, and that they are my poems,
Man's, woman's, child's, youth's, wife's, husband's,
mother's, father's, young man's, young woman's
poems,
Head, neck, hair, ears, drop and tympan of the ears,
Eyes, eye-fringes, iris of the eye, eyebrows, and the waking
or sleeping of the lids,
Mouth, tongue, lips, teeth, roof of the mouth, jaws and the
jaw-hinges,
Nose, nostrils of the nose, and the partition,
Cheeks, temples, forehead, chin, throat, back of the neck,
neck-slue,
Strong shoulders, manly beard, scapula, hind-shoulders,
and the ample side-round of the chest,
Upper-arm, armpit, elbow-socket, lower-arm, arm-sinews,
arm-bones,
Wrist and wrist-joints, hand, palm, knuckles, thumb,
forefinger, finger-joints, finger-nails,
Broad breast-front, curling hair of the breast, breast-bone,
breast-side,
Ribs, belly, backbone, joints of the backbone,
Hips, hip-sockets, hip-strength, inward and outward round,
man-balls, man-root,
Strong set of thighs, well carrying the trunk above,
Leg-fibres, knee, knee-pan, upper-leg, under-leg,
Ankles, instep, foot-ball, toes, toe-joints, the heel;
All attitudes, all the shapeliness, all the belongings of my
or your body or of any one's body, male or female,
The lung-sponges, the stomach-sac, the bowels sweet and
clean,
The brain in its folds inside the skull-frame,
Sympathies, heart-valves, palate-valves, sexuality,
maternity,

Womanhood, and all that is a woman, and the man that
  comes from woman,
The womb, the teats, nipples, breast-milk, tears, laughter,
  weeping, love-looks, love-perturbations and risings,
The voice, articulation, language, whispering, shouting
  aloud,
Food, drink, pulse, digestion, sweat, sleep, walking,
  swimming,
Poise on the hips, leaping, reclining, embracing,
  arm-curving and tightening,
The continual changes of the flex of the mouth, and
  around the eyes,
The skin, the sunburnt shade, freckles, hair,
The curious sympathy one feels when feeling with the
  hand the naked meat of the body,
The circling rivers the breath, and breathing it in and out,
The beauty of the waist, and thence of the hips, and thence
  downward toward the knees,
The thin red jellies within you or within me, the bones and
  the marrow in the bones,
The exquisite realization of health;
O I say these are not the parts and poems of the body only,
  but of the soul,
O I say now these are the soul!

HERMAN MELVILLE

[Sperm]

It had cooled and crystallized to such a degree, that
when, with several others, I sat down before a large Con-
stantine's bath of it, I found it strangely concreted into
lumps, here and there rolling about in the liquid part. It
was our business to squeeze these lumps back into fluid. A
sweet and unctuous duty! No wonder that in old times this
sperm was such a favorite cosmetic. Such a clearer! such
a sweetener! such a softener! such a delicious mollifier!
After having my hands in it for only a few minutes, my
fingers felt like eels, and began, as it were, to serpentine
and spiralize.

As I sat there at my ease, cross-legged on the deck; after the bitter exertion at the windlass; under a blue tranquil sky; the ship under indolent sail, and gliding so serenely along; as I bathed my hands among those soft, gentle globules of infiltrated tissues, woven almost within the hour; as they richly broke to my fingers, and discharged all their opulence, like fully ripe grapes their wine; as I snuffed up that uncontaminated aroma,—literally and truly, like the smell of spring violets; I declare to you, that for the time I lived as in a musky meadow; I forgot all about our horrible oath; in that inexpressible sperm, I washed my hands and my heart of it; I almost began to credit the old Paracelsan superstition that sperm is of rare virtue in allaying the heat of anger: while bathing in that bath, I felt divinely free from all ill-will, or petulance, or malice, of any sort whatsoever.

Squeeze! squeeze! squeeze! all the morning long; I squeezed that sperm till I myself almost melted into it; I squeezed that sperm till a strange sort of insanity came over me; and I found myself unwittingly squeezing my co-laborers' hands in it, mistaking their hands for the gentle globules. Such an abounding, affectionate, friendly, loving feeling did this avocation beget; that at last I was continually squeezing their hands, and looking up into their eyes sentimentally; as much as to say,—Oh! my dear fellow beings, why should we longer cherish any social acerbities, or know the slightest ill-humor or envy! Come; let us squeeze hands all round; nay, let us all squeeze ourselves into each other; let us squeeze ourselves universally into the very milk and sperm of kindness.

Would that I could keep squeezing that sperm for ever! For now, since by many prolonged, repeated experiences, I have perceived that in all cases man must eventually lower, or at least shift, his conceit of attainable felicity; not placing it anywhere in the intellect or the fancy; but in the wife, the heart, the bed, the table, the saddle, the fire-side, the country; now that I have perceived all this, I am ready to squeeze case eternally. In visions of the night, I saw long rows of angels in paradise, each with his hands in a jar of spermaceti.

—From "A Squeeze of the Hand," Chapter 94 of *Moby Dick*

JAMES KOLLER

Poem

Mars, opalescent orange, McIbbon's crystal ball
    reflects fire light
the sheen of ten brass shells whirring
she swings them over her very blond head

we dance as the moon disappears
howl & hoot dance drum
the orange moon disappears

she asks for a boy but I
bring none
she asks for a girl but I
only smile
                she writhes on her back
comes & comes
                  hears us

we fuck in high oat grass
children in a circle around us

     "Here the world ends, here
   it begins. I fly between. Bring word
     after the beginning, before the end."

wide wings thru dark trees

all that he could catch of her was white light
    & the black behind

owl, just returned from the dead

     "I wasn't really there"

GEORGE ECONOMOU

From Poems for Self-Therapy

Stand in front of a mirror
and declare
        I am the champ
I am
the champion
        (remove shirt or blouse
        if that will lend greater credence
        to your words and puff up)
Repeat: I am the
     champ
        have a champion champignon in my crotch
I was not a big man on campus
        but I have become a big man off campus
I am a big girl off and on campus
          off and on/off and on
Raise an eyebrow—purse your lips
murmur
     me a charming scamp
        I shall pursue lucrative campaigns
        (spoken with quiet resolve)
Toast yourself
A mes Victoires!
      with a glass of champagne.
            •
When despondency clogs your throat
coils around your heart
gets you by the ankles
because spouse to spouse correspondency
is not what it used to be
how do you respond?
        By taking to drink?
        (nicht gut)
        By making like a heartless beast?
        (nicht gut)
        By kicking a subordinate?
        (Ausflucht)

If all the voices insist
           "Respond to your responsibilities
           respond to your responsibilities"
and you reply
           perfectly spondaicly
                  "FUCK! YOU!"
Congratulations—
           you have made a start.
Be still
yourself's the thing
wherein you'll catch the power.
                •
Make positive and purposeful proposals
admitting no postponements
               or opponency
from yourself or anybody else
to yourself and everybody else
you care for.
           As for imposters
expose them.
           Despots
puzzle and depose them
               with deadly suppositories.
Above all
           in time of repose
                propound
superpositions—
              try the pseudo-Hellenic postposition
new and exciting juxtapositions
                 even a wicked contra-
position
     (providing it is not an imposition)
to give and receive
           Almighty Love's
sweet depositions.

HANIEL LONG

Heavenly Bodies

In the Hesperides the Atlantides
say that along with the arrow-heads of sex,
meteors of sea-blue and cinnabar
run this way and that in every group,
and certain important lines between heavenly bodies
are not to be descried without a microscope . .
They asked me if my heart was likewise a telescope,
whether I had studied light-lines. And if sex
is the line of light connecting two stars
and sex appears to stagger and go out
it is possible to twine something else with it——
for sex never goes completely out
in the Hesperides, or anywhere.

To seek out a corner of heaven with somebody
and possess that corner and that somebody
and cut the inter-stellar and inter-spacial
rights to light and gossamers of light——
it appears that this also has been tried;
and yet despite commandments, despite thugs,
sidereal longing apparently can never head off
the play of light between any star
and any other star . .
And to have inter-astral communication go wrong
would be a queer thing, they say; it would short-circuit
lights in unexpected places and faces . .
Love for everybody
in all the corners of heaven——
this also is to be tried some day . .

Halley's comet and Lucifer——
few can pretend to such careers.
We neophytes are only light-houses on a bad coast.
We revolve in our night and spray one another
with our thin streams of light:
on a bad coast one needs always
light from some quarter.

New perceptions——even light-houses
can throw them far inland . .

The light of the weird sisters
can be deadly, has such intensity——
to avert the prevalent homicide
such revolving lights in towers
are encouraged to turn more rapidly
hitting the same object recurrently
and never too long at a time.
In the Hesperides the Atlantides
wait till they see a light walking or streaming near by,
then go, and walk or stream with it;
they meet many lights out walking
and stream with many streams——
they call it being alive.
So they told me——
and being alight *may* equal being alive,
yet has another thing been known——
instead of real heart and real blood
to turn incandescence upon another.
But whether arc lights and search lights
can make seeds sprout
is a question——
for us, not for the Atlantides.

> From *Atlantides.* A largely forgotten poet of the thirties, HANIEL
> LONG wrote an extended work, *Pittsburgh Memorandum,* that
> seems now to anticipate WILLIAMS' *Paterson* and OLSON'S *Maximus
> Poems,* as an epic-like poem of the modern city, many-voiced and
> grounded in the realities of history.

CLAYTON ESHLEMAN

Ode to Reich

Wilhelm for you I would sit in the reverberation of the Last
    Supper
& still keep my eyes to the gentle look in the eyes of children,
for you I would make love to Caryl
would keep her as the vent thru which I experience the
    world,

for you I would make her the terminal,
the station in which all the trains unload
with girls upon girls upon girls & fathers & old men &
    mothers,
for you, I would keep her before me, keep
that need of the unknown unknown thru her,
& known in the rain that falls on me, in that sopping bed the
    poem is
alone in the landscape that you almost alone inhabit
We love & embrace in a lone bed set out in a meadow
Nearby a city of fire

Wilhelm four years I have watched you alone this century
kindling the heavens over that lone meadow bed,
four years I have watched you daily rub off the soot from
    Baudelaire's
immortal lines: "Real civilization consists not in gas,
not in steam, nor in turning tables, but in the diminution of
the traces of original sin."
                            Concerned doctor, in workpants &
workshirt, in the photo I have of you page 173 in your *People
In Trouble*
1934 in Sweden, in exile then in the full flow of your Arian
    arrow
sprung from the bow of your breeding laboratory for
    butterflies when you
were 10, your ax-head Arian profile looking intently then 37
    years old at
something we know off the page,
                        in the page of the youth breathing
fully for the first time in his life on a cot you in the late
    twenties
moved around from the chair placed behind him to sit
beside him, look him in the eyes & not use his dreams but
    confront him,
I have this photo of you with hollyhocks & forsythia in the
    background,
you are in a meadow in a room, yes! with insects buzzing in
    the dry rigid

proneness of the youth on a cot on a hillock, you are torridly
     maintaining
his emotions are an expression of his biology & that his
     biology is
expression of a cosmic energy, that
We love & embrace in a lone bed set out in a meadow
Nearby a city of fire

Wilhelm four years, but the count is for all men, four years
     Blake
with marginalia on Lavater, this like an advance on
     Baudelaire:
"But the origin of this mistake in Lavater & his
     contemporaries
is, They suppose that Woman's Love is Sin; in consequence all
the Loves & Graces with them are Sins."—you Wilhelm
making rain over these lines, scouring them from reason,
keeping the fine edges cut into stone sharp in man's infinite
times of trouble, in workpants & workshirt (this image is
very important)—your compassionate eye on Merton
soundlessly repeating his rounds in the circumscribed nature of
Trappist, Kentucky, speaking gently to him in your fury of
your text on Jesus: "The great mistake is not the curbing of
man's evil urges for free-for-all-fucking with dead genitals,
the great mistake is the burying of the very natural powers in
man's body which alone are capable of putting out of function
     the
perverted sex in mankind."
                           God, Wilhelm, what a tract your
arrowhead everywhere would lead me to, how difficult it is to
move you into the company of poets where for all centuries
     you
belong, there is so much cause, so much argument, so many
things to set straight; you with the medieval strangeness of
your simple frank theories, your orgone accumulator like a
     gigantic
slingshot before the Castle, your hollow metal pipes bringing
rain down on dubious Tim Reynolds visiting a farmer in
     Michigan,
Tim told me "I didn't believe he could make rain, he held the

pipes up to the bright sky and then we went in and drank
      beer,
it suddenly poured, an hour and when we left, a few miles
      away
the sun was again shining!"
                    To call you a poet
              is to deepen your place as an advance on
imagination, it is not to say you are not a doctor nor to slant
you so as to keep anyone from your meaning as a scientist;
it is the revolution of the identity of a person & his
      expression,
as such to make for Harry Lewis morality a function of
      intuition,
that these are not separable things, you urge me tonight
in a bar in New York City—as Breton felt Fourier in a fresh
bunch of violets at the foot of his statue in Paris, I feel you
before me in an unknown girl, she is your bunch of violets
      Wilhelm,
this girl in her voluptuous body & pretty face hard
with what you called "armoring" sipping brandy & wondering
What is my life? She came in her confusion to
enter the poem, for I would rather not go to Maine to stand
before your tomb, but allow her as the living violet to
enter the poem and say Yes—
I feel you most next to me in Caryl &
I feel you before me as emanation of something not
mine, and in this very wood bench
your imagination vibrating violets
at the foot of your statue which is
now at Vallejo's cross in the Andes
& in Baudelaire's prayer that he simply might be able to work
& in Breton's old manifestoed hand in New Mexico
writing his *Ode To Fourier,* these saints
poets recognize in their own trembling energies to be
Jesus in their own hearts, that pioneering
cosmic fateful strength we know of you
through Aries, your glyph in the pulsating zodiac of
expansion contraction, the body of man
you as a red red Mars come like Isaiah
out of the judgement of the wine vats of your own being,

you curved, as your arrow was not wont to curve, you
bent the drive of that arrow, how can I say it,—to bions,
to heat sand once you had seen what drove you, to
keep the thing out of system, to follow out the strange
crooked road, to keep moving outward, to keep perception
vital, to not backtrack in your later years & smudge
what I shall call your *clarification of Beulah.*

Wilhelm, what I am
getting to is to somehow honor the clarification you
gave us of self-sacrifice, that the substance of love is
kept fresh in the death of feminine form, this happens in
that meadow, in the giving up of pride & possession, of
man & woman allowing their bodies to convulse, to dissolve
truly thoughts & fantasies, this is the sacrifice Blake named
Eternal Death, to die there in joy with another, that that form
die, that the substance be liberated to find fresh form in
creation, We love & embrace in a lone bed set out in a
      meadow
Nearby a city of fire
our brother William Blake named Eden, is creation &
in your understanding of the creative process you embrace
the poets telling
them sexual hindrance is imaginative crippling,
how simply you now appear shoveling the hate out of our
      bodies,
you sturdy, in your workpants, with no mantle, no egg to
balance on your shoulders, you gazing intensely at
Vallejo's cross in the Andes on which you forever see
"Until I labor I in labor lie"
explaining to him in the ruins & dust that Beulah allows
the transmission, that creation is
not that struggle with the body,
that poetry is translation not just of language
but the passing of a psyche into new form.

DAVID MELTZER
From Yetsiradicals [Section One]

BOOK OF FATHERS

to father from Father. Farther & farther away. Down the
line. Draws closer. We return to letters. To ancient words.
New. Resources. Re, sources.

• • •

Create from all parts equal to each other.
Name them. Race them. Destiny them.
Thru union. Thru way. Thru Shekinah.
Soul of man in letter-fragments of his being
he daily links together, nightly
learns translation.
Hold back nothing not of breath.
The book forms itself as the body forms itself.
Within, without.
Skin-web both transmits & takes in light.
Light is broken into letters
re-circulated thru the body to immerge on the tongue.
To submerge on the page.
The book formation. Sefer Yetsirah.
Form, shape, give breath.
Forms within to without, without to within.
Name. Play. Dance the letters.
Maim the breath-less beauty.
Break the code. Imagine, create.

THOMAS McGRATH
From Letter to an Imaginary Friend

Wait for the Angel.
SAQUASOHUH:
the blue star
Far off, but coming.
Invisible yet.

Announcing the Fifth
World
(Hopi prophecy)
world we shall enter soon:
When the Blue Star kachina, its manifested spirit,
Shall dance the *kisonvi* for the first time.

In still light
Wait.

"But it's cold here!"
Hush.

I'll take you as far as the river;
But no one may dream home the Revolution today though we
offer
Our daily blood, nor form from the hurt black need
The all-color red world of the poor, nor in the soviet
Of students transform this might; nor alcohol compound
Manifestos; nor pot set straight a sleepy rifle's dream.

Still we must try.
S A Q U A S O H U H.

Far off: the blue
Star.
The Fifth World. Coming.
Now, try:
Necessary, first, the Blue Star kachina to dance the *kisonvi;*
Necessary that the *kapani* at the crown of the head must be
Kept open always.
Loosen your wigs.

I go to the far
Country
to the sacred butte and the empty land
I'll make
The kachina . . .

ORC: The god enraged by history; repressed love set free as molten
desire; political revolution as adjunct of a great awakening of human
powers, sexual and psychic. Such is the myth of fiery youth, whom
Frazer identified as the "dying-reborn god" (*The Golden Bough,*
1890): Tammuz, Adonis, Osirus, Zagreus, Dionysus, Soma, and Christ.

And in the New World, the many gods of fertility and renewal, often the threatening or violent figure characterized by Blake's Orc *(America a Prophecy)*: Tlaloc (see page 405); Huitzlopochtli (page 167); Coyote (page 157)—the latter also an analogue of Hermes the Thief and Magician (or, like Orc, Alchemist). Pound invokes his Zagreus-Dionysus in a rite of renewal "for the West" (page 319). And Olson, in the poem below, adds "Enyalion," and provides this context:

> Now, my argument would be, then, that the way the Earth gets to be attained is that we are born, ourselves, with a picture of the world. That there is no world except one that we are the picturers of it. And by world here I don't mean the Earth, I mean the whole of creation. And it seems to me that I, I don't know enough, but I think that the phrase *imago mundi* is as legitimate as the better known phrase *anima mundi*. . . . *We* are, *we* are spiritual exercise, by having been born. . . .
>
> . . . I found that in Crete, or in Greece at the time of Mycenae and Pylos and Tiryns, that the god who we know of as Ares or Mars was apparently called Enyalios. In this poem I abuse his name by using Enyalion. And it's directly connected now to the struggle of the *imago mundi,* as a child of Earth, with the bosses.
>
> —*Causal Mythology* (Four Seasons Foundation, San Francisco, 1969)
>
> (See also the commentary, "The Rape and Counter-Rape of America," page 161, above.)

CHARLES OLSON
Enyalion

       rages
     strain
   Dog of Tartarus
  Guards of Tartarus
Finks of the Bosses. War Makers

                    not Enyalion. Enyalion
has lost his Hand, Enyalion
is beautiful, Enyalion
has shown himself, the High King
a War Chief, he has Equites
to do that

                    Enyalion
is possibility, all men
are the glories of Hera by possibility, Enyalion
goes to war differently
than his equites, different
than they do, he goes to war with a picture

      far far out into Eternity   Enyalion,
the law of possibility, Enyalion

the beautiful one, Enyalion

who takes off his clothes

wherever he is found,

on a hill,

in front of his own troops,

in the face of the men of the other side, at the command

of any woman who goes by,

and sees him there, and sends her maid, to ask,

if he will show himself,

to see for herself,

if the beauty, of which he is reported to have,

is true

he goes to war with a picture

                              she goes off

in the direction of her business

      over the city   over the earth—the earth

is the mundus   brown-red is the color

                              of the brilliance

                              of earth

he goes to war with a picture in his mind
that the shining of his body

    and of the chariot
    and of his horses
    and of his own equites
  everyone in the nation of which he is the High King

he turns back

into the battle

             Enyalion

is the god of war   the color

of the god of war   is beauty

              Enyalion

is in the service of the law of the proportions

of his own body   Enyalion

            but the city

is only the beginning of the earth   the earth

is the world   brown-red is the color of mud,

              the earth
shines
      but beyond the earth

         far off Stage Fort Park

    far away from the rules of sea-faring   far far from
                      Gloucester

far by the rule of Ousoos   far where you carry

the color, Bulgar

far where Enyalion

quietly re-enters his Chariot   far

by the rule of its parts by the law of the proportion
of its parts

over the World   over the City   over man

A BOOK OF CHANGES

Behind all renewal is a tradition of metamorphosis,
which symbolizes the power of any creative
transformation of consciousness. **A Book of Changes**
attempts to reveal chronological keys to this process
by plotting, first, some of the traditions of
meditation inherited from pre-Columbian America and
from Europe, and, second, the development of these
and others along distinctively American lines over
the past three centuries. Special attention
is given to those modalities which contribute
to our knowledge of creative mind manifesting
itself in the "changes" undergone through language
(*metapoesis,* as described below). The present
Book of Changes ends with the final hexagram from
the *I Ching,* taken as a prophecy for an age of renewals.

Calligraphy by SHUNRYU SUZUKI, reading *nyorai* in Japanese or
tathagata in Sanskrit. "This is a name for Buddha which means
'he who followed the path, who has returned from suchness, or is
suchness, thusness, is-ness, emptiness, the fully completed one.' It
is the ground principle which makes the appearance of a Buddha
possible. It is Zen mind. At the time Suzuki-roshi wrote this callig-
raphy—using for a brush the frayed end of one of the large sword-
like leaves of the yucca plants that grow in the mountains around
Zen Mountain Center [California]—he said: 'This means that Ta-
thagata is the body of the whole earth.' "

—*Richard Baker, "Introduction," Zen Mind, Beginner's Mind*
(Weatherhill, New York, 1970)

■ *"Suppose there were in the ocean certain strong currents which drove a ship, caught in them, with a force that no skill of sailing with the best wind, and no strength of oars, or sails, or stream, could make any head against, any more than against the current of Niagara. Such currents, so tyrannical, exist in thoughts, those finest and subtilest of all waters, that as soon as one thought begins, it refuses to remember whose brain it belongs to; what country, tradition, or religion; and goes whirling off —swim we merrily—in a direction self-chosen, by law of thought and not by law of kitchen clock or county committee. It has its own polarity. One of these vortices or self-directions of thought is the impulse to search resemblance, affinity, identity, in all its objects . . ."*

   —RALPH WALDO EMERSON, *Poetry and Imagination* [1872]

■ *"My son, the ancient No-ho-zhi-ga have handed down to us, in songs, wi-gi-e, ceremonial forms, symbols, and many things they learned of the mysteries that surround us on all sides. All these things they learned through their power of wa-thi-gtho, the power to search with the mind. They speak of the mysteries of the light of day by which the earth and all living things that dwell thereon are influenced; of the mysteries of the darkness of night that reveal to us all the great bodies of the upper world, each of which forever travels in a circle upon its own path, unimpeded by the others. They searched, for a long period of time, for the source of life and at last came to the thought that it issues from an invisible creative power to which they applied the name Wa-ko-da. "*

   —PLAYFUL CALF, an Osage, as related to FRANCIS LA FLESCHE,
   early in the twentieth century

A TRADITION OF METAMORPHOSIS: In an American "book of changes," the first tradition to be charted is that of the pre-European practices of meditation, relating, in our minds, to a "poetry of changes" reaching into the present. A "law of metamorphosis," writes Ernst Cassirer, governs all "mythical thought," and by this law "life is felt as an unbroken continuous whole" in which "the limits between [its] different spheres are not insurmountable barriers [but] fluent and fluctuating," so that "by a sudden metamorphosis everything may be turned into everything." Such a process, present throughout the Indian oral tradition, is very like what Emerson spoke of for his own time as "the poetic perception of metamorphosis . . . [in which] every correspondence we observe in mind and matter suggests a substance older and deeper than either of these old nobilities."

CHILAM BALAM (literally, the Prophet Balam or Prophet Jaguar) was the last and greatest of the Mayan prophets. Inadvertently, it would seem, he prophesied the coming of the Christian conquerors (he apparently meant the return of the Mexican god-king Quetzalcoatl), and when they appeared in his lifetime, that "so enhanced his reputation as a seer," writes Ralph L. Roys, "that in later times he was considered the authority for many other prophecies" both before and after him. His name was put to various books (of prophecies, chronicles, rituals, almanacs, catechisms, etc.) written in the Mayan language but in European script.

After the Christian opening of the following section, the imagery and thought turn sharply Mayan. If the initial bridging is between two religious systems, the procedure after the ninth or tenth lines becomes one of generating sacred riddles—encouraging the mind to leap from thought to thought.

CHILAM BALAM [MAYA]
"A Chapter of Questions and Answers"

13 Etznab was the day when the land was established. 13 Cheneb was the day when they measured the cathedral off by paces: the dark house of instruction, the cathedral in heaven. It was also measured off by paces here on earth. . . .

Mani is the base of the land. Campeche is the tip of the wing of the land. Calkini is the base of the wing of the land. Itzmal is the middle of the wing of the land. Zaci is the tip of the wing of the land. Conkal is the head of the land.

In the middle of the town of Tihoo is the cathedral, the fiery house, the mountainous house, the dark house, for the benefit of God the Father, God the Son and God the Holy Spirit.

Who enters into the House of God? Father, it is the one named Ix-Kalem.

What day did the Virgin conceive? Father, 4 Oc was the day when she conceived.

What day did he come forth from her womb? On 3 Oc he came forth.

What day did he die? On 1 Cimi he died. Then he entered the tomb on 1 Cimi.

What entered his tomb? Father, a coffer of stone entered his tomb.

What entered into his thigh? Father, it was the red arrow-stone. It entered into the precious stone of the world, there in heaven.

And his arm? Father, the arrow-stone; and that it might be warmed in the sun, it entered the red living rock in the east. Then it came to the north and entered into the white living rock. After that it entered the black living rock in the west. Also it entered the yellow living rock in the south.

Son, how many deep hollows are there? These are the holes for playing the flute.

Son, where is the cenote? All are drenched with its water. There is no gravel on its bottom; a bow is inserted over its entrance. It is the church.

Son, where are the first marriages? The strength of the King and the strength of the other head-chiefs fail because of them, and my strength because of them also. It is bread.

Son, have you seen the green water-holes in the rock? There are two of them; a cross is raised between them. They are a man's eyes.

Son, where are the first baptized ones? One has no mother, but has a bead collar and little bells. It is the small yellow corn.

Son, where is the food which bursts forth, and the fold of the brain and the lower end of that which is bloated, and the dried fruit? It is the gizzard of a turkey.

Son, bring me that which hooks the sky and the hooked tooth. They are a deer and a gopher.

Son, where is the old woman with buttocks seven palms wide, the woman with a dark complexion? It is a certain kind of squash.

Son, show me the light complexioned woman with her skirt bound up who sells white flints. It is another kind of squash.

Son, bring me two yellow animals, one to be well boiled, and one shall have its throat cut. I shall drink its blood also. It is a yellow deer and a green calabash full of chocolate.

My sons, bring me here a score of those who bear

flat stones and two married ones. They are a quail and a dove.

Son, bring me a cord of three strands, I wish to see it. It is an iguana.

Son, bring me that which stops the hole in the sky and the dew, the nine layers of the whole earth. It is a very large maize tortilla.

Son, have you seen the old man who is like an overturned tortilla pan? He has a large double chin which reaches the ground. It is a turkey-cock.

Son, bring me the old farmers, their beards come to their navels, also their wives. It is a muddy arrowroot.

Bring to me here with them the women who guard the fields, white complexioned women. I will remove their skirts and eat them. It is a root like a turnip.

Son, bring me the great gallants that I may view them. Perhaps they will not dance badly when I see them. It is a turkey-cock.

Son, where is the first collector? The answer is to undress, to take off one's shirt, cape, hat and shoes.

Son, where was it that you passed? Did you pass to the high rocky knoll which slopes down to the door of heaven, where there is a gate in the wall? Did you see men in front of you, coming side by side? A god called Ninth Heaven and the first town councillor are there. It is the pupils of the eyes and any pair of eyes.

Son, have you seen the rain of God? It passed beneath the mountains of God; it entered beneath the mountains of God, where there is a cross on the savannah. There will be a ring in the sky where the water of God has passed.

Son, where has the water of God passed when it comes forth from the living rock? Father, from a man's head and all a man's teeth, passes through the opening in his throat and comes forth beneath.

Son, whom did you see on the road just now?
. . . .

Son, what did you do with your companions who were coming close behind you? Here are my companions. I have not left them. I await the judgment of God when I shall come to die. This is a man's shadow.

Son, whom did you see on the road? Did you see some old men accompanied by their boys? Father, here are the old men I saw on the road. They are with me; they do not leave me. This is his great toe with the little toes.

Son, where did you see the old women carrying their step-children and their older boys? Father, here they are. They are still with me so that I can eat. I can not leave them yet. It is my thumb and the other fingers.

Son, where did you pass by a water-gutter? Father, here is the water-gutter; it is right with me. This is my dorsal furrow.

Son, where did you see an old man astride a horse across a water-gutter? Father, here is the old man. He is still with me. My shoulders are the horse on which you say the old man sits astride.

Son, this is the old man with you of which you spoke: it is manifest truth and justice.

Son, go get the heart of the stone and the liver of the earth. I have seen one of them lying on its back, and one lying on its face as though it were going into hell. They are a Mexican Agouti and a Spotted Agouti, also the first local chief and the first Town Councillor. As for the heart of the stone, it is the tips of the teeth; and that which covers the opening of hell is a sweet potato and another kind of root to eat.

Son, go and bring me here the girl with the watery teeth. Her hair is twisted into a tuft; she is very beautiful. Fragrant shall her odor be when I remove her skirt and her other garment. It will give me pleasure to see her. Fragrant is her odor and her hair is twisted into a tuft. It is an ear of green corn cooked in a pit.

Son, then you shall go and get an old man the herb that is by the sea. The old man is the rushes, and the herb is a crab.

Son, then you shall go and get the stones from the bottom of a forest pond. It is a *tzac*-fish.

Son, then you shall bring here the stones of the savannah. It is a quail.

Also, bring the first sorcerers, there are four of them. They are the gopher, the Spotted Agouti, the Mexican Agouti and the peccary.

Son, then go and get the thigh of the earth. It is the cassava.

Son, go and bring here the green gallant and the green singer. It is a wild turkey hen and cock.

Son, you shall bring your daughter that I may see her in the sun tomorrow. First the smaller one shall be brought and behind her shall come the larger one. Her hair shall be bound with a feathered band; she shall wear a head-scarf. I will take off her head-scarf. Also the Town Councillor is behind her.

Son, then go and get a cluster of Plumeria flowers widely separated. They should be there where the sun is tomorrow. What is meant is roasted corn and honey.

Here I have rolled something that you have which is flat and round. There are many rolls of it in the cave where you live. Then you shall roll it here that we may see it, when it is time to eat. It is a fried egg.

—Translation by RALPH L. ROYS

HAKO (below) was the name given by Alice Fletcher to a Pawnee version of a ceremony once widespread among Plains Indians. On one level it functioned as a rite of adoption between groups and as "a prayer for children, in order that the tribe may increase and grow strong." Fundamentally *"hako"* means *sound.* Literally "a breathing mouth of wood" (i.e. the drum), it also includes the pulsation of voice generated in the throat and by the beating of a hand against the lips. Finally *hako* is everything in the ceremony, for everything, the leader tells us, *speaks:* "The eagle, Kawas, speaks; the corn speaks; so we say Hako—the voice of all these things."

In the version that follows, Tahirussawichi (himself a *ku'rahus,* or ceremonial leader) gives a syllable-by-syllable breakdown of the words, giving them ritual as well as lexical meanings. Thus *h'* is a breath and the breathing forth of life itself. What's revealed is a system of meditation—a change of state through concentration on the words and sounds. The process of transcription and of syllable-by-syllable and symbol-by-symbol exegesis then brings Tahirussawichi to a sort of meditation on the meditation itself.

TAHIRUSSAWICHI

From The Hako: A Pawnee Ceremony

THE MORNING STAR AND THE NEW-BORN DAWN

Explanation by the Ku'rahus

Now all have risen and have received the breath of the new life just born, all the powers above, all things below. Kawas has stood and spoken in the lodge; the Ku'rahus has heard and understood; the Son is awake and stands with the Ku'rahus awaiting the coming of dawn. The Ku'rahus has sent the server outside the lodge to watch for the morning star. We stand at the west and wait its coming. When it appears he sings the following song:

SONG

Words and Music

M. M. ♪ = 132.
• = Pulsation of the voice.

Transcribed by Edwin S. Tracy.

Ho-o-o-o! H'O - pi - rit ri - ra   ri - sha;   H'O - pi - rit ri - ra   ri -

Drum.
Rattles.

sha; H'O - pi - rit ri - ra   ri - sha;   H'O - pi - rit ri - ra   ri - sha.

I	III
578 Ho-o-o-o!	588 Ho-o-o-o!
579 H'Opirit rira risha;	589 Reshuru rira risha;
580 H'Opirit rira risha;	590 Reshuru rira risha;
581 H'Opirit rira risha;	591 Reshuru rira risha;
582 H'Opirit rira risha.	592 Reshuru rira risha.

II	IV
583 Ho-o-o-o!	593 Ho-o-o-o!
584 H'Opirit ta ahrisha;	594 Reshuru ta ahrisha;
585 H'Opirit ta ahrisha;	595 Reshuru ta ahrisha;
586 H'Opirit ta ahrisha;	596 Reshuru ta ahrisha;
587 H'Opirit ta ahrisha.	597 Reshuru ta ahrisha.

Translation of First Stanza

578   H-o-o-o! An introductory exclamation.
579   H'Opirit rira risha.
    h', the symbol of breath, breathing forth life.
    Opirit, the Morning Star.
    rira, coming; approaching toward one.
    risha, something seen at a great distance; it seems to
        appear and then to be lost, to disappear. The word

conveys the picture of a gradual advance, as from a great distance, where the object was scarcely discernable, to a nearer point of view, but still distant.

580, 581, 582 See line 579.

Explanation by the Ku'rahus

We sing this song slowly with reverent feeling, for we are singing of very sacred things.

The Morning Star is one of the lesser powers. Life and strength and fruitfulness are with the Morning Star. We are reverent toward it. Our fathers performed sacred ceremonies in its honor.

The Morning Star is like a man; he is painted red all over; that is the color of life. He is clad in leggings and a robe is wrapped about him. On his head is a soft downy eagle's feather, painted red. This feather represents the soft, light cloud that is high in the heavens, and the red is the touch of a ray of the coming sun. The soft, downy feather is the symbol of breath and life.

The star comes from a great distance, too far away for us to see the place where it starts. At first we can hardly see it; we lose sight of it, it is so far off; then we see it again, for it is coming steadily toward us all the time. We watch it approach; it comes nearer and nearer; its light grows brighter and brighter.

This is the meaning of this stanza, and the star comes as we sing it four times.

Translation of Second Stanza

583 H-o-o-o! An introductory exclamation.
584 H'Opirit ta ahrisha.
  h', the symbol of breath, life.
  Opirit, the Morning Star.
  ta, approaching.
  ahrisha, coming still nearer, but at the same time disappearing. The word conveys the picture of the morning star by its increased brilliancy coming nearer, and then fading, disappearing in the light of day.

585, 586, 587 See line 584.

Explanation by the Ku'rahus

As we sing this stanza the Morning Star comes still nearer and now we see him standing there in the heavens, a strong man shining brighter and brighter. The soft plume in his hair moves with the breath of the new day, and the ray of the sun touches it with color. As he stands there so bright, he is bringing us strength and new life.

As we look upon him he grows less bright, he is receding, going back to his dwelling place whence he came. We watch him vanishing, passing out of our sight. He has left with us the gift of life which Tira'wa atius sent him to bestow.

We sing this stanza four times.

Translation of Third Stanza

588   Ho-o-o-o! An introductory exclamation.
589   Reshuru rira risha
      Reshuru, the Dawn.
      rira, coming toward one.
      risha, something scarcely to be seen because of its
          distance; it eludes, seems to appear and then to
          disappear.
590, 591, 592 See line 589.

Explanation by the Ku'rahus

As we sing this stanza we are still standing at the west of the lodge, looking through the long passageway toward the east. Now in the distance we see the Dawn approaching; it is coming, coming along the path of the Morning Star. It is a long path and as the Dawn advances along this path sometimes we catch sight of it and then again we lose it, but all the time it is coming nearer.

The Dawn is new born, its breath has sent new life everywhere, all things stir with the life Tira'wa atius has given this child, his child, whose mother is the Night.

We sing this stanza four times.

Translation of Fourth Stanza

593   Ho-o-o-o! An introductory exclamation.
594   Reshuru ta ahrisha.

Reshuru, the Dawn.

ta, approaching, coming,

ahrisha, coming nearer but only to diappear. The
Dawn comes nearer, nearer, grows brighter, but
disappears in the brighter light of day.

595, 596, 597 See line 594.

Explanation by the Ku'rahus

As we stand, looking through the long passageway of
the lodge, watching and singing, we see the Dawn come
nearer and nearer; its brightness fills the sky, the shadowy
forms on the earth are becoming visible. As we watch, the
Dawn, like the Morning Star, recedes. It is following the
star, going back to the place whence it came, to its birth-
place.

The day is close behind, advancing along the path of
the Morning Star and the Dawn, and, as we watch, the
Dawn vanishes from our sight.

We sing this song four times.

—Recorded and translated, 1898–1902, by ALICE C. FLETCHER, assisted
by JAMES R. MURIE

ANAGRAM AS REVELATION: To speak of the poem as revelation im-
plies that the intricate operations of language have the power to bring
the mind to a deeper state of knowing. Without poets like John Fiske
(born 1608 in Suffolk, England; buried in Chelmsford, Mass., 1667),
we might more easily forget that even the apparently "mechanical"
procedures of the anagram figure in the sacred ways of poetry. A
"vortex" in Pound's sense (see page 417, above), the anagram was in
familiar usage from the tenth through the seventeenth centuries in
Europe as a spiritual exercise. There may be poetic justice in the fact
that Fiske's small body of anagrammatic poetry, intended for private
and occasional uses only, didn't come to public light till 1943, because
it belongs in an age which has relearned the values of meaningful
structure. (The concrete verbal structures, for example, of Emmett
Williams or the chance operations of Jackson Mac Low and John Cage
can in that sense provide a contemporary context in which to reevalu-
ate the uses of Medieval and Baroque modalities.) In the poem below,
Fiske laments the death of the poet John Cotton by making of his name

an anagram—"O, Honie Knott"—a node radiating through the poem as a "fugue of meanings" and a "heightened consciousness of the extremely subtle variant meanings of a single word." Like the magical words of the Jewish Kabbalah, "the anagram was intended to reveal aspects of a person's character that lay hidden in the letters of his name."—(Quotations from Harrison T. Meserole's *Seventeenth Century American Poetry,* 1968)

JOHN FISKE

Upon the much-to-be lamented desease
of the Reverend Mr John Cotton
late Teacher to the Church at Boston N. E.
who departed this Life 23 of 10. [16] 52.

John $\begin{cases} \text{Cotton} \\ \text{Kotton} \end{cases}$ after the old English writi'g
Anagr:
O, Honie knott

With Joy erst while, (when knotty doubts arose)
To Thee we calld, o Sir, the knott disclose:
But now o and alasse to thee to call
In vayne tis thou no Answer give or shall.
Could loud Shrickes, could crys recall thee back
From deaths estate we wold our eye ne're slack
O, this our greife it is, lament shall we
A Father in our Israel's cea'st to be.
Even hee that in the Church a pillar was
A gurdeon knot of sweetest graces as
He who set fast to Truths so clossly knitt
As loosen him could ne're the keenest witt
Hee who his Flesh together bound ful-fast
No knott more sure whilest his life did last
Hee who the knotts of Truth, of Mysteries
Sacred, most cleerely did ope 'fore our eyes
Even hee who such a one, is ceas'd to bee
'Twixt whose life, death, the most sweete harmony
Knotts we doe meet with many a cue daily
Which crabbed anggry tough unpleasing bee

But we as in a honi-comb a knott
Of Hony sweete, here had such sweetenes Gott
The knotts and knobbs that on the Trees doe grow
The bitterest excressences we know.

    his soule Embalmd with grace
        was fit to soare on high
    and to receive its place
        above the starry skie.
    now grant O G[od that we]
        may follow afte[r him]
    surviving worlds ocean unto thee
        our passage safe may swim.

A vine tree seene, a plant of Gods owne hand
In it this knott of sweetest parts did stand.
The knott in place sublime: most eminent
As, his, no Branch could challeng like extent
The knott sometimes seems a deformity
It's a mistake, tho such be light set by
The knott it is the Joynt, the strength of parts
The bodies-beauty, so this knott out-starts
What others in that place, they ought to bee
Even such a knott exemplar'ly was hee
Knotts now adayes affrayd of are most men
Of Hony if expose'd feare none would then
I guesse why knotty Learning downe does goe
'Twould not, if as in him 'twere sweetned soe
Meeknes Humility forbearance too
This lovely knott to love the most did woe
In knotts what greate adoe to gayne the hearte
Yee had it heere, he did it free impart
When knotty theames and paynes some meet with then
As knotty and uncouth their tongue and pen
So 'twas not heere, he caus'd us understand
And tast the sweetnes of the knott in hand.
When knotty querks and quiddities broacht were
By witt of man he sweetely Breathed there.

His charity his wisdom meeknes eke
Left none that loved light, in knotts to seeke
Hee tho invincible thrô softnes did
The knottiest peeces calme and cleave amid
Such was hee of such use in these last dayes
Whose want bewayle, o, and alas alwaies
This knott so we have seen lien broknly
By knotts so breathlesse, so crookt, crackt, or fly
This knott thereof so surfetted we see
By hony surfetted we know som bee
The cause nor in the knott nor hony say
Thro Temper bad, unskilfulnes this may
O knott of Hony most delightfull when
Thou livd'st, thi death a sad presage hath ben
Have Ben? yea is, and is, and is alas
For woe to us, so greate a Breach when was
Woe to that knotty pride hee ne're subdude
Woe they who doe his Truthes dispent exclude
And woe to them that factions there contrive
Woe them whose wayes unrighteous survive
Woe they that by him warning did not take
Woe to us all if mercy us forsake
A Mercy once New England thou hast had
(You Boston cheifly) in thi Cotton clad
Some 'gan to count't too meane a dresse and sought
Silk Velvetts Taffeties best could be bought
These last will soyle, if first doe soyle also
How can we think but Naked we shall goe
Must silken witts, must velvet tongues be had
And shall playne preaching be accounted bad
I feare a famine, pinching times t'ensue
Time Such may have, slighted mercy to Rue
My wakened muse to rest, my moystned pen
Mye eye, my hearte which powred out this have ben
Cease try no more, for Hee hath gayn'd his prize
His heavenly mansion 'bove the starry skie
Returne thee home and wayle the evills there
Repent breake off thi sins Jehovah feare

O Jehovah feare: this will thi wisdom bee
And thou his waies of mercy yet maust see
Returne thou mee;   And turned bie
Lord unto thee: even so shall I.
                      Jo: Fiske

THE MIND, THE SENSES, AND TIME: Our contemporary interest in "expanded consciousness" generally omits recognition of the long, distinctively Western tradition of meditation which influenced the "Metaphysical poets" and, with the *Preparatory Meditations* of Edward Taylor, entered a specifically New-World phase. Taylor was born about 1642 in Sketchley, England, and came to Boston in July 1688. A Calvinist minister in the frontier settlement of Westfield, Mass., and a poet detached from the literary and religious context of English meditative practice, he initiated a new modality for "open[ing] the door, between the Head and the Heart." As minister he wrote a sermon; then as poet he wrote a verse-meditation, to "prepare" him to enter into direct bond with the Divine, to administer the sacrament, and to address men with "the bloud and spirits of Affection." The advance on earlier Catholic and Puritan practice consists in the degree to which the senses are used to direct the mind and free the poem for a process of celebration. Thus the 217 *Preparatory Meditations* (1682–1725), undiscovered until 1937: one poem each two months for forty-three years; an open-ended serial form identical with the life-journey; a Western rite for invoking the powers of vision; the poetry of "the liveliest picture." A century before Blake's prediction, with an eye on America, that the infinite world would be realized through "an improvement of sensual enjoyment," Taylor was in Westfield praising the joys of Earth as the keys to Heaven.

EDWARD TAYLOR

Meditation 163. Cant. 2.3.
His fruit was Sweet to my Tast.

Sweet Lord, all sweet from top to bottom all
    From Heart to hide, sweet, mostly sweet.
Sweet Manhood and sweet Godhead and ere shall.
    Thou art the best of Sweeting. And so keep.
    Thou art made up of best of sweetness brast.
    Thy Fruit is ever sweet unto my tast.

Thou art my sweetest one, my Onely sweet.
From kirnel to the rinde, all sweet to mee.
Thy bitterness is sweet: no choaking reech
    Nor damping Steams arise to damp from thee
    The Sacred Spices. Muske * * * * * * them
    Are unto thee, sweet, like to faded gum.

Thou unto mee art onely sweet all sweet
    Sweet in the Virgin wombe and horses Manger.
Sweet in thy swath band and thy Childhood meete
    Yea, sweet to all, to neighbour and to Stranger.
    Sweet in thy Life and Conversation, friends.
    Thy Sweetness dropest from thy fingers Ends.

My Lord, my Love, my Lilly, my Rose and Crown
    My brightest Glory, and my Hony sweet
My Happiness, my Riches, my Renown.
    My Shade for Comfort, in thee good things meet.
    Not one thing in thee that admits of Spot
    All Heavens Scutchen, and a bright Love knot.

Heavens Carnation with most sweet perfume,
    Pinkes, Roses, Violets that perfume the Aire
Inchant the Eyes and fancy in their bloome
    Entoxicate the Fancy with their Ware
    That fuddled, turne and reele and tumble down
    From holly sweet to Earthly damps like Clowns.

It gathers not the Lillys nor doth Picke
    This double sweet rose in Zions Rose tree breede
Nor climbs this Apple tree, nor doth it sit
    At all in'ts Shade, nor on its Apple feed.
    Its lost within the fog and goes astray
    Like to a fuddled person out of's way.

But Oh! my Lord, how sweet art thou to mee
    In all thy Mediatoriall actions sweet

Most sweet in thy Redemption all way free
  Thy Righteousness, thy holiness most meeke.
In Reconciliation made for mee
  With God offended in the highst degree.

A Cabbinet of Holiness, Civit box
  Of Heavenly Aromatick, still much more,
A treasury of Spicery, rich knots,
    Of Choicest Merigolds, a house of Store
    Of never failing dainties to my tast
    Delighting holy Palates, such thou hast.

A sugar Mill, an Hony Hive most rich
  Of all Celestial viands, golden box
Top full of Saving Grace, a Mint house which
    Is full of Angells, and a cloud that drops
    Down better fare than ever Artist could,
    More pleasant than the finest liquid Gold.

Then glut the Lord, ev'n on this dainty fare,
  Here is not Surfeit; look upon this dish:
All is too little to suffice, this fare
    Can surfeit none that eatest; none eate amiss,
    Unless they eat too little. So disgrace
    The preparation of the banquit place.

While I sat longing in this Shadow here
  To tast the fruite this Apple tree all ripe
How sweet these Sweetings bee. Oh! sweet good Cheere
    How am I filld with sweet most sweet delight.
    The fruite, while I was in its shady place
    Was and to mee is now sweet to my tast.

■ *"KNOT OF ETERNITY—Symbol of meditation or the mind of the Enlightened One. It was the never-ending discriminating awareness of wisdom. It is the state of being fully true, a continuous flow with no beginning and no end.*

"Garuda is the celestial hawk [sun eagle] which hatches from the egg fully developed, symbolizing the awakened state of mind, Buddhanature. He destroys and eats the five nagas or snakes which represent the diseases, both physical and psychological to which all beings are prey. In his middle he holds the bodhi leaf . . . in the center of [which] is the knot of eternity. . . ."

> —CHÖGYAM TRUNGPA, from *Mudra* (1972) and *Garuda: Tibetan Buddhism in America* (published by Tail of the Tiger, Barnet, Vermont, 1972)

JONES VERY
The Hand and Foot

The hand and foot that stir not, they shall find
Sooner than all the rightful place to go:
Now in their motion free as roving wind,
Though first no snail so limited and slow;
I mark them full of labor all the day,

Each active motion made in perfect rest;
They cannot from their path mistaken stray,
Though 't is not theirs, yet in it they are blest;
The bird has not their hidden track found out,
The cunning fox though full of art he be;
It is the way unseen, the certain route,
Where ever bound, yet thou art ever free;
The path of Him, whose perfect law of love
Bids spheres and atoms in just order move.

A MAGICAL DIARY: *Hypothesis:* An unsuspected quantity of men's accurate attentions are hidden away in daybooks, notebooks, night-books, piled scraps of paper; the "experimental" poetry of the past two centuries was often confined to private quarters, occulted by the judgments of convention. A "magical diary" is a record of moments of special intensity, in which consciousness goes beyond apparent causalities to describe, in "random" order, a-causally related or "synchronous" events (see Jung, above, page xxxiii). Nathaniel Hawthorne's *American Notebooks,* written during the main years of his life, provide an often strange view of the mind, its mode of operation and its ecology. The following is a selection arranged in no specific order, though it would be rash to say it has none.

See also Melville's journal entry and the commentary on Dickinson that follow. The reader might note too that the situation is reversed in the twentieth century, where the "diary-poem" has become a common and sometimes powerful modality. Consider, as examples, Pound's journal-like *Pisan Cantos,* Stein's unmediated conversations and land-scapes (*Stanzas in Meditation,* below, as a modified instance), and, more recently, John Cage's *Diary: How to Improve the World (You Will Only Make Matters Worse),* Paul Blackburn's *Journals,* Denise Levertov's *From a Notebook,* David Antin's *November Exercises,* and many other works not identified as of this genre.

NATHANIEL HAWTHORNE
From The American Notebooks

The Magic Play of Sunshine for a child's story—the sunshine circling round through a prisoner's cell from his high and narrow window. He keeps his soul alive and cheerful by means of it, it typyfying cheerfulness; and when he is released, he takes up the ray of sunshine and carries it away with him; and it enables him to discover treasures all over the world, in places where nobody else would think of looking for any.

•

A dream, the other night, that the world had become dissatisfied with the inaccurate manner in which facts are reported, and had employed me, with a salary of a thousand dollars, to relate things of public importance exactly as they happen.

•

The situation of a man in the midst of a crowd, yet as completely in the power of another, life and all, as if they two were in the deepest solitude.

•

A person to be writing a tale, and to find that it shapes itself against his intentions; that the characters act otherwise than he thought; that unforeseen events occur; and a catastrophe comes which he strives in vain to avert. It might shadow forth his own fate—he having made himself one of the personages.

•

Four precepts: To break off customs; to shake off spirits ill-disposed; to meditate on youth; to do nothing against one's genius.

•

A story, the principal personage of which shall seem always on the point of entering on the scene; but never shall appear.

•

To think as the sun goes down, what events have happened in the course of the day—events of ordinary occurrence: as, the clocks have struck, the dead have been buried.

•

Two persons to be expecting some occurrence, and watching for the two principal actors in it, and to find that the occurrence is even then passing, and that they themselves are the two actors.

•

The journal of a human heart for a single day in ordinary circumstances. The lights and shadows that flit across it; its internal vicissitudes.

•

When scattered clouds are resting on the bosoms of hills, it seems as if one might climb into the heavenly region, earth being so intermixed with sky, and gradually transformed into it.

•

An article on fire, on smoke. Diseases of the mind and soul—even more common than bodily diseases.

•

An autumnal feature,—boys had swept together the fallen leaves from the elms along the street in one huge pile, and had made a hollow nest-shaped, in this pile, in which three or four of them lay curled, like young birds.

•

An ornament to be worn about the person of a lady—as a jewelled heart. After many years, it happens to be broken or unscrewed, and a poisonous odor comes out.

•

A company of persons to drink a certain medicinal preparation, which would prove a poison, or the contrary, according to their different characters.

•

A cloud in the shape of an old woman kneeling, with arms extended towards the moon.

•

An old looking-glass. Somebody finds out the secret of making all the images that have been reflected in it pass back again across its surface.

•

Men of cold passions have quick eyes.

•

Pandora's box for a child's story.

•

Moonlight is sculpture; sunlight is painting.

HERMAN MELVILLE

From Journal up the Straits

[Stones of Judea. We read a good deal about stones in Scriptures. (Stories of these) Monuments & memorials are set up of stones; men are stoned to death; the figurative seed falls in stony places; and no wonder that stones should so largely figure in the Bible. Judea is one accumulation of stones—Stony mountains & stony plains; stony torrents & stony roads; stony vales & stony fields, stony homes & stony tombs; (stony eyes & stony hearts). Before you, & behind you are stones. Stones to right & stones to left. In many places laborious attempts have been made, to clear the surface of these stones. You see heaps of stones here & there; and stone walls of immense thickness are thrown together, less for boundries than to get them out of the way. But in vain; The removal of one stone only serves to reveal those stones still lying, below it. It is like mending the old barn; the more you uncover, the more it grows.—The toes of every ones shoes are all stubbed to pieces with the stones. They are seldom a round......... stone; but sharp, flinty, & scratchy. But in the roads, such as that to Jaffa, they have been worn smooth by continuous travel.—To account for the abundance of stones, many theories have been stated; *My* theory is that long ago, some whimsical King of the country took it into his head to pave all Judea, and entered into contracts to that effect; but the contractor becoming bankrupt mid-way in his business, the stones were only dumped on the ground, & there they lie to this day [There is some prophecy about the highways being prepared for the coming of the Jews and when the "deputation from the Scotch Church" were in Judea, they suggested to Sir Moses Montefiore the expediency of employing the poorer sort of Jews in this work—at the same time facilitating prophecy and clearing the *stones* out of the way.

ENDLESS MEDITATION: There is a sense in which Emily Dickinson wrote only one poem, a "letter to the world" that ends not in aesthetic time but with biological time. Recording contours of the existential moment, each "unit" or separate poem is like her grammatically "lawless" but musically articulate hyphenization—a suggestion of intervals, silences, speech-like gaps, dreamtime. Nor does the process stop at the limits of verse (the apparent "poem") but continues through many of her letters, like that below (circa 1861), from which the following are the opening paragraphs.

EMILY DICKINSON

"To Recipient Unknown"

[excerpt]

Master.

If you saw a bullet hit a Bird—and he told you he was'nt shot—you might weep at his courtesy, but you would certainly doubt his word.

One drop more from the gash that stains your Daisy's bosom—then would you *believe*? Thomas' faith in Anatomy, was stronger than his faith in faith. God made me—[Sir] Master—I didn't be—myself. I don't know how it was done. He built the heart in me—Bye and bye it outgrew me—and like the little mother—with the big child—I got tired holding him. I heard of a thing called "Redemption"—which rested men and women. You remember I asked you for it—you gave me something else. I forgot the Redemption [in the Redeemed—I didn't tell you for a long time, but I knew you had altered me—I] and was tired—no more—[so dear did this stranger become that were it, or my breath—the Alternative—I had tossed the fellow away with a smile.] I am older—tonight, Master—but the love is the same—so are the moon and the crescent. If it had been God's will that I might breathe where you breathed—and find the place—myself—at night—if I (can) never forget that I am not with you—and that sorrow and frost are nearer than I—if I wish with a might I cannot repress—that mine were the Queen's place—the love of the Plantagenet is my only apology—To come nearer than presbyteries—and nearer than the new Coat—that the Tailor made—the prank of the Heart at play on the Heart—in holy Holiday—is forbidden me—You make me say it over—I fear you laugh—when I do not see—[but] "Chillon" is not funny. Have you the Heart in your breast—Sir—is it set like mine—a little to the left—has it the misgiving—if it wake in the night—perchance—itself to it—a timbrel is it—itself to it a tune? . . .

GERTRUDE STEIN

From Stanzas in Meditation   Part V

[Conclusion]

Alright let us think everything.
I have begun again to think everything.

STANZA LXXVI

I could not be in doubt
About.
The beauty of San Remy.
That is to say
The hills small hills
Beside or rather really all behind.
Where the Roman arches stay
One of the Roman arches
Is not an arch
But a monument
To which they mean
Yes I mean I mean.
Not only when but before.
I can often remember to be surprised
By what I see and saw.
It is not only wonderfully
But like before.

STANZA LXXVII

Now I wish to say I am uncertain if I will if I were every
day of any day.

STANZA LXXVIII

It is by no means strange to arrange
That I will not know
Not if I go or stay because that is of no importance
No what I wish to say is this.
Fifty percent of the roses should be cut
The rest should bloom upon their branch
By this means no one will mean what they pleased
And even if they are occupied they are content
To believe mind and wind, wind as to winding
Not as to rain and wind.

Because because there is very little wind here
Enough of rain sometimes too much
But even so it is a pleasure that whether
Will they remain or will they go even so.
I wish to know if they only mean to know
By me by you they will as readily maintain
That not by me by me as well remain
I wish to know if it is well to be by now to know
That they will remain if they might mean I know
If once if once if I might mean I know
That not which only if which only now to know
Know not in mean known if it is not only now
They could in gather mean if they meant mean
I mean.
This which I wish to add I wish to wish to add.
Can I can I be added which is not any wish.
To add.
I which I wish to add why should add not rhyme with
sad and glad
And not to talk to-day of wondering why away
Comes more than called to add obey to stay
I wish I had not thought that a white dog and a black
dog
Can each be irritably found to find
That they will call us if if when if added once to call
Can they be kind.
We are kind.
Can they be kind.
I wish no one were one and one and one.
Need they think it is best.
Best and most sweetly sweetness is not only sweet.
But could if any could be all be all which sweet it is
In not withstanding sweet but which in sweet
Can which be added sweet.
I can I wish I do love none but you

STANZA LXXIX

It is all that they do know
Or hours are crowded if not hours then days.
Thank you.

STANZA LXXX

Can she be not often without which they could want.
All which can be which.
I wish once more to say that I know the difference
between two.

STANZA LXXXI

The whole of this last end is to say which of two.

STANZA LXXXII

Thank you for hurrying through.

STANZA LXXXIII

Why am I if I am uncertain reasons may inclose.
Remain remain propose repose chose.
I call carelessly that the door is open
Which if they can refuse to open
No one can rush to close.
Let them be mine therefor.
Everybody knows that I chose.
Therefor if therefor before I close.
I will therefor offer therefor I offer this.
Which if I refuse to miss can be miss is mine.
I will be well welcome when I come.
Because I am coming.
Certainly I come having come.

These stanzas are done.

■ "*LOGOPOEIA, 'the dance of the intellect among words,' that is to say,
it employs words not only for their direct meaning, but it takes count
in a special way of habits of usage, of the context we expect to find with
the word, its usual concomitants, of its known acceptances, and of
ironical play. It holds the aesthetic content which is peculiarly the
domain of verbal manifestation, and cannot possibly be contained in
plastic or in music. It is the latest come, and perhaps most tricky and
undependable mode.*"

    —EZRA POUND, "How to Read," *New York Herald Tribune
    Books* [Jan. 1929], reprinted in *Literary Essays*

METAPOEIA: Of the three "kinds" of poetry distinguished by Pound—Phanopoeia, Melopoeia, and Logopoeia—the latter is least satisfactory in his application, being limited primarily to "satyric" and "ironical" modes (after Jules Laforgue). How to account for the analytic syntax and progressive modulations of Stein, or the "chain-grammar" and amphibolus phrase-torsions of Joyce's *Finnegans Wake* or Blake's *Jerusalem*—the verb of one "sentence" altering imperceptibly into the subject of the next? Or the "counter-pointing" and multi-directional puns of Mallarmé's *A Throw of the Dice Will Never Abolish Chance* or Robert Duncan's *Structure of Rime* series? (Pound's sympathies did not visibly attend any of these works—hence the lag in definition?) Let us consider a "Logopoeia of Changes" or "Metapoeia": a "kind," or, perhaps, a degree, of poetic structuring in which the formal center of gravity resides in the verbal process itself, the "hidden" resources of the language revealed in the *current* of mental operations. Such poetry is not subject to the usual techniques of textual analysis, but we may in time learn to apply the biologist's art of describing a growing form. Wallace Stevens speaks of metaphor as "the creation of resemblance by imagination, even though metamorphosis might be a better word" *(The Necessary Angel)*, reminding us that "meta-phor" is literally "change-bearer." The current interest in Tantric art from Tibet and India is one of those cross-cultural impregnations that help effect a reexamination of the roots of Western poetics: *Tan-tra* is literally "instrument of expansion." "Metapoeia" may be reserved for those modalities which expand the uses of language, the tools of thought. "The undeniable tradition of metamorphosis teaches us that things do not always remain the same. They become other things by swift and unanalysable process." (Pound, "Arnold Dolmetsch," 1918, in *Literary Essays*)

WALLACE STEVENS
The Rock

I SEVENTY YEARS LATER

It is an illusion that we were ever alive,
Lived in the houses of mothers, arranged ourselves
By our own motions in a freedom of air.

Regard the freedom of seventy years ago.
It is no longer air. The houses still stand,
Though they are rigid in rigid emptiness.

Even our shadows, their shadows, no longer remain.
The lives these lived in the mind are at an end.
They never were . . . The sounds of the guitar

Were not and are not. Absurd. The words spoken
Were not and are not. It is not to be believed.
The meeting at noon at the edge of the field seems like

An invention, an embrace between one desperate clod
And another in a fantastic consciousness,
In a queer assertion of humanity:

A theorem proposed between the two—
Two figures in a nature of the sun,
In the sun's design of its own happiness,

As if nothingness contained a métier,
A vital assumption, an impermanence
In its permanent cold, an illusion so desired

That the green leaves came and covered the high rock,
That the lilacs came and bloomed, like a blindness cleaned,
Exclaiming bright sight, as it was satisfied,

In a birth of sight. The blooming and the musk
Were being alive, an incessant being alive,
A particular of being, that gross universe.

    II   THE POEM AS ICON

It is not enough to cover the rock with leaves.
We must be cured of it by a cure of the ground
Or a cure of ourselves, that is equal to a cure

Of the ground, a cure beyond forgetfulness.
And yet the leaves, if they broke into bud,
If they broke into bloom, if they bore fruit,

And if we ate the incipient colorings
Of their fresh culls might be a cure of the ground.
The fiction of the leaves is the icon

Of the poem, the figuration of blessedness,
And the icon is the man. The pearled chaplet of spring,
The magnum wreath of summer, time's autumn snood,

Its copy of the sun, these cover the rock.
These leaves are the poem, the icon and the man.
These are a cure of the ground and of ourselves,

In the predicate that there is nothing else.
They bud and bloom and bear their fruit without change.
They are more than leaves that cover the barren rock

They bud the whitest eye, the pallidest sprout,
New senses in the engenderings of sense,
The desire to be at the end of distances,

The body quickened and the mind in root.
They bloom as a man loves, as he lives in love.
They bear their fruit so that the year is known,

As if its understanding was brown skin,
The honey in its pulp, the final found,
The plenty of the year and of the world.

In this plenty, the poem makes meanings of the rock,
Of such mixed motion and such imagery
That its barrenness becomes a thousand things

And so exists no more. This is the cure
Of leaves and of the ground and of ourselves.
His words are both the icon and the man.

III FORMS OF THE ROCK IN A NIGHT–HYMN

The rock is the gray particular of man's life,
The stone from which he rises, up—and—ho,
The step to the bleaker depths of his descents . . .

The rock is the stern particular of the air,
The mirror of the planets, one by one,
But through man's eye, their silent rhapsodist,

Turquoise the rock, at odious evening bright
With redness that sticks fast to evil dreams;
The difficult rightness of half-risen day.

The rock is the habitation of the whole,
Its strength and measure, that which is near, point A
In a perspective that begins again

At B: the origin of the mango's rind.
It is the rock where tranquil must adduce
Its tranquil self, the main of things, the mind,

The starting point of the human and the end,
That in which space itself is contained, the gate
To the enclosure, day, the things illumined

By day, night and that which night illumines,
Night and its midnight-minting fragrances,
Night's hymn of the rock, as in a vivid sleep.

■ *". . . I see [H. D.'s* War Trilogy: The Walls Do Not Fall, Tribute to
the Angels, *and* Flowering of the Rod] *develop along lines of an intuited
'reality' that is also a melody of vowel tone and rime giving rise to image
and mythos and out of the community of meanings returning to themes
towards its individual close. In her work she consciously follows the lead
of image to image, of line to line or of word to word, which takes her
to the brink (as 'gone' leads to 'guns' in the opening of [*The Walls Do
Not Fall])*of meaning, the poet establishing lines of free (i.e.,individual)
association within the society of conventional meanings. The form of
the poem, of the whole, is an entity of life-time, a 'biological reality,'
having life as her own body has life. "*
—ROBERT DUNCAN, *The H. D. Book* [1961]

H. D.

From Tribute to the Angels

29

We have seen her
the world over,

Our Lady of the Goldfinch,
Our Lady of the Candelabra,

Our Lady of the Pomegranate,
Our Lady of the Chair;

we have seen her, an empress,
magnificent in pomp and grace,

and we have seen her
with a single flower

or a cluster of garden-pinks
in a glass beside her;

we have seen her snood
drawn over her hair,

or her face set in profile
with the blue hood and stars;

we have seen her head bowed down
with the weight of a domed crown,

or we have seen her, a wisp of a girl
trapped in a golden halo;

we have seen her with arrow, with doves
and a heart like a valentine;

we have seen her in fine silks imported
from all over the Levant,

and hung with pearls brought
from the city of Constantine;

we have seen her sleeve
of every imaginable shade

of damask and figured brocade;
it is true,

the painters did very well by her;
it is true, they missed never a line

of the suave turn of the head
or subtle shade of lowered eye-lid

or eye-lids half-raised; you find
her everywhere (or did find),

in cathedral, museum, cloister,
at the turn of the palace stair.

    30

We see her hand in her lap,
smoothing the apple-green

or the apple-russet silk;
we see her hand at her throat,

fingering a talisman
brought by a crusader from Jerusalem;

we see her hand unknot a Syrian veil
or lay down a Venetian shawl

on a polished table that reflects
half a miniature broken column;

we see her stare past a mirror
through an open window,

where boat follows slow boat on the lagoon;
there are white flowers on the water.

     31

But none of these, none of these
suggest her as I saw her,

though we approach possibly
something of her cool beneficence

in the gracious friendliness
of the marble sea-maids in Venice,

who climb the altar-stair
at *Santa Maria dei Miracoli,*

or we acclaim her in the name
of another in Vienna,

Maria von dem Schnee,
Our Lady of the Snow.

     32

For I can say truthfully,
her veils were *white as snow,*

*so as no fuller on earth
can white them;* I can say

she looked beautiful, she looked lovely,
she was *clothed with a garment*

down to the foot, but it was not
girt about with a golden girdle,

there was no gold, no colour,
there was no gleam in the stuff

nor shadow of hem or seam,
as it fell to the floor; she bore

none of her usual attributes;
the Child was not with her.

35

So she must have been pleased with us,
who did not forgo our heritage

at the grave-edge;
she must have been pleased

with the straggling company of the brush and quill
who did not deny their birthright;

she must have been pleased with us,
for she looked so kindly at us

under her drift of veils,
and she carried a book.

36

Ah (you say), this is Holy Wisdom,
Santa Sophia, the SS of the *Sanctus Spiritus,*

so by facile reasoning, logically
the incarnate symbol of the Holy Ghost;

your Holy Ghost was an apple-tree
smouldering—or rather now bourgeoning

with flowers; the fruit of the Tree?
this is the new Eve who comes

clearly to return, to retrieve
what she lost the race,

given over to sin, to death;
she brings the Book of Life, obviously.

37

This is a symbol of beauty (you continue),
she is Our Lady universally,

I see her as you project her,
not out of place

flanked by Corinthian capitals,
or in a Coptic nave,

or frozen above the centre door
of a Gothic cathedral;

you have done very well by her
(to repeat your own phrase),

you have carved her tall and unmistakeable,
a hieratic figure, the veiled Goddess,

whether of the seven delights,
whether of the seven spear-points.

38

O yes—you understand, I say,
this is all most satisfactory,

but she wasn't hieratic, she wasn't frozen,
she wasn't very tall;

she is the Vestal
from the days of Numa,

she carries over the cult
of the *Bona Dea,*

she carries a book but it is not
the tome of the ancient wisdom,

the pages, I imagine, are the blank pages
of the unwritten volume of the new;

all, you say, is implicit,
all that and much more;

but she is not shut up in a cave
like a Sibyl; she is not

imprisoned in leaden bars
in a coloured window;

she is Psyche, the butterfly,
out of the cocoon.

39

But nearer than Guardian Angel
or good Daemon,

she is the counter-coin-side
of primitive terror;

she is not-fear, she is not-war,
but she is no symbolic figure

of peace, charity, chastity, goodness,
faith, hope, reward;

she is not Justice with eyes
blindfolded like Love's;

I grant you the dove's symbolic purity,
I grant you her face was innocent

and immaculate and her veils
like the Lamb's Bride,

but the Lamb was not with her,
either as Bridegroom or Child;

her attention is undivided,
we are her bridegroom and lamb;

her book is our book; written
or unwritten, its pages will reveal

a tale of a Fisherman,
a tale of a jar or jars,

the same—different—the same attributes,
different yet the same as before.

40

This is no rune nor symbol,
what I mean is—it is so simple

yet no trick of the pen or brush
could capture that impression;

what I wanted to indicate was
a new phase, a new distinction of colour;

I wanted to say, I did say
there was no sheen, no reflection,

no shadow; when I said white,
I did not mean sculptor's or painter's white,

nor porcelain; dim-white could
not suggest it, for when

is fresh-fallen snow (or snow
in the act of falling) dim?

yet even now, we stumble, we are lost—
what can we say?

she was not impalpable like a ghost,
she was not awe-inspiring like a Spirit,

she was not even over-whelming
like an Angel.

41

She carried a book, either to imply
she was one of us, with us,

or to suggest she was satisfied
with our purpose, a tribute to the Angels;

yet though the campanile spoke,
Gabriel, Azrael,

though the campanile answered,
Raphael, Uriel,

though a distant note over-water
chimed *Annael,* and *Michael*

was implicit from the beginning,
another, deep, un-named, resurging bell

answered, sounding through them all:
remember, where there was

no need of the moon to shine . . .
I saw no temple.

42

Some call that deep-deep bell
Zadkiel, the righteousness of God,

he is regent of Jupiter
or Zeus-pater or Theus-pater,

Theus, God; God-the-father, father-god
or the Angel god-father,

himself, heaven yet at home in a star
whose colour is amethyst,

whose candle burns deep-violet
with the others.

43

And the point in the spectrum
where all lights become one,

is white and white is not no-colour,
as we were told as children,

but all-colour;
where the flames mingle

and the wings meet, when we gain
the arc of perfection,

we are satisfied, we are happy,
we begin again;

I, John, saw. I testify
to rainbow feathers, to the span of heaven

and walls of colour,
the colonnades of jasper;

but when the jewel
melts in the crucible,

we find not ashes, not ash-of-rose,
not a tall vase and a staff of lilies,

not *vas spirituale,*
not *rosa mystica* even,

but a cluster of garden-pinks
or a face like a Christmas-rose.

This is the flowering of the rod,
this is the flowering of the burnt-out wood,

where, Zadkiel, we pause to give
thanks that we rise again from death and live.

LOUIS ZUKOFSKY

From Song of Degrees

William
   Carlos
Williams
    alive!

   Thinking of
Billy

The kid
shoots
to
kill,

But to
the expanse
of his
mind

who heard
that word
before,

scape
of a
letter

soars
with the
rest of
the letter

gulled by
the kid's
self-sacrifice:

reach
C
a cove—
call it
Carlos:

smell W
double U
two W's,
ravine and
runnel:

these
sink
high

in
high
fog

which
as
it
lifts,

the other
world
is
there:

the sight
moves—

open—

soothes

smoothes
over

the
same word

that
may have,
to touch,

two faces—
the heart
sees into—

of one
sound:

the
kid

's torn,
shot

so quickly
it sounds
water:

purls

a
high
voice

as with
a lien
on
the sky

that becomes

low now
frankly

water—

called also—

softly—

a kill.

■ *". . . There is some of the same fitness in a man's building his own house as there is in a bird's building its own nest. Who knows but if men constructed their dwellings with their own hands, and provided food for themselves and families simply and honestly enough, the poetic faculty would be universally developed, as birds universally sing when they are so engaged . . . ?*

". . . What of architectural beauty I now see, I know has gradually grown from within outward, out of the necessities and character of the

indweller, who is the only builder,—out of some unconscious truthfulness, and nobleness, without even a thought for the appearance; and whatever additional beauty of this kind is destined to be produced will be preceded by a like unconscious beauty of life. The most interesting dwellings in this country, as the painter knows, are the most unpretending, humble log huts and cottages of the poor commonly; it is the life of the inhabitants whose shells they are, and not any peculiarity in their surfaces merely, which makes them picturesque; *and equally interesting will be the citizen's surburban box, when his life shall be as simple and as agreeable to the imagination, and there is as little straining after effect in the style of his dwelling. . . . "*

—HENRY DAVID THOREAU, *Walden* [1854]

THE HOUSEHOLD: Thoreau's house, like Jefferson's plough or the furniture made by the American Shakers, embodies a way of mind that comes into being in relation to a way of living. Such a "way," celebrated by the ancient Sufis in a poetry that has parallels throughout the American tradition, bears upon contemporary consciousness generally in works like *The Whole Earth Catalog: Access to Tools* and *Domebook,* derived from Buckminster Fuller, a poet in his own right (see, e.g., *No More Secondhand God).* Gary Snyder, after ten years studying Zen Buddhism in Japan, returned to California to build his house in the back country out of materials at hand. James Agee, below, registers the meanings implicit in the building-as-meditation.

JAMES AGEE
From Let Us Now Praise Famous Men

1

. . . a house of simple people which stands empty and silent in the vast southern country morning sunlight, and everything which on this morning in eternal space it by chance contains, all thus left open and defenseless to a reverent and cold-laboring spy, shines quietly forth such grandeur, such sorrowful holiness of its exactitudes in existence, as no human consciousness shall ever rightly perceive, far less impart to another: that there can be more beauty and more deep wonder in the standings and spacings of mute furnishings on a bare floor between the squaring bournes of walls, than in any music ever made: that this square home as it stands in unshadowed earth between the winding years of heaven, is, not to me but of itself, one among the serene and final, uncapturable beauties of existence: that this beauty is made between hurt but unvanquishable nature and the plainest cruelties and needs of human existence in this uncured time, and is inextricable among these, and as impossible without them as a saint born in paradise:

2

There is plenty of time. We may stand here in front of it, and watch it, so long as it may please us to; watch its wood: move and be quiet among its rooms and meditate what the floor supports, and what is on the walls, and what is on shelves and tables, and hangs from nails, and is in boxes and in drawers: the properties, the relics of a human family; a human shelter: all in the special silence and perfection which is upon a dwelling undefended of its dwellers, undisturbed; and which is contracted between sunlight and a human shell; and in the silence and delicateness of the shame and reverence of our searching.

3

It is put together out of the cheapest available pine lumber, and the least of this is used which will stretch a skin of one thickness alone against the earth and air; and this is all done according to one of the three or four simplest, stingiest, and thus most classical plans contrivable, which are all traditional to that country: and the work is done by half-skilled half-paid men, under no need to do well, and who therefore take such vengeance upon the world as they may in a cynical and part wilful apathy; and this is what comes of it. Most naïve, most massive symmetry and simpleness. Enough lines, enough off-true, that this symmetry is strongly yet most subtly sprained against its centres, into something more powerful than either full symmetry, or deliberate breaking and balancing of 'monotonies,' can hope to be. A look of being earnestly hand-made, again, as a child's drawing, a thing created out of need, love, patience and strained skill in the innocence of a race. Nowhere one ounce or inch, spent into ornament, not one trace of relief or of disguise: a matchless monotony, and in it a matchless variety, and this again throughout restrained, held rigid: and of all this, nothing which is not intrinsic between the materials of structure, the earth, and the open heaven. The major lines of structure, each horizontal of each board, and edge of shingle, the strictness yet subtle dishevelment of the shingles, the nailheads, which are driven according to geometric need yet are not in perfect order, the grain, differing in each foot of each board and in each board from any other, the many knots in this cheap lumber: all these fluencies and irregularities; all these shadows of pattern upon each piece of wood; all these in rectilinear ribbons caught into one squared, angled and curled music, compounding a chord of four chambers upon a soul and centre of clean air: and upon all these masses and edges and chances and flowerings of grain, the chances and colorings of all weathers, and the slow complexions and marchings of pure light.

LORINE NIEDECKER
Wintergreen Ridge

Where the arrows
   of the road signs
      lead us:

Life is natural
   in the evolution
      of matter

Nothing supra-rock
   about it
      simply

butterflies
   are quicker
      than rock

Man
   lives hard
      on this stone perch

by sea
   imagines
      durable works

in creation here
   as in the center
      of the world

let's say
   of art
      We climb

the limestone cliffs
   my skirt dragging
      an inch below

the knee
   the style before
      the last

the last the least
   to see
      Norway

or 'half of Sussex
   and almost all
      of Surrey'

Crete perhaps
   and further:
      'Every creature

better alive
   than dead,
      men and moose

and pine trees'
   We are gawks
      lusting

after wild orchids
   Wait! What's this?—
      sign:

Flowers
   loveliest
      where they grow

Love them enjoy them
   and leave them so
      Let's go!

Evolution's wild ones
   saved
      continuous life

through change
   from Time Began
      Northland's

unpainted barns
   fish and boats
      now this—

flowering ridge
   the second one back
      from the lighthouse

Who saved it?—
   Women
      of good wild stock

stood stolid
   before machines
      They stopped bulldozers

cold
   We want it for all time
      they said

and here it is—
   horsetails
      club mosses

stayed alive
   after dinosaurs
      died

Found:
   laurel in muskeg
      Linnaeus' twinflower

Andromeda
   Cisandra of the bog
      pearl-flowered

Lady's tresses
   insect-eating
      pitcher plant

Bedeviled little Drosera
   of the sundews
      deadly

in sphagnum moss
   sticks out its sticky
      (Darwin tested)

tentacled leaf
   towards a fly
      half an inch away

engulfs it
   Just the touch
      of a gnat on a filament

stimulates leaf-plasma
   secretes a sticky
      clear liquid

the better to eat you
   my dear
      digests cartilage

and tooth enamel
   (DHL spoke of blood
      in a green growing thing

in Italy was it?)
   They do it with glue
      these plants

Lady's slipper's glue
   and electric threads
      smack the sweets-seeker

on the head
   with pollinia
      The bee

befuddled
  the door behind him
    closed he must

go out at the rear
  the load on him
    for the next

flower
  Women saved
    a pretty thing: Truth:

'a good to the heart'
  It all comes down
    to the family

'We have a lovely
  finite parentage
    mineral

vegetable
  animal'
    Nearby dark wood—

I suddenly heard
  the cry
    my mother's

there the light
  pissed past
    the pistillate cone

how she loved
  closed gentians
    she herself

so closed
  and in this to us peace
    the stabbing

pen
  friend did it
    close to the heart

pierced the woods
  red
    (autumn?)

Sometimes it's a pleasure
  to grieve
    or dump

the leaves most brilliant
  as do trees
    when they've no need

of an overload
  of cellulose
    for a cool while

Nobody, nothing
  ever gave me
    greater thing

than time
  unless light
    and silence

which if intense
  makes sound
    Unaffected

by man
  thin to nothing lichens
    grind with their acid

granite to sand
  These may survive
    the grand blow-up

the bomb
    When visited
        by the poet

From Newcastle on Tyne
    I neglected to ask
        what wild plants

have you there
    how dark
        how inconsiderate

of me
    Well I see at this point
        no pelting of police

with flowers
    no uprooted gaywings
        bishop's cup

white bunchberry
    under aspens
        pipsissewa

(wintergreen)
    grass of parnassus
        See beyond—

ferns
    algae
        water lilies

Scent
    the simple
        the perfect

order
    of that flower
        water lily

I see no space rocket
    launched here
        no mind-changing

acids eaten
    one sort manufactured
        as easily as gin

in a bathtub
    Do feel however
        in liver and head

as we drive
    towards cities
        the change

in church architecture—
    now it's either a hood
        for a roof

pulled down to the ground
    and below
        or a factory-long body

crawled out from a rise
    of black dinosaur-necked
        blower-beaked

smokestack-
    steeple
        Murder in the Cathedral's

proportions
  Do we go to church
    No use

discussing heaven
  HJ's father long ago
    pronounced human affairs

gone to hell
  Great God—
    what men desire!—

the scientist: a full set
  of fishes
    the desire to know

Another: to talk beat
  act cool
    release la'go

So far out of flowers
  human parts found
    wrapped in newspaper

left at the church
  near College Avenue
    More news: the war

which 'cannot be stopped'
  ragweed pollen
    sneezeweed

whose other name
  Ambrosia
    goes for a community

Ahead—home town
  second shift steamfitter
    ran arms out

as tho to fly
  dived to concrete
    from loading dock

lost his head
  Pigeons
    (I miss the gulls)

mourn the loss
  of people
    no wild bird does

It rained
  mud squash
    willow leaves

in the eaves
  Old sunflower
    you bowed

to no one
  but Great Storm
    of Equinox

THOMAS MERTON

From The Geography of Lograire

PROLOGUE: THE ENDLESS INSCRIPTION

1. Long note one wood thrush hear him low in waste pine
   places
   Slow doors all ways of ables open late
   Tarhead unshaven the captain signals
   Should they wait?

2. Down wind and down rain and down mist the passenger.

3. In holy ways there is never so much must

4. Should Wales dark Wales slow ways sea coal tar
   Green tar sea stronghold is Wales my grand
   Dark my Wales land father it was green
   With all harps played over and bells
   Should Wales slow Wales dark maps home
   Come go green slow dark maps green late home
   Should long beach death night ever come
   And welcome to dark father-mother land
   Simple white wall house square rock hill
   Green there low water hill rock square
   White home in dark bituminous con-
   Crete ways to plain of fates ways
   Fathers hill and green maps memory plain
   In holy green Wales there is never staying

5. Plain plan is Anglia so must angel father mother Wales
   Battle grand opposites in my blood fight hills
   Plains marshes mountains and fight
   Two seas in my self Irish and German
   Celt blood washes in twin seagreen people
   German Tristram is all mates' Grammer
   I had a toy called Tristram and Gurton's
   Needle in another sensitive place

What Channel bard's boarder house next sweet
Pub smell on cliff of winds Cliff was
A welshest player on the rugged green at Clare
Away next New Wood Forest fool on hunter map
Ship of forests masts Spain masts in Beaulieu wood
Minster in the New Wood Minster Frater in the grassy
Summer sun I lie me down in woods amid the
Stone borders of bards.

6. In holy walks there is never an order
   Never burden

7. Lay down last burden in green Wales seas end firs larches
   Wales all my Wales a ship of green fires
   A wall wails wide beside some other sex
   Gone old stone home on Brecon hill or Tenby harbor
   Where was Grandmother with Welsh Birds
   My family ancestor the Lieutenant in the hated navy
   From the square deck cursed
   Pale eyed Albion without stop.

8. In holy seas there is never so much religion.

9. On a run late hold one won
   Tarhead slaver captain selling the sables
   To Cain and Abel by design

10. Desire desire O sign of ire
    O Ira Dei
    Wrath late will run a rush under the
    Funnel come snow or deadly sign
    Design of ire rather I'd dare it not dare
    It not the ire run late hold strong Wales to a mast
    Young siren sexes of the green sea wash
    Hold captain home to Ithaca in a pattern of getaway
    Hold passion portion siren swinging porter
    Gutt bundle and funk gone
    Down slow mission done as possible

And another child of Wales
Is born of sea's Celts
Won rock weeds dragon designs
Missions capable defenders

11. In frail pines should they sometimes wait
Or ponds said one space cotton in captain design
Trace a dark pine fret way work walks
In soft South Pine house eroded away
Sweet smelling Virginia night and mint
Should they wet those cotton patches
Wash out a whole town

12. Wash ocean crim cram crimson sea's
Son Jim's son standing on the frigate
Jim Son Crow's ocean crosses a span
Dare heart die Spanish ram or Lamb Son's Blood
Crimson's well for oceans carnate sin sign
Ira water Ira will not wash in blood
Dear slain son lies only capable
Pain and Abel lay down red designs
Civil is slain brother sacred wall wood pine
Sacred black brother is beaten to the wall
The other gone down star's spaces home way plain

13. Dahomey pine tar small wood bench bucket
Under shadow there wait snake
There coil ire design father of Africa pattern
Lies all eyes awake eroded night
Traces gone tire far traces of dawn's fire
Dead rope hang cotton over captain branch

14. The willing night hides everything
Wills it tar face fret work wash out all chain
Saving all one country slave
Snake and tarheel minister and bat
And blood and ram and Isaac done in a dare.

15. Plain Savior crosses heaven on a pipe

16. Hay Abraham fennel and grass rain ram under span's star
    Red grow the razors in the Spanish hollow

17. Hallow my Savior the workless sparrow
    Closes my old gate on dead tar's ira slam
    Gone far summer too far fret work blood
    Work blood and tire tar under light wood
    Night way plain home to wear death down hard
    Ire hard down on anger heel grind home down
    Wary is smashed cotton-head beaten down mouth
    When will they all go where those white Cains are dead?

18. Sign Redeemer's "R"
    Buys Mars his last war.

W. S. MERWIN

Fear

Fear
there is
fear in fear the name the blue and green walls
falling of and numbers fear the veins that
when they were opened fear flowed from and
these forms it took a ring a ring a ring
a bit of grass green swan's down gliding on
fear into fear and the hatred and something
in everything and it is my death's
disciple leg and fear no he would not
have back those lives again and their fear as
he feared he would say but he feared more he
did not fear more he did fear more
in everything it is there a long time
as I was and it is within those
blue and green walls that the actual
verification has and in fact will

take the form of a ring a ring a ring
took I should say the figure in the hall
of the glass giants the third exhibition
on the right is fear I am I fear and
the rain falling fear red fear yellow fear
blue and green for their depth etcetera
fear etcetera water fire earth air
etcetera in everything made of
human agency or divine fear is
in the answer also and shall pierce thy
bosom too fear three gathered together
four five etcetera the brightest day
the longest day its own fear the light
itself the nine village tailors fear
their thread if not their needles if not
their needles in everything and it is
here this is New York and aside from that
fear which under another name in
every stone Abraham is buried it
is fear the infant's lovely face the
grass green alleys oh at about the third
hour of the night it being in those parts
still light there came fear my loving fear
in everything it is next the baker the
candlestick maker if you know what I
answer at that point and fear the little
cobbler his last is one fear and there is
fear in all shoes in the shoe line the clothes
line any clothes the blood line any in
everything it is the third button
the book books fear the bottle and what it
contains everything a life death the spirit
staring inward on nothing there and
the sunken vessel the path through the shadow
the shadow of me me or if I am not
suddenly fear coming from the west
singing the great song there was no need
fear no crying and others would sift

the salt in silence in fear the house
where I am familiar in all your
former lives remembered your parents
fear and fear theirs of your parents by
your parents and for your parents shall not
perish from this deciding everything
and it is deciding strike out Mr
Mrs Miss I am alone little stones
fear forgetting forgets remembering
it is my loving fear the mouth of my
seeing fear I am awake I am not
awake and fear no bones like my own
brother fear my death's sister and high on
the cliff face the small arched door from which
a man could fear or be in the winking
of an eye the tapping of the second
finger of the left hand the wind itself
fear I am alone forever I am
fear I am alone I fear I am
not alone couldn't tell your breath from fear
for it is your breath I do it and I'm
supposed to explain it too I fear I
completed my fear in everything there is
fear and I would speak for myself but fear
says logic follows but I advance in
everything and so discovery
geography history law comedy
fear law poetry major prophets
minor prophets that pass in the night
it is a mother and a guiding light
moving across fear before which they burn
in rows in red glass bleeding upwards their
hearts smoke in the gusts on earth as it is
in heaven with the sentence beginning
before the heavens were or the earth
had out of fear been called and any began
to be fear the bird feather by feather
note by note eye by eye pierced he is my

neighbor in the uttermost parts of aye
and shall I couple heaven when the fear
shall fear and those who walked in fear shall see
fear their very form and being for
their eyes shall be opened it was going
on in everything and I forgot but if you
stand here you can see fear the new building
starting to rise from which our children
will fear the stilted dogs the insects
who do not exist the dead burning
as candles oh dark flames cold lights in
everything without you the ship coming
in and a long way that I would never
traverse before fear had followed that
scent faster than a mortal bearing fear
I'm telling you I'm asking you I'm dying
I'm here today this is New York I'm more
than any one person or two persons
can stand fear the way down in everything
the way up is the same fear the next place
the next I said fear come on you it's you
I'm addressing get into line you're going
never fear there is a hair hanging by
everything it is the edges of things
the light of things do you see nothing
in them burning and the long crying
didn't you hear that either I mean
you again fear it's a strange name not
for a stranger ma'am he said lying I
mean there is you fear me fear but you
must not imagine fear through which the present
moves like a star that I or that
you either clearly and from the beginning
could ever again because from the beginning
there is fear in everything and it is
me and always was in everything it
is me

ROBERT CREELEY
People

ARTHUR OKAMURA
1.2.3.4.5.6.7.8.9.0

I knew where they were,
in the woods. My sister
made them little houses.

Possibly she was one,
or had been one
before. They were there,

very small but quick,
if I moved. I
never saw them.

How big is small. What
are we in. Do
these forms of us take shape, then.

Stan told us of the shape
a march makes, in
anger, a sort of small

head, the vanguard, then
a thin *neck,* and then,
following out, a kind of billowing,

loosely gathered *body,* always
the same. It must be
people seen from above

have forms, take place,
make an insistent pattern,
not suburbs, but the way

they gather in public places,
or, hidden from others,
look one by one, must be

me stories begin,
hen I was young—
is also. It tells

truth of things,
people. There used
be so many, so

ig one's eyes went
p them, like a ladder,
rouched in a wall.

Now grown large, I
ometimes stumble, walk
with no knowledge of
what's under foot.

Some small
echo
at the earth's edge

recalls
these voices,
these small

persistent
movements,
these people,

the circles,
the holes they
made, the

one
multiphasic
direction,

the going,
the coming,
the lives.

there to see, a record if
nothing more. "In a tree
one may observe the hierarchies

of monkeys," someone says. "On
the higher branches, etc." But
not like that, no, the kids

run, watch the *wave* of them
pass. See the form of their
movement pass, like the wind's.

I love you, I thought,
suddenly. My hands
are talking again. In-

side each finger must
be several men. They
want to talk to me.

On the floor the dog's eye
reflects the world, the people
passing there, before him.

The car holds possibly
six people, comfortably,
though each is many more.

I'll never die or else will
be the myriad people all
were always and must be—

in a flower, in a
hand, in some
passing wind.

These things
seen from inside, human,
a head, hands

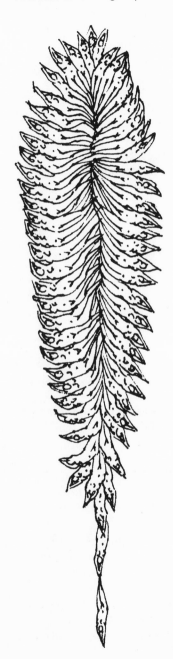

and feet. I can't
begin again to make
more than was made.

You'll see them
as flowers, called
the flower people—

others as rocks,
or silt, some
crystalline or even

a stream of smoke.
Why here at all
—the first question—

no one easily answers,
but they've taken place
over all else. They live

now in everything, as everything.
I keep hearing
their voices, most happily,

laughing, but the screaming
is there also. Watch
how they go together.

They are not isolated
but meld into continuous
place, one to one, never alone.

From whatever place
they may have come from,
from under rocks,

that moistness, or the sea,
or else in those
slanting places of darkness,

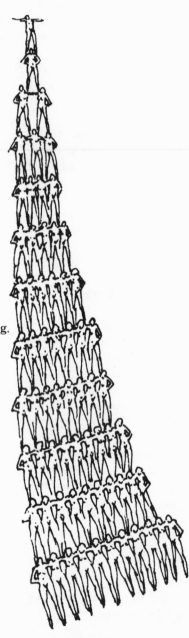

in the woods, they
are here and ourselves
with them. All

the forms we know,
the designs, the
closed-eye visions of

order—these too they are,
in the skin we
share with them.

If you twist one
even insignificant part
of your body

to another, imagined
situation of where it
might be, you'll

feel the pain of all
such distortion and
the voices will

flood your head with
terror. No thing
you can do can

be otherwise than
these *people,* large
or small, however

you choose to think
them—a drop of
water, glistening

on a grassblade, or
the whole continent
the whole world of *size.*

I
fails in
the forms

of *them,* I
want
to go home.

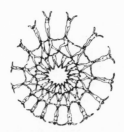

In its original form, "People" represents a collaboration between CREELEY and the artist ARTHUR OKAMURA. The latter's drawings (some fifty-six in the book-length version, *1.2.3.4.5.6.7.8.9.0,* Shambala Press, Berkeley, 1971) act upon the mind in a way similar to Tantric visualization exercises, awakening specific angles of knowing—as indeed do Creeley's word-people who "have forms, take place, / make an insistent pattern. . . ." An example of visual and vocal art, with numerous extensions in past and present (see, e.g., the section on image and hieroglyph, page 403 *et seq.,* above).

JOHN ASHBERY

Clepsydra

Hasn't the sky? Returned from moving the other
Authority recently dropped, wrested as much of
That severe sunshine as you need now on the way
You go. The reason why it happened only since
You woke up is letting the steam disappear
From those clouds when the landscape all around
Is hilly sites that will have to be reckoned
Into the total for there to be more air: that is,
More fitness read into the undeduced result, than land.
This means never getting any closer to the basic
Principle operating behind it than to the distracted
Entity of a mirage. The half-meant, half-perceived
Motions of fronds out of idle depths that are
Summer. And expansion into little draughts.
The reply wakens easily, darting from
Untruth to willed moment, scarcely called into being
Before it swells, the way a waterfall
Drums at different levels. Each moment
Of utterance is the true one; likewise none are true,

Only is the bounding from air to air, a serpentine
Gesture which hides the truth behind a congruent
Message, the way air hides the sky, is, in fact,
Tearing it limb from limb this very moment: but
The sky has pleaded already and this is about
As graceful a kind of non-absence as either
Has a right to expect: whether it's the form of
Some creator who has momentarily turned away,
Marrying detachment with respect, so that the pieces
Are seen as parts of a spectrum, independent
Yet symbolic of their spaced-out times of arrival;
Whether on the other hand all of it is to be
Seen as no luck. A recurring whiteness like
The face of stone pleasure, urging forward as
Nostrils what only meant dust. But the argument,
That is its way, has already left these behind: it
Is, it would have you believe, the white din up ahead
That matters: unformed yells, rocketings,
Affected turns, and tones of voice called
By upper shadows toward some cloud of belief
Or its unstated circumference. But the light
Has already gone from there too and it may be that
It is lines contracting into a plane. We hear so much
Of its further action that at last it seems that
It is we, our taking it into account rather, that are
The reply that prompted the question, and
That the latter, like a person waking on a pillow
Has the sensation of having dreamt the whole thing,
Of returning to participate in that dream, until
The last word is exhausted; certainly this is
Peace of a sort, like nets drying in the sun,
That we must progress toward the whole thing
About an hour ago. As long as it is there
You will desire it as its tag of wall sinks
Deeper as though hollowed by sunlight that
Just fits over it; it is both mirage and the little
That was present, the miserable totality
Mustered at any given moment, like your eyes
And all they speak of, such as your hands, in lost

Accents beyond any dream of ever wanting them again.
To have this to be constantly coming back from—
Nothing more, really, than surprise at your absence
And preparing to continue the dialogue into
Those mysterious and near regions that are
Precisely the time of its being furthered.
Seeing it, as it was, dividing that time,
Casting colored paddles against the welter
Of a future of disunion just to abolish confusion
And permit level walks into the gaze of its standing
Around admiringly, it was then, that it was these
Moments that were the truth, although each tapered
Into the distant surrounding night. But
Wasn't it their blindness, instead, and wasn't this
The fact of being so turned in on each other that
Neither would ever see his way clear again? It
Did not stagger the imagination so long as it stayed
This way, comparable to exclusion from the light of the stars
That drenched every instant of that being, in an egoistic way,
As though their round time were only the reverse
Of some more concealable, vengeful purpose to become
    known
Once its result had more or less established
The look of the horizon. But the condition
Of those moments of timeless elasticity and blindness
Was being joined secretly so
That their paths would cross again and be separated
Only to join again in a final assumption rising like a shout
And be endless in the discovery of the declamatory
Nature of the distance traveled. All this is
Not without small variations and surprises, yet
An invisible fountain continually destroys and refreshes the
    previsions.
Then is their permanence merely a function of
The assurance with which it's understood, assurance
Which, you might say, goes a long way toward conditioning
Whatever result? But there was no statement
At the beginning. There was only a breathless waste,
A dumb cry shaping everything in projected

After-effects orphaned by playing the part intended for them,
Though one must not forget that the nature of this
Emptiness, these previsions,
Was that it could only happen here, on this page held
Too close to be legible, sprouting erasures, except that they
Ended everything in the transparent sphere of what was
Intended only a moment ago, spiraling further out, its
Gesture finally dissolving in the weather.
It was the long way back out of sadness
Of that first meeting: a half-triumph, an imaginary feeling
Which still protected its events and pauses, the way
A telescope protects its view of distant mountains
And all they include, the coming and going,
Moving correctly up to other levels, preparing to spend the
        night
There where the tiny figures halt as darkness comes on,
Beside some loud torrent in an empty yet personal
Landscape, which has the further advantage of being
What surrounds without insisting, the very breath so
Honorably offered, and accepted in the same spirit.
There was in fact pleasure in those high walls.
Each moment seemed to bore back into the centuries
For profit and manners, and an old way of looking that
Continually shaped those lips into a smile. Or it was
Like standing at the edge of a harbor early on a summer
        morning
With the discreet shadows cast by the water all around
And a feeling, again, of emptiness, but of richness in the way
The whole thing is organized, on what a miraculous scale,
Really what is meant by a human level, with the figures of
        giants
Not too much bigger than the men who have come to petition
        them:
A moment that gave not only itself, but
Also the means of keeping it, of not turning to dust
Or gestures somewhere up ahead
But of becoming complicated like the torrent
In new dark passages, tears and laughter which
Are a sign of life, of distant life in this case.

And yet, as always happens, there would come a moment
    when
Acts no longer sufficed and the calm
Of this true progression hardened into shreds
Of another kind of calm, returning to the conclusion, its
    premises
Undertaken before any formal agreement had been reached,
    hence
A writ that was the shadow of the colossal reason behind all
    this
Like a second, rigid body behind the one you know is yours.
And it was in vain that tears blotted the contract now,
    because
It had been freely drawn up and consented to as insurance
Against the very condition it was now so efficiently
Seeking to establish. It had reduced that other world,
The round one of the telescope, to a kind of very fine powder
    or dust
So small that space could not remember it.
Thereafter any signs of feeling were cut short by
The comfort and security, a certain elegance even,
Like the fittings of a ship, that are after all
The most normal things in the world. Yes, perhaps, but the
    words
"After all" are important for understanding the almost
Exaggerated strictness of the condition, and why, in spite of
    this,
It seemed the validity of the former continuing was
Not likely to be reinstated for a long time.
"After all," that too might be possible, as indeed
All kinds of things are possible in the widening angle of
The day, as it comes to blush with pleasure and increase,
So that light sinks into itself, becomes dark and heavy
Like a surface stained with ink: there was something
Not quite good or correct about the way
Things were looking recently: hasn't the point
Of all this new construction been to provide
A protected medium for the exchanges each felt of such vital
Concern, and wasn't it now giving itself the airs of a palace?

And yet her hair had never been so long.
It was a feeling of well-being, if you will, as though a smallest
Distant impulse had rendered the whole surface
        ultra-sensitive
But its fierceness was still acquiescence
To the nature of this goodness already past
And it was a kind of sweet acknowledgment of how
The past is yours, to keep invisible if you wish
But also to make absurd elaborations with
And in this way prolong your dance of non-discovery
In brittle, useless architecture that is nevertheless
The map of your desires, irreproachable, beyond
Madness and the toe of approaching night, if only
You desire to arrange it this way. Your acts
Are sentinels against this quiet
Invasion. Long may you prosper, and may your years
Be the throes of what is even now exhausting itself
In one last effort to outwit us; it could only be a map
Of the world: in their defeat such peninsulas as become
Prolongations of our reluctance to approach, but also
Fine days on whose memorable successions of events
We shall be ever afterwards tempted to dwell. I am
Not speaking of a partially successful attempt to be
Opposite; anybody at all can read that page, it has only
To be thrust in front of him. I mean now something much
        broader,
The sum total of all the private aspects that can ever
Become legible in what is outside, as much in the rocks
And foliage as in the invisible look of the distant
Ether and in the iron fist that suddenly closes over your own.
I see myself in this totality, and meanwhile
I am only a transparent diagram, of manners and
Private words with the certainty of being about to fall.
And even this crumb of life I also owe to you
For being so close as to seal out knowledge of that other
Voluntary life, and so keep its root in darkness until your
Maturity when your hair will actually be the branches
Of a tree with the light pouring through them.
It intensifies echoes in such a way as to

Form a channel to absorb every correct motion.
In this way any direction taken was the right one,
Leading first to you, and through you to
Myself that is beyond you and which is the same thing as
     space,
That is the stammering vehicles that remain unknown,
Eating the sky in all sincerity because the difference
Can never be made up: therefore, why not examine the
    distance?
It seemed he had been repeating the same stupid phrase
Over and over throughout his life; meanwhile
Infant destinies had suavely matured; there was
To be a meeting or collection of them that very evening.
He was out of it of course for having lain happily awake
On the tepid fringes of that field or whatever
Whose center was beginning to churn darkly, but even more
    for having
The progression of minutes by accepting them, as one accepts
    drops of rain
As they form a shower, and without worrying about the fine
    weather that will come after.
Why shouldn't all climate and all music be equal
Without growing? There should be an invariable balance of
Contentment to hold everything in place, ministering
To stunted memories, helping them stand alone
And return into the world, without ever looking back at
What they might have become, even though in doing so they
Might just once have been the truth that, invisible,
Still surrounds us like the air and is the dividing force
Between our slightest steps and the notes taken on them.
It is because everything is relative
That we shall never see in that sphere of pure wisdom and
Entertainment much more than groping shadows of an
    incomplete
Former existence so close it burns like the mouth that
Closes down over all your effort like the moment
Of death, but stays, raging and burning the design of
Its intentions into the house of your brain, until
You wake up alone, the certainty that it

Wasn't a dream your only clue to why the walls
Are turning on you and why the windows no longer speak
Of time but are themselves, transparent guardians you
Invented for what there was to hide. Which has now
Grown up, or moved away, as a jewel
Exists when there is no one to look at it, and this
Existence saps your own. Perhaps you are being kept here
Only so that somewhere else the peculiar light of someone's
Purpose can blaze unexpectedly in the acute
Angles of the rooms. It is not a question, then,
Of having not lived in vain. What is meant is that this distant
Image of you, the way you really are, is the test
Of how you see yourself, and regardless of whether or not
You hesitate, it may be assumed that you have won, that this
Wooden and external representation
Returns the full echo of what you meant
With nothing left over, from that circumference now alight
With ex-possibilities become present fact, and you
Must wear them like clothing, moving in the shadow of
Your single and twin existence, waking in intact
Appreciation of it, while morning is still and before the body
Is changed by the faces of evening.

SPENCER HOLST

Three

The plants began to move, first withdrawing their roots
from the soil, they began to writhe on the ground, pound-
ing the earth with their leaves, bucking and jumping, and
finally waving, like wings, their leaves, they flew, flutter-
ing but a few feet at first, then soon the brown ground was
bare and the sky darkened with greenery.

The earth was covered with worms, all come to the
surface, standing on their tails, staring at the sky—like wet
dogs, the flying plants shook themselves free of beetles.

• • •

Holding cupped in his hands three pieces of dry ice
insulated by green napkins, the invisible man set them

afloat atop the tropical fishtank pool, like three smoking bars of bubbling soap.

A gramaphone was playing a one-time top tune on the Hit Parade.

A lemon fell onto the rug with such momentum it rolled out into the middle of the room, and it will remain there, unpicked-up, untouched, for at least fifteen minutes after this story is forgotten.

The man, whose hand was seen with green napkins dropping dry ice, now appeared above the water and rose to his feet from where he'd been kneeling behind the long empty fishpool.

●　　●　　●

He parted his beard in the middle and tied the ends to his two big toes, but this only a very ancient dwarf can do.

EDWARD DORN

The Lawg of the Winterbrook

the inside real
and the
outsidereal

Contained in the brain
like the nose was invented by cocaine
is the sum of What
Slam that filing cabinet shut!

Here Kums the Kosmos
Dont just stand there! (lookin dumb
Stick out your thumb.

The Body in winter is the hunting lodge
deep in the forest sheltered with a view
overlooking the full metaphor of the hart
and before all else in the winter interior
before winde and snowe
and before you goe
or when you suddenly are the guest of time

where the afterbirth of space hangs
in the mirror of rime
and where one place
is the center of this terrific actualism
  the waves of simplicity cross
   the shoals of destiny
    the shadows a
     cross the top of your grand desk
      are the numbers of your Winter Book
      the tumblers of the opening falling
     opening the Gates of Capricorn, the
    days have decreased as much as they ever will
   snowe covers living things with quietude
  Death rules over the visible, then,
Life surges with the Sunne out of decline
  the Sunne moves northward the light tauter
   spring spreads the New Life over cool death
    and the dissected earth includes the contrary
     over which our heads are not pervasive
      for there the nightforce increaseth
      "a rite
        not of passage
        but penetration

        a cellular destruction

        an act
        of will"

the maneuvers of a brilliant ghost
who returns with a longer stride
in his eye
          Apparently,
we wobble
several important periods show it
There is no vacuum in sense
connection is not by contact
sense is the only pure time
connection is a mechanical idea

nothing touches, connection meant is
Instant in extent a proposal of limit

    Dear lengthening Day
I have loved your apparencies since you created me

    From Book III of an ongoing work, *Gunslinger*, the first two books
    of which were published by Black Sparrow and Fulcrum Presses
    (1968, 1969) and later by Frontier Press, which is also issuing con-
    tinuing installments *(The Cycle, The Winterbook,* etc.).

DAVID ANTIN

7th separation meditation

merely the satisfaction
is the ordinary
remedy
for life
the spring
the water
suddenly turns round
helplessly
bearing on conduct and character
elsewhere
theoretical principles
are necessary
but a snare
this lie
or truth
seems more forcible
take these words as a sarcastic comment
the liar
maintaining fitting relations
with other men
the pupil of the eye
is corrupt
but inclines to what moves it
a man's powers include
reading

looking
freedom from judgment
stretching an obscene gesture
to spirit
as water
into which man returns at death
peace of mind
is common to man
is perverted
he
"the commissioner"
to set in order the affairs of the cities
we do not know who this commissioner is
this man
commanded an expedition
and died in the east
who was this corrector of cities?
the duty
of providing
management
is obscure
and not very relevant here
actions
have only a relative value
though
overmastering
which convinces those to whom it comes
of its truth
get a grasp on reality!
every town
in the provinces
has goods
of valuable material
but whether natural
or of glass
is uncertain
a palm tree
in winter
is of commanding importance
and accidental

in the arena
digging
would be
a breach of the rules
who is unskilled in the art of living?
those
who quarrel with good luck
Nowhere
is distinguished
by a more austere and isolated life
scout the land
discover forces
the world
is the only king
authority
goes about
destroying
beasts and men
recognize it in him
his attention to his self
from the beginning
without regard
for their houses

ROBERT KELLY

The Tower

three islands
in the sea
(she & her & me
three islands
in the sea
Atlantic himself
out there
over the edge
(the land
we've just

these few
million years
come in from the
wet
we'll be back
dolphins
be back

three islands
off the coast of Maine

I am a man
I am a woman
I came here to find bread
make bread
(bake bread

bake bread
for Kali Yuga
("credit,
not money"
for Kali Yuga
when the house
has glass walls
the tower
stands delectably up
everything can break
everything
built to fall
(I fall for you
day after day
fur around your
cunt the brightest
center of my eyes this
morning
third eye
for the fourth age
pale as you are
you're Kali
Kelly's shakti
white woman
with dark eyes

so the window
(the money
is all we've got
(the time

the house
under the mountain
"who hath time enough
hath none to lose"
face of a clock
standing there
two hundred years
to give me
that instruction
(took
the clouds
drift to sea
(may be four
islands
one darker
a shape
against the out
bending coast
(Poseidon weather
just
above freezing
everything
flows

Kali Yuga
credit
nobody bakes bread
(but the first
three ages
are man's
& this last
the age of woman
where her cunt
finally takes over
& we go
from there

& wind up
always here

(my cock
learn
tantra
of this yuga

(the cat
is brave
runs through the door
then stops to look
at where his feet
obedient
to his hunger
have taken him
past caution
out
where there might
be meat

down there
yellow house
green trim
grey house
with snow
sixteen
floors down
will I start
like Bruckner
counting leaves
to turn
everything to number
& number to music
the natural
world frozen
in human will

(more girls
no girls allowed
this male
tower
alone with its
sunrise
the world
is stone
(stone
grows

Kali Yuga
age of salt
skeletons locked
in yabyum
(embrace
beyond the flesh
we learn
to fuck bone

grey clouds over
us the white
over the sea
gone
to our home
brightness
(thin women
beautiful
in how they move
stripped
down to that
least
most
movement
dark
flesh inside you
the way you move

JIM HARRISON
Suite to Fathers

for D. L.

I

I think that night's our balance,
our counterweight—a blind woman
we turn to for nothing but dark.

*   *   *

In Val-Mont I see a slab of parchment
a black quill pen in stone.
In a sculptor's garden
there was a head made from stone,
large as a room, the eyes neatly hooded
staring out with a crazed somnolence
fond of walled gardens.

*   *   *

The countesses arch like cats in chateaux.
They wake up as countesses and usually sleep with counts.
Nevertheless he writes them painful letters,
thinking of Eleanor of Aquitaine, Gaspara Stampa.
With Kappus he calls forth the stone in the rose.

*   *   *

In Egypt the dhows sweep the Nile
with ancient sails. I am in Egypt,
he thinks, this Baltic jew—it is hot,
how can I make bricks with no straw?
His own country rich with her food and slaughter,
fit only for sheep and generals.

*   *   *

He thinks of the coffin of the East,
of the tiers of dead in Venice,
those countless singulars.
At lunch, the baked apple too sweet with kirsch
becomes the tongues of convent girls at gossip,
under the drum and shadow of pigeons
the girl at promenade has almond in her hair.

*   *   *

From Duino, beneath the mist,
the green is so dark and green it cannot bear itself.
In the night, from black paper
I cut the silhouette of this exiled god,
finding him as the bones of a fish in stone.

II

In the cemetery the grass is pale,
fake green as if dumped from Easter baskets,
from overturned clay and the deeper marl
which sits in wet gray heaps by the creek.
There are no frogs, death drains there.
Landscape of glass, perhaps Christ
will quarry you after the worms.
The newspapers says caskets float in leaky vaults.
Above me, I feel paper birds.
The sun is a brass bell.
This is not earth I walk across
but the pages of some giant magazine.

•　　•　　•

Come song,
allow me some eloquence,
good people die.

•　　•　　•

The June after you died
I dove down into a lake,
the water turned to cold, then colder,
and ached against my ears.
I swam under a sunken log then paused,
letting my back rub against it,
like some huge fish with rib cage
and soft belly open to the bottom.
I saw the light shimmering far above
but did not want to rise.

•　　•　　•

It was so far up from the dark—
once it was night three days,
after that four, then six and over again.
The nest was torn from the tree,

the tree from the ground,
the ground itself sinking torn.
I envied the dead their sleep of rot.
I was a fable to myself,
a speech to become meat.

III

Once in Nevada I sat on a boulder at twilight—
I had no ride and wanted to avoid the snakes.
I watched the full moon rise a fleshy red
out of the mountains, out of a distant sand storm.
I thought then if I might travel deep enough
I might embrace the dead as equals,
not in their separate stillnesses as dead, but in music
one with another's harmonies.
The moon became paler,
rising, floating upwards in her arc
and I with her, intermingled in her whiteness,
until at dawn again she bloodied
herself with earth.

• • •

In the beginning I trusted in spirits,
slight things, those of the dead in procession,
the household gods in mild delirium
with their sweet round music and modest feasts.
Now I listen only to that hard black core,
a ball harsh a coal, rending for light
far back in my own sour brain.

• • •

The tongue knots itself
a cramped fist of music,
the oracle a white-walled room of bone
which darkens now with a greater dark;
and the brain a glacier of blood,
inching forward, sliding, the bottom
silt covered but sweet,
becoming a river now
laving the skull with coolness—
the leaves on her surface
dipping against the bone.

Voyager, the self the voyage—
dark let me open your lids.
Night stares down with her great bruised eye.

DAVID HENDERSON
Egyptian Book of the Dead

pharisees come bloom
water eddys the twilight air
blue for music
red for fire
look out along the rooftops
ancient cities pop up
old testaments
tribes muster at grey street corners
sparks of cigarettes gleam the glass arcades
wine bottles libate the sidewalk
no more
the wine from palms
no more
the beer from bananas
but
easy now
easy
this night will turn you on/

where
death is a beautiful thing
done in the right way
and to die
tonight
in the street
on the radio
in the fire
will fare us well

we who are nothing
to the incarnate computers
save factors on a graph

we who are nothing
rescued by love
we cannot fathom
walk jaded neon jewelry
twinkling
twinkling
so delicate to the touch
to fall down
in a blaze of trumpets
in a blossom of fire
we
are from a place far off

GEORGE QUASHA

Somapoetics 45

for Susan

The Sphinx
sits sweating
in the Mohave
gazing at
steamy memories
of unlived ideas
century
within century of
tropism:
　　Helios
in the eye
blinding us
until the day
reaches mid-
point, the
　　Sphinx
is getting hotter
by the minute
just thinking of
　　My Lady
and the crevices
in Her hand's
crevices—

Meet my
Queen of Tentacles
twining a
record of these
thoughts, the
　　Stream
that is passing
us I claim is
mine
if I touch it, yours
if you catch Her, my
　　Lady is
at your disposal
for the Night, it's
the custom
in my Country, take a
dip in Her rivers
and listen to the song
of the one who saunters
from point to point
on the record, calling
it: American
　　Prophecy. Diction:

I have no desire
to go
to California or Pike's Peak, but I often
think at night with inexpressible
satisfaction and yearning of the
ARROWHEADIFEROUS
sands of Concord.
I have often spent whole afternoons, especially in the spring,
pacing back and forth over a sandy field,
looking for these relics of a race.
This is the gold
our land yields,
    confided Thoreau to his Journal,
artifacts
springing from the soil like mushrooms.
A red head, a look of being struck.
That savage over yonder has 20 noble words for *arbor vitae*—
have I 20 good ones
for the body of my woman?
    Barque. Blister. Bow. Bend
in my eyesight. Brain,
can you explore the Colorado
with Major Powell?
            The head faints
at the thought and
Wrong Way Corrigan is sung
as household hero.
        A seed or glance
of light, as Thomas Vaughan put it.
Put what?
      Life along the Merrimac.
Morning across the american plains
of my woman's body. Sweat
is juice on this
continent,
      and Canyon is rimmed
with 3 × 4 foot man-
shaped tuning forks
        8 times

8 octaves across Her
waiting.
       So take this glyph and plant it.
The *liat-god* is hiding again in old sticks.
I have agreed to be your handwriting
and persuade myself daily of the tale in all things.
Mars—even red Mars—is found here
wagging his dogtail, lounging and belching
in the aftertaste of immigrant garlic.
In one of the ancient Krepidian texts he steps aside to say:
In the Age of Horus, let the woman
be girt with sword before me. Here,
drink this lingual blood.
I take it this is the monthly message
with the smell of a seasonal fungus
ventriloquogrammicly rendered
by a vine
or snake, urgent
beyond belief, if a red dwarf
scuttles so far, the night
so cold, in such dark wood, so late
in the century.
       We've been waiting so long,
say the Redwoods of Canyon, *to get a word in*
your narrow ear, and whisper: We're here
at the rear of your wagging tongue
in secret bedrooms
of your personal pileus.
I lay in her lap, as instructed, fingered
the ivy that stains her back, and hung on
to a sound like the rolling of the left eye:
bla-ma bla-ma bla-ma, then *umbris*
and thru the gold light glancing from her body
I thought these seeded shadows
of ideas

T. S. ELIOT
From Little Gidding

We shall not cease from exploration
And the end of all our exploring
Will be to arrive where we started
And know the place for the first time.
Through the unknown, remembered gate
When the last of earth left to discover
Is that which was the beginning;
At the source of the longest river
The voice of the hidden waterfall
And the children in the apple-tree
Not known, because not looked for
But heard, half-heard, in the stillness
Between two waves of the sea.
Quick now, here, now, always—
A condition of complete simplicity
(Costing not less than everything)
And all shall be well and
All manner of thing shall be well
When the tongues of flame are in-folded
Into the crowned knot of fire
And the fire and the rose are one.

From the I Ching, *or* Book of Changes

64. Wei Chi / Before Completion

| | *above* | LI | THE CLINGING, FLAME |
| | *below* | K'AN | THE ABYSMAL, WATER |

This hexagram indicates a time when the transition from disorder to order is not yet completed. The change is indeed prepared for, since all the lines in the upper trigram are in relation to those in the lower. However, they are not yet in their places. While the preceding hexagram offers an analogy to autumn, which forms the transition from summer to winter, this hexagram presents a parallel to spring, which leads out of winter's stagnation into the fruitful time of summer. With this hopeful outlook the Book of Changes comes to its close.

THE JUDGMENT

BEFORE COMPLETION. Success.
But if the little fox, after nearly completing the cross-
    ing,
Gets his tail in the water,
There is nothing that would further.

The conditions are difficult. The task is great and full of responsibility. It is nothing less than that of leading the world out of confusion back to order. But it is a task that promises success, because there is a goal that can unite the forces now tending in different directions. At first, how-ever, one must move warily, like an old fox walking over ice. The caution of a fox walking over ice is proverbial in China. His ears are constantly alert to the cracking of the ice, as he carefully and circumspectly searches out the safest spots. A young fox who as yet has not acquired this caution goes ahead boldly, and it may happen that he falls in and gets his tail wet when he is almost across the water. Then of course his effort has been all in vain. Accordingly, in times "before completion," deliberation and caution are the prerequisites of success.

THE IMAGE

Fire over water:
The image of the condition before transition.
Thus the superior man is careful
In the differentiation of things,
So that each finds its place.

When fire, which by nature flames upward, is above, and water, which flows downward, is below, their effects take opposite directions and remain unrelated. If we wish to achieve an effect, we must first investigate the nature of the forces in question and ascertain their proper place. If we can bring these forces to bear in the right place, they will have the desired effect, and completion will be achieved. But in order to handle external forces properly, we must above all arrive at the correct standpoint our-selves, for only from this vantage can we work correctly.

The RICHARD WILHELM translation rendered into English by CARY F. BAYNES, Bollingen Series XIX [1950].

Index

The following isn't in any sense exhaustive, but is rather intended as a guide to poems, to free-standing quotes, and to other key quotations in the anthology. The listing is by author or by group, and includes translators as well, where such inclusion seemed of interest. Life dates, where available, are restricted to individuals with actual poem entries, or, if unavailable, have been replaced by significant years of the poet's activity. In a largely non-chronological work like this, it is the editors' hope that the dating will help to establish certain sequential perspectives for those who desire them.

Roger D. Abrahams 219

Louis Agassiz (b. 1807 d. 1873) 410, 411

James Agee (b. 1905 d. 1955) 555

Amos Bronson Alcott (b. 1799 d. 1888) 104

Arthur J.O. Anderson 86, 301

Sherwood Anderson (b. 1876 d. 1941) 151, 197

Edward Deming Andrews 110, 406

Jaime De Angulo (b. 1887 d. 1950) 117

Anonymous ("Boasting Drunk in Dodge," c. 1880) 153

Anonymous ("Horoscope of a Tentative N. American Republic") 239

Anonymous ("Revolutionary Pamphlet," 1774/1775) 179

Anonymous ("Schizophrenic Definitions") 90

Anonymous ("Sermon: Behold the Rib") 29

David Antin (b. 1932) 226, 585

Walter Conrad Arensberg (b. 1878 d. 1954) 423

Hans (Jean) Arp 339

Antonin Artaud 99

John Ashbery (b. 1927) 575

Aztec 85, 167, 301

Chilam Balam (15th/16th century) 516

Imamu Amiri Baraka [LeRoi Jones] (b. 1934) 161, 162

Owen Barfield 174, 408

Weston La Barre 99

Martha Warren Beckwith 175

Jimmy Bell (fl. 1960) 219

Ted Berrigan (b. 1934) 391

Harvey Bialy (b. 1945) 295, 374

William Billings (b. 1746 d. 1800) 325

William Blake xxiv, 130, 161, 324

Paul Blackburn (b. 1926 d. 1971) 284, 359

Black Elk [Hehaka Sapa] (b. 1863 d. 1950) 256

Blackfoot 175

Robert Bly (b. 1926) 159, 451

William Bradford 487

William Brandon 3, 189

Georges Braque 436

George Brecht (fl. 1955 to present) 96, 339, 438

Daniel G. Brinton 16

Bob Brown (b. 1886 d. 1959) 265

Norman O. Brown (b. 1913) 254, 436

William Cullen Bryant (b. 1794 d. 1878) 55, 409

Charles Bukowski (b. 1920) 223

Caddo 99

John Cage (b. 1912) 99, 106, 368, 369, 437

Jacob Carpenter (fl. late 19th century) 182

Ernst Cassirer 515

Carlos Castaneda xxi, 255, 402

Chippewa 335, 414

Noam Chomsky 81

Eldridge Cleaver 161

Michael Coe 403

Comanche 305

Confucius 402

Dane and Mary Roberts Coolidge 37

Gregory Corso (b. 1930) 83

Hart Crane (b. 1899 d. 1932) 71

Stephen Crane (b. 1871 d. 1900) 264, 413

Robert Creeley (b. 1926) 139, 570

Harry Crosby (b. 1898 d. 1929) 91, 249, 253, 428

E.E. Cummings (b. 1894 d. 1962) 119, 461

H.D. [Hilda Doolittle] (b. 1886 d. 1961) 8, 417, 544

Dakota 176

Delaware (*Walum Olum*) 15

Dekanawideh (c. 1450) 3

Frances Densmore (b. 1867 d. 1957) 33, 335, 414

Charles E. Dibble 86, 301

Harold Dicker (b. 1925) 218

Emily Dickinson (b. 1830 d. 1886) 244, 262, 329, 412, 536

Edward Dorn (b. 1929) 215, 583

John Dos Passos (b. 1896 d. 1970) 201

Marcel Duchamp (b. 1887 d. 1968) 93

Robert Duncan (b. 1919) 27, 211, 214, 355, 373, 445, 454, 543

George Economou (b. 1934) 499

Munro Edmonson 13, 124

Russell Edson (b. 1935) 287

Larry Eigner (b. 1925) 374

Mircea Eliade 402

T.S. Eliot (b. 1888 d. 1965) xxxiii, 597

Ralph Waldo Emerson (b. 1803 d. 1882) 59, 305, 515, 516

Theodore Enslin (b. 1925) 377

Max Ernst (b. 1891) 242, 426

Clayton Eshleman (b. 1935) 502

William Faulkner (b. 1897 d. 1962) 271, 430

Kenneth Fearing (b. 1902 d. 1961) 272, 273

Ernest Fenollosa (b. 1853 d. 1908) 415

Lawrence Ferlinghetti (b. 1919) 217

John Fiske (b. 1608 d. 1677) 525

Alice C. Fletcher 520

Charles Henri Ford (fl. 1930 to present) 435

David V. Forrest 89

Sigmund Freud 436

Else von Freytag-Loringhoven (b. 1874 d. 1927) 112, 247, 339, 426

Angel María Garibay 167

William Hamilton Gibson (b. 1850 d. 1896) 412

Allen Ginsberg (b. 1926) 32, 140, 284, 382, 383

John Giorno (b. 1936) 293

Arturo Giovannitti (b. 1884 d. 1959) 476

Delia Goetz 13

Battiste Good (fl. 1880) 176

Richard Grossinger 52
Jane Harrison 401
Jim Harrison (b. 1937) 590
Marsden Hartley (b. 1877 d. 1943) 68
Sadakichi Hartmann (b. 1869 d. 1944) 101
Nathaniel Hawthorne (b. 1804 d. 1864) 259, 309, 532
Lafcadio Hearn (b. 1850 d. 1904) 111
Ernest Hemingway (b. 1898 d. 1961) 199
David Henderson (b. 1942) 593
George Herriman (b. 1880 d. 1944) 434
Hidatsa 175
Dick Higgins (b. 1938) 105
Enoch Hoag (fl. 1890/1900) 99
Anselm Hollo (b. 1934) 115
Spencer Holst (b. 1926) 582
Hoodoo 269
John Lee Hooker (b. 1918?) 150
Hopi 52, 53
Lightning Hopkins 202
Langston Hughes (b. 1902 d. 1967) 350
George Hugnet 93, 247
Zora Neale Hurston 29, 269
Harry M. Hyatt 269
David Ignatow (b. 1914) 281
Kenneth Irby (b. 1936) 61
Iroquois 3, 109
William James 481
Ernst Jandl 443
Robinson Jeffers (b. 1887 d. 1962) 19
Richard Johnny John (b. 1914) 109
Eugene Jolas (b. 1894 d. 1952) 154, 267, 427, 428
Stephen Jonas (fl. 1950s/60s) 385
LeRoi Jones [Imamu Amiri Baraka] (b. 1934) 161, 162
Carl Gustav Jung xxxiii

Robert Kelly (b. 1935) 43, 448, 587
Hugh Kenner 417
Jack Kerouac (b. 1922 d. 1969) 385
Galway Kinnell (b. 1927) 289
Joanna Kitchel (fl. 1844) 302
James Koller (b. 1936) 33, 498
N.P. Krepid 80
Frank Kuenstler (b. 1928) 442
Philip Lamantia (b. 1927) 287, 435
Sydney Lanier (b. 1842 d. 1881) 331
Gerrit Lansing (b. 1928) 234
James Laughlin (b. 1914) 344
Denise Levertov (b. 1923) 158, 446
Vachel Lindsay (b. 1879 d. 1931) 317
Haniel Long (b. 1888 d. 1956) 501
Henry Wadsworth Longfellow (b. 1807 d. 1882) 403
James Russell Lowell (b. 1819 d. 1891) 409
Walter Lowenfels (b. 1897) 486
Mina Loy (b. 1883 d. 1966) 470
Fitz Hugh Ludlow (b. 1836 d. 1870) 261
Archibald MacLeish (b. 1892) 126
Jackson Mac Low (b. 1922) 114, 229, 372, 439
Garrick Mallery 51, 176
Mandan 175
Karl Marx 486
Edgar Lee Masters (b. 1869 d. 1950) 196
Cotton Mather (b. 1663 d. 1728) 86
Washington Matthews 453
Mayan (*Popol Vuh*) 13, 124
Mayan 13, 124, 403, 404, 516
Bernadette Mayer (b. 1945) 451
David P. McAllester 305

Michael McClure (b. 1932) 113
Thomas McGrath (b. 1916) 507
David Meltzer (b. 1937) 507
Herman Melville (b. 1819 d. 1891) 39, 243, 244, 496, 534
Menomini 175
Thomas Merton (b. 1915 d. 1968) 563
W.S. Merwin (b. 1927) 566
William Vaughn Moody (b. 1869 d. 1910) 192
Ajit Mookerjee 110
Marianne Moore (b. 1887 d. 1972) 342
Sylvanus G. Morley 13
Thomas Morton 487
Moundbuilders (c. 1000 B.C.) 54
Navajo 453
Nez Percé 126, 156, 189
John G. Neihardt 259
Lorine Niedecker (b. 1903 d. 1970) 557
Anaïs Nin (b. 1903) 274
Northern Ute 336
Frank O'Hara (b. 1926 d. 1966) 464
Arthur Okamura (b. 1932) 570
Charles Olson (b. 1910 d. 1970) xxxiv, 20, 243, 355, 357, 444, 509
George Oppen (b. 1908) 311, 394, 433
Joel Oppenheimer (b. 1930) 225
Simon Ortiz (b. 1941) 235, 238
Osage 51, 515
Rochelle Owens (b. 1936) 388
Papago 83, 336
Kenneth Patchen (b. 1911 d. 1972) 276
Charlie Patton (b. 1887?) 345
Pawnee 520
Andrew Peynetsa (b. 1904) 296
Allan Planz (b. 1937) 390
Playful Calf (fl. 1890/1900) 515
Edgar Allan Poe (b. 1809 d. 1849) 43, 123, 260, 327, 407

Ezra Pound (b. 1885 d. 1972) xxvii, xxx, xxxii, xxviii, 5, 34, 59, 164, 210, 252, 319, 337, 338, 409, 416, 418, 539
George Quasha (b. 1942) 37, 594
Boris de Rachewiltz 403
Paul Radin 157, 255
Carl Rakosi (b. 1903) 315
Man Ray 339
Red Corn (fl. 1880) 51
Ishmael Reed (b. 1938) 293
Wilhelm Reich 406
James Reuben (fl. 1880) 189
Kenneth Rexroth (b. 1905) 64, 103, 335, 423, 424
Charles Reznikoff (b. 1894) 137
M.C. Richards (b. 1916) 438
Theodore Roethke (b. 1908 d. 1963) 279
Jerome Rothenberg (b. 1931) 83, 109, 157, 167, 449, 477
Ralph L. Roys 516
Muriel Rukeyser (b. 1913) 207
Eric Sackheim 150, 202, 311, 345
Bernardino de Sahagún 85, 301
Sonia Sanchez (b. 1935) 386
Carl Sandburg (b. 1878 d. 1967) 195
Ed Sanders (b. 1939) 446
Hehaka Sapa [Black Elk] (b. 1863 d. 1950) 256
Santo Blanco (fl. 1930) 37
Carl Ortwin Sauer 59, 161
Gershom Scholem 122
Armand Schwerner (b. 1927) 396, 474
Laurette Séjourné 167
Seminole 337
Seneca 109
Seri 37
Shakers (United Society of Believers in Christ's Second Appearing) 100, 110, 302, 326, 406
J.D. "Jelly Jaw" Short 310

Eli Siegel (b. 1902) 481
Silu-we-haikt 156
Robert Silverberg 54
Charles Simic (b. 1938) 41, 309
Louis Simpson (b. 1923) 156
Sioux 33, 256, 336
Joseph Smith (b. 1805 d. 1844) 181
Smohalla (fl. 1890) 126
Gary Snyder (b. 1930) xxx, 32, 75, 117, 215, 307
Jack Spicer (b. 1925 d. 1965) 97, 365
Herbert J. Spinden 156
Daniel Spoerri (b. 1930) 88
Charles Stein (b. 1944) 393
Gertrude Stein (b. 1874 d. 1946) xxvii, 7, 74, 82, 87, 88, 265, 341, 407, 421, 455, 460, 537
Wallace Stevens (b. 1879 d. 1955) 9, 67, 429, 463, 540
George R. Stewart 59
Trumbull Stickney (b. 1874 d. 1904) 414
Sunryu Suzuki Roshi (b. 1905 d. 1971) 514
Wylie Sypher 420
Tahirussawichi (fl. 1900) 520
Nathaniel Tarn (b. 1928) 139
Edward Taylor (b. 1642? d. 1729) 303, 528
Dennis Tedlock (b. 1939) 296
Henry David Thoreau (b. 1817 d. 1862) xxxi, 312, 313, 410, 453, 554
Melvin B. Tolson (b. 1898 d. 1966) 206
Toltec 405
Torlino (fl. 1890) 453
Chögyam Trungpa (b. 1939) 108, 242, 437, 531
Mark Twain (b. 1835 d. 1910) 186

Ian Tyson (b. 1933) 109
Tristan Tzara 339
Ute 336
Jones Very (b. 1813 d. 1880) 327, 531
Jose García Villa (b. 1914) 351
C.F. Voeglin 15
Diane Wakoski (b. 1937) 147, 232
Frank Waters 53
Tom Weatherly (b. 1942) 29, 395
Philip Whalen (b. 1923) 116
Whales 40
Bukka White 123
Alfred North Whitehead 469, 473
Walt Whitman (b. 1819 d. 1892) xxxi, 4, 18, 48, 59, 81, 143, 185, 259, 328, 409, 410, 436, 454, 488
John Greenleaf Whittier (b. 1807 d. 1892) 183
Benjamin Lee Whorf (b. 1897 d. 1941) 95
Richard Wilhelm 597
Emmett Williams (b. 1925) 88, 390, 443
Jonathan Williams (b. 1929) 222
William Carlos Williams (b. 1883 d. 1963) 123, 133, 313, 328, 352, 430, 431, 488
Keith Wilson (b. 1927) 283
Winnebago 157
Yvor Winters 256
Wintu 256
James Wright (b. 1927) 450
Yaqui xxvii, 255, 336, 402
Louis Zukofsky (b. 1904) 347, 432, 553
Zuni 296

About the Editors

GEORGE QUASHA'S long "serial poem," *Somapoetics,*
recently began appearing in book form. His poems
and translations have been published in several collections,
including *Five Blind Men.* While teaching at The State
University of New York at Stony Brook, he independently founded
and edited *Stony Brook:* A Journal of Poetry, Translation
and Poetics. He has also edited a *Sumac Active Anthology* and
co-edited *Open Poetry:* Four Anthologies of Expanded Poems.
His critical writing includes a study of William Blake
printed in *Blake's Visionary Forms Dramatic.*
He lives with his wife in New York City.

JEROME ROTHENBERG has published twelve books of poetry,
the most recent being *Poems for the Game of Silence* and
Poland/1931; several volumes of translations and four anthologies,
including *Technicians of the Sacred:* A Range of Poetries from
Africa, America, Asia & Oceania, and *Shaking the Pumpkin:*
Traditional Poetry of the Indian North Americas. His translations
include several German works, among them Hochhuth's *The
Deputy* and *Gomringer by Rothenberg,* as well as a series of
experimental translations of American Indian poetry under a grant
from the Wenner-Gren Foundation. He is currently living with
his wife and son on the Allegany Seneca Reservation in
Western New York State and is co-editing, with
Dennis Tedlock, the first magazine devoted
exclusively to ethnopoetics, *Alcheringa.*